The Hague Conferences and International Politics, 1898–1915

The Hague Conferences and International Politics, 1898–1915

Maartje Abbenhuis

BLOOMSBURY ACADEMIC
LONDON • NEW YORK • OXFORD • NEW DELHI • SYDNEY

BLOOMSBURY ACADEMIC
Bloomsbury Publishing Plc
50 Bedford Square, London, WC1B 3DP, UK
1385 Broadway, New York, NY 10018, USA

BLOOMSBURY, BLOOMSBURY ACADEMIC and the Diana logo are trademarks of Bloomsbury Publishing Plc

First published in Great Britain 2019

A catalogue record for this book is available from the British Library.

A catalog record for this book is available from the Library of Congress.

ISBN: HB: 978-1-3500-6134-7
ePDF: 978-1-3500-6135-4
eBook: 978-1-3500-6136-1

Typeset by Newgen KnowledgeWorks Pvt. Ltd., Chennai, India
Printed and bound in Great Britain

To find out more about our authors and books visit www.bloomsbury.com and sign up for our newsletters.

Voor mam en pap

Contents

List of Illustrations viii
List of Abbreviations x
Acknowledgements xii

Introduction: For the Peace of the World 1
1 How the Nineteenth Century Shaped the Hague Conferences 9
2 The Tsar, the Rescript and the World 21
3 A *Coram Publies*: Planning the First Hague Conference, 1899 43
4 It Is Not Enough! The First Hague Conference, 1899 67
5 Civilization at War, 1899–1906 97
6 A Holy Duty: Activists for The Hague 121
7 When the World Showed Up: The Second Hague Conference, 1907 145
8 City of Peace: The Hague, 1907–15 169

Notes 185
Bibliography 244
Index 279

Illustrations

2.1 A peace dream, cartoon, 1899. *Puck* 5 April 1899, centrefold 35

2.2 A bear in sheep's clothing, cartoon, 1899. *De vredes-conferentie. Prentenboek voor oud en jong*. Amsterdam, H. Gerlings, 1899, 12 36

2.3 Rest in peace, cartoon, 1899. *De vredes-conferentie. Prentenboek voor oud en jong*. Amsterdam, H. Gerlings, 1899, 49 37

3.1 The great powers share a peace pipe, cartoon, 1899. Johan Braakensiek (1858–1940), *De Amsterdammer* 12 February 1899, centrefold 54

3.2 The American delegation attends the first Hague conference, cartoon, 1899. *Journal* (Minneapolis), 1899 62

4.1 The Hague's canals, cartoon, 1899. H. Jansen, 'Spotprent op de stank van de Haagsche grachten tijdens het bezoek van de leden van de vredesconferentie' *De Hofstad* 20 May 1899 69

4.2 High-Life Taylor, cartoon, 1899. B. Moloch (1849–1909), 'High-Life Taylor' in *La Vie Illustrée* 18 May 1899, 1 70

4.3 Horrors of war, painting, 1899. George Montbard (1841–1905), 'Horror of War' (1898) in *La Vie Illustrée* 18 May 1899, 8 71

4.4 Why are the doors of the peace conference shut?, cartoon, 1899. Cartoonist unknown, *Kikeriki* (Austria) 8 June 1899 75

4.5 The unsuccessful funeral of Mars, cartoon, 1899. Cartoonist unknown, *De vredes-conferentie. Prentenboek voor oud en jong*. Amsterdam, H. Gerlings, 1899, 21 93

5.1 The limits of 'civilized' war, cartoon, 1899. Johan Braakensiek (1858–1940), *Het jaar 1899*. Amsterdam, np, 1900, np 104

5.2 Queen Victoria's behind, cartoon, 1899. Crispin do Amaral (1845–1911) in *Caricature*. 26 November 1899, 1 110

5.3 The Netherlands' civilizing mission, cartoon, 1905. Albert Hahn (1877–1918) in *Het Volk* 3 September 1905, np 113

6.1 Christmas, cartoon, 1907. Albert Hahn (1877–1918) in *De Notenkraker* 22 December 1907, front page 127

6.2 Henri Danger's peace apostles, illustration, 1907. Henri Danger, 'The Hague delegates and their forerunners. Apostles of the world's peace throughout the ages' *Illustrated London News* 22 June 1907, 960–61 128

6.3 The grip of war, illustration, 1907. Artist unknown, 'The hand of war', *Illustrated London News* 24 August 1907, 265 129

7.1 A hard task, cartoon, 1907. Artist unknown, *Auckland Star* 11 September 1907, 6 149

7.2 The women at The Hague, cartoon, 1907. Artist unknown, *Amsterdammer* 21 June 1907, 11 149

7.3 In the international studio, cartoon, 1907. Johan Braakensiek (1858–1940), 'In the international studio' *De Amsterdammer* 14 April 1907 150

7.4 The peace tsar, illustration, c. 1907. Bertha Czegka (1880–1954) 'Der Friedenszar', c. 1914 [1907?] 152

8.1 Miss Peace of The Hague, cartoon, 1914. Henry Mayer (1868–1954) cartoon in *Puck* 75, 1950, 18 July 1914, centrefold 170

8.2 Cordonnier's design. Louis Cordonnier (1854–1940), architect, in *Internationale prijsvraag der Carnegie-Stichting. Het vredespaleis te 's Gravenhage*. Amsterdam, Elsevier, 1906, np 172

8.3 The peace palace, 1913. F., *Een bezoek aan het vredespaleis*. The Hague, Luctor et Emergo, 1914, 2 173

8.4 Holland 1913, advertising poster, 1913. Centraal Bureau van Vreemdelingenverkeer, poster, 1913 177

8.5 Neglecting The Hague, cartoon, 1917. Louis Denis Valvérane (1870–1943), cartoon, *Pêle-Mêle* 12 February 1917, 4 182

Abbreviations

AJIL	*American Journal of International Law*
AMRR	*American Monthly Review of Reviews*
AVG-CARHIF	Women's Archive, Brussels
BL	British Library
CAC	Churchill Archive Centre, Cambridge
CDT	*Chicago Daily Tribune*
COPD	*Organisation centrale pour une paix durable* (Central Organization for Durable Peace)
DE	*Daily Express*
DM	*Daily Mail*
FW	*Die Friedens-Warte*
HCCP	House of Commons, Parliamentary Papers, Britain
HGA	Municipal Archive of The Hague
HLH	Houghton Library
ICC	International Criminal Court
ICJ	International Court of Justice
ICW	International Council of Women
ILA	International Law Association
Institut	*Institut de droit international* (Institute of International Law)
IPB	International Peace Bureau
IPC	International Prize Court
IPU	Inter-Parliamentary Union
IPUA	Inter-Parliamentary Union Archives
IT	*Irish Times*
IVVT	*Internationale Vereeniging Vrede-Tentoonstelling* (International Association for a Peace Exhibition)
JT	*Japan Times*
LAT	*Los Angeles Times*
Ligue	*Ligue des femmes pour le désarmement* (Women's League for Disarmament)
LSE	London School of Economics and Political Science
NA	*Nationaal Archief* (National Archives), the Netherlands
NAA	National Archives of Australia
NAOR	*Nederlands Anti-Oorlog Raad* (Netherlands Anti-War Council)
NCH	*North China Herald*
nd	no date
NHZ	*Neue Hamburger Zeitung*
np	no page numbers or no publisher

NYT	*New York Times*
PCA	Permanent Court of Arbitration
PCAJ	Permanent Court of Arbitral Justice
PCIJ	Permanent Court of International Justice
PCSC	Peace Collection, Swarthmore College
POW	Prisoner of War
PPL	Peace Palace Library, The Hague
PRO	National Archives, Britain
SP	*Sumatra Post*
SWH	*Samoan Weekly Herald*
TT	*The Times* (London)
UNOG	United Nations Office at Geneva Archive
UP	University Press
WCTU	Women's Christian Temperance Union
WP	*Washington Post*

Acknowledgements

I am incredibly grateful to the Royal Society of New Zealand. Owing to their generous Marsden award, I was able to undertake numerous research trips to far-flung libraries and archives and obtain significant time off from my teaching and administration responsibilities. An equally large debt of gratitude goes out to my colleagues at the University of Auckland who accommodated my research needs, at quite some personal expense to themselves and to our department. Thank you.

There are numerous individuals who deserve mention here. As always, I cannot thank my husband, the wonderful Gordon Morrell, enough for his incredible historical agility. I am also indebted to my graduate students who shared their materials, insights, comments and encouragement. Here's to you Annalise Higgins, Leon Ostick, Chris Barber, Michael Moon, Merryn Ward, James Halcrow, Anthony Artus, Tiger (Zhifu) Li, Ozzy (Wang Shuo), Thomas Munro, Mark Stevenson, Bernard Marsh, Gordon Elder, Sam Jaffe, Tom Rosie, Harry Bloomfield, Harry Vossen, Steven Sheldon, Grace Jansen, Laura Staveley and Mathew Graham.

Among the wider scholarly community, I have further debts of gratitude to pay to Barry Reay, Lisa Bailey, Brian Boyd, Jonathan Burgess, Charlotte MacDonald, Tom Duurland, Arthur Eyffinger, Henk de Smaele, Vincent Genin, Jan Lemnitzer, Peter Holquist, Neville Wylie, James Crossland, Andres Sanchez, Anneleen de Jong, Wim Klinkert, Samuël Kruizinga, Ismee Tames, Chris Holdridge, Bjarne Bendtsen, Kenneth Keith, James Yeoman, Alexander Maxwell, Peter Romijn, Marjan Schwegman, Dominiek Dendooven, Damon Salesa, Glenda Sluga, Dirk Moses, Tony Ballentyne and Geoffrey Kemp. For research assistance and translation help I would like to thank Annalise Higgins, Marcelo Mendes de Souza, Maria Mitenkova, Michael Moon, Chris Barber, Harry Bloomfield, Harry Harknett, Steven Sheldon, Harry Vossen, Sarah Russell and Marie Kim.

In researching this monograph, I used the resources of numerous archives and libraries. I express my thanks to: the *Koninklijk Huis Archief* in The Hague; the National Archives of Australia; the National Library of Australia; the National Archives in Kew; the British Library; the Churchill Archive Centre at Cambridge University; the *Nationaal Archief* in The Hague; Philip Abela, Mandy Henk and the Interloans' team at the University of Auckland library; the *Haags Gemeentearchief*; Wendy Chmielewski and the Peace Collection staff at Swarthmore College; the United Nations Office at Geneva Library; Andy Richardson at the Inter-Parliamentary Union Archive in Geneva; the Roosevelt Study Centre in Middelburg; and Els Flour at the *ARV-Carhif* in Brussels. I am particularly appreciative of the support I received from the Peace Palace

Library in The Hague, including from its director Jeroen Vervliet, Jacobine Wieringa and Niels van Tol.

At the heart of all I do lives Gord, my glorious children, Joseph and Helena, my parents, Harry and Jacintha, and my sister, Wiesje, her husband, Tristan, and their children, Brianne and Kasper. This book is a testament to their love and support.

Introduction

For the Peace of the World

There's not room for everyone in the memory of men, time is a castle with restricted access, but the moat around it is crammed with shadows like ours.

– Jesus del Campo (2008)[1]

On 24 August 1898, Nicholas II, Tsar of Russia, circulated a statement of astonishing beauty to the governments represented at his court in St Petersburg. His appeal, or rescript – a word meaning 'official announcement' – urged them to consider how the ceaseless development of 'excessive armaments' had created a burden so great that it weighed heavily 'upon all nations'. He proposed an international conference of governments to 'put an end to these incessant armaments' and 'seek the means of warding off the calamities which are threatening the whole world'.[2] In the name of 'general peace', global stability and the future of humanity, the most powerful absolute monarch on earth, who commanded an army estimated at three million soldiers, urged military restraint and looked to negotiate some form of international cooperation to advance that end.

As extraordinary as the reception of the Tsar's note was among the diplomatic corps in St Petersburg, few were prepared for the scale of the press response that came with its public release four days later.[3] There was nary a newspaper that did not mention the rescript. Many printed its text in full. Most commented on its implications and assessed the Tsar's ambitions. In a world inundated with broadsheets, pamphlets, illustrated magazines and frequent telegraph news updates, most people who could read had access to an array of local, national and global news, advertisements and published ephemera. And as the Spanish newspaper *El Liberal de Reus* noted on 2 September 1898, the Tsar's rescript was the 'only subject of interest in the conversation of the foreign media' at a time when the Dreyfus affair, the Spanish-American War, the civil war in Samoa and the Fashoda crisis competed for headline space.[4]

The global media response to the rescript was as evocative as it was varied: while it inspired effusive praise and boundless hope in many editorials, others roundly dismissed the Tsar's initiative as humanitarian nonsense. Only by preparing for war, they urged, could general peace be maintained. What these oppositional commentaries had in common was their fascination with the Tsar's proposition. The newspaper record attests that the Tsar's rescript was not only considered a unique and peerless document, it also provoked controversy and generated exceptional levels of public responsiveness. In its wake, groups and individuals advocated for cooperation on an array of topics relating to war, peace and disarmament. They did so in the press, public meetings and petitions and by authoring resolutions, penning pamphlets, songs and poems, giving speeches and writing to the Tsar. Many encouraged their governments and the international community at large to consider ways of improving the world and its affairs in real and practical ways. Not only did people around the world read about the Tsar's unexpected declaration, they also framed their responses to that news in highly politicized ways. Those responses speak to the public and global power of the first Hague peace conference, which was held in 1899 at the Tsar's urging.

In his extraordinary book *A History of the World for Rebels and Somnabulists* (2008), Jesus del Campo reminds us that history is a construction that often foregrounds power and prestige. As del Campo describes it, there is little room for the voices, experiences and memories of those who are crammed in the moats of time's castle. In the writing of diplomatic history, the voices of the masses are rarely heard. The castle and its rulers have permanence. We tend to concentrate on the Tsar and his courtiers and not the people responding to his call for peace. Of course, since the social turn of the 1960s and 1970s, historians have done much to reject master narratives. They did (and do) so by rescuing the voices, experiences and agency of those previously silenced or under represented. Today, even diplomatic historians can point their lenses of enquiry almost anywhere and at anyone or anything, including in del Campo's moat. But how do we assess the importance and power of the voices of 'the people' in writing a history that appears initially to be about the power of states? And what happens when the voices from the moat offer contradictory versions of the past? How can we reconcile their perspectives? How do we make an argument for the power of public opinion in diplomatic affairs, for example, when that opinion was varied, incongruous, simultaneously globalized and local and altogether effusive in its magnitude and range? These questions inform the chapters that follow.

The first Hague peace conference held between May and July 1899 was a product of public agency as much as it was a diplomatic event shaped by the agency of state chancelleries. The diplomatic negotiations at The Hague in 1899 on disarmament, arbitration, the peaceful cooperation of states, the regulation of international order and the laws of war played to a transnational audience primed for action on these issues. The importance of the audience's existence and agency should not be underestimated. It was attentive and critical. It was globally alert. It looked for pragmatic achievement and voiced the diversity of its opinions loudly and proudly. It hoped to influence the governments attending the summit. As this book argues, it was highly successful in doing so.

The first Hague conference of 1899 marked a key shift in public perception about the function of international diplomacy and the conduct of warfare. After 1899, 'The Hague' permeated media discussions, endowed with a range of interconnected meanings relating to the concept of peace, the conciliation of conflict, the function of international law and international institutions, the limitation of warfare and state violence, and the amorphous concept of 'civilization'. The public spectacle that evolved around the 1899 conference ensured that 'The Hague', as a multidimensional international and internationalist ideal, would have a long afterlife.

The two Hague conferences of 1899 and 1907 played out as public spectacles on a global stage. They offer key moments of public reflection and evaluation of the contours of international affairs. They should also be seen as events that confirmed that public engagement was an essential element of diplomacy at the fin de siècle.[5] Between 1899 and the outbreak of the First World War, people around the world engaged with the Hague conferences as international developments that offered promise for improving the world and its affairs. Others looked to the conferences fearfully and argued that they endangered the sanctity of diplomatic practice and limited the sovereignty of states. Whether they were in favour or against, most of these individuals nevertheless hoped (and many expected) that their opinions would be noticed and acted upon by their political representatives.

The governments represented at the two Hague conferences (twenty-six states in 1899, forty-four in 1907) looked to exploit the events to advance their own foreign policy objectives. None of them, however, was immune to the levels of public pressure and expectation that built up around the conferences. They all had to adapt and engage with the public expectations that evolved around The Hague. The most adept of them attempted to manoeuvre the public discourse to their advantage. The world watched the events in The Hague and mobilized in varying degrees of excitement and desperation in response. Whether they wished to or not, the governments at The Hague were aware that they had to be seen to be listening to that public agency. At the very least, they had to look to be responsive.

This book charts the landscape of voices that emerged around the two Hague conferences of 1899 and 1907 and the third Hague conference planned for 1915 that was never held. It explains just how radical an impact the 1899 conference had on shaping public perceptions about the rightful limits of warfare and the conduct of states more generally. The public power of the first Hague conference not only inspired further Hague conferences but, in so doing, also fashioned twentieth-century international political values. It was the public engagement with the real and imagined promise and achievements of the three Hague conferences that fashioned a universally recognized set of norms. When referenced – as regularly happened after 1899 in relation to wars, peace treaties, international legal developments, arbitration cases, neutrality issues, militarism, peace activism, international institutions and international order – the phrase 'The Hague' invoked a set of ideas and standards relating to the conduct of states in times of war and peace. Those standards not only equated with the content of the Hague conventions formalized in 1899 (and expanded in 1907) but also with a more diffuse notion that 'civilized' states and people should behave in humane and orderly ways towards each other. These norms underwrote not only the ways in which newspaper-readers evaluated international affairs, but also how their political representatives shaped the public rhetoric of their diplomacy.

Historians traditionally struggle with the concept of public opinion.[6] Most agree that assigning relevance to expressions made in the public sphere, be they in a newspaper, pamphlet, book, speech, painting, song, petition or poem, is extraordinarily difficult.[7]

At most, the existence of a viewpoint can tell us something about the person who made it and possibly something more about the expectations of the audience for whom the piece was created. But we cannot, for example, note an idea published in an article in *The Times* (of London) in 1899 and assert that it reflected the opinion of the British people writ large without identifying who those Britons were and providing further evidence that these specific Britons agreed with the sentiment and engaged with the article in question. We cannot know for sure if anyone read the article, let alone what he or she thought about while reading.

Despite such challenges, I hope to show that historians can use media sources to reflect on public sentiment, opinion and agency, particularly when the quantity of sources is high, variegated and prevalent in both the elite and popular press. By representing the perspectives of dozens of newspaper editors (and other published authors) in a variety of languages from around the industrializing world and in making connections between them, it is possible to identify a sense of global public awareness. Today's historian is blessed in the availability of a rich range of digitally searchable newspaper databases. I used more than thirty newspaper search engines (as well as several microfilmed newspapers) as sources for this book, offering access to hundreds of contemporary press opinions. For each chapter, I picked case studies from around the world, often at random. Regardless of where I turned my gaze, I almost always found references to The Hague in news reports and editorial commentaries. The global pervasiveness of The Hague in the media commentary between 1899 and 1915 is astounding. By analysing the dynamics of that media engagement, it is clear that 'The Hague' had common currency and normative value yet also accommodated a range of contradictory opinions about its importance.

Alongside the normative framing of The Hague in the media, the conferences of 1899, 1907 and 1915 also presented internationalist organizations with the ideal forum to improve the world.[8] These organizations' archives are the other major source-base for this book. Many of these organizations, like the Inter-Parliamentary Union (IPU), the International Council of Women (ICW) and the *Institut de droit international* (Institute of International Law), looked to the first Hague conference as a turning point in improving international affairs, marking a shift to the legal framing of diplomacy. The Hague offered them boundless promise. Many recognized the conferences as foundational to shaping international organization and believed that they were a vital step in the path to effective world governance. Others lauded their value in promoting international law as a 'science of peace' that could revolutionize diplomacy and move it away from hard power and military action to judicial intervention and war avoidance. With the establishment of the Permanent Court of Arbitration (PCA) in 1899 – the world's first judicial tribunal – the city of The Hague also became a site of ongoing internationalist significance. By the time the ornate Peace Palace – home to the PCA – opened its doors in 1913, The Hague was recognized as the place where the international norms defining the parameters of war, peace and diplomacy were evolving. As such, the city itself had become a reference point for peace activists and a much used and discussed site of internationalist activism.

Charted through the lens of global news and internationalist agency, this book offers a history of the sociopolitical importance of The Hague as a city, as a series of conferences and as a normative idea between 1899 and 1915. At its heart, this is a story of the convergence of medium and message: where the medium for global connectedness (viz. the newspaper press) met with a powerful message of peace, disarmament and conflict resolution. It is a story that came about in large part due to the transformation of news media in the late nineteenth century, which enabled literate individuals to be made aware of world events regardless of their geographic location. It is also a story of the ways in which individuals at the fin de siècle engaged with their world and thought about their place in it. They did so as citizens of nations, as subjects of empires and as consumers of news and goods that traversed borders, seas, continents and oceans. They also did so as agents of international events, the movement of capital and the shaping of international developments. In other words, it is a story of globalization and of the understanding of how international affairs functioned and how individuals, societies, nations and states fit together. Above all, it is a story of how individuals considered their world and imagined its future, for good or ill. Their interactions with The Hague shaped their imaginings of how international relations between states and people might be improved, regulated and regularized.

While the book is presented as a global history of The Hague, I am fully aware of the limitations of being genuinely global or complete in writing this history.[9] What is offered here is not a history of how the whole world engaged with The Hague. Rather, it is a history of the multiplicity of transnational interconnections that existed around The Hague – as a text, as a place and as an idea – in a key period of world history. It casts its net far and wide from Europe to the Americas, from Africa to Asia, the Pacific and Australasia and offers a picture of how industrialized and industrializing societies and their imperial outposts engaged with The Hague in public life.

The book contends, as many histories of empire do, that the webs connecting people across the world can and should be studied although they were neither homogeneous nor monolithic.[10] As such, it uses The Hague as means of accessing a variety of places, publications, spaces, groups and values (individual, local, national, imperial, transnational) and charts the interconnections between them. It revels in what Antoinette Burton and Isabel Hofmeyr call the 'chaotically plural worlds of empire' and casts its net even wider into the 'crazy patchwork' of global connections that existed in the early 1900s.[11] It shows how The Hague was discussed, debated and invoked in complementary and globally responsive ways. Overall, the book argues for the utility of The Hague as a universally recognized concept, in the sense that it was understood and engaged with simultaneously by people all over the industrializing world. Of course, there were many people who were not literate or who were only marginally connected to the discourse that The Hague prompted at the turn of the century. But in 1900 more people were knowingly part of the globalized planet than ever before.

This book recounts the polemical public debates that evolved around the Tsar's rescript and the ensuing Hague conferences. In many ways, J.A. Hobson sums up some of the inherent contradictions at play in these debates best in his famous 1902 study on imperialism:

> Here is the significance of the recent Hague Conference, alike in its success and its failure. Its success, the mere fact that it was held and the permanent nucleus

> of internationalism it created, attests a real and felt identity of interests among different nations in the maintenance of peace; its failure and the open derision expressed by many politicians merely indicate the presence in high places of cliques and classes opposed in their interests and feelings to those of the peoples.[12]

These public debates mattered because contemporaries recognized that the Hague conferences offered a unique opportunity for governments to discuss key concerns that affected international affairs. They mattered because many newspaper readers saw in The Hague an opportunity to have their opinions on fundamental questions relating to war, peace and international stability acted upon by their governments. The debates mattered above all because they provided the catalyst and inspiration for heightened internationalist activism. They present an important step in the history of human rights and reflect on the 'soft power of humanity' as the historian Lynn Hunt so beautifully describes the public movement towards global empathy.[13] Or as Edwin Mead, the prominent American internationalist and husband of peace activist Lucia Ames Mead, explained in 1911, the Hague conferences remind us 'that in this time, when men the world over touch elbows as never before, and the interest of each is the interest of all as never before, very great things may be suddenly brought to pass in a very short time'.[14] That optimism infused the era before the outbreak of the First World War and influenced the activities of states and their leaders as much as (and often alongside) popular expressions of jingoism, ethnic nationalism and imperial pride.[15]

The following chapters also chart how the city of The Hague in the period 1898–1915 became a central focus for world attention. The book does not argue that the world was not part of people's consciousness before 1898 (that would be absurd) or that there were no attempts at world organization or universal congresses before this time: the whole nineteenth century was an age of congress and international engagement initiated by the grand spectacle that was the Congress of Vienna of 1814–15.[16] Rather, it suggests that the engagement and involvement with The Hague brought about an emerging awareness of a responsibility to the interconnectedness of the world in ways and to an extent that did not exist before. As such, it takes up Warren Kuehl's point that 'the meeting at The Hague' in 1899 'proved to be both a beginning and an end' as well as Madeleine Herren-Oesch and Cornelia Knab's more recent suggestion that The Hague has paradigmatic meaning for thinking globally.[17] The Hague conferences set into motion the twentieth century's obsession with global governance and international responsibility and left behind, even if ever so reluctantly, the understanding that diplomacy remained the preserve of diplomats alone.

Above all, the first Hague conference made clear that governments had no choice but to engage with public opinion or at least with the discourse created by press agencies. They necessitated a review of the 'old' ways of doing diplomatic business. Germany's Chancellor Bismarck had acknowledged the extraordinary power of the public domain during the negotiations of the 1878 Berlin agreement. The British Prime Minister Benjamin Disraeli was said to have commented at the time that the host of journalists invited to Bismarck's private residence (where the conference was held) was to 'publicly introduce' issues that would be 'privately settled' by the diplomats.[18] Of course, many of the great powers published careful selections of their diplomatic documents in compendiums and had done so for a long time. Britain's diplomatic blue books – called by one consul *les enfants terribles*[19] – certainly aimed at shaping popular opinion about Britain's international affairs.[20] However, The Hague not only signalled a rising public interest in world affairs, but also a sense of global public pressure. Barbara Tuchman describes the pressure as follows: 'delegates [at The Hague in 1899] were uncomfortably aware of the conscience of the world over their shoulder'.[21] The delegates could not safely ignore that conscience, however much they might have wished to. In this sense, the first Hague conference opened an era of public diplomacy that the second Hague conference extended.

The pressure on governments to accommodate the existence of public opinion certainly mattered to newspaper readers themselves. As a telling example consider this editorial printed in the *Thames Star*, the local newspaper of a small gold-mining town in New Zealand on 24 October 1907, six days after the conclusion of the second Hague peace conference and a few weeks after the signing of the Anglo-Russian *Entente* agreement. The article, entitled 'The Foreign Office and Democracy', suggested that

> [t]he British public are beginning to object at last to the undemocratic system on which the Foreign Office conducts its business. The accepted doctrine has been that Foreign Affairs should be kept separate from party politics and that the Foreign Office should be entirely independent of passing waves of public feeling. The fact that the Imperial Government concluded an important treaty with Russia without giving the public a hint of its terms has caused a great deal of adverse criticism.

The newspaper went on to cite Britain's *Daily Mail* and *Daily Chronicle*, both arguing that such conduct was an 'anomaly in our democratic Constitution'.[22] Whether or not the article reflected a will for change in the Foreign Office itself is almost beside the point.[23] Its dissemination in an outpost of empire attests to a growing awareness (or will) that public agency be influential to the agenda of governments.

Another major argument of this book is that the Hague conferences inspired an uptake in the ideals espoused by liberal internationalists. The 1899 conference not only witnessed extraordinary levels of private (non-government) agency but also affected universal support from liberal internationalist organizations in its aftermath. After 1899, they were all fixated on, and by, The Hague. They professionalized their organizations, planned carefully to maximize lobbying opportunities and aimed at improving the Hague conventions and the application of The Hague's 'peace through law' agenda. As such, The Hague offered liberal internationalists a framework of reference and a medium through which to advocate for future change. The Hague, then, helped to increase the importance of non-governmental political agency in affecting the dynamics of international diplomacy and politics.

Altogether, this book contests the assertion, first made by Merze Tate in 1942 and echoed by numerous subsequent historians, that the Hague conferences 'did not affect the public at large' and 'met with no general interest or encouragement'.[24] It also challenges other historical explanations, which frequently focus on singular aspects and often contradict each other. For example, the diplomatic and general histories of the 1899 and 1907 conferences tend to argue that they did not have much of an impact on international affairs and that their legacy was overwhelmed by more important events like the outbreak of the First World War. Stephen Kern calls the Hague conferences a 'collective failure',[25] a sentiment shared by Richard Langhorne, Margaret MacMillan and, less obviously, Daniel Hucker.[26] Sondra Herman repeats Calvin DeArmond Davis's assertion that the results of the first Hague conference were 'paper achievements masking failure',[27] while Nigel Brailey channels Sir Ernest Satow's contemporary opinions to suggest that the conferences were 'little more than a footnote *en route* to the 1914–18 war'.[28] Even Arthur Eyffinger's otherwise impressive studies at one point suggest that there was a 'ring of naiveté' about them.[29]

Quite in contrast, international legal histories of the Hague conferences present the events as foundational to the legal history of the twentieth century because they established the first international judicial system, legitimized the idea of international justice and formulated the first comprehensive law of war.[30] In the history of peace activism as well, the two Hague conferences feature brightly in legitimizing pacifist ideals, including those of disarmament, arbitration and humanitarian interventionism.[31] Largely contradictory, it is not surprising that these histories rarely meet. In response, this book develops on from the work of Inis Claude Jnr, Warren Kuehl, Ian Clark, Glenda Sluga and Mark Mazower, who argue that the Hague conventions and experiences helped to shape twentieth-century international organization and global expectation.[32] It does so by integrating various contemporary understandings and critiques of the conferences in what an intellectual of the time called the 'piping times of peace'.[33]

Altogether, this book complicates the existing narratives of the two Hague conferences and their legacies. In the process, it contributes to other historical narratives of the era, including those explaining imperialism, the origins of the First World War and the preponderance of nationalized militarism and xenophobia in Europe. Above all, this book suggests that for liberal internationalist contemporaries and a globally alert public, who had no foreknowledge of the First World War, the conferences did not fail. They offered impressive and important steps in the rational progress of international order, 'the significance of which', according to the prominent international lawyer Lassa Oppenheim, 'no one can underestimate'.[34] Only in July and August 1914, as the lamps went out all over Europe, did the ideal of The Hague waver. But even then, it did not wane. The Hague conferences and conventions did not prevent the outbreak of the First World War. They could never have done so and claiming they failed because they did not is very much like claiming laws and norms are unimportant because they are often broken.[35] There was a cost to breaking international laws and Hague norms in the Great War, though they were unevenly imposed. Throughout the 1914–18 conflict, the ideas of The Hague informed how people thought about war, how they ascribed responsibility for its violence and how they imagined a post-war world.[36]

1

How the Nineteenth Century Shaped the Hague Conferences

It is impossible to discuss international law without a reference to The Hague Conferences; it is impossible to conduct the foreign relations of nations without quoting the provisions of The Hague conventions; it is almost impossible to perform the duties of citizenship without knowledge of The Hague Conferences and their positive results.

– James Brown Scott, 1909[1]

The Hague conferences of 1899 and 1907 were products of their time. They were highly politicized events that engaged governments, their citizens and subjects in surprising ways. The importance of the Hague conferences in shaping contemporary understanding of international issues is hard to overstate. When it came to the conduct of war, the exercise of state violence, the resolution of conflict and the development of international law and organization, The Hague often featured. As the American lawyer, delegate to the 1907 conference and Hague scholar James Brown Scott explained in a lecture series on the subject, '[I]t is almost impossible [in 1909] to perform the duties of citizenship without knowledge of The Hague.'[2] This book explains how The Hague came to be so influential. This chapter shows how the globalizing process of the nineteenth century helped to make it possible for The Hague to become a powerful idea in the early twentieth century.

The 'long' nineteenth century, stretching from the end of the Napoleonic Wars in 1815 to the outbreak of the First World War in 1914, was filled with internationalist ventures. Historians often describe the century as one dominated by war and violent change, which came in the form of rampant imperialism, numerous revolutions, frequent conflict and a rising tide of militant nationalism. Yet it was also a century that witnessed concerted efforts to manage global affairs by means of peaceful interaction. The conservative supporters of the concert of Europe, for example, aimed at preventing war between the great European monarchies through mutual agreement. Free-trade liberals, in turn, successfully advocated for open access to the world's ever-growing network of seas, canals, railways, cables and roads so all humanity could (at least in theory) share in the economic prosperity offered by unrestricted global investment, travel and trade. The second half of the century witnessed the proliferation of institutions and societies, whose members looked to promote multilateral and transnational cooperation. Their existence highlighted what missionaries, merchants, diplomats, entrepreneurs and investment bankers had long been aware of: humanity was becoming more interconnected. For many internationalists, globalization offered the opportunity and, in some cases, the necessity to advance, even if very slowly and haphazardly, the ideal of global harmony. They hoped to revolutionize the corridors of power.

Today, 'world peace' tends to be considered an empty phrase infused with vain promise.[3] In our pessimism, we differ little from our nineteenth-century counterparts who argued in all earnestness *si vis pacem, para bellum* (if you want peace, prepare for war). Most internationalists at the turn of the nineteenth century were equally pragmatic, if more optimistic. The American scholar Paul S. Reinsch, for example, dismissed what he called the 'golden dream' and 'prophetic vision' of peace. As he explained it, '[T]he thought of world unity seems to lack relation to actual facts; it is at best a guiding hope, a generous aspiration by which the harshness of competition and strife may, in ordinary times, be smoothed over a little.'[4] He hoped to improve the 'constructive work' of international relations, by maximizing international cooperation, which he considered the 'centripetal force' of 'positive action'.[5] For, according to Reinsch, 'our destiny is a common one; whatever may happen to the nations of Africa or Asia affects *our* life [in his case, in the United States]'.[6] The Hague conferences offered an ideal medium to achieve Reinsch's ambitions for stabilizing international relations.

By 1900, there were few states not connected to networks of international trade, communication and empire. As a consequence, there were few people who did not understand that there was a wide world out there and, more importantly, that what happened elsewhere might and frequently did impact one's life at home. Furthermore, the communications revolution increasingly broke down the conception of near and far. It brought the 'other' into one's home either physically, as intercontinental travel became easier, or virtually through newspapers, telegraph communications and (later) telephone exchanges.[7] These tools of the new information age bolstered the forces that made the nineteenth century an age of globalization and migration. Certainly, few non-European communities escaped the 'civilizing' force of Western industrializers or the avalanche of white-faced traders, missionaries, investors, settlers, soldiers and colonizers that came with the opening up of the seas, the expansion of railway lines, the growth in manufacturing and the invention of new weapons and medicines.[8]

Given the simultaneous developments of rising literacy, cheap printing and faster communication systems, the dissemination of information and understanding of events and developments in other parts of the world became commonplace. In other words, if you had access to a newspaper, lived in a port city, near a railway station or telegraph office, you were connected to the world and could choose to interact with the people in it. Not everyone met those conditions, and large swathes of the planet remained isolated and most of their populations uninformed well into the twentieth century. Yet that reality takes little away from the fact that the nineteenth century witnessed a revolution in global interaction and with it a revolution in thinking internationally.

By necessity, most individuals caught up in the communications revolution had to consider local issues within a global context. Others looked to maximize their stakes in and improve the social, economic, scientific and diplomatic functioning of the international environment. The standardization of international relationships and norms became commonplace in the second half of the 1800s. These were often formalized by governments in multilateral agreements and resulted in the establishment of international institutions to manage their impact and scope. For example, the International Telegraph Union developed in 1865 to coordinate procedures for the relaying of telegraph messages across the globe.[9] The International Postal Union created similar guidelines for the circulation of mail in 1874.[10] The Union for the Protection of Industrial Property in 1883 instituted internationally binding criteria for patents and copyright.[11] Most important to establishing reliable trade, shipping and telegraph communication was the creation and then adoption of standardized universal time.[12]

These international institutions and agreements ensured that by 1900 millions of people worked within regulated webs of trade, communication and exchange.[13] While we should be wary of the suggestion that these international unions forced interaction to occur along uniform lines, they did ensure greater interconnectivity, heightened awareness and enabled transcultural interactions between individuals, communities and states.[14] At one level, these webs of interaction were dependent on governments and their willingness to accept and promote the regulation of international affairs. At another level, the webs were unregulated, complex and chaotic.[15]

The expansion of treaty law developed in tandem with these globalizing forces. International law offered an ideal tool for industrializing empires to make immutable their claimed rights to markets, trade, territory, resources and people.[16] It was through a legally binding treaty, then, that the British crown claimed sovereignty over New Zealand in the 1840s. China and Japan were subjected to what were known as 'unequal treaties' in the 1840s and 1850s, which opened both Asian regions to Western imperial expansion, trade incursions and, in the case of China, a loss of sovereignty over trade ports and territory.[17] The European conquest of large parts of Africa in the 1880s often came in the form of protectorate treaties or agreements signed with local chiefs and between the imperial powers.[18]

In the industrializing states, which by the 1890s included Japan, international law became a well-respected profession.[19] Universities endowed chairs in the field and governments employed lawyers to manage the small print of their treaty making.[20] But even outside the industrial metropoles, international law became an essential medium for cross-border interactions, be they commercial or diplomatic. For that reason, the Chinese and Korean governments trained diplomats in Western international law.[21] International law was as much a tool to justify and formalize global expansion, as it was a medium for negotiation about how that expansion might occur.[22] The Ottoman Empire certainly came to see international law as an essential tool of its foreign policy: as a defence against the expansionist aims of its great power rivals and to consolidate control within its own empire.[23] At the same time, it was the language of law – the legalese surrounding terms like 'treaty', 'sovereignty' and 'agreement' – that imbued the ways in which ordinary people considered the actions of 'civilized' states.[24] This same legalese influenced their consideration of the Tsar's rescript and the subsequent relevance of the Hague conferences.

It was the rise of literacy and cheap newspaper printing through the nineteenth century, however, that gave individuals access to information about world developments and each other. It was through newspapers that their understandings were shaped and their global imagination piqued. It was also through newspapers that people engaged first and foremost with the events surrounding the Hague conferences. That the newspaper industry underwent a transformation in the 1880s and 1890s is therefore vitally important.[25] By 1900, there were more newspapers in circulation in a greater number of languages (including indigenous languages) than ever before and their numbers kept rising.[26] According to the records of the *Institut international de bibliographie* (International Bibliographic Institute), for example, there were more than 52,000 newspapers in print in 1898. Ten years later that number had risen to almost 71,000, including several thousand in Asia, more than 300 in Africa and an astounding 1,175 in the sparsely populated territories of Australasia and the Pacific.[27] In other words, greater numbers of people had access to a range of printed information than ever before. On the one hand, these newspapers were audience specific and functioned as powerful platforms for the advance of the religious and political opinions and cultural biases of their editors and owners.[28] On the other, many of the periodicals were market commodities that aimed at a wide circulation. Their presentation of what was universally 'newsworthy' drove their content.[29]

To that end, a newspaper's reach was not restricted to its immediate audience or locality: they operated within a global web of information circulation.[30] The average newspaper included reports received by cable from a range of telegraph news companies such as Reuters, the Associated Press, Havas and Wolff, offering a mesmerizing array of information about global events.[31] Most newspaper editors were also voracious consumers of other journals, foreign and local. They published précis of other papers' contents, translated foreign-language articles and compared and contrasted views on domestic and international issues in their editorials. As an example, consider the ways in which the international press related Russia's use of floating mines, which sunk two Japanese battleships in Port Arthur in May 1904. Most newspapers reported the event. Many also documented a rising concern among the world's neutral governments about the safety of the seas and the security of neutral shipping. The Parisian paper *Le Figaro* explained on 26 May how many British and American newspapers criticized the Russians. It noted that President Roosevelt would address both belligerents and relayed that the American newspaper, the *Standard*, had solicited the opinion of an international lawyer, Professor Woolsey from Yale University, on the subject.[32] *Le Figaro* followed up with another article on 27 May, which explained that President Roosevelt would advise both belligerents of the dangers posed by floating mines to peaceful commerce. The British intended to lodge a formal complaint as well.[33] On exactly the same days, 300 kilometres north of Paris in Brussels, the editors of the *L'Indépendance Belge* iterated similar news to their readers. They also noted how 'most newspapers' expressed disquiet at Russia's indiscriminate use of the mines.[34] Half a world away, the *North China Herald*'s editors went much further and lambasted the Russians for their barbarous behaviour that so clearly endangered neutral shipping.[35] Meanwhile, the opinion piece written on the topic by the renowned British international lawyer T.E. Holland for *The Times* (London) not only served to inform its British audience but was also cited in newspapers in Australia, New Zealand, the Netherlands and the Dutch East Indies.[36]

By the outbreak of the Russo-Japanese War in 1904, the professionalization of journalism was well underway, even if many popular newspapers were not always picky in ensuring the veracity of their reporting.[37] Still, many editors employed 'special correspondents' to relay foreign news first hand, rather than rely on cablegrams. Newspaper readers, in turn, were both consumers of global news and participants in the web of international communication. When they reacted to news items – as they did in response to the Tsar in 1898 in the form of letters to the editor and as organizers of public meetings, petitions and entreaties – they themselves became the news. As the American H.S. Kerr noted in an article about his impressions of New Zealand in a Wellington newspaper in 1906:

> Newspaper offices fairly dot the country. The newspaper is a flag that flies in every breeze up and down dale. For a population of less than a million, there are over 60 dailies and about a hundred broad sheets which 'warn the Tsar' or somebody else two or three times a week . . . New Zealanders – and newspapers may claim the credit – are remarkable for their interest in the movements of the whole world. They are posted in the doings of the cosmos, the earth, sun, moon and stars.[38]

New Zealanders were certainly not unique in their greed for foreign news or in their reactions to that content. By 1899, newspapers were products of the nineteenth-century communications revolution as much as they were channels through which ideas about the world spread.[39] They offered a medium through which individuals consumed information about the world and considered the implications of global events for themselves and for others.

It was in the understanding that newspapers had the power to shape opinions and mobilize action that much of the agency for and against the Hague conferences formed: newspapers created the medium to advance The Hague's message.[40] As the Radical journalist H.N. Brailsford suggested in 1914: '[T]he real importance of newspapers depends less on their leading articles than on their power to present or colour or suppress facts. Here the masses are absolutely at their [the editors'] mercy.'[41] Obviously, we cannot equate the contents of newspapers with what individuals understood about their world. Still, newspapers give historians insight into the range of information available. For their part, contemporaries believed that newspapers were the way 'in' to the public's heart and to its opinion-making capacities.[42] Even in countries with harsh censorship restrictions, the force of public opinion mattered. The need to shape it was certainly felt by governments and interested parties alike.[43] In *The Great War for Peace*, William Mulligan shows that during the First World War governments used moralized ideas of 'right' to advocate publicly for their country's material interests. They also invoked abstract principles, such as those presented by international law, to frame their foreign policy. These 'rights' created a 'political vocabulary' for their public diplomacy.[44] This book argues that government advocacy for normative ideas relating to war and peace existed before the First World War. Many of those ideas were framed by the Hague conferences.

The rise of the popular press, the global focus of newspaper reports and the global interactivity of the media all emphasize that the 1890s witnessed the expansion of the power of public opinion. In a pivotal study, Paula Krebs contends that by the late 1890s, 'public opinion' in Britain was no longer defined by a handful of newspapers representing the perspectives of the political elite, but rather that the power of the people was expressed in and shaped by a widening press landscape.[45] Krebs also acknowledges the diffuseness of the idea of 'the public' having power, for 'the public' was not an amorphous whole, but consisted of all manner of subgroups and identities, which were not necessarily all represented in the press. Yet she reminds us that contemporaries were all too aware that 'the press' mattered both as a medium to reflect on public values and to shape them.[46]

But it was not in Britain alone that the emergence of newspapers as a 'fourth estate' counted.[47] Even in countries with restrictive newspaper cultures, most governments recognized the political power of the press and attempted to mould it to meet their needs. They understood all too well that the public sphere could be manipulated.[48] To that end, the Russian government published a French-language newspaper, the *Journal de St.-Petersbourg*, to proffer a Romanov-friendly version of events to the world. The German government, for its part, was one of the first to establish a press office, which aimed at shaping the content of German newspapers.[49] Other countries followed suit.[50] This book shows how the public and media responses to the Hague conferences helped to shape the diplomatic agenda of governments and highlights how 'The Hague' came to have widespread normative meaning.

The public engagement with The Hague from 1899 on should also be framed by other globalizing developments that pre-existed the rise of mass media in the 1890s. Global travel, for example, became relatively commonplace during the nineteenth century, both in the form of permanent migrations as well as casual travel by the well-to-do for business and pleasure.[51] The Great Exhibition, held in London in 1851, was one of the first coordinated events to profit from the global movement of people for entertainment purposes. It also sought to display a liberal vision of an integrated world and integrated humanity.[52] The World Fair held in Paris in 1889, which endowed the city with the Eiffel Tower, was even more globally aligned than its British predecessor. In all, sixty-nine international conferences were held in the course of that fair, all purporting to improve some element of international relations.[53] The 1893 Columbian Exposition held in Chicago, which was attended by twenty-seven million people, mooted a World's Congress Auxiliary and a World Parliament of Religion.[54] Meanwhile, the modern Olympic Games movement, formed in 1894 with the first events held in Athens in 1896, embodied the idealized possibilities of an interconnected world extraordinarily well.[55]

Unsurprisingly, the nineteenth century also witnessed numerous attempts at establishing new forms of international organization, some highly pragmatic, others more idealized. The Italian activist Guiseppe Mazzini, for example, advocated for the creation of a European union in the 1840s, as did Louis Napoleon after his ascension to power in France in 1851.[56] The Pan-American Union achieved a transnational organization of sorts when it formed in 1890 to link the United States and the Latin American states. Each member country agreed to resolve their commercial and juridical conflicts in amicable ways, especially by means of international arbitration.[57]

The European powers met at the Congress of Berlin in 1884 and 1885 to resolve their competing economic and imperial interests in the Congo basin.[58] Such developments aimed at finding ways of organizing and improving international relations and the international system more generally. They also sought to sustain the rising power of industrial empires.

Contemporaries attached the label 'internationalism' or 'internationalist' to the host of non-state organizations that sprang up through the course of the nineteenth century looking to improve the international condition.[59] Early on, Christian missionaries and church groups operated at the forefront of these movements. They also formed the first peace organizations – the American Peace Society and London Peace Society – in the aftermath of the Napoleonic Wars.[60] By 1900, the International Peace Bureau (IPB), housed in Berne, counted hundreds of peace groups as members.[61] An annual International Peace Congress was held in rotation in the major cities of Europe and the United States, attracting thousands of attendees.[62] As Martin Ceadel explains, we need to distinguish here between what we today would call pacifists and what he labels as 'pacifisists' in the late-nineteenth- and early-twentieth-century contexts.[63] The former were in the minority. They argued against the evil of war and idealized war-free utopias. The far larger movements of pacifisists certainly shared a deep concern about the inhumanity of war, but these groups looked for practical steps to reduce its occurrence.[64] Pacifisists, then, sought practical change embedded in the needs of the present.[65] The Tsar's rescript and the two Hague conferences offered ideal settings for these pacifisists to advance that cause.

Many nineteenth-century pacifisists were also ardent liberals. Liberalism, another early-modern ideology, offered a powerful motor for internationalist agency in the 1800s. Liberalism aimed at individual freedom and equality and encouraged new forms of international interaction. Free-trade liberals advocated for freeing up economic ties and access to the world economy for all 'civilized' people. Most liberals claimed they were proponents of universal peace and prosperity.[66] Many advocated for international arbitration and some were active members of peace organizations. They tended to be wary of the term imperialism, which they associated with costly, deadly and largely immoral acts of military take-over and colonization.[67] Still, they were ardent promoters of global interactivity and of what today is called 'informal empire': the building of inescapable networks of international and imperial trade, labour and exchange in which, inevitably, the rich benefit at the cost of the poor.[68]

Many liberals also aimed at the political organization of nation-states through the advancement of constitutions and representative parliaments. At the Paris World Fair of 1889, liberal politicians across Europe came together to establish the Inter-Parliamentary Union (IPU), an organization for public men to promote transnational cooperation.[69] The IPU became a powerful internationalist political body and saw itself as a conduit for peace. The Belgian international lawyer and IPU member Eduoard Descamps even coined the term *pacigérat* ('manager of peace') to describe the IPU's aims of advancing practical peace.[70] After 1899, the IPU embodied the principles and spirit of The Hague in their public advocacy.[71]

Many IPU members were also aligned with other internationalist organizations, including those promoting the regulation and standardization of international law. The

Institut de droit international (Institute of International Law), established in 1873, was the most important of these.[72] The *Institut* embodied the concept of international law as a 'science of peace' and aimed for the systematic regulation of international relations between 'civilized states' (by 'civilized' the lawyers meant countries that had recognizable governments, operated under recognizable standards of law and which advocated for the basic human rights of their citizens).[73] The *Institut*'s members believed that through proper international regulation, diplomacy could be constrained and foreign policy narrowed so that war would become a less likely outcome of diplomatic crisis.[74] International law also offered a mechanism through which to shape human society globally: a mould for civilizing states to adopt, to escape 'barbarity' and join the family of nations, as well as a rationale for 'civilized' states to intervene in the affairs of their 'uncivilized' neighbours.[75] The creation of universal standards of international interaction based on rational and well-considered norms offered what these lawyers considered a comforting progressive vision for the future of humanity. Like James Brown Scott, Paul Reinsch, members of the IPU and many peace activists, members of the *Institut* were also Enlightenment practitioners looking for the gradual improvement of global interaction. They were remarkably successful in achieving their ambitions and proved to be particularly adept at using the Hague conferences as a forum for advancing their ideas.

Nineteenth-century internationalist organizations also mobilized behind humanitarian action, another foundational context to consider the Hague conferences. In their drive to end the abhorrent African slave trade, for example, abolitionists were one of the first and one of the best organized humanitarian organizations of the era.[76] But most instances of conflict, war and imperial acquisition created critical public dialogues. During the first Opium War (1839–41) which Britain fought in China, a loud, if not overwhelming, critique of the enterprise begged Britons: 'let us be merciful in the prosecution of [the war], and not create any misery'.[77] After the 1848 revolutions, John Stuart Mill pronounced that 'it is too late in the day . . . to tell us that nations may not forcibly interfere with one another for the sole purpose of stopping mischief and benefitting humanity'.[78] The Crimean War (1853–56) and the Second War of Italian Independence in 1859 brought concerted attention to the plight and medical care of soldiers, which inspired the international organization of Red Cross units in 1863.[79] The first Geneva Convention of 1864, initially signed by twelve countries, formalized the rules for the care and treatment of the wounded in time of war.[80] Meanwhile from the 1860s on, the European press held little back in condemning the excesses of violence committed within the Ottoman Empire.[81] In the context of the Spanish-American War of 1898, some Americans debated the morality of their conduct towards Cubans and Filipinos.[82]

The last three decades of the century also witnessed an increase in the establishment of internationalist organizations, including the International Council for Women (ICW), founded in 1888. The ICW used the forums of the Paris World Fair of 1889 and the World's Columbian Exposition in 1893 to advance its causes.[83] The Women's Christian Temperance Union (WCTU) also connected up its many international branches in the English-speaking world from 1876 onwards and looked to advance issues of global importance, including women's suffrage, international arbitration and peace activism.[84] Speakers of Esperanto, an artificial language created in 1887 to enable international communication, met annually both to promote the spread of the language and to discuss means of improving the global condition.[85] By 1900, the International Association of Academies aimed to integrate scientific and academic enterprise globally, and universities in Europe and the United States initiated their own forms of international unions and exchanges.[86]

Significantly, many of the internationalist ventures noted above aimed at the improvement of the world through gradual change. They identified, by and large, with liberal and progressive ideas. Often, they were interconnected enterprises. Other forms of internationalism were much more radical. The Marxists, socialists, Fabians and anarchists, for example, were as internationally connected and globally minded as any of their liberal or religious opponents.[87] These radical internationals actively mobilized behind messages of anti-imperialism, anti-capitalism, workers' rights, the abolition of oppressive laws and even the abolition of the law-makers themselves.[88] For example, the First and Second Internationals, the latter established at the 1889 Paris World Fair (much like the IPU),[89] looked to unite the workers of the world behind socialist ideals. The Pan-African Association aimed to coordinate political activities and advance the welfare of African and indigenous peoples around the world.[90] Pan-Slavic movements had similar ambitions, namely, to advance the rights and prominence of Slavic peoples across Europe's many borders.[91] The Subject Races Committee, established in 1907 in The Hague, joined several committees of national self-determination together including the National Council of Ireland, the Egyptian Committee and the Georgian Relief Fund under the banner of democracy and civil rights.[92] In 1911, the First Universal Races Congress brought together academics, internationalists, government representatives and activists from around the world to discuss the relationship between the world's white and non-white races.[93]

Some of the most prominent activists in all these movements were internationally renowned figures, who travelled the world advocating for their causes in public addresses, newspaper articles and open-air meetings. The Russian author Leo Tolstoy, for example, was an ardent and prominent activist for radical pacifism. The Austrian Baroness Bertha von Suttner, best-selling author of the anti-war novel *Die Waffen nieder* (Lay down your arms, 1889), was a celebrated peace campaigner. After the publication of an abridged English-language edition of his *Is War Now Impossible?* in 1898, the wealthy Polish entrepreneur Ivan Bloch travelled the globe promoting the premise that the destructive power of industrial conflict made war too horrible to contemplate.[94] Prominent thinkers including Jacques Novicow, David Starr Jordan and Vernon Kellog all advocated that warfare was an outmoded and unnatural element of human society.[95] The name of the inventor of dynamite, Alfred Nobel, in turn, became synonymous with international respectability after he bequeathed an extraordinary sum of money to endow several international prizes for advances in science, economics and literature as well as to the person or institution that had done the most to promote practical peace.[96] The Nobel Peace Prize, awarded from 1901 on, offered the opportunity for noted peace activists and their organizations to receive press attention, recognition and a source of funding.[97]

Nobel was not the only wealthy benefactor at the fin de siècle who made internationalism a prime motivator for his philanthropy. The American steel magnate

Andrew Carnegie published treatises on worthy internationalist topics (including the *Gospel of Wealth* [1889] that called on the rich to use their riches to improve society) and supported several internationalist causes. He was a member of the American Anti-Imperial League and an admirer of international arbitration. He endowed the cities of The Hague and Washington D.C. with small fortunes to build peace palaces to house the Permanent Court of Arbitration (established at the first Hague conference) and the International Bureau of American Republics.[98] In 1910, he set up the Carnegie Endowment for International Peace, an organization aimed at promoting and studying internationalism and ending the blight of war.

The existence of all these internationalist groups and personages signal a growing awareness of international concerns in the late-nineteenth- and early-twentieth-century world. Of course, these internationalists did not represent everyone. They tended to come from Western societies that pigeonholed humanity into 'civilized' and 'uncivilized' categories. Still, to typecast the concern with international organization as a Western phenomenon alone fails to account for the extent of global interactivity. Chinese scholars in the 1880s and 1890s, for example, considered universalist solutions and sought viable pathways for China to engage with the world.[99] By 1900, citizens in Meiji Japan were known to voice their opinions against war and against the imperialist and nationalist policies of their government. Most Japanese Christians were liberal internationalists, while Japanese Buddhists developed their own transnational connections.[100] In the early 1900s, the Latin American states demanded representation at the second Hague peace conference to obtain a voice in the international arena. Meanwhile, in India, the Ahmadiyya movement stressed the peaceful nature of Islam, while proponents of the Bahá'i faith in Persia and the Ottoman Empire sponsored peace manifestos, including plans for arbitration and the establishment of a world court from 1873 on.[101] All these internationalists propagated their ideas far and wide through the dissemination of pamphlets, the publication of specialized newspapers and magazines and through public lectures and advocacy. Their existence suggests that there was a growing awareness of how the global arena mattered. After 1899, many of their discourses revolved around The Hague and sometimes were even conducted there.

Nevertheless, the internationalism of the late nineteenth and early twentieth centuries had a decisive Euro-centric and Anglo-centric flavour, which was an unsurprising consequence of the fact that European (including Anglo-American) standards dictated the form of most global interactions. While contemporaries were capable of and allowed extraordinary levels of local and even regional diversity, critique and action, Western models of political, economic, cultural and societal interaction nevertheless dominated world affairs.[102] During the 1800s, the non-European world was largely overwhelmed by the changes in the international system caused by the rapid impact of industrialization and the growth in economic, imperial and global power of the industrializing states (beginning with Britain, much of Europe and then Russia, the United States and Japan). Within the space of a few decades, the non-European world accommodated not only an influx of foreign peoples and their machines but was also confronted by an avalanche of foreign ways of thinking and engaging. In so many ways, then, the creation of nineteenth-century globalization – 'the first global international system in history' – came with extraordinary levels of 'cultural humiliation, dislocation and accommodation'.[103]

This is not to say that non-Europeans were not agents in international politics or that the cultural adjustment was a one-way process. Nor does it suggest that only Europeans advanced economic empires. At any rate, non-Europeans were all too aware of how their livelihoods and ways of being were challenged and undermined. They also came to realize that they had to both appropriate the standards of international interaction set by the Western world and attempt to break through the prejudices and restrictions of those standards before they could make a genuine impact on the world stage.[104] Much like Meiji Japan sought to westernize in order to be recognized as a 'civilized' state with equal status in the international system before it could become sufficiently powerful to resist Western power, so too were all other globalizing communities confronted with finding ways of operating within the Western global system.[105] For many non-European governments, participation in the Hague conferences offered the potential to not only become part of the international system but also shape it.

Altogether, the rise of internationalism offered both opportunities and challenges for governments. Frequently, they reacted to rather than shaped the sociopolitical forces in question. The media revolution of the 1890s, therefore, was particularly important. How might governments maximize their access to newspaper news to affect their domestic and foreign policies? How might they utilize the burgeoning media environment to promote their public diplomacy (which is broadly defined here as the ways in which governments openly communicated their foreign policy objectives and ambitions within and outside their country)?[106] The courting of public favour was a mainstay of diplomatic activity. But the profound explosion of public opinion and its dissemination in globally reactive ways were relatively new developments in the 1890s. How were these governments going to manage the potential backlash to events that were read and engaged with at home and abroad in increasingly diverse ways? The Dreyfus Affair was so profoundly embarrassing to the French government after Emile Zola's *J'accuse* article appeared in January 1898, in part because it heightened anti-French sentiment around the world.[107] The existence of a globalized media environment made the Dreyfus affair an extraordinary international issue, in much the same way as the first Hague conference was too. All governments had to find ways to cope with these realities.

Of all state actions, the most controversial was the waging of war. From the 1890s on, in fact, warfare dominated the news. In Europe, the United States and the British Empire, glorifications of military prowess and heightened militarized nationalism were on the rise. The idea that great nations and empires were built on great wars abounded. Masculinity and military service were intimately connected and the mass market for heroic war fiction pitting great power against great power bloomed.[108] While prestige, power and competition were acknowledged as dangerous combinations, they were also deemed inevitable, as natural outcomes of the Darwinian social order.[109] It is really no wonder that at the heart of many historical explanations of the origins of the First World War sits the idea that the European people were willing to risk war for national and imperial gain.

Yet to focus solely on the veneration of war themes in Western society at the fin de siècle is to miss a vital element of contemporary understanding. Many people also questioned the use of military power and aimed for its limitation and control.[110] They acknowledged war as a horror and considered ways of limiting its application. At a time when most European states were increasing their conscription quotas and purchasing massive industrial arsenals, it only made sense that the ordinary citizen and subject feared war.[111] Some of the turn-of-the-century war fiction, in fact, was purposely alarmist, warning of the dangers of a future war that might be avoided.[112] These war depictions also served the needs of 'civilization'. Some of them suggested that as the world was 'civilizing' faster and faster, new forms of global engagement would be found that would make human warfare a thing of the past. In the meantime, if it was impossible to prevent wars in the near term, then it made sense to humanize their conduct. Or, at the very least, steps could be taken to limit the impact of war on non-belligerents, thereby preventing the advent of global war. As David Bell explains, the nineteenth century was one of extremes and contrasts in which the 'vision of war' could feature as 'the sublime, redemptive, *desirable* exception' to the ideal of balance, order and stability.[113]

As a result, the idea that war could or should be regulated was considered by many as a rational and natural step in the progress of human civilization.[114] In this context, it is important to note the attempts made by governments to regulate the conduct of war, including the Geneva Conventions of 1864 and the St Petersburg Declaration of 1868. The Declaration of Paris of 1856 set rules for the conduct of war at sea and abolished the practice of privateering. It was the world's first multilateral law of war treaty.[115] The *Institut de droit international* formulated what came to be known as the Oxford Manual of 1880 to promote the standardization of the conduct of war between 'civilized' states. Its members did so in response to the Brussels Convention of 1874, which was not ratified, but which achieved agreement on the treatment of prisoners of war and internees and the rules of military occupation and engagement. The Hague conventions of 1899 and 1907 made considerable advances in developing these rules.

In 1898, the world's industrializing societies read each other's news and engaged with each other's issues. When Tsar Nicholas II invited the world's 'civilized nations' to a disarmament conference in August 1898, his rescript unleashed a public discourse on issues of war and peace that was diverse, complex and many-sided. The rescript inspired contemporaries to question the place of war, peace, arbitration and international organization at home and abroad. It also offered them an opportunity to voice their opinions, which they embraced. Their voices affected the course of the first Hague conference in fundamental ways. For the governments who could not avoid attending, the public attention given to The Hague was decisive. It ensured that The Hague would have an important influence on international politics in the era before the outbreak of the First World War.

2

The Tsar, the Rescript and the World

And the world has been shaken by burning news

– *Moscow Journal* 1898[1]

From the outset, the Tsar's rescript of 24 August 1898 was more than news.[2] It engaged widespread editorial commentary and conjecture, which turned to the ambitions of the Tsar, the possibilities of disarmament and the aspirations of those who, in the wake of the rescript, mobilized behind messages of peace and international cooperation. Unlike most of the other foreign events that preoccupied the press in 1898, the Tsar's declaration was unique and far-reaching. It had the potential to influence the future of almost every person on the planet. And it was the rescript's promised global impact that both excited and worried those who encountered the news. For as the Dutch weekly newspaper the *Vaderlander* suggested to its readers, the idealism embedded in the Tsar's call to bring about 'general peace' carried with it the potential of a utopian future. The paper cited Victor Hugo's edict that 'the utopia of today is the reality of tomorrow' (*les utopies sont der berceaux*, utopias are cradles) to make its point.[3] Its compatriot newspaper, the protestant *Nederlandsche Dagblad*, similarly editorialized that 'he who does not strive for the unreachable, will never achieve the achievable'.[4] It was in the spirit of what seemed achievable that much of the media discourse around the rescript evolved.

Few diplomatic announcements have caused as much international fervour as the release of Tsar Nicholas II's announcement. The foreign diplomatic corps stationed in St Petersburg received the message from Russia's Foreign Minister Count Mouravieff with incredulity. In flabbergasted tones, they forwarded it on to their home governments, with accompanying messages promising to uncover the meaning and intention of the document.[5] None of them could entertain the idea that the Tsar was serious in his hopes of guaranteeing general peace by reducing the strength of the world's military arsenals. They all understood that armaments control was the least likely platform for attaining diplomatic consensus. At best, the diplomats portrayed the Tsar as an idealistic young despot hoping to bask in history's glorious spotlight. At worst, they presented the declaration as a desperate attempt to correct Russia's shortfall in industrial-military production.

The world's statesmen responded in kind. Kaiser Wilhelm II dismissed the rescript as 'humanitarian nonsense'[6] and admonished his cousin Nicholas II for 'dissolving his regiments sacred with a hundred years of history and relegating their glorious colours to the walls of the armouries and museums (and handing over his towns to Anarchists and Democracy)'.[7] Britain's future King Edward VII equally scathingly pronounced that 'it is the greatest nonsense and rubbish I ever heard of. The thing is simply impossible'.[8] Even Russia's own diplomats quietly suggested among themselves that it was a 'childish and utopian' endeavour without any hope of success.[9]

Meanwhile, the governments' formal responses to the Tsar were conveyed in muted tones. The Japanese Prime Minister Marquis Shigenobu Okuma, ever wary of Russia's plans for Asia, lauded the Tsar's motivation but also warned that if his ambition in limiting armaments production failed, war may come, in which case Japan would be prepared.[10] The US President William McKinley explained that although his country applauded the Tsar's initiative, there was no way it could entertain the notion of disarmament while it was left reeling from the Spanish-American War.[11] The French government, Russia's staunchest ally, intimated that because France faced unique challenges, it could not promise to deliver on the Tsar's call to diminish its arsenal even if it gladly accepted the Tsar's invitation to confer on the issue.[12] More emphatic were the replies from the Ottoman Empire, the Macedonians and Serbs, who all proclaimed disarmament 'impossible'.[13] Perhaps China's minister to St Petersburg summed it up best when he asserted that 'everyone knows that Russia is "covering her ears to steal the bell" . . . but all the nations promote disarmament as a good topic'.[14] The reduction of armaments was a principle that governments could choose to pay public homage to, even if they had no intention of acting upon its ambition.

Beyond acknowledging that they could not turn down an invitation from the most powerful monarch on earth, most governments did little to encourage the Tsar's endeavour. The limitation of armaments was not a topic they would seriously consider for negotiation, at least not in an open multilateral forum.[15] Nevertheless, in January 1899, the Tsar sent Count Mouravieff on a tour of the European capitals, negotiating the possible agenda items of a 'conference of peace'. On 24 January, Mouravieff issued a second circular in the Tsar's name detailing the topics open for discussion at the conference. Extending well beyond the maligned subject of disarmament, the agenda looked to find common cause on the following issues: the limitation of armaments' production and invention, the application of the Geneva Conventions of 1864 to warfare at sea, the expansion of the laws of war (using the Brussels Conventions of 1874 as a starting point) and the application of 'good offices', arbitration and mediation.[16] By mid-February, the Dutch town of 's Gravenhage (The Hague), seat of the Netherlands government, was settled on as the host venue.[17] Amid much public aplomb, on 18 May 1899, the young Queen Wilhelmina opened the doors of her summer 'House in the Woods' (*Huis ten Bosch*) to twenty-six state delegations for a diplomatic conference lasting ten weeks.

The power of the first Hague conference lies not in the machinations of diplomats or the manoeuvrings of state chancelleries. The rescript's momentum was fuelled in the public sphere. The public release of the rescript in 1898 animated the world. As news of the rescript appeared in newspapers and featured in political debates around the planet, so too did engagement with the notion that 'the public' (as vague as that term is) could influence international developments. The world's statesmen had to consider the public profile of the rescript, the impact of any public mobilization behind various causes in the wake of its release and their own positions on the key issues to be discussed at The Hague. In the end, while the 1899 Hague conference was a diplomatic event, which only official government representatives could attend, it was also a public spectacle in which the weight of global and domestic opinion played a role in directing the hands of the states involved. Before the doors of the 1899 Hague conference closed, a new era of public diplomacy had opened.

The wider world's reception of the rescript was much more enthusiastic, although no less incredulous, than that of Europe's statesmen. Cast in an array of religious, nationalist, internationalist, imperial, pacifist, socialist, liberal, radical and conservative hues, their opinions on the rescript and why it mattered varied wildly. In a pamphlet addressed to the nation, for example, the French politician and journalist Georges Fonbelle suggested that, thanks to the rescript, the twentieth century would be baptized with peace.[18] In direct contrast, an editorial in the Parisian newspaper *Le Temps* reminded its readers that 'as long as the injustice of [the Franco-Prussian War of] 1871 has not been righted . . . the true heirs of the Revolution cannot subscribe to the principles of Count Mouraviev'.[19] As long as the lost lands of Alsace-Lorraine remained in German hands, France could not disarm.[20] In the United States, the Unitarian minister and prominent peace activist Edward Everett Hale urged that the rescript 'should be printed in the calendars of the new-born year . . . The words of it should be remembered by all children in the schools, as they remember the words of the Declaration of Independence'.[21]

Across the Atlantic, Hale's compatriot and renowned author of *Tom Sawyer, Huckleberry Finn* and a lesser-known work on the horror of war entitled *A Connecticut Yankee in King Arthur's Court* (1889), Mark Twain, comically responded by offering up his penknife to the Tsar's disarmament appeal during a lecture in Vienna.[22] Many months later he quipped that 'the Czar is in favour of peace . . . and so am I. There ought to be no difficulty about the other people'.[23]

In more hostile tones but echoing Twain's sentiment, the Austrian newspaper *Linzer Montagpost* argued that the rescript belonged 'to the realm of wild fantasies',[24] while socialists and anarchists everywhere proclaimed it a giant waste of time.[25] The British *News*' editor further hinted that behind the rescript it was 'not difficult to discern a man who shrinks from the fearful responsibility of holding in check millions of soldiers'.[26] The Indian Muslim barrister Rafiuddin Ahmed further exclaimed that 'the Tsar appealing to Muslim monarchs for disarmament is like the wolf desiring the sheep to get rid of their horns'.[27]

To illustrate the extent of the global engagement with the rescript, it is useful to consider the ways in which six different colonial newspapers presented it to their readers. The reportage of the rescript in the liberal English-language *Friend of India & Statesman* (published in Calcutta), the illustrated *Australasian* weekly (which aimed at an Australian and New Zealand readership and was published in Melbourne), the *Samoan Weekly Herald* (Apia, which in 1898 and 1899 was published in English),[28] the French-language *Courrier de Tlemcen* (Algeria) and *Gazette Algerienne* (Bône), and the Dutch-language *Surinamer* (Paramaribo) contained many similarities.[29] As they gained access to cablegrams and postal news from 1 September on, the six newspapers all noted the Tsar's announcement, explained the content of the rescript (some quoting it in detail, some in full) and referenced the opinions of the major newspapers of Europe on the issue. They also documented the concerns of France with regards to Alsace-Lorraine, reflected on Russia's position in Europe and Asia and assessed the impact of the news on Europe's stock markets.

While the content of their news reporting was noticeably similar, there were striking differences between the editorial commentaries of the six newspapers. The *Friend of India* first mentioned the rescript in its 'Latest Foreign Intelligence' section on 1 September 1898 paraphrasing the thrust of the Tsar's announcement along with notifications of how Europeans responded to the news.[30] The newspaper returned to the subject of the rescript repeatedly between September 1898 and May 1899. Throughout, its editorial comment was largely cynical and presented any public agitation in favour as nonsensical. On 29 September, in an article entitled 'Universal Peace', it commented that

> [t]he most striking feature of this remarkable document is still to be found in the fact that the head of the greatest army in the world has invited all the nations to lay down their arms and to establish a permanent peace. Whether his motives are purely humanitarian or mainly political, we are still left in doubt. That the former view is possible, no one need be concerned to deny. The Emperor of All the Russias can hardly fail to be aware of the misery which is inflicted on the Continental nations of Europe by the existing military systems.[31]

Two pages later, the *Friend*'s London correspondent suggested that on 'second' and 'third consideration . . . the warm greetings in store for [the rescript] were exhausted within forty-eight hours of its publication'.[32] On 10 November 1898, the same correspondent called a public demonstration, held in Exeter and chaired by the Bishop of London, as lukewarm and effeminate while exalting the enthusiastic crowds that lined the streets in London to welcome back Lord Kitchener after the Sudan offensives. The correspondent further exclaimed that 'whatever resolutions may be passed [at the forthcoming conference] will mean little. In sentiment we are all for the Czar. We shall go to his Conference. But we cannot help retaining a lively recollection of the events of the past three or four years'.[33] By January 1899, a three-column editorial questioned 'Is it peace?' and argued that '[t]he famous Rescript of the Czar was a proposal of despair . . . No self-respecting Power can begin to disarm until the causes which may in the near future lead to war are removed'.[34] Altogether, the readers of India's oldest and widest circulating weekly, which aimed at educating Indians about liberal politics,[35] presented the Tsar, the rescript and the Hague conference in Realist terms: disarmament would be impossible and popular agitation in favour of the rescript was futile.

The Melbourne newspaper, the *Australasian*, first noted the Tsar's rescript on 3 September 1898. It declared the announcement as 'remarkable' and agreed that armaments were a 'crushing burden'.[36] Its editors praised any popular support for the rescript, including from the Trades Union Congress held in Bristol. They commended

Bishop Kennon, the former Bishop of Adelaide, for noting 'this noble proposal' as 'the highest water-mark in the tide of Christianity'[37] and in March 1899 enthused that statesmen everywhere 'had grown eloquent on the advantages of peace'.[38] For the *Australasian*'s readers, The Hague brought hope: 'To believe that civilised mankind will not be able to evolve some better method of maintaining the peace of the world than the present monstrous system of gigantic armaments is absurd. It is equivalent to saying that a general bankruptcy of reason is about to occur.'[39] It was, then, in the spirit of reason and reasonableness that the *Australasian*'s editors looked to the possible achievements of the Hague conference.

The *Samoan Weekly Herald* received news of the rescript from Reuters, from Australian and New Zealand newspapers arriving by ship and from the west coast of the United States via the Pacific telegraph cable. Despite their relative geographic isolation in the middle of the Pacific Ocean, the Samoan islands were incredibly well connected and the *Samoan Weekly Herald* was particularly thorough in its foreign news coverage. It first mentioned the rescript on 10 September 1898 with the headline 'Sensation in Europe', noting not only European but also American opinions on the matter and, like the *Australasian*, acknowledging Bishop Kennon and the Trades Union Congress.[40] It reprinted the *North German Gazette*'s view that the rescript was a noble and philanthropic act and documented that the Women's Christian Temperance Union convention held in Sydney forwarded a resolution to the Tsar thanking him for his peace proposal. The *Herald*'s editorial that same day was reprinted from the *Auckland Star*, which both commended the Tsar for his initiative, especially as 'our noblest instincts plead for it', but also feared that expediency and suspicion would overwhelm any achievements. The 'civilized world' would not allow for a limitation of armaments. Still, the editorial continued, 'universal disarmament offers the only chance of peaceful escape [from war], but apparently it is not a chance that is likely to be taken advantage of yet awhile at any rate'. The *Herald* further suggested that Europe expected war and that astute commentators saw in Russia's move an attempt to gain real advantage. Given the developments in Asia, 'the present time seems singularly inopportune for the Colossus of the North to make overtures of the kind he [the Tsar] has made'.[41]

Over the following months, the *Samoan Weekly Herald* returned repeatedly to the topic of the rescript. It reflected on the likelihood of any success of a Hague conference with a pragmatic and occasionally cynical eye. It acknowledged its readers' interest in the issues involved, including an article on 17 December 1898 that offered 'a few statistics . . . to which the peace letter of the Czar gives a temporary interest', namely, that across the nineteenth century Turkey conducted the most wars (thirty-eight in total), Spain (thirty-two), France (twenty-seven), Russia (twenty-four), Italy (twenty-three), Britain (twenty-one) and Germany far fewer. It concluded that 'there has been more warfare, at least less continuous peace than one would, at first hand, have supposed'.[42] Wars certainly mattered to the *Herald*'s Samoan audience, who were themselves recovering from a civil war that had also involved German, American and British interests.

In northern Africa, the Algerian press was equally interested in the Tsar's message. Much like the *Samoan Weekly Herald*, the *Courrier de Tlemcen* used statistics to explain why a European war would be so destructive, and, by implication, why the Tsar's call for disarmament was so important. It noted that when counted together the size of Europe's armies equalled 14.5 million men.[43] It also remained sceptical about the possibility of any achievements on general peace, for while the Tsar suggested a grand conference, Britain was making steady advances in and around Khartoum.[44] Still, by May 1899, the *Courrier* reflected that of all the surprises facing the world at the end of the century, the Hague conference was certainly not the least surprising and that the topics in discussion at The Hague had 'stupendous importance' for the stability of all Europe and thus the world.[45]

The *Gazette Algerienne* worried in September 1898 about the impact of a general disarmament ruling on the safety and security of Europe's colonies.[46] In March 1899, however, it published an editorial on its front page by Raoul Benoit. In it, Benoit despaired that while all the powers would attend the conference, that the Pope was favourable, that mothers everywhere were thankful for it, that economists applauded the move and that philanthropists were hopeful for its success, the European governments were nevertheless increasing their military budgets and raising their conscription quotas. Benoit urged that the Tsar's mission must not fail, that Europe must dispose of its arms, that the destructive power of the latest military technology was so great that humanity faced a prospective cataclysm and that the art of killing was continuously being perfected by means of monstrous cannons, fantastical weapons of the air, airborne dynamite and incendiary balloons. Benoit finished with the exhortation that the avoidance of a *guerre terrible* was a collective humanitarian duty.[47] A month later, another editorial (not written by Benoit) began with the hopeful assertion that not long ago the power of monarchs was absolute and could command people to war whenever they liked. The times were changing. The Tsar's conference was a massive step in the evolution of civilization. The imperative behind the conference lay in the fact that if a European conflict occurred it would generate a terrible tragedy and occasion *un formidable tremblement de terre* (a formidable trembling of the earth). The frightening logic of this reality must, so the *Gazette*'s editor explained, spur along the diplomats at The Hague.[48] Fear, more than reason, compelled achievement.

Of the six colonial newspapers surveyed here, the *Surinamer*, published in Dutch in the Caribbean port of Paramaribo, was the most detailed and complete in its reportage. It explained on 22 September 1898 that the entire European press 'naturally' focused on the Tsar's 'peace message'. It then recounted with an extraordinary level of profundity the nuanced differences in French, German, Austrian and British media perspectives. According to the *Surinamer*, Germans were by and large in favour of the disarmament conference for, as the *Kölnische Zeitung* noted, any disadvantage to France was an advantage for Germany. At any rate, Germany only armed itself to secure its own peace. The liberal-leaning *Berliner Tageblatt* paid its honourable respects to the Tsar, whose message was so beautiful that one's heart shrank from the fact that disarmament was unattainable. The *Surinamer* further observed that not all French newspapers were negative and that concerns for the future of Alsace-Lorraine and the Russo-French alliance did not preclude several French editors from welcoming the Tsar's news. *Le Figaro* (Paris) hoped a disarmament conference might keep British imperialism in check. The *Journal Gaulois, Petite République, Siècle* and *Echo de Paris* all considered the rescript a noble act and Édouard Drumont's anti-Semitic *Libre Parole* attached the title of 'the Great' to Nicholas II in response. Pierre Veuillot in the Catholic periodical *l'Univers* disagreed, suggesting that France was wealthy enough to sustain the burden of armaments and that the country needed its arms to protect its security. The *Journal des Débats*, in its turn, considered disarmament unattainable.

According to the *Surinamer*, the British press was more universally supportive of the Tsar and his message, although *The Times, Daily News, Standard* and *Morning Post* all expressed doubts about the practicalities of disarmament, especially for the future of the Royal Navy. The *Surinamer* also noted that the Italian media covered a spectrum of opinions and that the rescript had initiated a lively debate: some were jubilant, others reserved and many distrustful of the Russian emperor's motives. The Austrian press represented by the *Neue Freie Presse, Neue Wiener Tageblatt* and *Vaterland* urged their readers to consider the Tsar's action as an olive branch lessening tensions in Europe and Asia, while the *Indépendance Belge* hailed the rescript as the 'first step towards a peace union [*vredesbond*] between all the peoples of earth'. The *Surinamer* finished its detailed assessment with the claim that the Pope was also in favour.[49] Between September 1898 and May 1899, the *Surinamer*'s editor offered his readers a relatively balanced account of European opinion on the forthcoming Hague conference. He steered away from presenting his own assessment of the event but frequently noted that few realists held out hope for the achievement of any practical result at The Hague.

The diversity of opinion noted in this handful of far-flung newspapers represents the gamut of attitudes that traversed the planet about the Tsar and the potential impact of his rescript. The most important statement to make about the Tsar's rescript, then, is that it was reported on, seriously considered, debated, condescended, critiqued and argued about from the moment of its release.[50] Many newspaper representations prioritized local, national and imperial concerns. There was, however, no universal response or national consensus anywhere. In other words, although the reactions to the rescript often focused on issues of national security and imperial interests, they were not defined by the nationality or imperial affiliation of the commentators alone. The German press was not, as some historians claim, universally dismissive of the rescript or the upcoming Hague conference, nor were Britain and the United States the only countries who showed a level of public support for these events, as others suggest.[51] Rather, it would seem that the engagement with the rescript was defined more by an editor's political affiliations, religious beliefs, moral aspirations and a sense of optimism or pessimism about diplomatic and geostrategic realities.

To that end, militarists and conservatives everywhere were most likely to dismiss the disarmament cause as unworkable, while liberals tended to hedge their bets on the need for military power but hoped for the progressive promise of the judicial ordering of the world.[52] Socialists were inclined to dismiss the Tsar's peace initiative as sentimentalism, although numerous labour associations and trade unions went out of their way to profess their favour for the event.[53] The German socialist Karl Liebknecht nevertheless called the rescript and the Tsar 'a fraud'.[54] Laced through almost all these responses were realistic assessments of the international environment, the likelihood of disarmament working and the ambitions of the Tsar himself. There were very few naïve responses. As the German peace activist Alfred H. Fried publicly reflected: there was nothing in the rescript about 'eternal peace' or, for that matter, about the complete demilitarization of nations. Instead, Nicholas II asked governments to consider the possible limitation of armaments.[55] For Fried, the upcoming conference offered the perfect opportunity to consider the improvement of international relations and to minimize and limit the outbreak and spread of war. It offered the first step of many he hoped would be taken in the future towards a more rational and peaceful international order.[56]

That the rescript was deemed important is particularly clear from the negative responses to it. Many military-minded individuals looked upon the conference and any planning to advance it as dangerous, risking global stability, national interests and war. They sought to prevent the conference or, if that proved impossible, to limit its impact. The most vociferous of such responses came from Baron Karl von Stengel, Professor of Law in Munich, who published a small treatise entitled *Der ewige Friede* (Eternal peace) in December 1898.[57] The treatise was a hurried retort to what Stengel believed was a pressing threat to Germany's security. In it, he argued that any approval by the German government of disarmament or of the peace movement's agendas would lead to disaster. Germany's security, and its very existence, relied on military might and peace was guaranteed best by protecting that might. In other words, Stengel advocated strongly for the principle that *si vis pacem, para bellum*. Predictably, peace activists everywhere dismissed Stengel's work as a harangue.[58] Kaiser Wilhelm II, in contrast, was so impressed by the pamphlet that he appointed Stengel to the official delegation for The Hague.[59]

The most important aspect to note about Stengel's response to the rescript is not that he represented the views of most Germans or that his perspective was unique. Similar opinions were held by all manner of people convinced of the necessity of guaranteeing national security by deterrent military means.[60] Even the British Prime Minister, the Marquis of Salisbury, publicly acknowledged in February 1899 that while Britons could work for a peaceful world, 'we must follow the example of other nations, and . . . obey the proverb and prepare for war'.[61] For sure, *Der ewige Friede* and the concept of 'armed peace' found favour with many Germans, especially those closely aligned to the country's imperial heart. But it did not represent them all. In Germany, as elsewhere, the rescript caused debate. To that end, Stengel's treatise is important because he felt the need to publish it quickly to counter those who responded with favour to the rescript.[62] Stengel not only opposed any steps made towards arms limitation but he also sought to demean, even demonize, the platform of the peace activists. He was all too concerned that the rescript had caused enough public momentum in Germany for the issue of disarmament not to have important political repercussions. Stengel's work thus offers an excellent example of how in the wake of the rescript, the German public sphere became an arena of competing visions of national priorities within a global setting. It would remain so throughout the first Hague conference and in its aftermath.

In Britain too, a public frenzy developed in the wake of the rescript. Historians often credit Britain's leading newspaper sensationalist, W.T. Stead, for this success.[63] But the mobilization of peace and charitable organizations like the London Peace Society, the Society of Friends and the International Arbitration and Peace Association (formerly the Workmen's Peace Association) needs to be acknowledged. Still, the public agency in favour of the rescript exceeded the activities of even these organizations. Hundreds of town meetings, trades and trade union gatherings and church congregations signalled their approbation of the rescript by petitioning the British government. The *Arbitrator* logged 38 town council resolutions and a further 91 public appeals in favour of the Tsar's conference in its December 1898 issue.[64] By June 1899, the *Herald of Peace* accounted for 348 town meetings, 79 trade union and labour association gatherings, 605 church and religious groups, 132 local government board meetings and 38 appeals from other organizations in support of the Hague conference.[65] More than 1,400 official resolutions landed on Foreign Secretary Salisbury's desk between August 1898 and May 1899.[66] Stead's International Peace Crusade also amassed 160,000 signatures appealing directly to the Tsar, which it bound in thirty volumes of red leather and handed over to the Russian ambassador in London in April.[67]

The meetings that inspired these resolutions were well attended and well reported, featuring local celebrities and dignitaries.[68] As an example, note the gathering held in the village of Hindhead, Surrey, in January 1899. According to the local paper, '[T]he hall was filled with villagers and gentry', Arthur Conan Doyle (of Sherlock Holmes fame) 'proved an admirable chairman' while playwright George Bernard Shaw gave a characteristically engaging speech about stockpiling armaments. The newspaper further noted that Mr Justice Wright (future Lord Chief Justice), Sir Frederick Pollock (noted jurist), Sir Robert Hunter (co-founder of the National Trust), Lord Russell (present Lord Chief Justice) and Hon. Rollo Russell (his son) regretted they could not be in attendance.[69] Meanwhile, another publication claimed that over 300,000 pamphlets circulated around the country promoting the Tsar's event.[70]

But not all Britons were enamoured with the Tsar or his message. There was plenty of critique both of the rescript, the Tsar and of the public's approval of his proposed conference. In March 1899, the conservative politician Sir Henry Howoth advocated with vehemence that the rescript was nothing more than effeminate sentimentalism, buffoonery and pantomime. He did so in large part to discredit the high levels of public agency behind the Tsar's proposals, which he labelled 'hysterical', and extended the hope that the Tsar was prudent enough not to confuse public opinion with good sense.[71] The equally conservative commentator Sidney Low offered another withering assessment of the prospects of the 'affair', as he put it: everyone knows that 'little will come of it'.[72] He nevertheless dedicated nine pages to explaining why.

Consideration of the Tsar's rescript was a global activity. In the hub of American industry and commerce,[73] for example, the *Chicago Daily Tribune* was quick to publish the Tsar's news on the front page of its 29 August 1898 edition and did so with a series of headlines: 'CZAR URGES ALL EUROPE TO DISARM. Proposes an International Conference to Consider Reducing Large Military Forces. MOVE TO INSURE PEACE. Text of the Note Handed to Accredited Representatives of the Various Powers. PROJECT WELL RECEIVED.' Two tables detailing the size of Europe's 'enormous armies' and the 'naval strength of Europe' and a word-for-word translation of the rescript followed.[74] The next day's issue sampled available opinion from around the world, including an accolade from the Salvation Army General William Booth and the announcement from 'eminent Hungarian historian' Emil Reich that the Tsar was a dreamer: 'this scheme for universal peace is one of his dreams. It is also a feint'.[75]

The paper also sent a correspondent to the home of Reverent Benjamin T. Trueblood, Secretary of the American Peace Society, who was convinced of the Tsar's genuine and sincere intentions with regard to peace. The 'public men in Washington', however, had 'little faith' in the proposed conference's success.[76]

On 31 August, the *Tribune* noted the editorial opinions of other American publications, including the claim in the *New York Times* that the conference's pragmatic ambitions may spell 'the beginning of the most momentous and beneficent movement in modern history, indeed, of all history'.[77] The *Milwaukee Sentinel*, however, feared that

> [t]he most effective opposition to the Czar's plan is likely to come from men who question his motives . . . This kind of opposition is likely to be effective because the world contains many persons who believe that a reform good in itself becomes less good if the man who suggest it acts from motives which he does not care to make public.

Taking a more practical approach, the *Philadelphia Press* pointed out that 'uniform change could be made' to the constituency of Europe's armies and navies.[78] Another day on, the *Tribune* printed the editorial responses of nine further newspapers, all subtly different in their interpretations.[79] It also explained why 'English residents in Peking' saw the rescript as a diplomatic move to 'checkmate Great Britain' and that the American Social Science Association meeting in Saratoga sent a message of approval to the Tsar.[80] By 3 September it acknowledged that, as the *New York Herald* reported, 'the Czar of all the Russias has created the sensation of the era'.[81]

Unsurprisingly, the Russian press proffered a favourable view of the Tsar's enterprise suggesting it will 'constitute a turning point in history'[82] or, as one of Moscow's journals poetically emphasized: 'the world has been shaken by burning news'.[83] Yet even in the Russian empire there were nuanced differences in the editorial commentary. The *Novosti*, for example, explained in a pragmatic tone that 'the disarmament question cannot be solved without a previous removal of the causes of the armaments. The conference must . . . propose means for a peaceful arrangement, and it may come to pass that at the close of the nineteenth century a liquidation may be effected of the international policies which are so prolific in troubles and dangers'.[84] Meanwhile, the *Sviet* lauded the Tsar with the words: 'If all the powers accept Russia's proposal with the same earnestness with which it was made the dawn of the twentieth century will see the idea of universal peace triumphant over that of unrest and discord.' The *Vledomosti* more reflectively suggested that the note of the Czar is essentially 'an attempt to introduce the element of trust into international relations' adding: 'Who-ever believes in the creative power of ideas propounded with conviction and clearness must rejoice that the note brings a new and beneficent course into the world's life and groups anew the participants in that life.'

In Asia, the *North China Herald*'s London correspondent, admittedly writing for an English-language publication aimed at ex-pats, claimed that few people had a 'very extravagant hope' that the Tsar's conference would achieve 'a practical result'. Still, 'we must in fairness give the young Tsar credit for humanitarian motives'.[85] Two months later, the paper's editors proclaimed even more condescendingly that the rescript was 'simply' the 'Utopian notion of a well-meaning young gentleman',[86] yet they also conceded a few pages on that its existence might suggest that Russia was not hell-bent on Europe-wide war.[87] The newspaper also published several odes to Nicholas II, including a poem entitled 'A dream of peace' in which the hope that the Russian endeavour may guarantee the 'Orientals' peace' firmly resounded. It ended with the couplet: 'How strange to think that War should cease / Because a Czar just whispered "Peace"!'[88]

On the other side of the Pacific Ocean, the Latin American newspapers showed equally mixed responses to the rescript and the Tsar. Brazil's *Revista Moderna* argued that a sincere commitment to peace was sure to create disagreements between the powers.[89] In January 1899, Mexico's *El Correo Español* presented its readers with a collection of newspaper perspectives from around the world and editorialized that the rescript was badly timed, was unlikely to lead to any practical results but that once the conference arrived there would be time to discuss and consider the 'important facets that it has to offer'.[90] The Argentine *El Sol del Domingo*'s editors both urged an 'end to innumerable armies' and issued an emphatic rejoinder that they did not praise the Tsar, who made his appeal not on 'superior moral' grounds but rather to 'calmly rule his enslaved people'.[91]

The enormous output of news and opinions surrounding the Tsar, his rescript and the lead-up to the first Hague conference in May 1899 begs the question: why did these developments warrant so much attention? The answer seems to lie in the understanding of contemporaries that the Hague conference had the potential to seriously impact the direction of international diplomacy. They also understood that the conference could have a decisive influence on the future of warfare: its scope, frequency and the likelihood of it erupting in the first place. That the world worried about war is all too evident from the global media responses to the rescript. They did not need to read all 3,084 pages of Ivan Bloch's *Is War Now Impossible?* (1898) to comprehend the destructive potential of industrial warfare. As the Constantinople correspondent of the British *Speaker* argued in January 1899:

> We cannot foresee how or when war will come, but what we can see clearly is this: when it does come, under the new conditions in which we live, in this new era upon which we have entered, a general war in Europe will mean universal war on every sea, and on every continent. Asia, Africa, the islands of the sea, Pagan and Mohammedan, will improve the opportunity to rise against their rulers, and return to their old ways. Europe will have conquered the world only to destroy herself and spread ruin and desolation over all the earth.

The correspondent then urged his readers to 'use all our influence to make the coming Peace Conference something better than a farce'.[92]

It is therefore particularly relevant that Ivan Bloch received considerable media attention in the wake of the rescript and that his international fame spread and the legitimacy of his views improved as reports circulated that he was the original inspiration for the Tsar's announcement.[93] Bloch himself made full use of the attention. He travelled widely, wrote numerous articles and offered a series of lectures during the Hague conference itself, aimed at ensuring that future war would be avoided.[94]

Leo Tolstoy also received considerable public notice, especially after he sent a letter to the Swedish Peace Party in which he advocated that only through complete disarmament and an end to military service could war be circumvented.[95] Tolstoy's letter was censored in Russia as were his reports on the starvation of peasants in Russia's 'black earth' districts.[96] Yet the Tsar visited Tolstoy for the express purpose of obtaining his approval for the conference, which was then communicated to the press.[97] Like Bloch, Tolstoy also continued to use his public fame to promote his own ideas on war and peace.[98] The public relations surrounding the rescript ensured that the opinions of well-known peace activists, including the novelists Bertha von Suttner and George Bernard Shaw and painters Vasily Vereshchagin and Felix Moscheles, were commented on as often as those of well-known detractors, like Mark Twain, Rudyard Kipling and Joseph Conrad.[99] Tolstoy was both lauded and demeaned, depending on the editorial bent in question. The *Liberty Review*, for example, called Tolstoy 'Europe's official Court Fool' and ranked him alongside Britain's 'own fools', including W.T. Stead and Bernard Shaw.[100] As the *Liberty Review* saw it, their actions could be dangerous: Tolstoy was responsible for the Tsar's ridiculous armaments programme after all.[101]

The most extraordinary result of the rescript, however, was the fact that it was not forty-eight-hour news, as the *Friend of India* correspondent predicted. While most governments did not expect any practical results to arise from their discussions on disarmament at The Hague, they nevertheless all agreed to attend the conference. Furthermore, the expectation that real progress could be made at The Hague, be it on the issue of disarmament, arbitration or the laws of war, increased significantly after the release of the second circular in January 1899 and did so among an eager public who mobilized behind the Tsar's message at a local, national and international level. For so many people, the Tsar's message was powerful and its ambitions achievable.

Despite the powerful message, however, few people were convinced by the Tsar's apparent altruism in calling for an armaments conference in the first place. When historians consider the origins of the rescript, they offer various explanations.[102] Using sources from the Russian archives, most credit the development of the rescript to the machinations of three prominent individuals, namely, Russia's Foreign Minister, Count Mikhail Mouravieff; its Finance Minister, Count Sergei Witte; and its Minister of War, Count Alexei Kuropatkin. In combination, the three ministers advised the Tsar about the economic and military realities facing Russia and explained that they were unable to technologically advance their armies at the rate of their rivals.[103] More specifically, Kuropatkin explained that Russia had no answer to Austria-Hungary and Germany's new quick-firing artillery.[104] Witte promoted a reduction in military expenditure to enable investment in the expansion of railways and communication lines eastwards into Asia,[105] while Mouravieff advised that a disarmament conference would offer a 'brilliant diplomatic' manoeuvre.[106] Other historians ascribe more noble origins to the Tsar's motivation by emphasizing Nicholas II's meetings with Bloch or his attentiveness to the anti-war paintings of Vereshchagin and the workings of the Inter-Parliamentary Union.[107] Certainly, the humanitarian deeds of his imperial forebears, including Catherine the Great, Alexander I and Alexander II, provided ample inspiration for the young Tsar as did previous Russian initiatives in the limitation of armaments, like the 1868 St Petersburg Declaration that outlawed the use of exploding bullets.[108] As Dan Morrill explains, a combination of factors motivated the Tsar to issue the rescript. He certainly prevaricated on the subject before its release, which ensured that the announcement was repeatedly delayed between April and August 1898.[109]

'What moved the Tsar?' was a contemporary question that caused an extraordinary amount of conjecture in the press.[110] Media opinions on the subject ranged from the pragmatic to the cynical. W.T. Stead suggested in January 1899 that '[t]here is one thing about the rescript that no one can deny. It was splendidly audacious as well as magnificently ambitious. Wise it may be or foolish, but mean, petty, or unworthy it was not'.[111] Many of Stead's colleagues favoured realistic assessments of Russia's geopolitical situation for explaining the Tsar's action.[112] Other evaluations were more self-serving. Nicolas de Basili suggested that his father, Alexander Basili, one of the Russian delegates at The Hague in 1899, provided the Tsar's inspiration.[113] A.C.F. Beales indicated that his own pacifist associates – Bloch, Suttner and the IPU – all inspired the Tsar.[114] Edwin D. Mead more magnanimously hailed his friend William Ellery Channing as having suggested a similar idea years earlier.[115] More imaginatively, the British *Sunday Times* conjectured in its 'Court and Society' pages in 1903 that a spiritualist had enthused Nicholas II, much like Alexander I had been transfigured to suggest a Holy Alliance at the Congress of Vienna.[116] A year later, Allan Upward fabricated a fantastical account in his illustrated novel *The Secret History of Today: Being the Revelations of a Diplomatic Spy*, in which he journeyed to the depths of Siberia to uncover a massive hidden arsenal and army complex. His conclusion: 'While appearing to disarm in concert with the rest of Europe, Russia's intention was secretly to withdraw her enormous forces to this unsuspected retreat, from when, at the decisive moment, they would issue like a creation of magic, to overwhelm the defenceless continent'.[117] One must beware the slumbering Russian bear.

More grounded in reality were the contemporary publications that reflected on earlier attempts to advance disarmament and international organisation. These assessments aimed at advancing the national prowess of one or other great state. Thus the (later discredited) peace activist Lewis Appleton suggested that only Britain had focused the world's attentions on disarmament before 1898.[118] He also reminded his readers that the British Foreign Arbitration Society had presented a request for disarmament to Kaiser Wilhelm II in 1891.[119] The biographer of Dimitri Stancioff, the young Bulgarian diplomat who attended the conference in The Hague in 1899, explained that in 1863, Napoleon III had called for a general disarmament conference and that it was Britain's reluctance that prevented it from occurring.[120] Yet others looked to Bismarck's coordination of the Berlin Conference of 1884 or the United States' role in the Pan-American Conference of 1889 as key models for the Tsar's plans for The Hague.[121]

While conjecture about the Tsar abounded both in the contemporary and (later) historical record, neither tended to reflect on why the public mobilized behind the rescript and the ensuing Hague conference. Most historiography, in fact, suggests that the Tsar's message was not well received outside internationalist circles.[122] The newspaper record, however, indicates that the rescript and the first Hague peace conference were not uniformly dismissed or universally welcomed anywhere. Certain sectors of the British and American press were, by and large, very good at mobilizing behind the message of peace. Their well-aligned peace organizations made sure of that. But even these organizations were amazed at the amount of popular support for the Tsar's circular. The *Advocate of Peace*, for example, acknowledged in October 1898 that 'the flood of thought and hope awakened by the Russian Emperor's trumpet call has been almost unparalleled'.[123] It was discussed everywhere and opinions fluctuated wildly.

Questions of war and peace were as topical in the United States, fighting its first 'foreign war' against the Spanish, as they were anywhere (Figure 2.1). On the European continent, a questionnaire, in the form of a circular letter of which 2,000 copies were dispersed before the announcement of the rescript in 1898, was published in pamphlet form in its aftermath. The initiative, organized by *Les annales de la jeunesse laïque* (Annals of Secular Youth), *La Vita Internazionale* (International Life) and the socialist *L'Humanité nouvelle* (New Humanity), resulted in the publication of a 262-page booklet, including several overview schemas, explaining the array of existing opinions on the role war played in society.[124] Some of the questionnaire's respondents, who came from a variety of countries, wrote lengthy treatises, others shorter exposés. Their answers varied appreciably: some held war to be a natural state, others that it was an injustice that could be righted. The respondents were divided in their opinions not as much by nationality as by explanatory framing: some approached the question anthropologically, others from the position of ethics, yet others from a socialist perspective. Nikolai Notovich, the (now) noted con artist, parading as a Russian noble and journalist, also collated an overview of responses to the Tsar's rescript late in 1898, richly interspersed with his own analysis.[125] While his 224-page brochure existed first and foremost as an ode to the Tsar and as a means of countering any anti-Tsarist perspectives, what is most telling is that Notovich presented a spectrum of opinion for and against the rescript among the populations of all the major powers, including Germany, France, the United States, Great Britain and Italy.[126]

As another example, Rudyard Kipling authored a poem in honour of the rescript. The poem, entitled 'The Truce of the Bear', offered a derisive assessment of the Tsar:

> When he stands up like a tired man, tottering near and near;
> When he stands up as pleading, in wavering, man-brute guise,
> When he veils the hate and cunning of his little, swinish eyes; . . .
> When he shows as seeking quarter, with paws like hands in prayer
> *That* is the time of peril . . .
> *There is no truce with Adam-zad, the Bear that looks like a Man!*[127]

Written around the same time as his famous poetical polemic 'The White Man's Burden', Kipling argued with *Adam-zad* that no matter what the Tsar might propose for a world congress, at heart, his ambitions were dangerous. His only interests were imperial and aimed at Russian domination of the world (Figure 2.2). Many years later, James Joyce referred back to the rescript and Tsar Nicholas II in equally derisive tones. In his *Portrait of a Young Artist* (1916), the character Stephen refuses to sign a petition

Figure 2.1 This American cartoon from April 1899, depicts Europe dreaming of a peaceful millennium, with thanks to the Tsar's rescript (in her hand). The gunpowder barrel on which she has fallen asleep is about to blow, however, lit by a candle called 'ambition' (*Puck* 5 April 1899, centrefold, Library of Congress).

in support of the rescript, referring to Nicholas II with the words, '[I]f we must have a Jesus, let us have a legitimate Jesus!'[128]

The militant socialist Charles Guieysse was as determined to dismiss the legitimacy of the rescript in a lengthy tome published in 1905, in the aftermath of the Russo-Japanese War and Russian revolution.[129] He looked to persuade the French public that alongside any promise they saw in the Tsar, they must also remember that Russia was not a modern state and could not accommodate the interests of modernity. When the Russians spoke of pacifism, they meant something quite different from the French. Guieysse suggested that the Tsar's call for disarmament in 1898 was a banality brought on by massive popular enthusiasm for the idea (in so doing, he confused the response to the rescript as the reason for its release). He furthered that in their assessment of the rescript, as in so many other situations, the public was wrong. Any reading of the history of modern nations attested to the fact, so Guieysse suggested, that wars of nationhood require arms as much as revolutions do. The inheritors of the French revolution should not accept the premise of arms control. They should also be wary of the Russian bear.

Figure 2.2 This Austrian cartoon was one of several contemporary representations of Tsar Nicholas II as a bear in sheep's clothing, in this case handled by Russia's Foreign Minister, Count Mouravieff. The caption read: Mouravieff: 'See here, oh noble Tsar, the new symbol of the twentieth century'. Tsar: 'As long as I can put it down when I need my weapons. They may come especially handy in Finland' (*De vredes-conferentie. Prentenboek voor oud en jong*. Amsterdam, H. Gerlings, 1899, 12).

Few satirical newspapers failed to offer contemptuous assessments of Russia. These were particularly fierce after the Tsar's move to forcibly Russify Finland in February 1899. At that stage, the Dutch cartoonist Johan Braakensiek published a mocking cartoon of Nicholas II beating a Finnish maiden with an olive branch. Its caption read: 'Oh Majesty, peace can be cruel'.[130] The British *Pick Me Up* magazine depicted the Tsar skewering a poor Finnish person with a sword in triumphant fashion (Figure 2.3).[131] Another cartoon in the Dutch weekly *Uilenspiegel* displayed the Tsar wielding a large whip over not only the Finns, but also the Siberians and Russian Jews, referencing recent pogroms. Behind the suffering people a glorious sunrise proclaimed 'peace'.[132] When it came to Korea too, the Tsar was presented in an Italian publication standing behind a line of massive cannons aimed at the peninsula, with the sarcastic headline: 'In an effort to set a good example, the Tsar is disarming Korea'.[133]

Figure 2.3 This cartoon appeared in Britain's *Pick Me Up* magazine in February 1899 in the wake of the 'Russification' of Finland. It depicted Tsar Nicholas II as the angel of peace impaling the Finns with a long sword (*De vredes-conferentie. Prentenboek voor oud en jong.* Amsterdam, H. Gerlings, 1899, 49).

Of course, the world of 1898 and 1899 came replete with international events and Russia's conduct was certainly not the only act of power that engaged the press or invited its cynical and critical eye. But if we were only to focus on these critical reflections on the exercise of power in the fin-de-siècle world, we might miss the more important point that many contemporaries also understood that the Tsar's proposed conference could make a difference. Even those who claimed the conference was impractical also acknowledged the possibility of its impact. As a result, the rescript, the second circular and the announcement of the first Hague conference were rarely treated as news alone, namely, as events that might be of interest to the reader but otherwise have little relevance. Rather, the commentary on the Tsar and The Hague was so wide-ranging, diverse and prolific because the importance of the proposed event was understood. The potential achievements of the conference were gauged both in terms of the perceived realities of the present and the expectations of an as yet undetermined future. The global reactions to the first Hague conference reflect an understanding that 'whatever may be' could be influenced and directed by governments (especially by the European governments) and therefore also by their citizenry.

It is really no wonder then that for peace activists, the rescript was heard as a clarion call to action.[134] 'It is a gigantic step', Henri Dunant exclaimed in a letter to Bertha von Suttner in September 1898. The instigator of the Red Cross movement went on to suggest that the peace agenda was no longer a utopian pipe dream of a small group of ardent believers, but had become legitimized as a workable ambition for diplomatic action. It was the Tsar who should receive all the praise.[135] The Norwegian author and poet Bjørnstjerne Bjørnson equally emphatically delighted that 'the air is throbbing with thoughts of peace, even where yesterday they were deemed impossible'.[136] The *Advocate of Peace*, the main journal of the American Peace Society, went even further: 'All good men everywhere will watch with the greatest interest the developments which the Czar's move brings about. It may be, we can not help believing that it is, the beginning of one of the grandest and more beneficent movements which history has ever recorded.'[137] They had reason to rejoice. For the first time their most treasured ambition for world peace – general disarmament – was deemed realizable. Needless to say, they mobilized to promote the forthcoming event and heaped lavish praise on its instigator, 'the Tsar of peace'.

But these pacifisists (as Ceadel would have us call them) were not alone in their optimism and this is where the existing historiography gets it so wrong. Contemporary opinion on the rescript was wide-ranging, diverse and voluminous. It was expressed in cartoons, editorials, commentaries and brochures. The Tsar's rescript was addressed from church pulpits, in public meetings, at trade union events and political rallies. It was voiced in petitions, resolutions and open letters addressed to the Tsar, his representatives and to governments around the world. And the global debate around the forthcoming Hague conference only increased as the event drew closer. In other words, many Europeans did not believe, as I.F. Clarke suggests, 'that they could have their wars and enjoy them' nor were all European reactions to war defined by jingoism, distorted concepts of Darwinism and defensiveness towards the concept of peace, as Brian Bond surmises.[138] Fin-de-siècle Europeans worried about war as much as they considered its alternatives. The rest of the industrializing world worried alongside.

The content of the media debate certainly became more nuanced after the release of the second circular in January 1899.[139] By extending the agenda of the conference to a series of key international issues, including international arbitration, the Geneva Conventions of 1864 and the codification of the law of war, not only did the prospects of the upcoming event increase but so too did media approval of it. The second circular made the conference 'respectable' according to the German international lawyer Hans Wehberg. In that 'respectability' lies an explanation as to why Mouravieff issued it in the first place.[140] Where disarmament was a problematic platform for diplomats and could easily be dismissed by anyone with an interest in military deterrence, these other issues were not only much more popular but also thought by some to be more practical. As the *Hawke's Bay Herald* (New Zealand) noted in a fine editorial in March 1899:

> Few people, we imagine, expect much result from the conference of representatives of European Powers on the Czar's proposals. Perhaps one reason for this scepticism is that they have been wrongfully described as disarmament proposals . . . But a perusal of a summary of the text of the proposals which were made public just before the last mail left shows that if some of them are impracticable, others come well within the scope of reasonable discussion . . . The publication of the Count's [Mouravieff's second] circular, we are told, has revived interest in the Czar's proposals, which are not all so impracticable as a bald proposition for disarmament.[141]

Of the agenda items, the concept of international arbitration was the most significant. Public advocacy for international arbitration had existed in many countries, and especially in Britain and the United States, since the early nineteenth century. It had advanced apace during the 1860s.[142] By the 1890s, arbitration was the most prominent and publicly acceptable idea for improving international relations, with adherents across the political spectrum. Many politicized groups, from the International Council of Women (ICW) and Women's Christian Temperance Union (WCTU) to peace organizations, the IPU and *Institut de droit international*, mobilized behind its potential. Governments also utilized international arbitration in a variety of forms as a pragmatic solution for settling financial, territorial and legal disputes.

It is telling then that international arbitration made it on to The Hague's agenda. According to the Belgian diplomat in St Petersburg, it did so because of the recognized public appeal of the move.[143] This admission is particularly important, as the work of Vincent Genin shows, because when the Belgian government sent a missive to a number of foreign governments early in 1898 requesting their opinion on regulating arbitration, it received only one positive response and that from the Duchy of Luxembourg.[144] In other words, there was little, if no, state support for an international initiative in establishing workable rules for international arbitration when the Belgians proposed it in private. However, in the aftermath of the release of the rescript, amid the widespread public appeal for the success of the promised event, international arbitration was able to make it on to the Tsar's agenda, where it would have significant results.

But beyond arbitration, which remained a controversial topic, there was also considerable public support for the other agenda items included in the second circular. Particularly engaging was the ambition to extend the rules of the Geneva Conventions to warfare at sea and to develop the international law of the conduct of war. Even Karl von Stengel, who was as hostile to the cause of disarmament as he was to that of international arbitration, reflected in 1908 that the first Hague conference made valuable progress in delineating the laws of war.[145] Through the nineteenth century, there had been several attempts at regulating the laws of war, of which the St Petersburg Declaration of 1868 and Brussels Convention of 1874 were the most notable. Both these treaties stumbled due to the proclaimed national interests of the governments involved. By 1898, the debate around the possibility of creating an international law of war was heated and many-sided in numerous countries and had been for years. After the release of the second circular, however, opinions in favour of achieving some agreement on key principles advanced in diplomatic circles. As the following chapters show, it was on the 'law of war' front that the great power governments were particularly keen to protect their vital interests.

The editorial debate about The Hague certainly expanded in the weeks after the release of the second circular. Careful thought went into considering the potential outcomes of the impending event. In March 1899, the *American Monthly Review of Reviews* offered a useful overview of some of these global perspectives. It began by acknowledging Arthur Desjardin's January 1899 editorial in the *Revue des Deux Mondes*, which advocated that while disarmament would achieve little in world affairs, arbitration was a worthy cause for the world's statesmen to consider.[146] It went on to highlight American missionary and anti-imperial activist Edwin Munsell Bliss's opinion that

> [t]he very fact that the officially accredited representatives of so many governments should meet for such a purpose is perhaps the most significant fact of the times. It must not, however, blind the vision to other facts, and those who fix their eyes upon The Hague alone may suddenly find themselves out of focus. Imperial extension is not a matter to be decided in the courts.[147]

It also reprinted the editorial of Leopold Maxse, the ultra-conservative editor of Britain's *National Review*, in full, including Maxse's analysis that '[u]niversal peace will be as far off as ever after the Czar's conference, and universal disarmament no nearer. But a serious consideration of the possibility of revising the rules and conditions of warfare is really called for, and there is no reason why the discussion of this subject should not produce some practical and beneficial results'.[148] In France, too, the *Journal des Économistes* repeatedly returned to the topic of the Tsar's conference. In September 1898, its editors congratulated Nicholas II for bringing the question of disarmament to world attention and forcing it as a subject of diplomatic negotiation.[149] By May 1899, the journal assessed the importance of the items on the agenda and reiterated that readers must pay close attention to what was happening in The Hague.[150] The Italian jurist Pasquale Fiore, writing in the academic publication *Nuovo Antologia*, agreed by suggesting that the best way of achieving any success in ensuring that the 'extreme expedient of war before all means for avoiding it are exhausted' was by gradual steps. Fiore continued, '[T]his conference could propose establishing a set of rules which should form the common law of civilized nations'. To that end, 'the present conference can perhaps initiate this evolution, leaving its unfolding to future ones . . . we shall then have the firm confidence in greater progress for the future'.[151]

Between February and May 1899, the world awaited the opening of the first Hague peace conference. Governments prepared delegations, considered policy directives and tried to accommodate divergences in their national and imperial interests when it came to the conference's agenda. They noted, with varying degrees of despondence, the public momentum behind the upcoming event. Activists with a variety of agendas also planned to go to The Hague to influence the course of events. They hoped to persuade delegates and the world's media alike of the righteousness of their causes. As the following chapter shows, it was in terms of this media context that these preparations for The Hague had the greatest influence.

3

A *Coram Publies*: Planning the First Hague Conference, 1899

The Conference will meet at a Palace in a beautiful forest two miles from The Hague . . . It is a beautiful, quiet spot, a fit place for a Peace Conference.

– *Poverty Bay Herald*, 9 May 1899[1]

As evocative as it was lengthy – Germany's Count Eulenburg called the rescript 'curiously impulsive and somewhat crude'[2] – the Tsar's rescript clearly aimed at provoking a public response:

> This Conference should be, by the help of God, a happy presage for the century which is about to open. It would converge in one powerful focus the efforts of all States which are sincerely seeking to make the great idea of universal peace triumph over the elements of trouble and discord. It would, at the same time, confirm their agreement by the solemn establishment of the principles of justice and right, upon which repose the security of States and the welfare of people.[3]

The context of the rescript's media release on 28 August also spoke volumes as to the public message Nicholas II looked to advance. Its release coincided with the Tsar's dedication of a new memorial to his grandfather, Alexander II, the 'Tsar Liberator' who had emancipated Russia's serfs in 1861. The congruence of the two events aimed at forging a cultural legacy between the two emperors. The court's official newspaper, the *Journal de St-Petersbourg*, certainly presented the two moments as complementary. Its edition of 28 August included not only a 'special bulletin' quoting the full text of the rescript, but also detailed accounts of the Tsar's schedule of celebratory events in Moscow.[4]

Still, although considerable forethought and preparation went into the wording and announcement of the rescript, neither Tsar Nicholas II nor his ministers had distinct plans for their proposed disarmament conference. The details of that event – where it would be held, who it would involve and what it would entail – remained undetermined for months. While exalting the power of peace and the necessity of arms control, the vagueness of the Tsar's text allowed for a variety of responses and enabled a range of Russian replies. There is substantial evidence to suggest that even Nicholas II himself became more reluctant to pursue the conference between August and December 1898, fearing a diplomatic fiasco if it went ahead.[5] Mouravieff and Russia's Foreign Ministry had a rather challenging time handling the wavering emperor and the avalanche of requests for conference details. Obviously, once the rescript was released, some kind of conference had to happen. Once the governments who had received an invitation accepted it, their diplomats in St Petersburg also sought assurances that the conference would serve their interests. For all of them, the upcoming event was an unknown and uncertain quantity.

It is in the context of the Tsar's ambitions and the lukewarm responses from the foreign governments that the sizeable transnational movement in favour for the Tsar's peace appeal must be considered. Between August 1898 and May 1899, the prospects of the Hague conference were assessed, praised, celebrated, planned for and liberally dismissed in a multitude of different public and private forums. For every person who agitated in public in support of the conference, another existed who dismissed the endeavour as either pointless, impossible or dangerous. Yet the voices in support of The Hague were loud and prolific enough to influence the conference agenda. In the end, the world's governments actively planned for and tried to shape the coming event to achieve the best possible outcome for themselves. They did so well aware that the world was watching and assessing their every move.[6]

Altogether, the public power of the rescript's appeal proved difficult for diplomats to manage or curtail. Influencing how the public interpreted the rescript and ensuing conference, nevertheless, became a key task for these statesmen.[7] The first Hague peace conference, as the event officially came to be known in April 1899, could not be seen to fail, if only because the Tsar was too important a figure to lose face.[8] As Théophile Delcassé, France's foreign minister, explained in a private letter to Count Herbert von Münster, the irascible German ambassador in Paris:

> We [the French government] have quite the same interest in this Conference that you [the German government] have. You do not wish to limit your power of defense at this moment nor to have anything to do with proposals for disarmament . . . We both wish to spare the Czar and to seek a formula for side-stepping this question . . . In order to avoid a complete fiasco, we shall possibly be able to make some concessions with reference to arbitration.[9]

Delcassé continued: 'Besides the Czar, we must also spare the public opinion of Europe, since this has been aroused by the senseless step of the Russians.'[10] Münster agreed with Delcassé's sentiment, as did Kaiser Wilhelm II and many other European diplomats.[11] While they were willing to attend a conference on disarmament to save public face, none of them looked for any real achievement on the subject.

For his part, Mouravieff took full advantage of the groundswell of public support for the disarmament conference to make it a reality. Although he was wary of the power of the press, he also hoped that power could be harnessed to meet Russia's need. As early as 1 September 1898, Mouravieff explained to Britain's ambassador in St Petersburg that whatever form the disarmament conference would take it would need to be held in a *coram publies* (public court or forum).[12] He deemed frank and open discussions in a public setting as vital to the interests of all states involved and expressed it as a direct desire of the Tsar himself. Russia's Minister of War A.N. Kuropatkin also stressed the necessity of engaging public opinion. On 22 September 1898, he noted in his diary that '[t]he enthusiasm of the peoples [for the Tsar's rescript] is premature. Expectation of rapid results. They push disarmament. There will be disenchantment and reaction. It is necessary to avert this'.[13] Although most diplomats disagreed with Mouravieff, Kuropatkin (and the Tsar) about the appropriateness of open negotiations between great powers about their military concerns, they well understood that the issues to be discussed in The Hague were of public interest and deemed a public matter. As a result, they also recognized that the conference's achievements would be framed in the arena of public diplomacy. They were increasingly aware that their public diplomacy required as much attention as did their ambitions for what might be achieved (or not achieved) in the conference's debating chambers.

The public's engagement with the rescript had its own energy that developed quite independently from that of the bureaucratic mechanisms of government affairs. Diplomats worked in an environment of protocols, proposals and carefully worded announcements that kept their state's interests firmly in mind. The groups and individuals who mobilized in support of the Tsar and The Hague in the 'real' world, however, imposed themselves on these bureaucratic processes. They signed petitions, voted for resolutions and sent letters. They lobbied their political representatives and organized meetings, concerts and rallies. They published manifestos, composed songs, wrote editorials and circulated pamphlets. They organized themselves locally and transnationally and did so in overwhelming numbers. Their petitions were signed by millions of people. Their resolutions represented countless others. Their governments had no choice but to listen. As a result, between August 1898 and May 1899, the public debate on issues of war and peace were of immediate concern to these governments.

From August 1898 to May 1899, the gaze of the international press also fixated on the public and private activities relating to the upcoming conference. Editorial opinion was as varied as the opinions on the likely success of the conference itself. The newspaper record attests that contemporaries were aware of the importance of the convergence of the public's interest in and the 'private' world of diplomacy. Their governments also carefully assessed public opinion within their own countries and elsewhere and used newspaper coverage to gauge its importance. For example, the American ambassador in St Petersburg, Herbert H.D. Peirce, wrote to Secretary of State John Hay on 9 November 1898 that aside from the merchant and educated classes, most Russians were not interested in the peace conference. Their respect for the Russian military, the 'bulwark and safety of the nation', far outweighed any humanitarian or economic sensibilities.[14] In other words, the Tsar's ambitions for the disarmament conference were far from altruistic in intent. No Tsar would undermine the military power underpinning Russia's imperial strength, particularly not if the people were not on board. Note, however, how Hayashi Tadasu, the Japanese ambassador in St Petersburg, wired the following message to his government on 1 September 1898: '[I]t appears that the European press welcomes the Russian proposal with almost unanimity, and considers it as one of the most important acts of international policy of this century'.[15] In so doing, he reaffirmed the importance of Japan's presence at the event. The Japanese government was, in fact, eager to attend, not so much to discuss disarmament but rather to solidify its position as a key member of the diplomatic family of nations. For the Japanese government, the global profile that Japan would obtain by negotiating at The Hague had far greater value than any conventions it might sign up for during the conference.[16]

In fact, no foreign ministry left public opinion off their radar. Britain's Foreign Office correspondence was particularly prolific in commenting on press reports relating to the rescript and The Hague.[17] By implication, the British government well knew that public opinion mattered in shaping the foreign policy of all states. It also utilized British public activism for the conference to advance its own diplomatic ends. Its ambassadors presented the public appeal of the conference as a reason for Britain to be, in the words of the Dutch Foreign Minister Willem Hendrik de Beaufort, 'magnificently represented' at the event.[18] In so doing, Britain's cabinet tried to carry forward the public momentum circulating around The Hague and win approval for their actions. Yet few of these ministers looked for fundamental change at the Hague conference itself. As the Marquis of Salisbury explained to the House of Commons sitting on 7 February 1899: 'I shall myself be heartily pleased if the results of this conference . . . are capable of a somewhat humbler aim [than disarmament].'[19] Public expectations – whatever they might be – had to be tempered in part to meet their governments' more subdued expectations.

Public support for the rescript and the Hague conference nevertheless increased as the event drew nearer and this momentum served to raise expectations in many quarters. People not only read the news circulating around the Tsar and The Hague, they also acted upon what they read. Initially, most responses came from private individuals or groups inspired by the Tsar's act. They sent letters and announcements directly to the Tsar or as public declarations in favour of the sentiment of the rescript in general. New Zealand's newspapers alone noted dozens of such acts, including the resolutions sent by the Trades Union Congress in Bristol (representing 1.25 million 'workmen') on 1 September 1898, the Women's Christian Temperance Union in Sydney on 2 September 1898 and the Canterbury Women's Institute a day later.[20] The National Council of Women of New Zealand sent several resolutions in support of peace including one on 4 October that lauded the Tsar's 'peerless proposal'.[21] At its annual meeting in Christchurch in April 1899, the Council sent a further resolution in support of The Hague and called all women in Australasia to advocate for the Tsar's cause.[22]

The Wellington *Evening Post* further noted the resolutions sent by the Society of Friends in November 1898,[23] while the *Thames Advertiser* observed how Britain's populist *Daily News* urged its readers to get behind a national movement in support of the Tsar's disarmament scheme.[24] In December 1898, the *New Zealand Herald* mentioned how the National Liberal Federation (in Britain) had formally approved the Tsar's conference, as did a Cobden Club manifesto in early January 1899.[25] On 8 February, the *Evening Star* also recorded that the Congregational Union of New Zealand met to praise the Tsar's wonderful manifesto.[26] The Wesleyan Conference held in Melbourne in early March passed a similar resolution that was sent directly to the Tsar.[27]

According to the historian A.S. Rybachenok, between August 1898 and May 1899, hundreds of thousands of people from around the world signed petitions or sent personal messages and resolutions to Nicholas II.[28] They also sent proposals for improving global affairs, schemes for disarmament and designs for an international court of arbitration. They set forth solutions to the world's pressing problems and forwarded the details of their hobby-horse projects, which they hoped would influence the conference ahead. These documents suggest that their authors believed that the Tsar had made an open call to them, as citizens of the world, to help with improving its condition. For them, the Tsar's rescript signalled that diplomacy could be shaped by the agency of thoughtful individuals.[29]

Others mobilized their own governments to support the Tsar's initiative. Such movements were particularly strong in countries with parliamentary traditions and long-standing political freedoms. As noted in Chapter 2, British public activism behind the Hague conference was particularly prolific and wide-ranging. In the Netherlands too, the public drive to support peace was as frenetic as anything witnessed across the Channel. Much of this frenzy was helped along by the activism of Baroness Johanna Waszklewicz van Schilfgaarde, who established the Dutch branch of the *Ligue des femmes pour le désarmement* (Women's League for Disarmament) in July 1898 under the banner *vrede door recht* (peace through law). She exerted all her energies to promote the Tsar's conference.[30] Her efforts began with a public petition, released on 30 August 1898, which expanded into a national campaign endorsing W.T. Stead's pilgrimage of peace in December.[31] No Dutch newspaper left Waszklewicz van Schilfgaarde's movement unreported, and many international papers commented on her activities as well.[32] She organized for copies of her petition to be sent to 1,121 municipalities, and acquired nearly 225,000 signatures in support.[33] Her petition even reached the outposts of the Dutch empire in Surinam.[34] Some of the events held in support of the conference were incredibly rewarding: in the small fishing town of Terschelling, for example, 1,334 residents out of a total of 4,000 signed the petition. The mayor of the town commented that there would have been more signatures if the men had not been out at sea.[35]

Peace issues dominated the Dutch press in 1899. A comical editorial in the *Echo* on 5 April 1899 suggested that one encountered 'peace' everywhere, even in the bookshop and delicatessen. It went on to suggest that there must be more addresses on the topic of peace in existence than there were poor oppressed Finns.[36] The *Hollandia* began one of its articles on 22 April with a headline 'The peace manifesto once more', which betrayed its exasperation with the topic.[37] The editor of *De Amsterdammer*, Johannes de Koo, published a tongue-in-cheek response using his pseudonym Julius Pruttelman Brommeijer on 6 March: 'From all sides they appear. Countless brochures, articles, letters, visits. And all of them about the peace conference.' He continued: 'if I do not watch out, Waszclewicz-van Schilfgaarde will write to me personally'.[38] Meanwhile, the *Centrum* organized a counter-petition asking signatories to lament the lack of character exhibited by the international peace crusade and affirm that diplomacy existed only to advance national interests, not to break them down as Stead and Waszclewicz-van Schilfgaarde were trying to do.[39]

Despite the fact that there was some backlash to Waszclewicz-van Schilfgaarde's peace campaign, most Dutch newspapers seriously considered the practical possibilities of the Tsar's call for peace. They did so even before The Hague was identified as the host site for the conference. On 26 January, for example, *De Tijd* editorialized that while world peace was an illusion – the 'civilized' world would always need to keep the 'uncivilized' world in check by military means – Europe's wars should be restrained.[40] A day earlier, the *Familie Blad* explained that since the Tsar's announcement the meaning of peace had changed. Serious men, according to the magazine, used to think of war as good, solid and important and of peace as 'something for cowardly people, for sentimental, fearful women, who'd faint at the sight of a single drop of blood', but they did not do so any longer. The magazine urged everyone to carefully consider supporting Waszclewicz-van Schilfgaarde's campaign.[41] The lawyers J.M. van Stipriaan Luiscius and J.B. Breukelman also made headline news when they proposed that the forthcoming disarmament conference should establish an international court of arbitration.[42]

In Scandinavia too, peace activism became commonplace in the wake of the rescript. The desire that the conference in The Hague might find a solution for the long-term security of the Scandinavian region by permanently neutralizing all three kingdoms was a particularly powerful motivator.[43] Tens of thousands of signatures adorned a Norwegian petition, which was sent on to the secretariat of the Hague conference in May 1899.[44] The petition sought both to support the conference's peace cause and to promote the permanent neutralization of Norway by great power decree. Another petition signed by 286,000 Danes urged their king to promote the permanent neutrality of Denmark at The Hague alongside compulsory arbitration and a continent-wide reduction in arms.[45] However willing they were to negotiate arbitration and disarmament at the conference, the Scandinavian governments understood that the topic of their permanent neutrality was unlikely to be discussed.[46] That reality, however, did not prevent the Scandinavian people from promoting the cause.

In France, Belgium and Germany there were nationwide drives to collect signatures in favour of the conference. The Belgian *Croisade de la paix* (Peace Crusade) offered a statistical review of the 105,900 signatures collected in favour of peace from 1,026 towns and villages. These were collated in a booklet and forwarded on to The Hague in May.[47] The French *La paix par le droit* (Peace through Law) organization asked the country's first delegate, Léon Bourgeois, to present another sizeable petition to the Hague conference with tens of thousands of appended signatures, which asked both the French government and the rest of the nations gathered at The Hague to succeed in their appointed tasks.[48] An appeal from the *Gesellschaft für Reform und Kodification des Völkerrechts* (Association for the Reform and Codification of International Law) was sent to the German government. It represented the signatures of thousands of people who attended a large public meeting in Munich, which resolved that while demilitarization was not an option for Germany, the German government should do everything in its power to create an international framework for war avoidance at the coming Hague conference.[49] Other public meetings in favour of The Hague's general mission were held around Germany, as they were around Europe.[50]

Within a month of the rescript, a massive peace meeting was held in Torre Pellice (Turin, Italy) including some of the biggest names in the global peace movement. Frédéric Passy, Élie Ducommun, William Evans Darby, Gaston Moch and Felix Moscheles all attended.[51] The meeting was commemorated in a full colour pamphlet, sixty-five pages in length, intended to promote the Tsar's peace message.[52] Meanwhile, Arthur Kirchhoff published his own propaganda pamphlet entitled *Männer der Wissenschaft über die Friedens-Konferenz. Gesammelt von der Berliner Wissenschaftlichen Korrespondenz* (Men of science on the peace conference. Collected from Berlin's scientific correspondence) which showcased the opinions of Europe's most educated men, all university professors in Germany, Switzerland, Austria, Russia and France.[53] Kirchhoff's aim was to present practical solutions for peace and to dismiss Stengel's claim, made in *Der ewige Friede*, that the concept of peace was a farce. Kirchhoff's collection represented dozens of perspectives that focused on peace as a *Leitmotiv* for the rescript, not as an end in itself. His contributors did not all agree with each other but the pamphlet nevertheless presented a compelling range of practical solutions to improve global affairs including to international arbitration, the international law of war, the international coordination of military first aid as well as the international organization of states. Altogether, Kirchhoff's publication aimed to counter what he saw as rising popular chauvinism and nationalism in the German-speaking world.

In the United States, the call to support the peace conference resulted in a variety of activities. On 31 December 1898, as the Wellington *Evening Post* reported it, a deputation of 145 churches, representing eight million Christians, handed over a 'monster' petition to President McKinley to support the Tsar's peace conference. McKinley responded by praising the Tsar's message although he also reiterated that disarmament was an impossible task.[54] Many American churches preached in favour of peace, especially on Sunday 14 May 1899, four days before the opening of the Hague event. Hundreds of these parishes subsequently sent peace resolutions to The Hague or directly to the Tsar. No less than twenty-six organizations in the city of New York, including the New York Bar Association, presented resolutions in favour of the conference.[55] The *Women's Tribune* noted ninety meetings on the topic of The Hague in the state of Utah alone.[56] Edward Everett Hale, already a prolific activist, organized the Boston Peace Crusade and edited twelve issues of a special bulletin, the *Peace Crusade*, to promote the conference. In doing so, he copied W.T. Stead's activities in Britain.[57] Hale's activism helped to spur the creation of the Universal Peace Congress, which met three times a week while the Hague conference sat to remind the American delegation about its responsibilities and to lend moral support to the event.[58] Hale also met with high-ranking government officials, including Secretary of State John Hay, his assistant, David Jayne Hill, and Russia's ambassador in Washington, Count Cassini, to advocate for the peace cause at The Hague.[59]

Although most efforts in support of the rescript and the Hague conference were organized at a local or national level, the most significant characteristic of the public agency was the realization that their messages were communicated to a global audience. In that respect, the public mobilization for the Tsar's message was a transnational phenomenon. It crossed borders in part due to the globalized nature of news: the world read about the range of activities occurring in support of the disarmament conference in their newspapers and that helped to motivate their own popular agitation at a local level. Furthermore, the transnational activities of a range of internationalist organizations, such as the Inter-Parliamentary Union, the Women's Christian Temperance Union, the various affiliations of the International Peace Bureau and the International Council of Women, also inspired a range of cross-border activities in support of the Tsar's appeal.

In the historiography on the first Hague peace conference, the actions of one individual, controversial journalist named W.T. Stead are particularly foregrounded. Stead was an active promoter of the Tsar's message, the idea of disarmament and the movement of peace. He was also transnationally aligned. Stead had an innate sense of how to maximize the power of the press and to create sensation.[60] Under his mentorship in the 1880s, the British *Pall Mall Gazette* had become a popular daily filled with exciting investigative news, even when illegally acquired.[61] In so many ways, Stead was the perfect example of a Victorian gentleman who understood how to make a spectacle in the nineteenth-century age of spectacles.[62] And as Stead described it, the Tsar's conference offered the 'opportunity of the century'.[63]

As early as September 1898, Stead headed off on a highly publicized 'pilgrimage of peace', in which he visited the capitals of Europe and sought to meet with heads of state and like-minded pacifists to persuade them of the value of the Tsar's disarmament appeal.[64] Stead's crusade aimed to raise the international profile of the upcoming conference and further the peace cause in Britain. He published liberally exaggerated accounts of his travels in the *Review of Reviews* and wrote a lengthy and heavily illustrated book entitled *The United States of Europe* in its wake.[65] Stead's reports on his meetings with high-ranking officials were so embellished, in fact, that many diplomats refused to talk with him, lest their words be minced unrecognizably.[66] On reaching the Crimean peninsula, Stead nevertheless managed to be received twice by the Tsar at the Romanov's imperial summer retreat, which lent cachet to his campaign.[67] Stead understood all news was good news. He was also convinced that as long as people clamoured for the Tsar's ideas then progress on peace, disarmament and arbitration would be made.

In late December 1898, Stead, in conjunction with a number of British peace groups, launched the International Crusade of Peace. The Crusade sought to court public favour for the rescript and the Hague conference by planning town meetings and public rallies across the United Kingdom, inviting individuals to sign petitions and send resolutions. Stead also launched a unique weekly publication, *War Against War*, to propagate the message of peace. The publication circulated widely (although not as widely as Stead might have liked)[68] until May 1899 at which point Stead relocated to The Hague to further his campaign. There is no doubt that Stead aimed for his crusade of peace to make headline news globally. He succeeded in large part, although he alienated many supporters along the way, including the London Peace Society, which issued a scathing attack on Stead's principles in the April 1899 edition of the *Herald of Peace*.[69]

Before 1898, W.T. Stead was famous within the British empire. By May 1899, he had attained global fame, even if that fame was not always presented in flattering terms.[70]

In a long editorial published during the second Hague conference in 1907, the *Japan Times* exposed W.T. Stead as a self-interested fraud and used press commentaries from around the world to back up its argument, including this extract from the Chicago *Chronicle*:

> It ought to be clear to the dullest understanding that Stead considers himself the superior and the condescending patron of any American community that he visits, that the only objects he has in view are the collection of money and the advertisement of himself and his absurd schemes, and that he is utterly unworthy of the hospitality and respectful consideration which is everywhere shown him.

It further noted Dr Buckley's view that Stead's 'credulity is as gluttonous and undistinguishing as the appetite of a shark' and finished with *Current Literature* magazine's assessment that 'William T. Stead does not write about William T. Stead through lack of something to write about. He does it merely because the things which pertain to himself are the best possible illustrations of anything that can concern the human race . . . Stead, in a word, is his own best topic'.[71] Stead certainly believed himself to be important. In 1909, he even claimed that he was solely responsible for ensuring that the first Hague conference came about, a claim some contemporaries blindly accepted.[72] Many colleagues, however, perceived Stead as a schemer, inclined to boom and bust.[73] As the *Spectator* described him in December 1898: 'Mr Stead's screaminess, and the entire absence in his mind of any sense of proportion, always offends us, but in this proposal of his to popularize the cry for peace . . . he has shown more judgment than usual, and may in the end accomplish some little good . . . He has probably strengthened the Czar's hands'.[74]

Stead's omnipresence has resulted in numerous historians fastening on to Stead as an explanatory factor in accounting for Britons' widespread support for the rescript and conference. Annalise Higgins's recent work revises this Stead-centric historiography. She shows that the extraordinary levels of British public support for the Tsar, his rescript and the proposed disarmament conference exhibited between August 1898 and May 1899 transcended the work of one man and exceeded the capabilities of the existing networks of peace activism.[75] Higgins highlights how hundreds of thousands of individuals in Britain mobilized politically behind the message of disarmament, the promise of arbitration and the need for the peaceful interaction of civilized nations. Much of that agitation was religiously motivated, yet it defied traditional social divisions, involving men and women from a variety of classes and backgrounds. Altogether, Higgins argues that in Britain, the public's mobilization for The Hague was a far bigger phenomenon than Stead.[76]

That public mobilization was also remarkably successful. As Sir U. Kay-Shuttlesworth reminded the House of Commons on 13 March 1899, the rescript 'has aroused hopes in this country of which the Government should take note . . . if Her Majesty's Government should fail to offer every assistance in promoting the object of the Tsar of Russia the country will be of the opinion that a great opportunity has been lost'.[77] The British government believed it needed to be seen to be listening to the public. But so did the rest of the world's governments, at least to some extent. For it was not only the British public that agitated for their government to take a positive role in the 1899 Hague conference and they certainly did not do so only because W.T. Stead asked it of them.

Through May and June of 1899, numerous petitions, appeals, letters and telegrams arrived in The Hague from all manner of places: from Sophia the Bulgarian Protestant Churches sent their salutations; from the 1.6 million members of the Cooperative Societies in the United Kingdom came a resolution for The Hague to bring 'a great extension of the Principle of Conciliation and Arbitration'; from the worldwide Epworth League fellowship (representing 6 million members) arrived an appeal that 'war should end'; and from the 'chess players of many nations' meeting in London a telegram 'to express their sympathy with your efforts which they trust will prove the first step to the eventual peace of the world'.[78] The delegates at The Hague were targeted in similar ways. Before he left his ambassadorial post in Berlin for The Hague, for example, the United States' first delegate, Andrew D. White, was inundated with '[b]ooks, documents, letters, wise and unwise, thoughtful and crankish, shrewd and childish . . . in all classes of society there seemed fermented a mixture of hope and doubt'.[79] The Secretary of the American delegation, Frederick W. Holls, spent hours every day answering the deluge of letters, telegrams and suggestions for the conference made by patriotic Americans.[80] Even the French socialist journal *Humanité Nouvelle* printed a supplement addressed to the delegates at The Hague offering ideas and proposals for the improvement of global relations.[81] The supplement was one of dozens of publications attempting to promote the value of international law and international order to the delegates.[82] It seemed that the world was on high alert.

Unsurprisingly then, contemporaries and historians have noted how in the aftermath of the rescript, public support for peace organizations and peace causes grew in many countries.[83] Yet few historians acknowledge how widespread the agitation for peace actually was and tend to undervalue its impact and importance.[84] In general, the amount of attention afforded to topics of pacifism, disarmament and arbitration in the mainstream press heightened everywhere in the weeks leading up to the Hague conference. Moreover, after the release of the second circular in January 1899, planning for the conference developed apace among internationalist groups. As the British activist Hodgson Pratt reminded the secretary-general of the Inter-Parliamentary Union Albert Gobat on 3 February 1899, the Tsar had placed the subject on the agenda for The Hague and the IPU should make the most of this opportunity.[85] In the end, several prominent members of the IPU were represented among the formal delegates at The Hague, including Baron Eduoard Descamps and Auguste Beernaert (Belgium), Baron d'Estournelles de Constant (France), Philipp Zorn (Germany), Heinrich Lammasch and Count Albert Apponyi (Austria-Hungary) and Eduard Rahusen (the Netherlands).[86] Several other delegates were members of the *Institut de droit international* including Louis Renault (France), T.M.C. Asser (the Netherlands) and Fyodor Martens (Russia). Altogether, their collective expertise in international law and internationalism more widely had a significant impact on the achievements of the conference itself.

The most successful transnational mobilization for The Hague, however, came from women's organizations. The International Council of Women (ICW), the Women

Christian Temperance Union (WCTU) and the *Ligue des femmes pour le désarmement* had developed strong and vibrant transnational links over the previous decades. The Tsar's conference offered an ideal moment for these organizations to present peace as a women's issue and to mobilize women, most of whom had no suffrage or political representation at a local level (outside New Zealand, parts of Australia and Scandinavia), globally. These women were not only inspired by the Tsar's words, they also saw in his rescript an opportunity to affect change on issues for which they had long campaigned. Their success in doing so not only spoke to the power of the message of peace, but also to the high levels of women's participation in political affairs at the fin de siècle, particularly in Europe and the United States. Their actions in support of peace, disarmament and arbitration were not ephemeral. Each organization had dedicated sections aimed at promoting these ideas and had already worked for years on advancing them. The Tsar's rescript gave these women an opportunity to make their opinions count locally and globally. They embraced that opportunity with fervour.

One of the most significant and public movements in favour of the peace conference was organized out of Germany by the anthropologist Margarethe Lenore Selenka.[87] Late in March 1899, Selenka mobilized the *Ligue* and other women's groups, including the German Women's Association, the American Women's Council and the International Council of Women, to host simultaneous meetings in support of the upcoming Hague conference. On 15 May 1899, 565 such meetings were held in 18 different countries, including Japan, Spain, Hungary, Serbia, Austria, Italy and Russia, attended by more than 200,000 women in person, who, so the organizers claimed, represented a constituency of three million others.[88] Prominent peace activist and ICW member May Wright Sewall helped to organize 163 meetings across 21 American states that day with a collective attendance of more than 73,000 women, which capped off several weeks of public events to promote the Hague conference in the United States.[89] As Selenka herself described it, these global events represented 'the first truly international public act among women, and their first resolute entering into the domain of international politics'.[90] The activities of these women highlight how strongly they felt that their fates as women and as citizens of the world were intimately tied to the waging of war and the conduct of states. All the meetings on 15 May advocated affirmative action and resulted in resolutions in support of peace, salutations to the Tsar and expressions of support for the delegates gathering at The Hague for the opening of the conference three days later. Their resolutions were bound in a large volume and personally taken to The Hague by Selenka, who handed them over to the president of the conference, Russia's Baron Georges de Staal.[91]

The events of 15 May were an extraordinary expression of the inspiration provided by the Tsar's rescript to the power of the people. The 15 May celebrations and the accompanying resolutions received extensive press coverage in each of the nations involved, albeit not always in positive terms (Figure 3.1). The events themselves were impressive public spectacles. In Denmark, for example, the newly formed branch of the ICW organized a performance of Bjørnsterne Bjørnson's new oratorio 'Peace', which Edvard Grieg was initially to have composed the music for. In the end, a choir of 80 women, dressed in white, sang the piece to a packed audience in a Copenhagen music hall. In Norway, a festival of celebration held on 15 May in Stockholm resulted in 50,000 signatures for Selenka's peace appeal.[92] In Russia, women succeeded in overcoming the existing prohibition against political meetings in order to support the 15 May peace initiative: fifty public meetings were held across the empire attended by more than 24,000 women.[93] Meanwhile, the 15 May initiative ensured the first public displays of women's political activism behind an international cause in both Spain and Japan.[94] In Tokyo, 2,000 women met to express their 'heartiest gratitude to his Imperial Majesty the Czar of Russia'. They also wished to give expression to their 'deepest hope, that the conference may advance the realization of the great aims for which it has been called together and that thus the brutalities of belligerent acts may vanish more and more and peace and justice established among nations. Then only shall the continued prosperity of countries and the undisturbed happiness of families be attained'.[95] The Japanese women's peace petition carried more than 6,000 signatures.[96] From this point on, the Japanese women's peace organizations became transnationally aligned too, attending the ICW's conference in 1899.[97]

Throughout the British empire, too, women's groups mobilized for the 15 May campaign, although few public gatherings were held in British India due to an outbreak of the plague.[98] Unsurprisingly then, the ICW's 1899 conference in London, which coincided with The Hague conference, witnessed extraordinary agency for peace and disarmament among the women in attendance. The ICW also hosted a mixed-gender public meeting on 27 June 1899 to promote the cause of international arbitration.

Figure 3.1 This Johan Braakensiek cartoon from 1899 mocked the women's peace cause. It depicted prominent peace activists Baronesses Bertha von Suttner (standing on the left) and Johanna Waszklewicz van Schilfgaarde (on the right) as they watch Europe's heads of state sharing a peace pipe. The caption read: Mrs Waszklewicz: 'Oh, Bertha, that smells so good!' (*De Amsterdammer* 12 February 1899, centrefold, IISG BG D23/625).

According to the ICW's records, the meeting at Queen's Hall involved 'an immense concourse of people'.[99] Bertha von Suttner, Waszklewicz-van Schilfgaarde, Ishbel Aberdeen and May Wright Sewall all attended.

The statesmen whose job it was to plan for the Hague conference were well aware of these global events in favour of the Tsar's peace. Needless to say, they were not particularly supportive of such 'popular' involvement. Count Münster was particularly scathing of the activities of what he called 'the rabble'.[100] The Russian government nevertheless made good use of the public attention and attempted to court it in its own favour: it was the reason the Tsar met with Stead, Bloch and Tolstoy. It was the reason why Mouravieff, Witte and Kuropatkin visited Vienna and Paris in September and October 1898.[101] It was also the reason why in December 1898, Mouravieff co-opted the international lawyer and Russian bureaucrat Fyodor Martens to create a workable agenda for the conference. With Martens's involvement, it was clear that the programme would morph away from the single-issue concern of arms control to a range of issues relating to the conduct and prevention of warfare. As one of the authors of the Brussels conventions of 1874, Martens had considerable experience in the creation of the international law of war. His function was to make the agenda for The Hague comprehensive enough that something useful could be achieved.[102]

That the Russian government sought achievement from the Hague conference is crystal clear from Mouravieff's second trip around the European continent in January 1899. During the trip, Mouravieff called on diplomats, heads of state and politicians but also on well-known public figures related to the peace movement. On meeting Mouravieff in Vienna, Baroness Bertha von Suttner was surprised by the attention: 'All in all, *odd* that we are being received'.[103] But Mouravieff's purpose was not so odd at all. Although officially aimed at setting the agenda and achieving agreement from the major powers on the terms of reference for the conference, Mouravieff's unofficial task on his European tour was to court public favour and to minimize overzealous expectations for the peace of the world. Who better to help him achieve this aim than the author of a best-selling anti-war novel?[104]

Mouravieff's second circular, released on 11 January 1899, certainly spoke to a diplomatic and public audience. It represented not only the issue of disarmament as vital, but also those of arbitration, 'good offices', the regulation of the international law of war and the extension of the Geneva Conventions to maritime conflict. The second circular was broad enough to allow the delegates in attendance the security of having something to negotiate. It was, as the Dutch Minister of Foreign Affairs saw it, a 'beneficial start' (*heilzaam beginsel*).[105] The world's governments were all pretty much unanimous that arms control was unachievable but the Russian authors of the circular hoped that some diplomatic unanimity could be achieved on the other issues, many of which were long-standing concerns in international relations and broadly popular. Many governments worded their replies to the second circular to make precisely this point. For example, the French government failed to mention disarmament in its response to the circular but, nevertheless, intimated its support for the conference by praising the Tsar for conferring on diplomats a new power to prevent conflict by regulating good offices and arbitration.[106] Delcassé subsequently instructed the French delegation to focus their efforts at the conference on arbitration, for which, as he stated, there would be a ready and supportive audience in France itself.[107]

The preamble of the second circular openly referenced the importance of the public's support: 'the Imperial Cabinet has been also able to collect, with lively satisfaction, evidence of the warmest approval – which has reached it, and continues to be received, from all classes of society in various parts of the globe'.[108] For her part, Bertha von Suttner bemoaned the second circular for giving governments the ability to evade the issue of disarmament. She recognized that the second circular admitted the defeat of the peace movement's most treasured concern: the end of warfare.[109] But in general, most newspaper commentaries praised Mouravieff's agenda. Mouravieff and Martens had succeeded in presenting a document that the world's public and its diplomats could get behind.

Above all, the second circular signalled how aware the Russian government was of the power of the public sphere to influence the diplomacy of the moment. The circular reiterated that The Hague's agenda looked to practical solutions for complex issues and would, as a result, avoid negotiating political issues. Russia had agreed to this stipulation as early as 3 September 1898, in order to ensure that the other great power governments would accept their invitations.[110] To guarantee the success of a conference of peace, it could not (and therefore would not) become a forum to revisit or renegotiate the status of Alsace-Lorraine, the borders of Alaska or the permanent neutralization of the Scandinavian states.[111] Nor would the conference discuss anarchism, which the Italian government had briefly promoted as a potential focal point in October 1898.[112] In other words, the peace conference at The Hague was not called to negotiate the actual limits of state power. Principles rather than crises were to be the focus of The Hague.

For the public reading about the upcoming conference in their newspapers, however, separating the acts of states from the principles to be discussed at The Hague was nigh impossible.[113] The German *art-nouveau* magazine *Jugend* satirized the problem incisively when one of its covers represented world leaders in an impossible 'egg dance', carefully stepping around a precarious quantity of fragile 'eggs' each labelled with key international concerns of the day: the Bosphorus, China, Tripoli, the Afghanis, Transvaal, Samoa, Macedonia, Persia, Bosnia, Rome and a small red-coloured egg branded 'revolution'.[114] No conference of states, the magazine suggested, could avoid the delicate issues plaguing global diplomacy.

Unsurprisingly, newspaper commentaries also reflected critically and cynically on the decisions of governments that seemed to contradict their commitments to the principles of the forthcoming Hague conference, especially those relating to disarmament. Thus on 21 January 1899, the *Mataura Ensign* found it hard to accept the logic in a speech made by the Swedish King Oscar II in which he announced an 'experimental' mobilization of Swedish troops as being in keeping with the ambition of the Tsar's conference, for a conference of peace did not imply a neglect of defences.[115] Similarly, the Wellington *Evening Post* sarcastically reminded its readers on 17 January 1899 that the Ottoman Empire's answer to the second circular was to order the construction of 162 Krupp cannon and 30,000 shells.[116] That almost all European states, including Russia, augmented their military budgets between August 1898 and

May 1899 is telling. At one level, the increases signalled how serious the military establishments in these states considered the threat of armaments control and the potential success of the Tsar's conference. At another, they set a new base line from which negotiations about military limitations could begin. Each state wanted that base line to be as high as possible.

The extent to which governments actively pre-empted the outcome of The Hague's disarmament negotiations by manipulating their military budgets is debatable. They certainly used their budgets to manage their public and private diplomacy surrounding the forthcoming discussions at The Hague. The British cabinet, for example, considered the implications of its proposed naval budget in a private letter sent to Britain's ambassador in St Petersburg on 1 March 1899: 'We have discussed in The Cabinet the possibility of the Russian government, or the Czar himself, being startled at the very large increase in our Naval Estimates for 1899–1900'. It went on to explain that the budget increases were to cover liabilities not the augmentation of the fleet. Furthermore, the Russian government should see nothing 'inconsistent' in these increases with 'our readiness' to attend his disarmament conference.[117]

That the 'very large increase' to Britain's naval estimates was a potential headache for the British government became all too clear when its details were 'accidentally' released to *The Times* on 9 March, resulting in an unprecedented speech made in their defence by the First Lord of the Admiralty, G.J. Goschen, in the House of Commons.[118] While the members of the House were willing to listen to the Goschen's justifications for demanding a 'colossal sum' (an increase of three million pounds), they were not so keen on accepting the underhand method by which his estimates found their way into the press. According to Goschen, there 'must have been some breach in trust in some quarter or other' for which he was willing to apologize. But he did not apologize for reminding the House that the Tsar's disarmament conference posed a threat to the security of the British empire.[119]

Few in the British Admiralty or War Office were enamoured with the Tsar's disarmament appeal.[120] Utilizing the press to advance their message of military preparedness was their way of influencing the public's understanding. The Admiralty's position was particularly significant as the House of Commons had already witnessed a serious challenge to an increase in the army budget. As the Liberal MP Henry Labouchere noted on that subject: Britain's 'responsibilities' to the Tsar's conference precluded the expansion of the military budget for Egypt and the Sudan.[121] On 13 March, when the naval estimates were further debated, other MPs noted their concern that the Admiralty's 'gigantic' budget threatened the very principles of the Hague conference, which Britain was committed to supporting.[122] The battle lines over the British public's interpretation of The Hague were thus drawn across a stark divide between those who dismissed the premise of armaments limitation in favour of armed peace and those who were wary of war and military procurement. Above all, the public assessment of these military budgets speaks to the realization that every issue up for discussion at, or with regards to, the forthcoming conference was loaded with political meaning and had the potential to impact diplomatic relations in public and private.

As a result, all the major decisions relating to the planning for the Hague conference, including the decision to host it in that city in the first place, played out in the international press and were commented on within the framework of international and domestic interests. Within and outside diplomatic circles, questions abounded about the forthcoming conference: Would it be an ambassadorial meeting? Would it be held in St Petersburg? Who would be invited? How would it proceed? What would be on the agenda? The answers to these questions were frequently contested. For statesmen, the level of public scrutiny of their activities was discomforting. Diplomatic protocol was already difficult enough to manage without the additional concerns created by the public's attention. Pleasing the world's newspaper readers was, at any rate, impossible. Shaping how they might think about the upcoming event was, nevertheless, important.

Aside from the negotiations around the content of the agenda, which preoccupied Martens and Mouravieff in December 1898 and January 1899, the composition of the conference was of equal concern to diplomats and journalists alike. Early in May, the Netherlands announced that governments could send delegations consisting of diplomats and technical experts. Each government could send multiple representatives but each state would only receive one vote in decision-making moments.[123] The great powers all expressed some concern that such an organization would give undue power to the small states. The democratization of multilateral negotiations sat uncomfortably with the notion of great power diplomacy so entrenched in the concert system that had steered European diplomacy since 1815.[124]

The location of the proposed conference posed another key concern. None of the great power governments, including that of Russia, felt comfortable with holding the conference in a major capital, let alone in St Petersburg, because it might skew the diplomacy in favour of the hosts or embarrass them unduly if the conference failed.[125] The fear that the conference may end up as a 'giant fiasco' was widespread.[126] As a result, the shortlist of likely locations concentrated on small neutral states, with the cities of Copenhagen, Berne, Geneva, Brussels and The Hague prominently featured. In the end, the Russian government chose The Hague in part because the Swiss cities were deemed unsafe (the Austrian Empress had been murdered in Geneva by anarchists in September 1898), the Danish government was uninterested and, at least according to the Catholic press, Brussels was too closely aligned to the Pope.[127] A more likely explanation for Brussels's exclusion was the existing political stalemate between the Belgian king and his parliament.[128] At any rate, both Martens and Mouravieff had strong connections to The Hague: the former visited often and was close friends with the Dutch international lawyer T.M.C. Asser. Mouravieff had served as a diplomat in the Dutch administrative capital years earlier as well.[129]

Persuading the Dutch Queen Wilhelmina to agree to host the event was more difficult. From the Russian viewpoint, it was an advantage that Wilhelmina was Tsar Nicholas II's niece.[130] She could not very well deny his request, but she did need persuading. Although in public Wilhelmina graciously accepted the duty, in private she seethed that the situation removed all her agency and that the conference 'pressed upon us the stamp of insignificance'. She did not want to be reduced to the status of 'making tea and arranging flowers', let alone pay for the costs involved of offering up one of her palaces for the event. Above all, she was annoyed at her uncle for placing her in this impossible situation.[131] Germany's *Lustige Blätter* magazine satirized the implications of the Queen's dilemma on its front cover in May 1899: depicting Queen

Wilhelmina and her mother, Queen Emma, packing away their porcelain in *Huis ten Bosch*.[132] In general, the Dutch public was both flattered and sceptical about hosting the conference in The Hague. They recognized the conference would be costly – the Dutch parliament approved a special budget of 75,000 guilders to enable the event to go ahead – and it would require active diplomacy to make it work.[133] Still, much of the foreign press was enamoured with the choice of The Hague. As far away as New Zealand, the *Poverty Bay Herald* enthused: 'It is a beautiful, quiet spot, a fit place for a Peace Conference.'[134]

Issues of protocol complicated the organization of the conference as well.[135] As host nation, the Dutch government was responsible for issuing invitations, but as the originators of the event and authors of the agenda, the Russian government took charge of most organizational decisions. Who to invite was a particularly delicate issue, in part because not all the governments represented in St Petersburg were recognized by the Dutch state. Geopolitical considerations invariably affected the composition of the invitee list and caused significant levels of scrutiny. Three potential invites drew particular attention, namely, those of the Vatican, the South African republics and Bulgaria.

Pope Leo XIII was a highly vocal and prolific advocate of global peace and made no secret of the fact that he encouraged the Tsar's disarmament proposal and sought an invitation to attend. As the Vatican was formally represented at The Hague and in St Petersburg, an invitation was not inappropriate. However, the Italian government was not impressed.[136] Arguing that public opinion in Italy would not allow for papal representation, the Italians pressured the great powers to prevent the Pope from attending.[137] In private, however, the Italian leadership worried whether they had played the right hand. Acknowledging that Russia would have trouble excluding the Pope, the Italian Foreign Minister Felice Napoleone Canevaro also recognized that if Italy abstained from the conference, it would cause public embarrassment and might occasion an unpredictable backlash among Italians, who were generally supportive of the Tsar's conference.[138] In the end, the German government sided with the Italians, in part because it feared that through the Pope the interests of Catholic Bavaria might obtain too much international credence.[139] With Germany's official support for the Italian position, the Pope could credibly be left off the invitation list.[140]

In the public arena, the papal controversy played out along predictable denominational lines. Catholics everywhere were disgusted with the decision, but in Britain it raised less than an eyebrow. As the *Daily News* commented: if the Pope was invited why not the Archbishop of Canterbury too?[141] In contrast, the American *Catholic World* editorialized that 'to bar Leo's representative from the Congress is to invite defeat' and that his non-attendance signalled that the conference would be 'strangled in its birth'.[142] In the Netherlands, the level of Catholic dismay was so considerable that a political furore ensued. The Roman Catholic *Volksbond* publicly resigned its membership of the Dutch Peace Society because it continued to support the conference despite the Pope's lack of involvement.[143] During the conference itself, the papal nuncio in The Hague absented himself, while the Dutch Queen attempted to placate the international (and local) controversy by thanking the Pope for all his work on peace, an initiative which the Pope warmly and publicly endorsed.[144] Yet the issue of the Pope's non-involvement in The Hague would plague Catholic press opinions of The Hague for years to come. In the midst of the second Hague conference in 1907, for example, the *Venloosche Bode* returned to the issue with the claim that it reflected an international pettiness and narrow-mindedness (*kleingeestigheid en kleinzieligheid*) among the world's powers.[145]

The decision not to invite the South African republics of Transvaal and Orange Free State was even more heated and globally controversial. For the British government, the invitations were out of the question. Both regions were firmly part of the British empire: they were not recognized nation-states and should, therefore, not receive any representation. The republics, however, were represented diplomatically in the Netherlands. Many Dutch were also strong advocates of Boer independence. The Dutch government realized the bind: it could not placate public opinion within the country and keep Britain from demanding that the South Africans not attend. To defuse the situation, the Dutch Foreign Office tried to get the German government to negotiate with the Transvaal on their behalf. The Germans politely refused: the issue was a political hot potato.[146]

In the end, de Beaufort, the Dutch Minister of Foreign Affairs, addressed the Dutch parliament about the situation on 2 May 1899. He explained that other states, including Venezuela, Bolivia, Liberia, Abyssinia and the Congo, had not been invited 'without any question being raised as to whether they felt affronted or not'. The conference will not, as Beaufort described it, be a 'friendly meeting' and while some non-European states would be present at Russia's request, it was largely a European affair. He further acknowledged the Dutch people's great sympathy for the South African republics but that the government of the Netherlands was not in a position to extend a protectorate over the Transvaal or the Orange Free State, nor could it advocate on their behalf unconditionally. Beaufort further conceded that while his government had conveyed the level of public support for the inclusion of the two states to the Russian emperor, in the end, the general opinion of the world's governments was that such a move would be unwise.[147]

Unsurprisingly, de Beaufort's speech did little to stem the tide of public sentiment in the Netherlands and abroad. The issue of the Boer states remained controversial throughout the conference and in its aftermath. In June 1899, a massive Anti-Peace League rally was planned for The Hague, organized by socialist labour agitators to protest the fact that the Transvaal was not represented at the conference. How, so the protestors claimed, could peace be achieved if the world's under-represented peoples were not given a voice?[148] When Britain went to war with the Boer republics later that year, the lack of representation given to the Transvaal and Orange Free State at The Hague was one of the many points on which Britain was roundly condemned.[149]

Bulgaria's representation at the Hague conference was less publicly divisive although no less diplomatically strained. While Bulgaria had official representation in St Petersburg, the Dutch were wary of extending an invitation without consulting the Ottoman Sultan first. As long as Constantinople was happy with the invitation, Bulgaria could attend, but as the Dutch government saw it, without the Sultan's approval, its attendance might upset the whole event.[150] After all, the purpose of the conference was to bring the world's powers to The Hague in the spirit of cooperation, not confrontation.[151] Furthermore, the Dutch government was wary of the great number of Muslim subjects in its own East Indian colonies, who might protest in solidarity with the Ottoman Sultan, if he expressed his displeasure at Bulgaria's inclusion.[152] In the end, the Sultan accepted Bulgaria's invitation, as long as its delegation was seated at all official events after that of the Ottomans. In this way, protocols and diplomatic decorum would offer powerful symbols of Ottoman imperial power.

The press interest in The Hague's plans also ensured that considerable attention was given to the delegates who would attend. A minor cult of celebrity grew around the delegates sent to The Hague. In appointing them, governments kept in mind both the public appeal of the delegate and the private diplomatic needs of the state. Britain's delegation, for example, consisted of some of the country's most decorated diplomats and military leaders. Its lead delegate was Sir Julian Pauncefote, ambassador in Washington, ardent advocate of arbitration and co-author of the Hay-Pauncefote agreement. To balance Pauncefote's pro-arbitration diplomacy with Britain's strong stand on naval power and the protection of military might, Admiral Jacky Fisher and Major John Ardagh were appointed as technical delegates.[153] Admiral Fisher, future First Sea Lord, was keenly aware of how tough his responsibilities were at The Hague. As Director of Military Intelligence, Major Ardagh was another important choice. Both Ardagh and Fisher had little compunction in advocating for 'might makes right' during the conference itself – Ardagh himself was unsympathetic to the very idea of regulating warfare by international agreement.[154] Importantly, within the British ambitions for the conference at The Hague, arbitration and militarism could sit comfortably side by side.[155]

The American delegation was equally as impressive. The *American Monthly Review of Reviews* noted of the delegation that they 'will place the United States in a very favorable light', while the *New York Tribune* gushed that the delegation represented an 'exceptionally strong body' (Figure 3.2).[156] The American delegation consisted of Andrew D. White: historian, experienced diplomat and ambassador to Berlin. The second delegate, Seth Low, was president of Columbia University. He was sent off from the docks of St Louis by 300 of his students as was the third delegate, Captain Alfred Thayer Mahan.[157] Mahan's fame as the author of *The Influence of Sea Power upon History* (1890) offered kudos to the delegation, although his intransigent behaviour during the conference itself would cause the American delegation numerous diplomatic headaches. The other members of the delegation included international lawyer Stanford Newel, the inventor of the Buffington-Crozier disappearing gun carriage Captain William R. Crozier, and the ambitious Captain Frederick W. Holls, as secretary.[158]

Germany sent the experienced diplomat and its ambassador in Paris, Count Münster, as its lead delegate for, as Kaiser Wilhelm II noted, attendees at The Hague needed 'common sense . . . [and Münster] has lots of it'.[159] Münster had no inclination to support any multilateral agreements that limited Germany's sovereignty or global power. Two lawyers went to The Hague in support: Baron von Stengel, author of the anti-pacifist pamphlet *Der ewige Friede*, and Philipp Zorn, who (at least in 1899) denied that international law had any qualification as real law.[160] The delegation clearly signalled Germany's intentions at The Hague not to allow the conference to interfere

BE IT PEACE OR WAR, UNCLE SAM WILL BE WELL REPRESENTED AT THE HAGUE.

Figure 3.2 The Minneapolis *Journal* cleverly illustrated the depth of expertise of the US delegation to attend the first Hague conference in this cartoon published in April 1899 (*Journal* [Minneapolis], 1899, available in 'William Frederick Holls Papers' MS Am 1308 (362), Houghton Library, Harvard University).

with Germany's sovereign rights.[161] Yet even the Kaiser had to be seen to be taking the conference seriously. He would not have appointed Count Münster otherwise.

France's delegation was particularly impressive, consisting of former Prime Minister Léon Bourgeois, the French ambassador in The Hague Georges Bihourd and the member of parliament and noted internationalist Baron Constant d'Estournelles. Louis Renault, the renowned international lawyer, attended as one of France's three technical delegates. The other two represented the French army (General Mounier) and navy (Rear Admiral Péphau). Italy also sent its highest-ranking and most experienced diplomat, Count Constantino Nigra, who, at the time, served as ambassador in Vienna. Nigra was renowned for his pleasantries, keen insight and unhappiness at being chosen to undertake an impossible task at The Hague. Yet he, like the rest of the Italian delegation, were adept at ingratiating and endearing diplomacy.[162] The Austro-Hungarians were not outdone. The Emperor Franz Joseph sent a practiced diplomat, Count Rudolph von Welserheimb, the Foreign Ministry's Kajetan Mérey von Kapos-Mére, Lieutenant-Colonel Victor von Khuepach zu Reid, the rather lazy Alexander von Okolicsány and his most trusted international legal adviser, Heinrich Lammasch.[163]

The delegations of the smaller and extra-European states were equally noteworthy. The Japanese government ensured its delegation was both linguistically and culturally adept and well-read in international law and treaty-making. It consisted of the noted international legal scholar Ariga Nagao, Japan's Minister in St Petersburg Baron Tadasu Hayashi, and the lawyer-cum-diplomat Ichiro Motono. The Japanese also appointed two military advisers: Toshiatsu Sakamoto and Yusaka Uehara. Not to be outdone, the Chinese delegation arrived in The Hague consisting of three foreign diplomats: Ambassador Lou Tseng-Tsiang, Yang Yü and Hoo-Wei-Teh. Meanwhile, the

Belgians were particularly concerned about the long-term viability of their permanent neutrality and sent its most renowned international lawyers and politicians to make their case, including its former Prime Minister Auguste Beernaert, the international lawyer Baron Eduoard Descamps and the diplomat Count de Grelle Rogier. The Bulgarian king, altogether wary of the controversy over his country's inclusion, chose for his representative in St Petersburg, the keen-eyed and youthful Dr Dimitri Stancioff, along with Major Christo Hessaptchieff, who served as military advisor.

That Russia sent a high-powered delegation was particularly important. Its first delegate (and president of the conference), Baron de Staal, was a highly respected albeit aged career diplomat, who enjoyed his function as Russia's ambassador in London very much. Although de Staal had no experience running a democratic forum, he was an astute negotiator, even if he stumbled on words in his public speeches and enjoyed the occasional snort of opium.[164] It was no coincidence that de Staal met with Count Münster in Paris six weeks prior to the conference to discuss a common approach. Neither diplomat held out any ambitions or hopes for the conference. In fact, neither wished to attend.[165] They agreed that disarmament was impossible although they both agreed that some boons could be allowed in the regulation of the international law of war and to the Red Cross statutes.[166] Count de Basili and Fyodor Martens made up the rest of the Russian delegation, the latter taking full responsibility for pushing the agenda along.[167]

Most of the delegations that attended the first Hague conference were publicly impressive and diplomatically adept. Given the stakes, it was essential that the delegates understood the implications of their involvement. As the US Assistant Secretary of State David Jayne Hill impressed on his delegation, the key concern was that they avoid a 'flapdoodle': disarmament might be impossible but something could be achieved on arbitration and on the regulation of the law of war. Above all, Hill surmised that the United States was to be presented as a 'friend and promoter of peace'.[168] It is clear that the public profile offered by The Hague to the delegations, and thus to the governments they represented, mattered very much. Many delegations, including the one from the United States, had detailed instructions outlining the nuances of a variety of issues from the adoption of compulsory arbitration to the implications of extending the Geneva Conventions to naval warfare. Most governments obtained advice on the implications of the second circular from a range of government departments and their country's military establishment.[169] Many of the delegates were also appointed because of their expertise as well as their ability to toe the government's line.

However, because the nature of what would happen at The Hague was unknown, the event was hard to anticipate. Julian Pauncefote, for example, was given a mandate by his government to pursue the regulation of arbitration, but exactly how he might do that was left entirely open. As Keith Hamilton suggests, '[F]ew envoys in modern times could have embarked on so major a negotiation [as establishing an international court of arbitration] with so little briefing or so broad a mandate.'[170] Kaiser Wilhelm II went as far as to instruct his delegation to stay out of the limelight, interact as little as possible with the other delegations and 'remain in the shadows and let others pull the chestnuts out of the fire'.[171] For Wilhelm II, the Hague conference represented, at best, a public nuisance that needed to be kept under control and, at worst, a potential challenge to the power of state sovereignty. He believed that the other governments would have instructed their delegations in a similar way. Either way, his delegates were to give away little diplomatic ground and avoid negotiations and compromises as much as possible. Count Münster was the ideal person to ensure these ambitions were met. But Münster was no public diplomat. In not courting the public sphere during the conference at The Hague, Germany encountered numerous problems. While their actions played well in the German (and to some extent Austrian) press, they did not communicate well in the global media. In stark contrast, the British and American delegations looked to coordinate at least some of their activities at The Hague in part to advocate for international arbitration and to reap reward in the public sphere.[172] In 1899, they were much more successful in playing the public relations' game.

The smaller European states also worried about the impact of the Hague conference on their diplomacy and future security. The Belgians feared that their permanent neutrality was in jeopardy if limitations on armaments were introduced. The Scandinavian states were happy to support arbitration measures and looked to achieve greater recognition of the importance of international law. The Portuguese government, however, made no effort to hide its disinterest in the event and, much like Serbia, argued that the conference was really only of concern to the great states.[173] The Dutch government was equally wary. As Beaufort put it in a private letter, the conference imposed all manner of 'difficulties and objections' on his government. Altogether he expected little success: 'nothing will come of disarmament but arbitration may receive a small push'.[174] It seemed a lot of effort for little hope of achievement. But for many of these governments small achievements were exactly the desired outcome.

Despite these governments' reluctance, the Hague conference had captured the world's imagination and the contrast between these public expectations and those of the diplomatic corps were profound. The conference attracted dozens of internationalists, peace activists and other interested parties to the city. They arrived in The Hague in May 1899 to advance the peace cause, to circulate materials to the delegates and journalists gathered there and to witness what they perceived as a momentous occasion. W.T. Stead was there, as was Bertha von Suttner, Ishbel Aberdeen, Johanna Waszklewicz-van Schilfgaarde, Alfred Fried, Felix and Greta Moscheles, William Evans Darby, Charles Richet, the sociologist Jacques Novicov, IPU member Baron Pirquet, Zionist activist Theodor Herzl and Ivan Bloch. The latter worried about the pragmatics of solving the world's problems at such short notice and urged a postponement of the event so governments would have 'time for arranging investigations and preparing public opinion'.[175] The American Universal Peace Union claimed twenty of its representatives were in The Hague during the conference, including the Quaker Dana Boardman and the editor of the *Friend's Intelligencer*, Howard M. Jenkins.[176] Benjamin M. Trueblood, chair of the American Peace Society, was there and would write a comprehensive history of the conference soon after, as were Archbishop Ireland, the historian James Ford Rhodes and the Speaker of the US House of Representatives Thomas B. Reed.[177] All three came to see history being made. At the other end of the spectrum, the Dutch anarchist leader Domela Nieuwenhuis arranged for a series of protest meetings in the city that would highlight the fruitless nature of the task ahead.[178]

That something phenomenal was about to happen dawned on the residents of The Hague and its environs too. Their hotels bulged with foreign visitors. A. Gall, the manager of the Rotterdam fireworks factory, asked for special permission to let off fireworks on 18 May to celebrate the opening of the event (the request was denied).[179] Various establishments and organizations commissioned commemorative plaques and earthenware. The diamond, gold and silver traders J.M. van Kempen and Sons crafted a red and bronze shield emblazoned with the words 'Hommage au Congres de la Paix' (Homage to the peace congress) which they displayed in the vitrine of their city shop.[180] The Dutch artist Jan ten Kate completed a series of paintings entitled *Voor den vrede* (For peace) which were exhibited at the famous Pulchri gallery for the duration of the conference, after which time it travelled through Europe and Britain before ending up in Ivan Bloch's Peace Museum that opened in Lucerne in 1902.[181] Others wrote to the Dutch Minister of Foreign Affairs offering to take delegates on special excursions to show them their cities or their factories or to invite them out for soirées, special performances and theatre shows.[182] So began The Hague's flirtation with the concept of peace. Two decades before Wilson arrived in Paris, this small Dutch city ushered in the era of public diplomacy.

4

It Is Not Enough! The First Hague Conference, 1899

Little by little, the diplomats became prisoners of opinion

– Géraud de Geouffre de Lapradelle, 1900[1]

With the same degree of optimism with which it had welcomed the Tsar's rescript, the *Australasian* opened its 27 May 1899 edition with a lengthy editorial. Across three columns of fine newsprint, the editorial explained the stakes at play. The conference then sitting in The Hague was 'a sign of the times . . . In the midst of warlike preparations, the feeling of humanity is towards peace'. Nevertheless, the newspaper's editor gauged the Hague conference's chances of success as bleak:

> It must be confessed that, in the interval between the original invitation and the assembling of the guests at the Hague, the prospects of success have been dwindling . . . The delegates at the Hague are, doubtless, fettered by instructions from their Governments, and it will be an unexpected triumph of diplomacy if, in the face of so many obstacles, they arrive at any practical conclusion.

Still, and here the editorial showed a remarkable degree of prescience:

> [S]hould the conference fail to arrive at any agreement, it raises questions that cannot die, and must lead to a more imperative expression of the desire that peace shall be maintained.

For, in the end:

> The pacification of the world must spring from some mightier source than the bargainings of interested Governments . . . The reign of universal peace . . . is now included as a matter of course in our ideal of civilisation; and such an ideal lends to realise itself . . . In all probability it is only by slow degrees that the nations will be induced to lay down their arms. But, even if unfruitful in immediate results, the Peace Conference of 1899 may serve to mark a stage in our onward progress.[2]

For the *Australasian*, at least, the Hague peace conference of 1899 harkened the power of progress and bode well for the future of the world.

The *Australasian*'s interpretation of the opening of the Hague peace conference offers a stark contrast to the way many of its delegates experienced the event first-hand. Admiral Jacky Fisher acknowledged a 'grey cloud' of 'cynicism and defeatism' that lay over the House in the Woods.[3] His son, Cecil, wrote in a letter on 16 May 1899: 'I can imagine you are just starting off for the Peace Conference. I don't suppose any one has the slightest idea that it will come to anything.'[4] Equally pessimistically, the US delegate Andrew D. White described the atmosphere at a pre-conference party held in The Hague on 17 May as follows: 'never has so large a body come together in a spirit of more hopeless scepticism as to any good result'.[5] White also documented how a 'senior diplomat' at the gathering derisorily predicted that the conference would mark the failure of his own career, which would now descend into ignominy.[6] Italy's Count Nigra expressed similar sentiments.[7] So did Austria's Count Welsersheimb and Germany's Count Münster, who wrote to his friend Whitelaw Reid in April 1899: 'I could not refuse and have to obey orders, although I think it is a most difficult and ungrateful task.'[8] Russia's Baron de Staal was also pessimistic as was Andrew White himself, who, on being asked to represent the United States in April 1899, wrote in his diary: 'Am in much doubt'.[9] Prince Ferdinand of Bulgaria summed up his distaste for the affair most decisively when he wrote to Dimitri Stancioff, his country's first delegate, on 29 April 1899: 'Alas, what can I write about this Peace Conference, which seems to have been created to produce exactly the opposite of all the ideals of its programme? This assembly of rancid diplomats . . . is according to me one of the greatest impositions of the nineteenth century.' As for any advice: 'Well, I feel I am a useless sort of chief, unable to give instructions to his representative; but I really have nothing to tell you.'[10]

None of these delegates' feelings were on public display on 18 May 1899, when the city of The Hague welcomed them. Crowds gathered at the gates of the *Huis ten Bosch* to witness the arrival of the carriages and ogle at the exalted guests in their formal attire. As one newspaper described the atmosphere: the city 'usually so calm' took on an air of 'unaccustomed animation'.[11] All in all, the day was inaugurated well. The city basked in brilliant sunshine. Its gardens, woodlands and nearby beaches charmed its guests. Meanwhile, the locals hoped that the canals would keep their usual malodourous damp at bay (Figure 4.1).[12] The regional papers also delighted in the festivities. One commented that '[t]he Hague recommended itself dressed in green, with flags arrayed as on a memorable public holiday [*feestdag*]. The *driekleur* [Dutch national flag] flutters not quite from every home but in abundance around the centre of town and in no suburb is it missing'.[13] The police had extra guards on duty.[14] Journalists from all over Europe and the Americas were in attendance. They sent out their photographers to capture the image of the hundred or so delegates and urged the secretariat of the conference to impart information about the House in the Woods, its royal history as well as that of the city.[15] The Russian delegation made special arrangements, including the celebration of an intimate mass at a local Orthodox chapel that morning, which coincided with Tsar Nicholas II's birthday.[16]

The fact that many newspapers were enamoured by the opening of the Hague conference is well illustrated by the special edition of the French periodical *La Vie*

Figure 4.1 This comical sketch, published on 20 May 1899 in the local newspaper *De Hofstad*, depicted the delegates at the first Hague conference taking a gondola ride around the city cheered on by an excited crowd. Its caption read: 'The Hague is truly beautiful . . . but those canals . . . *enfin*, it's a good thing we have Sanders' *eau-de-cologne* with us!' (H. Jansen, 'Spotprent op de stank van de Haagsche grachten tijdens het bezoek van de leden van de vredesconferentie' *De Hofstad* 20 May 1899, in Haagse Beeldbank, Haags Gemeentearchief, kl. B 4418).

Illustrée (Life Illustrated), issued on 18 May. The magazine's cover depicted The Hague's picturesque parliamentary buildings (*Het Binnenhof*) and lake. The next page rather comically advertised the made-to-measure garments available at the High-Life Tailor on Rue de Richelieu in Paris by presenting the heads of state at the 'disarmament conference' in their formal best admiring the shop's window displays (Figure 4.2).[17] The following three pages offered photographs and short biographies of the main delegates, beginning with France's delegation. The former Prime Minister Léon Bourgeois received pride of place. The magazine then presented a richly illustrated three-page history of the city of The Hague, the Dutch royal family and the Queen's summer palace. Its final two pages juxtaposed a painting hanging in the main room of the *Huis ten Bosch*, of a lavish seventeenth-century royal ball, with a tableau from George Montbard's 1898 'Horror of War' painting depicting the four horsemen of the apocalypse riding forth (Figure 4.3). In a mere eight pages, *La Vie Illustrée* summed up the various public messages circulating about the conference: its pomp and circumstance warranting cynical humour; the uniqueness of the event justifying special attention to the delegates and to The Hague as a city of diplomatic significance; and the ultimate stakes at play at the conference, namely, the prospect of looming war. It was this final message of war and pestilence that *La Vie Illustrée* chose to leave with its readers. For its editors understood, much as those of the *Australasian* did too, that the Hague conference's relevance was first and foremost related to the serious subject of war.

Figure 4.2 *La Vie Illustrée* opened its special edition for 18 May with this comical advertisement for the Parisian made-to-measure store, High-Life Tailors. The advertisement depicted the sovereigns of the world meeting in front of the shop, decked out in their formal best. The illustrator, the well-known French caricaturist B. Moloch, offered a nod to the wider issues at stake by depicting an urchin harassing the Ottoman Sultan while carrying a petition advocating for the rights of Armenians (bottom left-hand corner). The drawing's caption, loosely translated, read: 'At the conference of disarmament in The Hague. Thinking of their people and in contemplation of their own merits, the sovereigns decide unanimously to compliment the High-Life Tailor for his marvellous suit [*complet*] made to measure for 69 francs 50 and to order it in advance of the [forthcoming] Paris Expo' (*La Vie Illustrée* 18 May 1899, 1).

At first glance, the first Hague conference that met between 18 May and 29 July 1899 was a diplomatic gathering involving duly qualified government representatives. Yet the local and global media contexts for the event belie a straightforward interpretation. Most newspapers followed the developments in The Hague with immense interest and attention to detail. It would not have mattered whether they picked up the *La Vie Illustrée*, the *Australasian* or, for that matter, the *Los Angeles Times*, *Le Matin*, the *Wiener Zeitung*, the *Japan Times* or the *Telegraaf* in The Hague itself. In almost every issue of these newspapers between May and July 1899, readers were confronted with the Hague conference, its developments, predicaments and political concerns.[18] As long as they read the news, they could not escape the conference nor fail to consider its achievements. It is, therefore, particularly relevant that the *Los Angeles Times*, the *Japan Times*, *Le Matin*, the *Wiener Zeitung* and the *Telegraaf* all published lengthy editorials

Figure 4.3 Printed in *La Vie Illustrée*'s special edition on 18 May 1899 to celebrate the opening of the first Hague conference, this tableau from George Montbard's 'Horror of War' painting depicts the four horsemen of the apocalypse wreaking havoc. Including the painting in the magazine reminded readers of the high stakes involved at the Hague conference (*La Vie Illustrée* 18 May 1899, 8).

on the merits of the conference, noted local and international public agitation in its favour and referenced the finer details of its agreements.[19]

A typical case study of how the 1899 Hague conference featured in newspaper reports around the world is presented by the *Los Angeles Times*. On 18 May 1899, the newspaper offered an account of the opening ceremony in The Hague and noted the efforts by May Wright Sewell to bring tens of thousands of women out in support.[20] On 19 May, it published W.T. Stead's account of the Tsar's ambitions as well as news from the 111th Presbyterian Convention in Minneapolis, including a message of support sent to the delegations in The Hague.[21] On 20 May, the newspaper published an irate comment on its front page about the lack of media access to conference negotiations. It also explained that the American delegation was greatly surprised at the flood of 'telegrams from all parts of the United States' supporting their efforts.[22] The following day, an editorial lauded that 'it is a hopeful sign that the peace conference now in session is a reality rather than a barren ideality'.[23] Over the ensuing weeks, the Californian daily commented in detail on the programme of the conference, the activities of the delegations, the tensions involved in conference diplomacy and the complexity of the negotiations about key issues (especially those relating to arbitration, disarmament and the laws of war). It also offered detailed analyses of the various agreements made during the negotiations. The *Los Angeles Times* repeatedly emphasized that many delegates were 'hopeful' of practical results and that, if anything, the mere fact that the conference was held ensured that international law was now recognized as a legitimate force in international affairs.[24]

The *Wiener Zeitung*, *Matin*, *Japan Times* and *Telegraaf* were as fascinated by The Hague's events as the *Los Angeles Times*. So was the *Friend of India*, whose editor explained on 6 July: 'Nothing strikes the newspaper reader more at the present moment than the progress of measures taken to promote international peace. Day by day the deliberations and decisions of The Hague committees are reported'.[25] A *Los Angeles Times* editorial joked on 23 June that 'whatever else the Czar's disarmament scheme may have failed in, it certainly has not failed in being a prolific theme for the paragraphers and editorial writers of the world'.[26] In analysing this coverage collectively, it is impossible to argue, as some historians do, that public interest in The Hague waned as the conference proceeded.[27] It is also not possible to argue that the world was only informed about the conference through the reportage of a few select individuals, such as W.T. Stead.[28] In fact, the high levels of global reporting on the conference reminds us how alert the world's media was for news from The Hague. To that end, it is significant to note that where newspapers differed was not in their fascination with The Hague, but rather in the tone of their editorial commentary. Of the five newspapers surveyed above, the only newspaper that posited any real difference in terms of its coverage was the *Telegraaf*. As a Dutch newspaper, it not only reported on the diplomacy of the Hague conference but also on local news: the outings made by delegates, the public events held in their honour and the activities of publicists and activists in support or as a critique of the conference. The newspaper even included a particularly scathing review of the uninspiring classical concert presented by The Hague's municipal council to the delegations.[29]

This chapter charts the public ideas that shaped the first Hague peace conference of 1899. It analyses the negotiations of the delegates and situates them within a global media context. It suggests that the intensity of the media's gaze during the conference mattered because it impacted on the negotiations in direct ways. As such, the chapter does not argue that ordinary diplomacy ended in 1899 nor does it suggest that the diplomats at The Hague did not have full agency to shape the terms of the ensuing Hague conventions. The diplomatic history of the conference is, at any rate, well charted.[30] What the chapter does argue is that the public environment in which the diplomacy of the conference took place mattered to its outcomes. The existence of an acknowledged public movement for disarmament and arbitration inspired many delegates to advance these ideas during the negotiations. They did so with zeal and resolve. The rest of the delegates, with some obvious exceptions, worked hard at attempting to look like they considered the merit of these proposals. At a bare minimum, then, the ongoing public interest in The Hague's happenings explains why the delegations had to succeed at least in some of their work. They could not indulge their cynicism in public and had to aim for consensus and agreement. Where in August 1898 their governments felt compelled to attend the Tsar's disarmament conference, by May 1899, many of them also felt compelled to achieve something to warrant the public's support of their endeavours.

The delegates' hard work paid off. Whatever critics said at the time (and would say later), the first Hague conference achieved some remarkable feats. It established the world's first international judicial forum (the Permanent Court of Arbitration, PCA). It instituted a code of military conduct for warfare on land. It extended the Geneva Conventions and, in so doing, ensured their legitimacy.[31] It created numerous principles for the conduct of international diplomacy, including the expectation that conflict resolution mechanisms be utilized, that the conduct of war be limited and that disarmament was a worthwhile end for states to pursue. All of these developments were dependent, at least in part, on the understanding that they would be welcomed. While the Hague conventions of 1899 were the product of extended diplomatic negotiation among the official representatives of twenty-six sovereign states, who took their task of protecting their state's interests very seriously indeed, the public context in which those negotiations took place played a role in how they panned out.

Furthermore, at some point between August 1898, when the Tsar released his rescript, and late July 1899, when the first Hague conference wrapped up its business, the concept of 'The Hague' entered everyday media parlance as a term that reflected the issues up for negotiation at the conference, namely, conflict resolution, the regulation of warfare and the limitation of military might. As the following chapters show, in the aftermath of the conference, the media continued to use and refer to 'The Hague' and, in so doing, attached normative expectations to the term, suggesting not only that wars fought by 'civilized' states should be conducted in 'civilized' ways as defined by the Hague rules but also that conflict should be avoided where possible. Within this framing of 'The Hague', it was the duty of governments to engage in mediation, arbitration and other 'good offices'. Contemporary newspaper readers also encountered the idea that the power of the Hague conventions lay not only in their content but also in how states applied them. If governments did not ratify or abide by the conventions, they might appear to have little value, but such failure could also have consequences. Ultimately, it was in the public sphere that states were held accountable to 'The Hague'.

It is, therefore, highly significant that the term 'The Hague' (or 'La Haye', 'Den Haag', 'L'aia' etc.) entered the lexicon of most newspapers in 1899 as a phrase that summed up the key ideas up for negotiation at the conference. It is also noteworthy that the public's power in framing the content of the Hague negotiations was recognized by contemporary commentators, and particularly by those who had something to gain from the development. For example, in 1900, the French international lawyer Géraud de Geouffre Lapradelle enthusiastically explained in a 260-page exposé that public opinion was 'responsible' for the Hague conference's results. He further suggested that the event made diplomats the prisoners of public sentiment.[32] For Lapradelle, the fact that the causes up for negotiation at The Hague had wide public appeal was a positive development. It heightened, so he hoped, the legitimacy of international law as a mitigating force in international affairs. It also recognized the potential of progressive change and, thus, bode well for the future of international diplomacy. Similarly, the American peace activist William Evans Darby noted in 1900 that 'the Conference was not controlled by the Tsar, or Muravieff, or the Kaiser, but by the people'.[33] Even if Lapradelle and Darby exaggerated the power of public opinion on actual diplomatic decision-making, their statements nevertheless recognized the wider relevance of public agitation for and media coverage of the negotiations at The Hague. The Hague conference of 1899 made public relations on issues relating to war and peace a priority for all governments, even if many of them were altogether reluctant to accept that reality and others ignored it entirely.

There were dozens of foreign journalists in The Hague in May 1899.[34] They all covered the opening session of the conference on the 18th. That session was largely ceremonial and lasted a mere thirty minutes. The delegates were all present along with a select few outside guests, including, as the sole woman, Baroness Bertha von Suttner. The addresses, given first by the Netherlands foreign minister and then by president Baron de Staal, were short, aimed at the message of peace and set in motion the formal business of the conference. These speeches were faithfully reprinted and commented on in newspapers around the world. The real business of the Hague conference began two days later on 20 May.

Two issues stood out during this first plenary session: the need for procedural clarity and what to do about giving the press ongoing access to conference proceedings. Unanimity on process was quickly achieved. On 19 May, de Staal met with the principal delegates. They agreed to form three commissions. The First Commission focused on the question of arms limitation and was chaired by Belgium's Auguste Beernaert. Russia's Fyodor Martens presided over the Second Commission on the law of war. France's Léon Bourgeois took charge of the Third Commission on international arbitration. Each government could choose whom they wished to have represented on the commissions, although their delegations could only vote as one. The framing of the content of the final conventions occurred in a series of plenary sessions with all delegates in attendance.[35]

The question of media access to the daily discussions was a more controversial matter. For most delegates, conference diplomacy could only work effectively if it occurred behind closed doors, out of the public gaze. While the conference secretariat run by J.C.N. van Eijs kept a record of speeches, resolutions and decisions, these accounts were intended for the use of the attending delegations only.[36] From their perspective, the conference had to proceed as all other international negotiations had done in the past, namely, as an in-committee enterprise. Only after the fact, so many of the diplomats thought, could their achievements be publicly explained and framed in appropriate ways.[37] The press was thus told that they would not receive any information about the ongoing negotiations. They would have to wait, along with everyone else, until the conference's end to ascertain the merits of its results.

Needless to say, the announcement did not sit well with the journalists gathered in The Hague nor with the peace activists and internationalists who had come to the city to witness history being made. How could they bear witness from behind closed doors? Unsurprisingly, newspaper editorials around the world quickly condemned the development.[38] The German social-democratic magazine *Der Wahre Jacob* satirized the situation when it depicted the peace angel herself barred at the conference door as an uninvited guest (see also Figure 4.4). An editorial comment in the *Los Angeles Times* lambasted the conference for ignoring the fact that 'the public [which] has to do the fighting when war begins would be glad to hear these murmurings of the peacemakers, in order to know if they are big and adroit enough to carry out the contract'.[39] The

Figure 4.4 This drawing, published in the Viennese satirical magazine *Kikeriki*, asked why the press was denied entry to the Hague negotiations. The two signs on either side of the doors read 'To the peace conference', 'entry forbidden' (*Kikeriki* [Austria] 8 June 1899, 3).

Washington Post reminded its readers that keeping the press out came at a considerable cost to the delegations:

> When the delegates at The Hague decided to close the doors during their sessions they put a premium on outside speculation and opened the way to all sorts of reports about the nature and progress of business . . . There are some clever men on the scene taking notes, and they are in commission to keep the public, at least, interested in the conference. And there need be no doubt that they will discharge their duty well, whether the delegates do or not.[40]

The *Post*'s boast was particularly important, suggesting that whether the diplomats and their governments liked it or not, the public would find a way into the conference chambers.

The conference secretariat was at a loss on how to respond to the media backlash. There was no precedent. At no previous juncture had media interest in a diplomatic event been so profound, global or demanding. In an attempt to alleviate the critique, a compromise decision was reached on 20 May. The secretariat established a press bureau, which offered a daily summary of conference developments to journalists. Yet the compromise was unsatisfactory.[41] The daily briefings were perfunctory, only noted the decisions made during the discussions and did not give any depth or nuance to what was discussed. Journalists, then, had to find their own 'news' by interviewing delegates and other prominent individuals. They did so with considerable determination. By the time the Third Commission held its first meeting on 23 May, some of the delegates expressed their distaste of the press situation.[42] Sweden's Baron Carl Nils Daniel Bildt, for example, asked for the work of the commission to be made public, given that its focus on arbitration was of such great international interest. Nevertheless, the established diplomats, including Bourgeois, Nigra, Martens, Descamps, Zenil, van Karnebeek and Okolicsány, all rebuffed Bildt's proposal.[43]

Ultimately, the *Washington Post*'s boast proved true: keeping the public's gaze out of the *Huis ten Bosch* was an impossible and fruitless task. Journalists not only actively sought out information from delegates, it was often readily given and, at other times, purposely leaked by the delegates themselves. Bertha von Suttner's memoirs note several incidences where she became the conduit for such leaks. For example, on 22 May at a lunch given by Felix and Greta Moscheles, Andrew White offered up the US plan for a full arbitration tribunal. He further commented: 'I cannot as yet give the details, but the fact itself will and should, be no secret'.[44] Two days later, Sir Julian Pauncefote imparted to Suttner that Britain too would propose a court of arbitration.[45] Both diplomats wished that news to circulate and looked for their countries to be given due credit. They fully recognized how the rhetoric around the conference mattered to the audience reading the news. Belgium's Éduoard Descamps also sought out Suttner's help in preventing the French peace activist Émile Arnaud from attacking the establishment of the PCA in the *Indépendance Belge*. For, as Descamps saw it, any negative publicity towards the principle of arbitration had the potential of influencing the outcome of the Hague negotiations.[46]

The internationalists and peace activists gathered in The Hague fully understood how the conference offered an excellent opportunity to influence and shape mainstream media representations in favour of their ideas. They did not squander any opportunity to advance them. They accepted, as many delegates did too, that newspapers not only informed the public of what was happening in The Hague but also shaped their assessment of that information. It was no surprise then that on 5 June Romania's delegate Alexander Beldiman complained in a meeting of the Third Commission that the contents of the United States' proposal for an arbitral court had been published in *The Times* (London) and *Cologne Gazette*, and intimated that perhaps the media restrictions on access to the conference should be lifted as they seemed rather pointless.[47]

Certainly, the Dutch journalists baulked at the lack of open access. Their *Journalistenkring* (Council of Journalists) lobbied the Dutch Ministry of Foreign Affairs to revoke the closed-door policy. They were particularly galled at the fact that foreign newspapers carried more information about conference deliberations than they could. They refused to be lowered to the position of spies or to cajole delegates into breaking their confidence. The council further argued that the delegates must also be unhappy as there were so many informers among them leaking information. At any rate, so much of what happened in the sessions was publicly disclosed that the notion that the conference operated under the veil of secrecy was a fallacy. The journalists also noted that the Dutch press was cutting a bad figure in the international arena: with the existing restrictions in place it could not operate at the forefront of news reporting, where it ought to be. At any rate, so the complaint continued, the public was not well served by the decision, which prevented the circulation of good information about essential issues of concern to them all.[48]

In the end, there was very little kept secret about the conduct of the conference. Whatever decisions were made in confidence, ended up being those made after-hours, in daily telegram exchanges with home governments, during lunch or dinner, while promenading along Scheveningen beach or strolling the woodlands around Queen Wilhelmina's summer abode, but not in the debating chambers of the *Huis ten Bosch* itself. The wording of the speeches and debates offered in the commissions and subcommittees (as reported in the conference record) were certainly declarative of a public audience, however hidden from immediate view. That the delegations were aware of the public duty attached to their mission was made all too obvious by Baron de Staal when he reminded the plenary session on 20 May that

> [t]he name 'Peace Conference', which the popular mind, outstripping the decision by the Governments in this respect, has given to our meeting, well indicates the mission incumbent upon it; its deliberations must lead to a tangible result which the whole human race confidently expects . . . the general goal toward which we are to direct our efforts [is]: *the prevention of conflicts by peaceful means.*[49]

De Staal's message could be read both as a threat and an opportunity. He effectively warned that none of the governments present would be able to bear the weight of the public's disapprobation if they failed in at least achieving partial results on the Tsar's agenda.[50] It is significant then that de Staal neglected to mention arms limitation in this speech. He firmly focused on Russia's expectations for arbitration, mediation and the humanization of warfare through law.[51] The delegates listening to Staal were thus also made to understand that their efforts had to achieve something on these issues particularly. Across the following ten weeks, many of them exerted a considerable effort to fulfil this mission, within the limits of their government briefs. Their results were substantive and many of them took great pride in those achievements.

At any rate, the diplomats could not escape the public's insistent gaze. There were too many visitors in The Hague, who looked to influence the conference's outcome and shape its public legacy. To that end, between 18 May and 29 July 1899, The Hague was a city of advocacy. Around town, ideas, concepts and plans were bandied about, applauded and dismissed. As the secretary of the London Peace Society noted in his reports to the *Herald of Peace*, there was little the activists could do to affect the deliberations, other than to engage in an 'act of presence': to promote their cause as publicly and actively as possible.[52] The visitors shared the same hotels as the delegations, attended the same parties and met each other in the streets. Given that many delegates brought their families with them, the social life of The Hague's first peace conference spurred interaction between delegates and non-delegates. Of course, throughout history, congresses and multilateral negotiations have always involved much more than the formal element of treaty making and diplomatic negotiation. After-hours diplomacy – the quality of the entertainments, dinners, balls, soirées and royal receptions – played as great a hand during this 1899 conference as it had in the past. The delegations were also well aware of the public attention paid to them. As Andrew D. White put it, '[T]here is, of course, a mass of social business . . . but these, of course, have their practical uses.'[53]

Yet the sheer volume of public advocacy was significant, as was the ongoing attention of the world's media. Newspapers even commented on the kinds of literature delegates had made available to them and Martinus Nijhoff, a prominent local publisher, reprinted the most significant of these for public purchase, including A. van Dhaene van Varick's sizeable compendium, which the Dutch government had commissioned for the delegates.[54] The *Journal de St.-Petersbourg* offered a lengthy précis of its content.[55]

Meanwhile, the commentators who had been so busy in the lead-up to the conference continued publishing their viewpoints and critiques.[56] The Hague's many activist visitors also made the most of the opportunity to advance their cause in person. Ivan Bloch offered a public lecture series, which many delegates attended.[57] W.T. Stead lauded the conference at length in a well-attended event at the Diligentia theatre, while Domela Nieuwenhuis offered his critiques at a rival theatre, Concordia, to an equally large audience.[58] Various visiting preachers offered sermons in favour of peace and brotherly cooperation at the English Church in The Hague.[59] Inter-Parliamentary Union (IPU) member H. Zillesen promoted the work of the Union in a public seminar aimed at making connections between the IPU and the objectives of the conference.[60] Jan ten Kate's exhibition of peace paintings at the Pulchri studio was regularly frequented (and commented on), while other artists flocked to the city to expound their talents on the topic of peace.[61]

These visitors also encountered the delegates at other social events, including at the ill-reviewed classical concert organized by the city's municipal council,[62] and at the town of Haarlem's 'festival hippique', which entertained delegates on 4 June with hurdle races, traditional peasant dances and refreshments.[63] Queen Wilhelmina hosted a lavish reception for lead delegates at her residence in The Hague.[64] She also invited them on a day-trip to Amsterdam, where she presided over a state banquet.[65] The Dutch government offered a festival of celebration on Saturday 17 June.[66] The Dutch Foreign Minister de Beaufort, for his part, held a weekly Friday soirée at his home in The Hague, enabling delegates, local dignitaries, journalists and visiting celebrities to mix, mingle and discuss international affairs.[67] Along with lunches, afternoon teas, concerts, dances and parties offered by local worthies, embassies, hotels and the visiting activists and the delegates themselves, the first conference of The Hague was a social success.[68] Count Nigra called it a 'delightful family party'.[69] Bulgaria's Dimitri Stancioff considered it 'one of the most interesting and congenial of the many international gatherings he had attended'.[70] Jacky Fisher left The Hague with the affectionate nickname, the 'dancing Admiral'.[71]

One Dutch editorial commented that many delegates travelled the country by rail and bicycle and were enamoured by the people, the landscape and culture. The rest spent their summer days at the beach in Scheveningen. It suggested that with all this holidaying, maybe 'little work' was actually being done.[72] Andrew White, for his part, lamented that '[t]he number of people with plans, schemes, notions, nostrums, whimsies of all sorts, who press upon us and try to take our time, is enormous; and when this is added to the pest of interviewers and photographers, life becomes serious indeed'.[73] Julian Pauncefote's staff often had trouble locating the British delegate 'for the delegates of the other countries were continually paying visits at his hotel to have his opinion'.[74] Meanwhile, Bertha von Suttner lapped up the attention, hosting a series of salons attended by delegates, journalists, locals and activists alike. She was boasted to be the most interviewed person at The Hague and her admirers extolled her virtues as 'the unofficial focal point, as it were, of the whole thing'.[75]

For delegates, there was no escaping the public context of the conference. They could not escape the attention of the media, the locals or the city's many foreign visitors. At any rate, journalists were invited to most of the conference-related social occasions.[76] Their newspapers also sought photographs of the delegations and notable dignitaries.[77] Local businesses made the most of the commercial possibilities. They advertised 'peace' paraphernalia, including 'peace pipes', 'peace flowers' and 'peace bread'.[78] Local bookshops sold conference photographs, while local cafés, attractions and sports facilities offered appropriate specials for delegates and their families.[79] As a particularly self-interested letter to the editor of *De Tijd* suggested, the hosting of the conference brought wealth and prosperity to the city of The Hague, which 'can never hurt' its commercial interests (*kan nooit kwaad*).[80] Still, the city's telegraphists complained about all the extra work they had to do over their summer to meet the needs of the foreign delegations.[81]

The more socially adroit of the delegates made the most of these public opportunities to ingratiate themselves with the various peace causes. The American delegation was particularly accomplished at schmoozing. With what some of their European colleagues disdainfully considered as acts of American pomp and circumstance, the US delegation hosted a series of public events to celebrate Independence Day on 4 July 1899. The day's festivities began with a formal wreath-laying ceremony at the tomb of international law's most famous son, Hugo Grotius, at the Nieuwe Kerk (New Church) in Delft, a small town within a short train ride of The Hague.[82] Lunch for 350 guests followed in Delft's medieval town hall. The celebrations finished with an 'American concert' in Scheveningen.[83]

The Grotius ceremony offered solemnity to the day. The wreath made of oak and laurel (symbols of civic virtue and victory) was adorned with silver-gilded leaves, acorns and berries. A choir of a hundred voices sang the hymns along with the United States, Russian and Dutch national anthems. Despite inclement weather, the church filled to the brim.[84] The audience included the entire Dutch cabinet, much of the diplomatic corps accredited to The Hague and many of the delegates at the conference. The first delegate of the Netherlands, A.P.C. van Karnebeek, presided and offered a suitably impressive opening speech. Andrew White's much longer speech[85] honoured Grotius's work, which offered, as he saw it, the 'greatest blessing to humanity'.[86] He continued that 'the time and place are well suited' to acknowledge that [i]n this town Grotius was born; in this temple [the Nieuwe Kerk] he worshipped; this pavement he trod when a child; . . . at his death his mortal body was placed in this hallowed ground. Time and place, then, would seem to make this tribute fitting'. For, as White explained, all nations owe a 'vast debt' to Grotius and thus to the city of The Hague.[87]

In making this speech, White achieved many important things. First, he ensured the public legacy of the United States' mission at the Hague conference was confirmed. David Jayne Hill's request that the delegation come away from the event as a 'friend and promoter of peace' was firmly substantiated.[88] The public rhetoric of peace and international cooperation would serve the US government well for the foreseeable future.[89] It also ingratiated the Americans to the Dutch public. Second, the wreath-laying ceremony proffered an important accolade to the public agency surrounding the conference. The press reported the event around the world, often quoting White's speech in detail. The *Manchester Guardian* even reprinted it in full.[90] The journal of the *Institut de droit international* used the Grotius celebration as a catalyst to consider the importance of Grotius to modern international law, while the *Journal des débats politiques et littéraires* suggested that the United States had occasioned a 'lasting souvenir' (*souvenir durable*) of their time in The Hague.[91]

Unsurprisingly, the Delft ceremony received special attention in the United States. On 5 July, the *Los Angeles Times* headlined with 'Impressive ceremonies at Delft'.[92] The *Chicago Daily Tribune*'s special correspondent acclaimed 'All Honor to Grotius' and quoted White's call to action for the delegates at the Hague conference: 'Go on in your labor to search out facts and develop principles which shall enable future conferences to build more and more broadly, more and more loftily for peace.'[93] Meanwhile, the *New York Times* finished its conference analysis on 26 July 1899 with another extract of White's 4 July speech, in which he urged the delegates to

> [g]uard well the treasures of civilization with which each of you is entrusted, but bear in mind that you hold a mandate from humanity. Go on with your work. Pseudo philosophers will prophesy malignantly against you; pessimists will laugh you to scorn; cynics will sneer at you; zealots will abuse you for what you have not done . . . Heed them not; go on with your work.[94]

The article finished with the exhortation: 'The voice of Grotius has been heard and heeded'.[95]

Above all, the Grotius ceremony forged a mythical connection between the city of The Hague and the concept of peace and international law. By honouring Grotius at his grave, White helped to fashion a legacy for the city as a site of internationalism, peace activism and international regulation. In making his speech, White was well aware of the historical links he was fashioning in the public imagination, although he may not have imagined their longevity. Undoubtedly, he understood the excellent public press it would give him and his delegation in the immediate term.[96]

Not all of the public causes on display in The Hague were as easily accommodated by the delegations or the local authorities as these ingratiating acts of public diplomacy. It was one thing to agree with von Suttner over dinner that world peace was a worthwhile cause, as Count Nigra was so adept at doing,[97] to engage Bloch on the future of modern warfare after one of his public lectures or even to pay homage to Grotius. It was quite another to confront the Zionist ambitions of Theodor Herzl[98] or the claims for independence made by the representatives of the Armenians, Georgians, Macedonians, Serbs, Poles, South African Boers and Finns, who also sent representatives to The Hague in 1899.[99] The city attracted a world of causes, many of which were communicated in print, some of which were delivered in person.[100] Many of these petitions were founded on desperation. For those that arrived by post, the secretariat of the conference wrote suitably dismissive answers. They acknowledged that they could not ignore them.[101] For those who arrived in person, more decisive action was occasionally necessary. When a delegation of Young Turks sought an audience among the delegations in early June, for example, they were received with disdain in some quarters and dismissed in others.[102]

For the Dutch government, the Armenian Minas Tcheraz posed a particular problem, especially since the Armenian cause was well reported in the world's newspapers.[103] Tcheraz had come to the Netherlands in 1899 to promote the cause of the Armenians and to highlight their persecution under Ottoman rule. He went about his business in suspect ways, apparently presenting himself as a formal delegate to the peace conference.[104] In the end, the Dutch government had the police keep a close eye on his activities, which they officially restricted when he attempted to give a series of public speeches.[105] Undoubtedly, the Ottoman Empire was unimpressed with Tcheraz's presence in The Hague. With an eye to avoiding a diplomatic embarrassment, the Dutch police quietly removed him from the country. However, when the Dutch press caught wind of this fact, it erupted. The *Telegraaf* editorialized that it was ridiculous that in a country famous for celebrating the right to free speech, a man with a legitimate cause was kept from speaking.[106] In the end, and at the instigation of Abraham Kuijper, the leading politician in the Protestant Anti-Revolutionary Party, Tcheraz was given a formal platform and attracted considerable crowds in Amsterdam and The Hague.[107] In the process, Tcheraz became a cause célèbre.

What the Tcheraz incident also brought to the fore was the fact that the Dutch press was disconnected from the world by the barrier of language. While the polyglot Dutch newspaper editors readily read and borrowed 'news' from all over the world, few foreign journalists could access the content of the Dutch-language newspapers.

Given that the eyes of the world were trained on The Hague, the concern was pressing. As the *Telegraaf* put it, if the world read our newspapers, then we could let the world know of our stand on all manner of issues from Tcheraz to the Transvaal.[108] That the *Dagblad van Zeeland en 's Gravenhage* published several columns of 'official' news on the conference in French each day was not enough to make Dutch 'news' accessible to the foreign media. A proffered solution was the creation of a French-language *Journal de l'Haye* that could engage the foreign media. Above all, the debate about how to make the Netherlands more prominent brought out how aware newspaper publishers were of their potential global relevance.

That the eyes of the world's media were trained on The Hague obviously mattered to the delegations at the conference as well. It is highly significant then that, as Julian Pauncefote described it, 'a remarkable change came over the spirit of the conference' within days of its opening.[109] Of course, in bringing the world's best diplomats, their lawyers and military advisors to The Hague, all men with experience, ideas and a desire to be useful, perhaps it was inevitable that progress was made. Yet previous conferences on similar issues had stalled or failed. By 1899, most governments considered the Geneva Conventions of 1864 as shambles and reworking them highly problematic. Their thoughts on the St Petersburg Declaration of 1868 were not much better and everyone was aware that despite the official goodwill on show at the Brussels Conference, the conventions of 1874 were never ratified.[110] That the 1899 Hague conference achieved any agreement on genuinely controversial issues like arbitration, the Geneva conventions, the law of war and the extension of 'good offices' is, therefore, particularly remarkable. That success speaks to the genuine efforts made by the delegations in The Hague and to their willingness to accept the principle that some consensus was essential.

The success of the conference was in no small part due to the immense effort put into planning, drafting and mobilizing assent among the delegations by a set of key individuals, most notably Fyodor Martens, Andrew White, Julian Pauncefote, Léon Bourgeois, Auguste Beernaert, T.M.C. Asser, Count Nigra, Baron de Constant d'Estournelles, Édouard Descamps and Alexander Beldiman.[111] At stake were principles of sovereignty and military strength (might makes right). In the balance hung the promise of humanitarianism, international cooperation, regulation and organization. Among the delegates were powerful proponents of international law, international arbitration and the humanizing of war, who faced off against equally powerful proponents of state sovereignty and the military principle *si vis pacem para bellum*. Yet the animosity one might suppose to develop by such contrasting viewpoints, although not non-existent, was rarely on display. Recent work by Alan Anderson, for example, revises the perception of Admiral Fisher as a hard-nosed militarist who only threatened hell and damnation.[112] Fisher worked hard at the conference and kept to his government's brief: to protect the power of the Royal Navy and avoid offending the other delegations.[113] He co-authored the report on the application of the Geneva Conventions to warfare at sea and made serious and thoughtful contributions to the discussions at hand.

The First Commission had undoubtedly the hardest task reconciling the public promise of disarmament and the reality that none of the governments in attendance had any inclination of limiting their armed forces. Aimed at Articles 1, 2, 3 and 4 of the second circular, it was obvious from the opening session on 23 May that very little real progress would be made on general disarmament principles. Still, Auguste Beernaert, the Commission's president, tried. He reminded the meeting that they had a sacred duty endorsed by the public's spirit. He also noted that the mere summoning of a conference of disarmament was, in itself, a 'stupendous fact'.[114] The Russian delegation made a substantial effort to advance the agenda as well. Its representatives proposed a moratorium on the development of new weaponry and on the expansion of military budgets. As Baron de Staal reminded the Commission on 23 June: 'What we are hoping for is to attain a limitation – a halt in the ascending course of armaments and expenses.'[115] All that was needed was one small step.

The Dutch military delegate, General de Beer Poortugael, reinforced de Staal's motif by arguing that keeping millions of soldiers armed in Europe was an unsustainable expense. He continued: 'Please understand me. I am far from being a Utopian. I do not believe in an eternal peace, I even think that wars can in exceptional cases be inevitable and salutary, by purifying, like a storm, the political atmosphere . . . [but] there are limits to everything, and we have already passed them a long time ago.'[116] So: 'Let us make a united effort, let us halt on this edge of the abyss, if not, we shall perish!'[117] Russia's military delegate General Gilinsky then asked the all-important question: 'Will the peoples represented in this Conference be satisfied if, in going hence, we take them arbitration and laws of warfare, but nothing for times of peace?'[118]

Only one objection was made to the above speeches. Germany's Colonel Gross von Schwarzhoff reminded all that his country was 'not hanging on the edge of the precipice' nor 'hastening towards exhaustion and ruin. Quite the contrary . . . As for compulsory military service, which is intimately associated with these questions, the German does not regard it as a heavy burden but a sacred and patriotic duty, to the performance of which he owes his existence, his prosperity, his future'.[119] A.P.C. van Karnebeek, the first delegate of the Netherlands, had no qualms in expressing his dismay at von Schwarzhoff's declaration, which seemed to imply that the question of disarmament did not 'merit the most serious attention of the Conference and even of the entire world'. He asserted not only that von Schwarzhoff was wrong, but also that there were many delegates in the room who condemned von Schwarzhoff for his pronouncement.[120]

Nevertheless, by 30 June, it was clear that the First Commission was unable to agree on any form of armaments limitation. At this point, Beernaert suggested a compromise, namely, that each government should take up the burden and study the topic of disarmament in house. In support, Sweden's delegate, Baron Bildt, made an impassioned plea: '[W]e are about to terminate our labors recognizing that we have been confronted with one of the most important problems of the century, and that we have accomplished very little towards its solution.' He furthered:

> Let us not indulge in illusions. When the results of our deliberations shall become known, there will arise . . . a great cry: It is not enough! And this cry: 'It is not enough,' most of us in our conscience will acknowledge to be just. Our consciences, it is true, may also tell us in consolation, that we have done our duty, since we

> have faithfully followed our instructions. But I venture to say that this duty is not fulfilled and that there still remains something for us to do.[121]

Bildt then noted that 'the Czar's proposal has been strewn with all the flowers of rhetoric by men more eloquent than I', so the least he and the other delegates could do was to give shape to the rhetoric and help the future of these grand endeavours by not only supporting Beernaert's resolution but also explaining the justness of the cause of armaments control to their home governments. Bildt's speech met with concerted applause.[122]

The Danish delegate E. Bille seconded Bildt's plea as did France's Léon Bourgeois, who also reminded the German delegation that he too represented a country with a proud tradition of military service. However, he hoped that von Schwarzhoff might agree that 'if the considerable resources that are devoted to military organization were in part put to the service of pacific and productive activities, the total prosperity of each nation could not but increase at a much more rapid pace'.[123] He further asked that a declaration be accepted: 'that the restriction of military charges, which are at present a heavy burden on the world, is extremely desirable for the increase of the material and moral welfare of mankind'.[124] This resolution passed into the final act of the conference and, in so doing, firmly embedded the concept of disarmament into the diplomacy of states. It also legitimated the first Hague peace conference as a conference of disarmament, even if no arms agreements were actually entered into.[125]

The other subcommittees of the First Commission had somewhat more to show for their deliberations, although their final set of resolutions offered meagre pickings. While they considered limitations on the introduction of new types of rifles, small arms, naval cannon and battering rams (all dead-end discussions, although a vast amount of energy and time was exerted in having them),[126] they only forwarded three articles for consideration to the plenary session of 21 July[127]: the first to prohibit the launch of projectiles from balloons or 'analogous new ways',[128] the second to outlaw the release of asphyxiating gases by armies in the field and the last to prevent the use of hollow-nosed or perforated 'bullets which expand and flatten easily in the human body'.[129] More commonly known as dum-dum bullets, their prohibition was roundly contested by the British delegation. In the subcommittee, Sir John Ardagh leapt to the defence of the bullets and their use. Arguing that the traditional Lee Metford bullet failed to render soldiers encountered in colonial battles *hors de combat* (outside combat) fast enough, the bullet had been invented in the eponymous Dum-Dum arsenal near Calcutta.[130] The British Army considered its utility against 'savages' as exemplary.[131] Ardagh's opinion was not only in line with War Office thinking, it also represented the perspective of the British Admiralty, who had advised the Foreign Office that any proposal to 'restrict improvements in weapons . . . would favour the interests of savage nations, and be against those of the more highly civilized'.[132]

Ardagh's plea, much like von Schwarzhoff's cited above, caused general consternation. The Russian delegate Arthur Raffalovich, for example, responded that Ardagh's ideas were altogether 'contrary to the humanitarian spirit which rules this end of the nineteenth century'.[133] Others noted that experiments undertaken at the University of Tübingen showed hollow-tipped bullets causing excruciating internal wounds. These injuries, along with the accounts of battles in which the real dum-dum bullets (as opposed to the replicas used in the Tübingen experiments) were used, rendered them needlessly cruel. The 1868 St Petersburg Declaration had already imposed a requirement for states to ensure that 'the only legitimate object' of war was 'to weaken the military forces of the enemy' and 'that the employment of such arms', 'which uselessly aggravate the sufferings of disabled men, or render their death inevitable . . . be contrary to the laws of humanity'.[134] In keeping with the spirit of the 1868 agreement, all the delegations present, excepting the United States and Britain (with a further abstention registered by Portugal), voted to proscribe the dum-dum.

At the plenary session on the subject, it was the United States who lobbied to revise or revoke the declaration prohibiting the hollow-nosed bullet, having persuaded the British delegation to vote against the asphyxiating gas embargo in return.[135] As the Dutch delegate van Karnebeek then rather exasperatingly reminded the gathering, if either article was revised then 'no result will be reached'.[136] For the sake of consensus and achievement, all three declarations (on gas, aerial bombardment and dum-dums) formed part of the final Hague conventions of 1899. At the same time, they also passed into public parlance and understanding.

The Second Commission, presided over by Fyodor Martens, proved much more productive than the First. Aimed at dealing with the laws of war (articles 5, 6, and 7 of the second circular), the Commission sought ways to extend the Geneva Conventions of 1864 to warfare at sea and the regulation of the international law of war on land. It was in the subcommittees of the Second Commission that the role of the technical delegates came into their own. To regulate the laws of war, expertise was essential. It was also in these subcommittees that vital interests were potentially at threat. As the American representative William Crozier noted, he 'had to be constantly on guard that something unfavourable to the United States should not find its way into the agreements'.[137] Britain's Sir John Ardagh, for his part, attempted to placate his War Office by suggesting from the outset that the Second Commission might recommend guiding principles rather than binding articles.[138] Martens forcefully countered the request and reminded the commission that the Brussels Conventions would form the 'solid basis' of their discussions and that any regulation, once ratified, would have the binding force of a treaty.[139] Martens's intervention put an end to Ardagh's attempt to jeopardize the Commission's brief.

On 20 June, the Second Commission recommended a set of regulations to augment the Geneva Conventions. They looked to neutralize hospital ships, guarantee their safety from naval attack, protect medical staff and enable them to offer succour to shipwrecked, sick and wounded sailors during battle.[140] These rules were particularly pertinent: the recent Spanish-American War had created questions about the legitimacy of hospital ships and the rights to medical aid in neutral waters. Furthermore, as the report to the conference explained, the expansion of the Geneva rules was 'earnestly desired by public opinion' as it extended charitable and humanitarian assistance in time of war.[141] Broadening the Geneva rules to apply to naval warfare was a significant development. It not only legitimated the existing Geneva Conventions (which not all states had signed up to before 1899) but also recognized that there was scope to improve them. As a result, pressure was brought to bear on Switzerland to take a lead in that process.[142] As Neville Wylie suggests, without the first Hague conference there may not have been a Geneva law tradition in the twentieth century.[143]

On 5 July 1899, Martens presented a further sixty articles in a convention for the conduct of war on land.[144] The articles regulated invasion and military occupation, the treatment of besieged civilian populations and their rights to self-defence (which were not endless), capitulation and armistice, as well as the capture and incarceration of prisoners of war (POWs) and internees. While these rules avoided any mention of the principle of military necessity (a heavily debated subject among the delegates),[145] they did delineate terms for attacking undefended towns, the misuse of flags of truce and succour (such as the Red Cross flag) and the protection of religious, cultural, scientific and medical facilities. The convention for the conduct of warfare on land was a remarkable achievement. It established a standardized and universal code of military conduct that applied to all armed forces whose states were signatories.

The convention was made possible in part because the circumstances of recent conflicts, including the Franco-Prussian War, the Sino-Japanese War and the Spanish-American War, brought out common concerns relating to the conduct of war, the treatment of its victims and the protection of neutral territorial sovereignty. At another level, the new Hague rules reflected, as Isabel Hull explains, 'the consensus . . . among most nation-signatories about what was [already] legal in wartime'.[146] In other words, the convention was a product of pragmatism and the military and strategic needs of armed forces. It could not be classified as a product of pacifist idealism or of humanitarian ambition. Still, the creation of the rules was, in itself, significant. After 1899, there was no escape from them.

Yet the delegates also realized that their war code was incomplete and ignored the regulation of warfare at sea almost completely. Furthermore, as Beernaert warned the Second Commission, the regulation of warfare might have the unforeseen consequence of legitimizing the act of war and occupation. His question was an essential one, and spoke directly to the elephant in the room: 'whether the fear of appearing by an international regulation to legalize as a right the actual power exercised through force of arms should be a good reason for abandoning the invaluable advantage in a limitation of this power?'[147] The ensuing debate was heated and protracted and pitted the proponents of military necessity against those advocating for the humanization of warfare.[148] It resulted in two important suggestions: first that another Hague conference be held to advance the discussions and to improve the existing regulations, especially to cover topics that were not on the agenda (such as the regulation of neutrality and the exemption from capture of private property at sea);[149] and second that the conference adopt a generic principle. The principle was embedded in the preamble of the final Hague conventions, and became known as the Martens Clause (Fyodor Martens authored it). Its final version stated that the signatories

> clearly do not intend that unforeseen cases should, in the absence of a written undertaking, be left to the arbitrary judgement of military commanders. Until a more complete code of the laws of war has been issued . . . the inhabitants and the belligerents remain under the protection and the rule of the principles of the law of

> nations, as they result from the usages established among civilized peoples, from the laws of humanity, and the dictates of the public conscience.[150]

If anything, the Hague conventions that followed this preamble only heightened the expectation that all 'civilized' peoples would conduct their wars accordingly.

While on the one hand, the Martens Clause was easily dismissed as having little real impact on the conduct of war – it was purposely vague on the issue of military necessity – the clause nevertheless permeated through public and legal debates from 1899 on (and continues to do so today).[151] The clause underwrote the idea that 'civilized' states could not wage unlimited warfare, at least not without risking public disapprobation and international sanction. How individual states and their armed forces interpreted the clause and its 'silences' was, however, another issue.[152]

In the end, it was the work of the Third Commission on international arbitration, mediation and the regulation of 'good offices' that spoke best to the 'peaceful' ambitions of the conference agenda.[153] Many of the delegates understood that if something could be done to temper the global disappointment at the (inevitable) lack of success on armaments control, it would be by regulating international arbitration. Arbitration was a powerful internationalist idea with proponents in most countries. It had also been utilized effectively by governments in the past. By 1899, bilateral arbitration treaties were common.[154] Even Britain and the United States attempted to finalize a compulsory arbitration treaty in 1897.[155] Promoting both the utility of arbitration as a tool of conflict resolution and offering a process to affect its use by states preoccupied the Third Commission.

As early as 26 May, at the second meeting of the Third Commission, Sir Julian Pauncefote filed a motion to establish in The Hague a 'permanent international tribunal which can assemble instantly at the request of contesting nations'.[156] The American, Italian and Russian delegations also offered up their plans for an arbitral tribunal, which they called the Permanent Court of Arbitration (PCA).[157] Over the course of dozens of meetings amid much debate and contending viewpoints, the delegates fine-tuned the workings of the PCA. They also framed the situations that might see governments send their disputes to the court in the first place. Most contentious of all was the question of whether, in circumstances not ruled by 'vital interests' and 'national honour' (in other words those that covered legal or pecuniary concerns alone), a dispute might be forcibly sent to the PCA.[158] While many governments represented at The Hague were wary of any compulsion, they nevertheless allowed their delegates considerable leeway in discussing its potential.

At this point, Germany's delegate Philipp Zorn announced that his government did not sanction obligatory arbitration or 'justify a more general and immediate development of these conventions' at all.[159] Germany's uncooperative position almost deadlocked the Commission for without its participation, the regulation of international arbitration would carry no weight. The impasse resulted in Zorn (the only German delegate who believed that arbitration might prove useful)[160] and Frederick Holls (the American delegation's ambitious and well-connected secretary)[161] setting off to Berlin on 18 June to persuade Kaiser Wilhelm II to change his instructions.[162] The Kaiser, however, was in Hamburg, which enabled the Foreign Office to avoid an embarrassing outburst.[163] Instead, Germany's foreign minister Count von Bülow met with the delegates and reluctantly conceded to the creation of the PCA as long as no obligation was imposed on any state to use it. As he explained to the Kaiser: 'The idea of arbitration is in every aspect unattractive. Through your Majesty's firm and decisive attitude, it has, however been possible to persuade the remaining states to abandon all that there was of importance in the idea.'[164]

In the end, the PCA was formed on the basis of voluntary utilization. All signatories to the convention nominated judges for the PCA's roster and paid for its operation. Each state could send a dispute to the court, but it was under no obligation to do so. An International Bureau was established in The Hague to administer the court's affairs. To heighten the value of the court, the Third Commission enabled the use of the PCA for investigative purposes as well, in the form of commissions of inquiry.[165] The signatory powers also recognized that, in questions of a legal nature, arbitration was 'the most effective, and at the same time the most equitable, means of settling disputes which diplomacy has failed to settle'.[166] Furthermore, the Commission regulated the concept of mediation and urged 'good offices' on neutrals: neutral states would become, as the Swiss delegate Edouard Odier noted, the 'managers of peace' (*pacigérants*).[167] To that end, the new conventions advocated that 'strangers to the dispute, should, on their own initiative, and as far as circumstances may allow, offer their good offices or mediation to the States at variance'.[168] Such interventionism could 'never be regarded . . . as an unfriendly act'.[169] Altogether then, the regulations heightened the expectation that in time of international crisis, the duty of an outside government was to intervene to pacify the situation. The PCA offered a useful medium for achieving that end.

Many delegates hoped that the PCA might have had an even greater jurisdiction. The formal report tabled at the plenary session on 25 July contained a wealth of information about the advantages of compulsory arbitration. In an address clearly aimed at countering Germany's recalcitrance on the topic of arbitration, Count Nigra also exclaimed that

> [t]he impatience with which public opinion awaits the results of our labors has become so great that it would be dangerous to refuse to accept an arbitral tribunal. If the Conference should meet this impatience with a *non possumus*, or fail to satisfy it, it would really be guilty of deceit. In that case the Conference would incur a grave responsibility to history, to the nations, and to His Majesty the Emperor of Russia himself.[170]

Most delegates acknowledged that Germany was responsible for 'the collapse of a generous initiative'.[171] Still, as the diplomatic record attests, many governments were secretly pleased that the issue of compulsory arbitration was avoided.[172]

Germany's seeming volte-face on the topic of arbitration, nevertheless, needs an explanation. Neither Kaiser Wilhelm II nor his cabinet had any inclination to support the arbitral cause before the conference.[173] Von Bülow's delegates were also told to shun conference affairs and let other delegations do the dirty work of negating those developments that threatened state sovereignty.[174] Count Münster, for one, made no secret of his anti-arbitration views. On 14 June, he wrote to his friend Friedrich von Holstein:

> On this question [or arbitration] nearly all the delegates fail to see the wood for the trees. If the Conference does not result in some sort of Court [of] Arbitration, they will consider themselves dishonoured in the eyes of public opinion . . . Being sensible, we [the Germans] are pretty well isolated . . . We shall soon be in a position where we shall have to accept some utterly worthless compromise proposal or else be looked upon as the rock on which the good ship 'Conference' foundered . . . The question for us will be simple: do we accept this bad Court of Arbitration out of consideration for Russia and public opinion artificially roused by her, and later refuse to ratify the Conference decisions; or do we stick to a completely negative attitude? I can hardly wait to learn what the wise men in Berlin are deciding?!![175]

Meanwhile, the German government worked hard to promote its uncompromising vision of The Hague in the national newspapers.[176] Zorn's intervention on behalf of the PCA reflected how isolated the Germans were on the subject.[177] There were, of course, detractors in all governments, but only Germany officially positioned itself against the principle of any and all arbitration.[178]

That von Bülow overturned Germany's position on the PCA in July 1899 is, therefore, an important reflection of the public power of the moment.[179] Von Bülow was well aware that if Germany was held responsible for the failed arbitration negotiations, it would create a public relations disaster.[180] At the time, many newspapers reported on the sudden halt to the Third Commission's negotiations and noted that the envoys were on their way to Germany's capital.[181] Some of them commented on Germany's recalcitrance at the conference in general and on the topic of arbitration in particular.[182] The *Los Angeles Times*, for example, turned to the subject repeatedly from 11 June onwards,[183] including in an editorial comment on 13 June that 'the failure of the peace negotiation, which is now probable, will be due to the inflated medieval ideas of the young Emperor of Germany'.[184]

The Kaiser also recognized that he needed to make good in public on the subject. He offered a suitable toast at a Wiesbaden dinner, which the *Berlin Post* reported and which was republished around the world on 22 June, in which he announced that Germany had been the first nation to support the Tsar's rescript, that he and all Germans sought achievement from the event and that the accomplishments of the Hague conference were a shared and global venture.[185] It was also telling that it was Count Münster who, during the closing addresses of the conference, responded to President de Staal's exclamation that 'the first step has been taken . . . The good seed is sown. Let the harvest come' with the somewhat less than convincing statement:

> It is very rare that an assembly which has lasted two and a half months can show such perfect harmony as that which has always reigned in this hall . . . If the Conference has not realized all of its wishes – and its desires and illusions ran high – it will at least have a great influence upon the future, and the seeds which

> it has sown are sure to germinate . . . This Conference will be one of our most beautiful memories.[186]

In private, he wrote to Whitelaw Reid that 'we thrashed peacefully and did not much good but *no harm*'.[187]

Altogether the Final Act of the first Hague conference resulted in the signing of three conventions: the Convention for the Pacific Settlement of International Disputes (I), the Convention Respecting the Laws and Customs of War on Land (II) and the Convention for the Adaptation to Maritime Warfare of the Principles of the Geneva Convention of 22 August 1864 (III). It also issued three declarations relating to the prohibition of aerial bombardment, the dispersion of asphyxiating gases and the use of dum-dum bullets. It registered the resolution that 'the restriction of military charges' was desirable and issued six other *voeux* (literally 'wishes') for consideration at the next Hague conference.[188] The *voeux* highlighted how the work of this first peace conference had initiated so many useful and important discussions that they necessitated a future conference.

Many delegates and their governments, although by no means all, were impressed by their achievements at The Hague.[189] In a private letter to his brother-in-law, Dimitri Stancioff explained:

> We have had 'diplomacy at its best'. It is too soon to judge the results of the work accomplished by prominent men from international, diplomatic and financial circles from all quarters of the globe with so much learning and integrity to support their pacific aims . . . Baron de Staal's closing address was admirable . . . these were the final words: 'the work we have accomplished . . . is sincere, practical and wise'.[190]

Stancioff also noted that he had the honour of an appointment to the PCA and thought Bulgaria might send their Macedonian concerns to the court for consideration.[191] Louis Renault opined that he went to The Hague as a Frenchman and left as a 'citizen of the world',[192] while for Austria's Heinrich Lammasch the first Hague conference was a turning point as he leapfrogged from his career as a university professor into international public life.[193] Both these men also served as judges on the PCA.[194] Fyodor Martens was ecstatic about the laws of war conventions, or as he put it: 'I myself did not expect such a brilliant success. The Brussels Declaration – my beloved child – has been adopted'.[195] Even Sir John Ardagh, who had advocated so loudly and strongly for the rights of armed forces to decide on their own military codes, wrote to a friend that the conference had many practical results and while it 'has done much good work in dissipating unrealistic conceptions' it was also 'a monumental work' in which the codification of the laws of war were a 'considerable step in advance'.[196]

While many delegates were optimistic about their achievements at The Hague, the public interpretation of the signing of the Final Act on 29 July tended to focus on all that was not achieved. Bildt's warning that the public would cry 'It is not enough!' was all too evident in media reports. Bertha von Suttner considered 4 July as a 'melancholy, gloomy day', in part because the rumours that the disarmament negotiations had stalled were rife.[197] Many newspapers, including a number from Germany, expressed their condescension with a series of dismissive headlines: 'The disgusting drama at The Hague', 'Noxious nuisance now under way' and 'comedy at The Hague'.[198] On 4 July, *Der Wahre Jacob* offered a scathing front-page cartoon in which a gluttonous god of war seated on the ruins of *Kultur* (civilization) and *Volksfrieden* (the people's peace) received bags of cash from the world's great powers, including Germany.[199] By 10 July, the *Spectator* (Britain) labelled the conference 'a failure', as did the *Anglo-Saxon Review* who derided the failure as being 'ceremoniously veiled' and offering no 'practical validity'.[200] On 3 August, the *Friend of India* condemned the conference as having 'ended in universal indifference', although the editorial also iterated that there was no reason to despair and that Britain could do much with arbitration to solve some of India's pressing concerns.[201]

Blackwood's Edinburgh Magazine offered another scathing assessment of the 'woe-begone' and 'ill-used assembly' at which all the Tsar's proposals, except for arbitration, were dropped 'at the door'. As for the PCA, *Blackwood's* suggested that because it was 'established by the "conscience of Europe"; its doors open; its halls swept and garnished; its judges pathetically waiting, [it] would appeal so strongly to our sentimentalism that a weak, chicken-hearted responsibility-dreading Government would never lack excuses enough for committing honour and interest to the dice-box'. The PCA was then a useless and pointless institution.[202] More despondently still, the *Grazer Tageblatt* invoked a funerary metaphor by suggesting on 30 July that the Hague conference was the event that saw mourners take peace to its grave.[203] Other Austrian newspapers proclaimed that Great Britain was the villain of the event: its delegation had weakened the utility of the conference by reducing its issues *ad absurdum*, and cited the dum-dum deliberations to make their case.[204]

Outside Europe, pessimism also prevailed. The Japanese newspaper *Kokumin* described the conference as a 'failure', although with some recompense offered by the establishment of the PCA.[205] The *Los Angeles Times* noted on 27 June that '[t]he Hague peace conference is settling down into a discussion of the best way to kill an enemy without hurting him, but there is precious little talk about peace on any terms. The Czar's scheme looks like a miscarriage of good intentions'.[206] Two days later it despondently reflected that

> [t]he Russian scheme for universal disarmament has been declared unacceptable to the Peace Conference at The Hague; in other words, the Peace Conference, as such, is a failure, and it is not too much to say that it was foredoomed to that end. When all the earth has been brought into the light of civilization, and when man has had all the fight evoluted out of him, universal disarmament may be possible, but until that extremely remote time comes, the nations of the world will continue to accept the advice of Debs 'Save your money and buy a gun'.[207]

A useful perspective on the public despondency on show in 1899 is offered by the French author Paul Adam.[208] Adam was one of many individuals lured to The Hague in May 1899 to witness the making of a historic moment. While there, he stayed with the French delegation at the Hotel des Îndes and volunteered his time undertaking administrative duties for Bourgeois. In 1908, he published a memoir entitled *Les impérialismes et la morale des peuples* (The imperialists and the morality of the people). In it he chastised the Germans and British for their imperial ventures, advocated for the rights of all human beings (regardless of race) and made a strident call for the rights of Afrikaners against the oppression of the British empire. Above all, his book begged for the acceptance of human equality. It was not only a treatise against imperialism, but also a deeply cynical reflection of state power. Adam's rebukes came out most strongly when he recalled his impressions of the first Hague conference. He quoted from his journal of May 1899 that he witnessed the spectacle of the first meetings in the *Huis ten Bosch*. He discussed the 'great hope' of the people and of some of the delegates, like Bourgeois, who looked to the conference for great achievements for the good of humanity. But the whole experience left Adam angry and dejected. None of the diplomats were there to achieve peace, he wrote: they were there to achieve whatever their governments desired. None of them wanted peace: they were militarists, warmongers, imperialists and conquerors. He concluded that the conference was a *chimère*, a façade that communicated no meaning.

Adam also laughed condescendingly at the peace activists gathered in the city, whom he described as 'active, bearded and with good heads of hair, their arms weighed down by their files'. Among their ranks he included W.T. Stead, Alfred Fried and Frédéric Passy,[209] all of them 'learned humanitarians' who misunderstood the purpose of their governments' business. He was particularly scathing of Bertha von Suttner, whom he depicted as 'opaque, veiled, shaded by vast hats, weighed down by the fat of her age, but running from door to door, at a trot' and who lived under the impression that she was making a difference (Figure 4.5). During the conference, Adam preferred the company of the Dutch socialists and anarchists, men like Domela Nieuwenhuis, who gathered his numerous supporters in The Hague to propagate the message that the conference was a useless venture, a great lie told by governments to their people, where they flirted with peace all the while planning for war.[210] Adam finished his account with the words, 'I am at a loss. I am saddened.' His hopes for universal peace and the *grand désir des peuples* (grand desire of the people) were dashed.[211]

It would be a mistake, however, for historians to place too much emphasis on the exhortations of failure that circulated around the world in July and August 1899. Despite the despondency of many, the world was not, as Suttner had it, 'indifferent or unfriendly in its attitude towards the Hague Conference'.[212] For example, the *Japan Times* both described the event as a failure and important beginning and did so by reflecting on French newspaper reports of the time.[213] Arthur Desjardin, reporting in the *Revue des deux mondes*, further suggested that progress on essential issues be it the abolition of slavery, privateering or war was always slow and measured. The Hague conference was therefore a significant step in the right direction.[214] In the German press, too, the conference was not rejected off-hand. The *Cologne Gazette* talked of the conference acting as an effective 'barrier' to the outbreak and spread of war, while the *Berlin Tageblatt* considered arbitration 'an important step to securing the peace of the world'.[215] In an editorial written on 23 July, Arthur Levysohn exclaimed that the conference had ensured a more 'peaceful attitude' (*friedfertige Haltung*) among Germans and that they were now more attuned to the practical nature of the politics

Figure 4.5 Originally published in the German magazine *Der Lustige Blätter*, this cartoon from 1899 depicted the funeral procession of the god of war, Mars, heralded in jubilation by Bertha von Suttner, who is blissfully unaware of the reawakening of Mars. The thunderbolts in the sky denote war-like speeches made by the German Kaiser. The caption read: 'Deathly shock in the procession. "My goodness, he's alive, the guy was only faking it!"' (*De vredes-conferentie. Prentenboek voor oud en jong.* Amsterdam, H. Gerlings, 1899, 21).

of peace (*Friedenspolitik*).[216] The *Norddeutsche Algemeine Zeitung* also lauded the conference for its civilizing mission and suggested that its achievements ensured it a 'honourable place in history'.[217]

In Britain, the *Economist* explained in a page-long editorial that 'we write in no mood of cynicism', the 'peace conference . . . has advanced the limits of international law . . . we do not doubt that the conference will have useful results, and that everyone will discover that is so'.[218] The Anglican newspaper, the *Church Times*, echoed a similar sentiment, suggesting on 8 August that '[i]t is impossible to pass over the results of the Conference at the Hague without one word of satisfaction . . . The establishment of a permanent Court of Arbitration is an admission by the civilised world that reason and justice ought to prevail'.[219] In the Netherlands, the *Leeuwarder Courant* suggested that arbitration was the most important legacy of the conference and that the 'softening of war' made by the various conventions was a 'priceless legacy' given by 'this century to the next'.[220] The *Elseviers Geillustreerd Maandschrift* editorialized that the work of the conference had not failed: although we are 'too close to the cradle' the future will show its long-term relevance.[221] Meanwhile, in a lengthy editorial, the *Algemeen Handelsblad* précised an exposé published in the *Edinburgh Review* suggesting that the achievements of The Hague should be read within the context of recent literature on war, peace and arbitration. It concluded that although the ambitions of the Tsar were not met in The Hague the issues up for discussion, including disarmament and arbitration, were now part of practical international politics. At the very least the conference's achievement was to familiarize the people of the world with arbitration.[222] The Russian press also offered a positive spin. The *Petersburgskija Vledomosti* suggested that the 'meeting at The Hague will exercise an important and beneficient effect . . . Every new idea requires time to mature'. It was particularly taken by the establishment of the PCA, which indicated that the 'impossible has become possible'.[223]

Andrew White recorded in his diary as he was leaving The Hague on 3 August 1899 that 'I feel that in spite of the general disappointment of the world at what is generally considered the meagre result of this conference, we have done much – but time will tell which is right'.[224] White planned to use his public profile to advocate for The Hague and to mould public opinion in its favour. As early as 20 July, he considered writing a speech 'which, . . . may be published, and, perhaps, aid in keeping public opinion in the right line as regards the work of the conference after it has closed'.[225] Many delegates, including France's Baron d'Estournelles and Léon Bourgeois, the Americans Frederic Holls and Seth Low, Russia's Fyodor Martens and Arthur Raffalovich, Italy's Count Nigra, the Hungarian Count Albert Apponyi and even Germany's Philipp Zorn were also convinced that they had a public responsibility to explain the achievements of the conference both at home and abroad.[226] They did so by writing articles for newspapers and journals, offering public speeches and authoring books on the topic.[227] Some did so anonymously, others proudly, prominently parading their delegate credentials.[228] James Harris Vickery, an attaché to the American delegation, for example, wrote a series of articles in 1899 and 1900 explaining that the delegates at The Hague had worked hard and pragmatically for real ends, but also that the lack of agreement on disarmament illustrated their 'eminent good sense' as they understood what was 'practical and possible'.[229] Vickery hailed the first Hague conference as a 'step in a natural, healthy, and orderly evolution of the forces of peace which have so effectively asserted themselves in the improvement of international relations'.[230]

Many governments also promoted The Hague as a successful venture. In so doing, they looked to reclaim the public diplomacy of the event and to frame it in their own way. To that end, the Dutch Minister of Foreign Affairs de Beaufort emphasized in his closing remarks that while the conference may not have achieved all the desires of the 'utopianists', it nevertheless 'dented the sombre predictions of pessimists'. He finished by declaring that the moral reaction exercised around the world during the conference will return and be fortified in public opinion. He argued that all governments would now take even disarmament seriously.[231] The French, British and American official reports written at the end of the conference also focused on a message of optimism and achievement.[232]

The German government was particularly adamant in selling a hard-line approach to the conference and the issue of arbitration in particular to the German public as righteous and appropriate. There were numerous references in the German press and assertions by members of the German delegation that it was unlikely that Germany would ratify the Hague conventions (it ratified all of them in December 1899).[233] In March 1900, when the conference was finally discussed in the *Reichstag*, Count von Bülow announced that by denying compulsory arbitration and freeing up the PCA (both in its membership and the voluntary nature of arbitral procedure), the German delegation had guaranteed the public safety (*salus publica*) of the German people. The political existence of the German state, and therefore the 'vital interests' (*Lebensinteressen*) of the German people required full sovereignty. No international agreement, however exalted, should endanger that sovereign authority.[234] Yet by signing the Hague Conventions, Germany lent legitimacy to their content.

The theatrics of selling The Hague's success in these 'official' state productions were not lost on commentators. Hungary's Count Apponyi explained the stakes well in a letter he wrote to Bertha von Suttner:

> The optimism which I display [in my article about the Hague conference published in the *Budapest Tagblatt*] is . . . a tactical maneuver more than actual conviction. The great powers at The Hague were less than lukewarm, and I am not sure their assent to The Hague conventions . . . will be given. The rulers do not want the thing to succeed . . . any limitation of their absolute power (to do either good or ill) is instinctively repugnant to them.[235]

In the United States, Seth Low also advocated strongly for the 'public opinion of the United States' to 'address itself to securing the ratification [of the Hague conventions] . . . by Senate' for it was a 'happy augury' that the conference left the 'vitalization of its work' to public approbation.[236] By actively promoting the value of the conventions, delegates like Apponyi and Low not only hoped to make an impression on public opinion but also to make it difficult for their governments to backtrack from ratification. Even the Dutch Queen promoted ratification (despite her own misgivings about the value of the conventions) in her annual address from parliament.[237]

That most of the Hague conventions were ratified by most of the participating governments is, therefore, important.[238] Ratification was not automatic and had stalled previous internationalist endeavours, most notably the Brussels Conventions of 1874. After the first Hague conference, many countries witnessed considerable backlash to its terms from within their ministries of defence, their armed forces and among conservative elites.[239] Still, that all bar two governments ratified most of the conventions speaks volumes.[240]

As the following chapter shows, it was mainly in the immediate aftermath of the first Hague conference and especially within the context of Boer War that contemporaries presented the first Hague conference as a disappointment. Over the longer term, the global press repeatedly reinforced the content of the Hague conventions and used the ideas of the Hague conference to frame their representations of international concerns, especially those relating to war and peace. As a result, the Hague conference of 1899 and its conventions came to be the lens through which state behaviour in time of war was read by an increasing number of people. Ongoing interest in the prospect of another

Hague conference also ensured that the principles of humanitarianism, international organization and international regulation continued to hold public interest. As a result, public agitation for the principles of The Hague did not end in 1899. As the twentieth century dawned, such agitation only grew in importance. Pandora's box was well and truly open and no one could now close the lid.

5

Civilization at War, 1899–1906

It may be true . . . that after the Hague gathering every nation will go on exactly as it did before it, making just what provisions it thinks needful for war, aggressive or defensive. But the world will not be in the same condition as if the Hague Conference had never met.

– William Evans Darby, 1900[1]

Historians have long considered the second Anglo-Boer War (1899–1902)[2] as a defining moment in Anglo-European perceptions of war and imperialism.[3] This war enabled outsiders to critique and demonize Great Britain as an imperial fiend unleashing unnecessary warfare on a defenceless population. Yet the fact that Britain was so readily vilified during the conflict was more than an indulgence of Anglophobia. For one, many Britons and other subjects of the British crown were also highly critical of their government's conduct in the war. The timing of the Boer War, coming so close on the heels of the first Hague conference, was important not only because most governments ratified the Hague conventions in the course of the war but also because contemporaries interpreted the conflict in terms of what they knew about The Hague.[4] Those Hague ideas endowed the Boer War with new meaning, which complicated its antagonists' conduct in it.

As many European newspapers almost gleefully noted, the onset of war in October 1899 seemed to mark the ultimate failing of the Hague conference. In light of the conflict, the *Telegraaf* in the Netherlands lambasted the conference as a 'farce' and 'bagatelle', the *Neue Hamburger Zeitung* described it as little more than a 'spectacle' (*Schauspiel*), while a Russian newspaper derided the 'great contradictions between the Hague conference and its solemn declarations in the spirit of peace and humanity, and the slaughter undertaken by the government of the most cultured and civilized power in the world [Great Britain]'.[5] The *Sumatra Post* not only lambasted the conference as 'bad comedy' but also described 1899 as a 'hypocritical' year during which the spectre of world peace was overwhelmed by the Russification of Finland and the onset of the Anglo-Boer War.[6] That war, fought by the Afrikaner populations of the Transvaal and Orange Free State against the British empire, seemed to negate the principles of peace and conciliation that Britain's delegates had advanced while they were at The Hague. To the newspaper-reading public in most parts of the world, Britain's decision to go to war in southern Africa belied any commitment to the Tsar's ambition for the Hague conference of 'insuring to all peoples the benefits of real and durable peace' or to the idea that international arbitration might prevent unnecessary conflict.[7]

Despite the obvious despondence and cynicism, these same newspapers also read the violence enacted during the Boer War as falling within the purview of the Hague conventions. They held the belligerents, and especially Great Britain, accountable for their unwillingness to arbitrate the crisis. Rather than demonstrating the failure of The Hague conference, the Boer War actually signalled that the Hague conventions represented standards by which the public could (and did) judge the behaviour of states. In the process, 'The Hague' was normalized as a reference point to consider the implications, applications and prevention of war and state violence more generally. The South African war was certainly savage. Fought largely by guerrilla tactics, it witnessed the decimation of villages and farms, saw local African and white populations incarcerated in concentration camps and resulted in the capture of thousands of prisoners of war (POWs), some of whom were interned overseas.[8] The global media reported and commented on all these developments.

Britain's ultimate victory came at the expense of the lives and livelihoods of tens of thousands of soldiers and civilians. The conflict also adversely impacted Britain's international credibility. There was little support for Britain's position.[9] The French, Germans, Russians and Dutch populations pressured their governments to utilize 'good offices' to advocate on behalf of the Boers.[10] Within Britain, a vociferous anti-war lobby also voiced its disapproval.[11]

It is not surprising then to find commentators like the German jurist Carl Ludwig von Bar exclaiming in 1900 that Britain had a 'moral obligation' to prevent the war precisely because it had attended the Hague conference.[12] By using The Hague to validate his opinions, von Bar, and others like him, lent *gravitas* and moral weight to the idea of international law and to the terms of the Hague conventions. In codifying the laws of war and formalizing principles of 'good offices', the 1899 Hague conference not only established a code of conduct for states when war threatened but also forged a public understanding that there were limits to what a country could and could not do in time of war, even within the boundaries of its own empire. Those limits may have been ill defined and their terms contested but their applications were nevertheless considered unassailable. Perhaps the most noteworthy success of the first Hague conference, then, is that, as W.E. Darby suggested, the world was no longer in the 'same condition' as it had been before 1899. It had a moral language authenticated by the Hague conventions to assess the behaviour of states.[13] That language permeated media representations of warfare from 1899 on and framed them within a wider discourse about the acceptable limits of 'civilized' and 'barbaric' state conduct.

What constituted 'civilized' conduct was, of course, a loaded term that meant different things to different audiences.[14] For Europeans and Anglo-Americans, the concept of 'civilization' was defined both anthropologically and in terms of international law. At a base level, a state was classified as 'civilized' either because of the racial profile of its population (it was white), its commitment to Christianity or its ability to apply Western principles of domestic law and order. Non-white societies were, by and large, classified as 'barbaric' or 'semi-civilized' in part because of their racial and religious profile but also in relationship to whether they accepted or instituted state sovereignty, sustained familiar (Western) rules of law and protected the property of foreign (Western) visitors.[15] Above all, a state could not join the 'family of civilized nations' until its people cooperated in the international economy and its government signed up to international agreements and accepted the tenets of treaty law advanced by the Western states.[16] Western hegemony across the world was conterminous with the expansion and application of this version of 'civilized' international law as a moral concept.[17]

The first Hague conference of 1899 was a product of the diplomacy of 'civilized' states and, as a result, its rules applied only to those states. The Hague's regulations did not apply to warfare outside the norms of 'civilization', in other words between 'non-civilized' societies or between 'civilized' and 'non-civilized' people within an empire. To that end, the United States could advance stringent rules of warfare at the 1899 Hague conference and readily decimate First Nations' societies while also engaging in pernicious warfare in the Philippines.[18] The blanket of 'civilization' covered a multitude of Western sins, especially in the acquisition and maintenance of empire.[19] Nevertheless, after 1899 the binary oppositions between supposedly 'civilized' and 'barbaric' peoples were muddied in a media environment that commented on all warfare and assessed those conflicts along moralized lines of acceptable behaviour. These commentaries often did not distinguish between interstate wars (fought between 'civilized' nations) and imperial conflict, internal disorder or civil war. They invoked the Hague conventions liberally and, in so doing, blurred some of the expectations attached to the West (as opposed to the 'rest').[20] While the 1899 Hague conference enabled the ongoing legal dominance of the West in terms of the international laws created at The Hague, the conference also opened up the possibility of the inclusion of other voices and perspectives in the media dialogues that existed around state violence and imperialism.

Scholars have long debated the value of legalese in setting frameworks for facilitating excessive levels of state violence in the modern era. International law, as Bourke, Hull, Jochnik and Normand all argue, exists first and foremost to enable states, not to restrict them.[21] This was also true of the Hague conventions. Joanna Bourke contends that international law presents a veil hiding caustic government actions from public view and a language of legitimacy to enable them.[22] Isabel Hull makes an excellent case for the silences in the Hague conventions expediting Germany's use of 'military necessity' as a rationale for excessive military action during the First World War.[23] Certainly, the language of international law validated imperial acquisitions and the expansion of economic and military power for many industrializing states in the 'long' nineteenth century. In the Anglo-European world, the language of international law also maintained the differentiation between 'civilized' and 'non-civilized' people, thereby legitimating the ongoing subjugation and brutal treatment of the latter. For Bourke, the twentieth century offers countless other examples of governments exploiting the normative power of international law to deceive their subjects into accepting the exercise of extreme violence by their own state, all the while referencing the same laws to condemn the violence employed by others.[24]

These scholars remind us that states are not (and never were) benign entities. Yet it would be wrong to suggest that the Hague rules came into being solely to enable hard power or that they were created primarily to act as smokescreens for a pliant public.[25] In sending their delegations to the Hague conferences, few governments looked forward to creating rules that bound them. Even so, they went and created rules that applied to state-to-state behaviour. The regulations they developed were substantive and spoke as much to general principles as they did to specific rules. The Hague rules were a product of public expectation as much as of diplomatic negotiation and in this sense the wider public was never limited to 'legalese' to bring judgement against those who violated their understanding of 'The Hague'. While the laws' silences enabled states, their content also tied governments to a range of actions. Most importantly, the Hague conventions presented a set of standards that ordinary people could appeal to and hold a government accountable for in the public sphere. Whether states abused the rules or not, The Hague signalled that conceptual restraints existed and that, at the very least, governments had to be seen to apply them. When they did not, there were consequences both for their relationships with other states and for their public diplomacy. The Hague rules, therefore, signalled that the purview of international law extended well beyond the relationships of states and their diplomats.

Before the first Hague conference met in May 1899, the British Admiralty had all too presciently forecast that if the conference succeeded in regulating the laws of war it would lead to an environment of reproach and accusation.[26] The Admiralty's warning echoed ominously in October 1899 when the world's media fixated on the South African war. It did not matter if a newspaper was British or if it professed pro- or anti-Boer sentiments, in their representations of The Hague their coverage was remarkably similar.[27] That is to say, when these newspapers invoked the Hague conventions, their reporters usually did so by advocating that those conventions represented an established and expected standard of behaviour. In almost all cases, such reports implied that 'civilized' states, like Great Britain and the Transvaal, should avoid war if possible. If a war did erupt, it should be conducted in line with The Hague's rules, even if the state in question had not signed up to them.[28]

It is not surprising then to find that the Hague conventions also played a prominent role in the public discourse of governments after 1899. As the Swedish foreign minister suggested to the Dutch ambassador in Stockholm, the Hague conference functioned 'as advertising work for the Russian government'.[29] But the Russians were not the only ones to promote The Hague to their own advantage. In their public diplomacy, governments often drew on references to The Hague to rebuke their adversaries and promote their own virtue. The Afrikaner leader Paul Kruger was particularly adept at mobilizing the principles of The Hague in the public sphere.[30] The British government also took care to present itself as keeping to the principles of the Hague conventions. The world's neutral governments did likewise.[31] The Hague both carried *cachet* and enabled the demonization of an enemy or the censure of a neutral. Such developments had long-lasting effects. During the Boxer Rebellion (1899–1901) and the Russo-Japanese War (1904–1905), for example, belligerent and neutral states alike framed their public diplomacy in terms of The Hague's expectations. They would continue to do so well into the First World War.

In 1900, von Bar analysed the impact of the Hague conference on public diplomacy in a polemical pamphlet. He suggested that the conference produced a schism

(*Zwiespalt*) between the expectations of states and those of their subjects. He cited the Boer War as an excellent example: while the British government felt no obligation to avoid the conflict merely because it had attended the Hague conference, the general public within and outside Great Britain felt differently. The whole 'civilized' world, in von Bar's eyes, was convinced that responsibility for the war lay with Britain and that, as a result, the British government should be held accountable for its results. In a similar way, von Bar explained that while the Tsar's rescript had not prevented Russia from subduing Finland in February 1899, the public communicated their disapproval in part because the action did not befit Nicholas II's role as the inaugurator of the peace conference. Furthermore, so von Bar explained, the schism between how states behaved and how their people expected them to behave was heightened by the 'glaring humanity and sense of justice [*Rechtsgefühl*]' inspired by the wording of the Hague conventions. The conventions strengthened the idea that states had a responsibility to humanity at large.[32] Accordingly, The Hague fortified the concept of ethics in international affairs and signalled that governments had to recognize and adapt to that development.[33] Or to paraphrase the German pacifist, Ludwig Quidde: the 1899 Hague conference heralded the public's expectation that warfare should be the last act of a state, not its first.[34] Perhaps, governments were less prisoners of public opinion after The Hague, as Lapradelle suggested,[35] but they were more aware of the need to engage with public dialogues on international and imperial affairs, framing them optimistically where possible and managing opprobrium where necessary. After 1899, The Hague featured prominently in governmental attempts to manufacture public consent for issues relating to war and peace within and outside their empires.[36]

While Quidde, Lapradelle and von Bar were all committed internationalists and hopeful of the judicial promise of the 1899 conference, they were not alone in suggesting that the Hague conference had shifted public expectations with regard to war and violence. Contemporaries encountered extraordinary amounts of state violence in their newspapers. The Boer War, the Boxer rebellion, the atrocities committed in the Belgian Congo, the massacre of the Mahdi, the Ottoman suppression of the Armenians and the Dreyfus affair all ensured that turn-of-the-century editorials discussed military authority and moralized about its importance. The advent of photography, lithograph printing, lantern slide shows and moving pictures enabled greater access to visual representations of war and state violence as well. Unsurprisingly, many commentators lamented the destructive power of modern warfare. Even style-conscious *Vogue*, the American weekly aimed at New York's elite, editorialized about the carnage of war. In 1901, an article entitled 'A Word with the Pessimists' exhorted the importance of the Hague conventions. While the end of the century 'finds not the ploughshares of peace, but blood-dripping swords of revolt', its editor nevertheless reminded pessimists that they should not ignore the accomplishments of the Hague peace conference for 'this was not a gathering of sentimental women but a congress officially recognized by the most powerful nations of the world'. As such, it affirmed the 'world's recognition of the passing of the war ideal'.[37]

Such commentary signals that the rise of popular reporting on war and military violence in the latter half of the nineteenth century helped to make the Hague conference a compelling event for contemporaries. That same media attentiveness also offers vital context for explaining why, as William Mulligan, Daniel Segesser and Solomon Wank remind us, Anglo-European governments could not go to war, even within their empires, without offering an adequate justification to their subjects. Increasingly, such justifications were tied to the expectation that wars should be defensive in nature and that they should be conducted within the confines of international law.[38] After July 1899, those expectations were bound to the terms of the Hague conventions.

From the moment the British government denied Transvaal the right to attend the Hague conference in early 1899, the fate of the conference and the fate of the Anglo-Boer crisis became interconnected in the media. Well before the outbreak of armed conflict on 11 October 1899, newspaper editorials lamented the impasse. Where they laid the blame depended on their editorial position. In September 1899, for example, the Bordeaux newspaper *La Gironde* depicted Britain as a 'devouring ogre' and chastised the other great powers for not intervening in the crisis in the spirit of The Hague. If, as *La Gironde* suggested, 'there was a Europe worthy of the name she would not permit such a criminal policy [as Britain's in the Transvaal] to bask in the sun of humanity'.[39] The Liberal Leader of the Opposition Sir Henry Campbell-Bannerman was also deeply critical of the British government's role in bringing about the war. In a speech made in early October 1899, he questioned 'what is it that we are going to war about'? He hoped that 'at this eleventh hour even, there might not be some means of reaching a peaceful settlement'. He appealed 'to save, if possible, the States of South Africa and the Empire, and indeed, the civilized world, from so dire a calamity incurred on grounds so wholly insufficient'.[40]

What irritated its critics most was that the British government, which proudly associated itself with the establishment of the Permanent Court of Arbitration (PCA), refused to arbitrate the Boers' demands. In Europe and the United States, numerous editorials were published, public meetings held and signatures collected to promote an arbitral solution to the crisis.[41] The French peace movement, in turn, amassed nearly 300,000 names on a petition in favour of ending the war using The Hague's arbitration mechanisms.[42] In 1901, a transnational gathering of the Committee for Boer Independence, including members from the United States, Germany, Africa, Spain, Belgium, France, Italy, Russia, the Netherlands and Switzerland, met in Paris to promote the Hague rulings and turn the Boer conflict over to the PCA. Their aim was to mobilize global opinion and thereby put pressure on the British government to act.[43]

The debate about arbitration even entered the British houses of parliament.[44] On 17 October 1899, the Irish MP John Dillon made an impassioned plea that the government's depiction of a 'malignant' global pro-Boer movement misconstrued the 'opinions of the civilised world', which 'rightly' saw the Boer War as avoidable. Dillon urged that before 'any more bloodshed takes place proposals should be made in the spirit of the recent Peace Conference at The Hague, with the view of finding . . . a settlement'. He claimed that his was a 'modest' request and that at a time 'when the dogs of war have been let loose' it would be hard 'to get a hearing for the voice of reason, of justice, and of humanity' but that 'the overwhelming majority of the civilised world outside this Empire' begs us to consider the question.[45]

Kruger himself made much of Britain's unwillingness to arbitrate, as did the President of the Orange Free State Martinus Theunis Steyn. They both accused

Britain of a breach of faith. War, according to Steyn, was an 'insult to religion and civilisation'. It was especially maddening as the points of difference in the Transvaal crisis were capable of settlement by arbitration.[46] Steyn's and Kruger's appeals to reason, arbitration and the use of the PCA pervaded the global press. The Transvaal leader also spent much of his time travelling around Europe, meeting with government leaders and presenting the plight of his people to sympathetic audiences.[47] As a result, the Boer War offered ongoing attention to the potential value of the PCA, so much so that one internationalist pamphlet suggested that Kruger's diplomacy was a 'natural and necessary sequel of the Hague Conference'.[48] Even the Ottoman Empire weighed in on the topic, at least to a special correspondent from the French monarchist newspaper *Le Gaulois*, who claimed in December 1900 that the Sultan supported the cause of arbitration (although he had not signed the Hague conventions) and that Britain should bring the South African conflict to a peaceful end.[49]

Whether the complicated issues at hand suited an arbitral settlement was often, although not always, ignored in these reports. What galled the critics most was that warfare had resulted from a negotiable dispute between 'civilized' states. It was particularly important then that the British government presented its involvement in the war in terms of the norms of 'civilization'. For example, in December 1899, Prime Minister Arthur Balfour expounded that the corruption of the Transvaal government had caused the war.[50] In turn, pro-British papers like the populist *Daily Mail* explained not only the lengths to which the British government went to obtain a suitable diplomatic settlement but also that the South African issues were impossible to arbitrate.[51] According to these papers, it was Boer recalcitrance that caused the war. They held the Boers responsible for the lapse in 'civilized' conduct.

Once war broke out, newspaper commentary within and outside Britain invoked the Hague conventions to make sense of the conflict and to indict its agents. Considerations of what befitted the conduct of a 'civilized' state at war sat at the heart of such representations.[52] Both the Boer and British forces came under repeated attack for exercising unwarranted levels of violence in contravention of international law. The British were accused of the mistreatment of POWs, of unnecessarily interning civilians, of slashing and burning Boer property and of shooting at Boer hospital stations (Figure 5.1). When British soldiers captured a Dutch ambulance unit and imprisoned the staff as POWs on Cyprus, an already incensed Dutch public sought revenge. Their government sent warships to the region to rescue refugees and offered free passage to Kruger to return him to Europe to advance a diplomatic solution.[53] Sympathy for the sufferers of the Boer War resulted in charitable activity around the neutral world to support its refugees and Afrikaner victims.[54] Even in Britain, the war elicited charitable responses, including by the South African Women and Children's Distress Fund and the Stop the War Committee.[55] For Europeans, the white casualties of this 'civilized' war deserved care and attention. These same newspapers, however, largely failed to notice the thousands of black African victims.[56]

As might be expected, the pro-British papers focused on the excesses of Boer soldiers, censuring them for ignoring flags of truce, utilizing bands of brigands, arming civilians as *franc-tireurs*, using dum-dum bullets and attacking British non-combatants. It is particularly significant, then, that assertions of Boer barbarity were

Figure 5.1 This Johan Braakensiek cartoon from 1899 (published in the Netherlands) suggested that the British willingly exceeded the limits of 'civilized' conduct in the Boer War, under the guise of religious righteousness, when they shot at defenceless Afrikaner enemies and Red Cross hospital stations (J. Braakensiek, *Het jaar 1899.* Amsterdam, np, 1900, np).

also countered in the pro-British press. For example, the young Winston Churchill, special correspondent for the *Morning Post* in South Africa, assured his British readers that while he was wounded during a campaign he could categorically state that 'the Boer methods of war are certainly humane'.[57]

How central the Hague conventions were to these commentaries for and against the 'civilized' conduct of the Boer War is well illustrated by W.T. Stead's pamphlet, *Methods of Barbarism*, which he published in July 1901.[58] In it, Stead presented a lurid picture of Britain's barbarous treatment of Afrikaners and reminded his readers that all Britons 'shall have to answer at the Day of Judgment' for the acts committed by their soldiers. At any rate, no one could ignore them:

> For to-day the nation at home witnesses every morning and evening, in the camera obscura of its daily press, the whole hellish panorama that is unrolled in South Africa . . . We seek the smoke of the burning farmstead; we hear the cries of terrified children, and sometimes in the darkness we hear the sobbing of the outraged woman in the midst of her orphaned children, and we know that before another sunset British troops carrying the King's commission, armed and equipped with supplies voted by our representatives, will be steadily adding more items of horror to the ghastly total which stands to our debit in South Africa.[59]

He further chastised the government for brainwashing the population into accepting the necessity of these 'methods of barbarism', which were outlawed by the 'universal agreement of civilized nations'.[60] War may be war, but the Hague conference 'found it possible, but also necessary, to restrain the beast and fiend in men'.[61] Across several chapters, Stead exposed Britain's breaches of the Hague conventions. He concluded that the public must place pressure on the British government to seek redress for 'this is an international question, and one upon which it is the right and interest of every State to have an opinion, and make that opinion felt'.[62]

Stead's pamphlet bolstered support for the globalized pro-Boer campaign.[63] Unsurprisingly, it incensed those in opposition. Arthur Conan Doyle, Stead's erstwhile friend, was particularly angry.[64] Having witnessed the South African conflict first hand, Conan Doyle vehemently disagreed with Stead's representation. Early in 1902, he published a counter entitled *The War in South Africa: Its Cause and Conduct*.[65] In measured tones, the pamphlet explained why Britain was at war and corrected Stead's excitable version. Most importantly, Conan Doyle also proffered the Hague conventions as a guide for assessing the war. He noted that while other states might submit *franc-tireurs* and brigands to torture, Britain treated them as combatants and placed them in POW camps, as the Hague rules required. He personally accounted for British troops as respectful of private property and argued that the internment of civilians was essential to keep the people out of harm's way. Given the wartime conditions, he regretted that the deplorable conditions in these camps were unavoidable, but 'every effort has been made to keep the war as humane as possible'. He also exhorted that 'if the Boers claim the advantages of the Conventions of the Hague', then they were also liable for any breaches, of which he enumerated a number. Altogether, Conan Doyle surmised that while he considered the Hague conventions important and that every effort should be made to abide by them, no armed force could ever live up to The Hague's 'counsel of perfection'.[66] By implication, warfare could never be fully 'civilized'.

Both belligerent governments also went out of their way to assert that they abided by the Hague conventions. They did so in part to moderate any claims of barbarity. When it came to the treatment of POWs, for example, the British War Office assured the public that its forces kept to The Hague's stipulations.[67] To that end, the government reprinted 300,000 copies of Conan Doyle's pamphlet, translated into seven languages, which it circulated around the world.[68] The pamphlet received a mixed reception. The

Chicago Daily Tribune's London correspondent, for example, lauded the publication as doing 'a great deal of good in spreading the real truth about the war . . . written by a man in whose word every one must have complete confidence'.[69] In opposition, the Dutch socialist newspaper *Het Volk* called Conan Doyle's study a 'toxic, repugnant, intolerant thing' purposely misrepresenting the Boer War.[70] The *Algemeen Dagblad* expended three columns of its front page on 23 February 1902 to explain that Sherlock Holmes and Conan Doyle's representation of the Boer War had one thing in common: their fantastical fiction.[71] The *Soerabaijasch Handelsblad* was equally incensed and republished an editorial from the *Nieuwe Rotterdamsche Courant* that expounded its astonishment that Conan Doyle would stoop so low as to argue for such 'brazen untruths'.[72] In contrast, these Dutch-language newspapers readily vaunted Stead's version of the war's events.[73]

Thus, when Lord Kitchener announced on 10 August 1901 that all Afrikaners 'still engaged in resisting his Majesty's forces . . . [after 15 September] . . . shall . . . be permanently banished from South Africa',[74] his proclamation came under intense editorial scrutiny. On the one hand, pro-British newspapers, like the Christchurch *Star* in New Zealand, reinforced the necessity of the measure and demeaned British critics of the policy as 'good, loyal Britons, who want to wage war nicely', when wars cannot be waged by niceties.[75] On the other hand, many newspapers within and outside the empire roundly critiqued the move as overly brutal. Even the Tsar was quoted by the *Neue Hamburger Zeitung* reflecting that Kitchener's proclamation 'decays the collective work of the Hague peace conference' and brought the world to the edge of the abyss.[76] Participants in the Tenth Universal Peace Congress held in Glasgow in September that year passed a strongly worded resolution that any state that transgressed the Hague regulations lost its right to be considered as 'civilized'. Furthermore, according to the congress, every citizen of an offending state carried the burden of that 'uncivilized' status on behalf of his or her government.[77]

These commentaries reflect that after July 1899, states and their citizens were increasingly held accountable for the violence they exacted on others. The ubiquity of such conceptualizations is well illustrated by a front-page editorial in the *Daily Express* published early in 1902. Opening with the headline 'Britons and Boers and the Hague Convention', the editorial reflected on the (delayed) release of the Hague conventions in Britain's *Parliamentary Papers*. It did so by asking the question: 'whether the British or the Boers are the greater offenders in abusing the customs of war?' Point by point, it noted how the laws and customs of war as decided by The Hague were violated during the war by both sides.[78] The *Neue Freie Presse* in Austria also focused on the transgression of international law in South Africa to ascertain the rightful limits of military violence in a 1901 article, subsequently republished in the Dutch East Indies.[79]

Importantly, the media commentary around the Boxer Rebellion developed in tandem with that on the Boer War. The uprising, which began late in 1899 as members of the Yihequan (Righteous and Harmonious Fists) movement attacked foreigners in China's treaty ports, was finally quashed in 1901 by a coalition of forces, including British, German, Russian, American, French, Italian, Austro-Hungarian, Dutch and Japanese.[80] In the public relations campaigns conducted by the great powers during the crisis, The Hague featured prominently. Both President McKinley and Tsar Nicholas II suggested that indemnity claims for any damage done to foreign property by the Chinese rebels should be sent to the PCA, to avoid further confrontations with the Qing dynasty.[81] The *Neue Hamburger Zeitung* saw in these calls the possibility of the PCA having a beneficent effect on international relations and returning peace to China.[82] For his part, Fyodor Martens asserted the sovereign rights of the Chinese 'to a national and independent existence' and determined that Russia behaved itself with regards to Chinese subjects in line with the Hague conventions.[83]

Significantly, the Anglo-European press also critiqued the conduct of the coalition forces in terms of The Hague's rules. An editorial by a Canadian minister in the *Calgary Weekly Herald*, for example, condemned the outbreak of war in China and likened it to the conflict in South Africa. His sermon began with a quotation from the Tsar's 1898 rescript and then coupled the Boer and Boxer conflicts in a scathing assessment of the British imperial cause: 'Meantime in two continents, Anglo-Saxon nations are spending the closing hours of the existing century . . . shedding the blood of their own armies and also the blood of people who look upon themselves as fighting for their freedom and resisting for their lives.'[84] He looked for more humanity from his Christian coreligionists. Elsewhere, editorials scrutinized the ways in which coalition soldiers obtained retribution in China, reporting on rapes, looting, vandalism, pillaging and the confiscation of private property.[85] The polyglot Irish journalist E.J. Dillon worked as a special correspondent for the *Daily Telegraph* in China during the rebellion. His thirty-two-page report on the war noted all the above 'outrages' but focused particularly on looting as that act was 'expressly forbidden' by the Hague conventions. He admitted that no British soldiers took part in these events, but that the other nationalities that made up the coalition forces (including Japanese, Russians and Germans) were involved in this 'apocalypse of crime' which caused 'the gutters of the city of Tung-chow' to run 'red with blood' at the hands of so-called civilized men. Britain's consular representative in China, Sir Robert Hart, confirmed the reports: 'From Taku to Peking, the foreigner has marched triumphantly', leaving a wake of destruction and terror.[86] That this behaviour was deemed inappropriate was made all too clear by pointed questions made in the House of Commons asking the British government for reassurance that no Britons engaged in these abhorrent acts.[87]

The use of non-white troops by the foreign forces in China was another controversial issue. In the Boer War, the global press critiqued Britain for arming local Africans against white Afrikaners, thereby blurring distinctions between 'civilized' and 'non-civilized' combatants and complicating the applications of the Hague law. How could 'black' troops be held responsible for their actions against their 'white' adversaries? There was no international law to cover that scenario, so Britain should cease the practice.[88] Still, when 'coloured' troops were used against the Boxers in China, the *Sumatra Post* argued against the double standard in a deeply sarcastic tone: '*Those* people [the Chinese] are yellow, one can do with them what one will. One can also send brown or other-coloured *luidjes* ['little peoples'] to kill them'.[89] By implication, the terms of 'civilization' did not apply, yet the *Sumatra Post*'s editor surely thought they ought.

The same editor also criticized his chauvinist compatriots in the Netherlands for loudly supporting the Boer cause, while conveniently forgetting that the native populations in the Dutch East Indies had no political rights and were violently oppressed by the Dutch authorities. He suggested that the double standard was hard to bear for locals and Dutch settlers alike.[90] In a similar vein, he argued that the European imperial powers were violating China's sovereign rights in suppressing the Boxer rebellion.[91] If The Hague defined the limits of 'civilized' warfare then, for the *Sumatra Post*, The Hague complicated any assessment of state violence, its agents and victims.

The essentiality of The Hague to shaping the media commentary on war is particularly evident from an analysis of newspaper reporting on dum-dum bullets. The prohibition of the bullet at the Hague conference was not a bolt out of the blue. Ever since its invention and first use in India in 1897, the bullet received considerable public scrutiny. Given that the 1868 St Petersburg Declaration prohibited 'any projectile of a weight below 400 grammes, which is either explosive or charged with fulminating or inflammable substances', the dum-dum already seemed illegal to many.[92] It certainly was presented as inhumane in newspapers within and outside Britain.[93] Still, the British government defended its right to use the bullet. Sir John Ardagh repeated the sentiment at the 1899 Hague Conference.[94] For the War Office, the bullet was an indispensable weapon. For the other governments at the Hague conference, a ban of the dum-dum offered an effective achievement on arms limitation without great cost. Few armies outside the Britain empire utilized the ammunition, so the cost would be largely Britain's to bear.

Most newspapers fixated on The Hague's dum-dum prohibition and on Britain's defence of the bullet at The Hague. The *Journal de Débats* (Paris), for example, satirized Britain's position as follows:

> England is a great country, and exports humanity, whisky, and cottons. Sometimes it may appear that England does not carry out her own humanitarian ideals, but that is only because England is very humble. She does not wish to push herself forward. Do you know the genial, gentle, graceful Dum-Dum bullet? England has given the Hindus a taste of it. But their humanitarian zeal does not stop here. The excited Boers, who are white men, will also be pacified with it . . . Let us all be grateful that once more England, strong in her goodness of heart and the gentleness of her manners, leads the world in civilisation.[95]

Other papers included detailed descriptions and diagrams of the bullet and its wounding effects.[96] These descriptions stood in sharp contrast to the British newspapers that applauded Ardagh's impassioned defence at The Hague.[97]

For historians, the dum-dum bullet offers an enigma. According to Joanna Bourke, its prohibition enabled the British government to employ even more devastating exploding bullets (Mark V) that did not fit the description of the Hague declaration.[98] For Bourke, the imprecise language of the Hague law undercut its moral authority to restrict soft-nosed bullets.[99] Andrew Scott Keefer also contends that the impetus for any arms regulation at the 1899 conference came from military necessity, not humanitarianism.[100] By implication, the British could not accept a ban on the dum-dum bullet for the War Office expected to need the technology. Jochnik and Normand go even further by arguing that the Hague laws were 'permissive, enabling powerful states to use the latest military technology with little regard for humanitarian consequences'.[101] According to Jochnik and Normand, the Hague conventions existed solely to legitimate military power, offering a 'veil of justice' to facilitate its violence.[102] According to all three explanations, the prohibition of the dum-dum at The Hague offered up a red herring, empowering armed forces to use new technology, not restricting them from inhumane weaponry.

These interpretations are excessive. While Ardagh was pleased that no one asked questions about the Mark V bullet at the Hague conference, the War Office nevertheless officially recalled all Mark IV and Mark V ammunition from South Africa in July 1899.[103] The dum-dum was, in fact, no longer being produced.[104] Lord Lansdowne accepted the military rationale for continuing with the alternate hollow-nosed bullets, which technically did not breach the terms of the Hague declaration, but he also noted that his government had to take into account the 'political and sentimental as well as purely military considerations' of their use. As the Under-Secretary of State George Wyndham stated at the time: the public 'did not distinguish between forms of hollow-nosed bullets'.[105] The government could not afford to risk public opinion on the subject.[106]

That the British government had reason to worry about media representations of dum-dums is clear from the *Journal de Débats* comment cited above. In fact, most newspapers studied here made at least some comment on the Boer War and dum-dums.[107] The French were particularly adept in their satirical depictions. For example, when *La Caricature* published a libellous image of Queen Victoria with 'dum-dum' emblazoned on the cheeks of her bared behind (Figure 5.2), not only was the magazine censored in France, illegal copies of the illustration were sold for exorbitant prices around Europe.[108] In the end, even though it did not sign up to The Hague's dum-dum declaration, the British government nevertheless restricted its military use. While there is evidence to suggest that both armies in South Africa toyed with soft-nosed bullets, the global media's presentation of the bullet as a barbaric weapon contributed significantly to its restriction.[109]

It is particularly telling, then, that media reflections on the dum-dum changed in the aftermath of the Hague declaration. Even though there was a media debate in 1899 about the humanity (or lack thereof) of the ammunition, during the Boer War almost no newspaper came to the bullet's defence. Reporting in the popular British *Daily Mail* offers a telling case study. In 1897 and 1898, the *Daily Mail* commented on the bullet on several occasions, noting both its effective stopping power against 'the rush of hordes of fanatics' and its 'simply dreadful' wounding capacity.[110] It reported on French and German condemnations of the bullet and the House of Commons' debate on the issue in February 1898.[111] During the Hague conference in 1899, however, the newspaper defended Britain's right to the ammunition and presented a case for its necessity: 'Let the Peace Conference keep to its work, and not make itself ridiculous by going outside its "sphere of influence" in attempting to discredit England. Our soldiers know how to observe the rules of war . . . The Dum-dum projectile never has been and never will be employed in European war.' The *Mail* further suggested that British troops needed to be adequately armed against 'savage and barbarous tribes' and repeatedly announced that the bullet's cruelty was overstated.[112]

Figure 5.2 This Crispin do Amaral cartoon, featuring the Boer leader Paul Kruger 'correcting' Queen Victoria for Britain's apparent use of dum-dums during the South African war of 1899–1902, was censored in France. The cartoon breached libel laws that prevented newspapers from publishing demeaning representations of monarchs. Illegal copies of the cartoon soon circulated around Europe at exorbitant prices (*Caricature* 26 November 1899, 1. Bibliothèque Nationale de la France).

Yet after The Hague's ruling on the dum-dum and despite the fact that Britain did not sign up to the declaration, the *Daily Mail* lauded the British government for returning to the traditional Lee Metford bullet in the Boer War. Its readers were reminded that '[i]n civilised warfare the employment of the Dum-Dum bullet is prohibited. For this reason, accordingly, our troops are restricted to the use of ordinary ball ammunition while fighting against the Boers'.[113] It also lambasted the Boers for using soft-nosed bullets while shooting at British soldiers digging graves.[114] Nevertheless, by the time the newspaper reported that police opened fire with dum-dums against rioters in Bangor City in November 1900, the *Daily Mail* protected the reputation of the India Office by noting that as soon as Office heard about the uprising it ordered Enfield cartridges to the region to replace the dum-dums.[115] In other words, the dum-dum was no longer deemed an appropriate weapon of war or for colonial police work, at least not as far as this newspaper's editors were concerned. In their eyes, the dum-dum's reputation as cruel and uncivilized was sealed by the Hague conference.[116] And they extended the application of the dum-dum's barbarity to all other soft-nosed projectiles. While Ardagh may have sighed in relief that the delegates at The Hague fixated on out-dated dum-dum technology, in the end the British government restricted the use of hollow-nosed cartridges any way, even if it did not outlaw them outright.

The successful application of The Hague's dum-dum declaration during the Boer War was recognized by contemporaries as a most important result. At a meeting of the *Société d'économie sociale* in 1900, for example, Charles Dupuis and Arthur Desjardins discussed the importance of the Hague conference. Neither commentator felt particularly pessimistic about the achievements of The Hague. While they agreed that 'without a doubt the [Hague's] work is imperfect', they also accepted that 'all human work is imperfect'.[117] Above all, the Hague conventions gave them hope. Britain's rejection of dum-dum bullets during the Boer War highlighted that the conventions changed the behaviour of states. For Dupuis and Desjardins, this development was 'the greatest tribute to the conference of peace'.[118]

Military commentators were also cognisant of the importance of the dum-dum regulation. Major Thomson of the 1st Bengal Lancers noted in an article published in India, Britain and the United States that while Britain was able to recall soft-nosed bullets in southern Africa in keeping with the Hague law, the Boers were not so lucky. Due to shortages, they resorted to using hunting ammunition, including soft-nosed ones, in contravention of the Hague conventions. Thomson argued that 'we cannot seriously blame them as necessity has no law, but the fact shows how difficult it is to make binding laws of war'. Still, he finished with the statement that these war laws 'are a good example of the progressive spirit of humanity' and that, as a result, the attempt of the conference to 'set up a standard which is desirable' to restrict the expansion of warfare is commendable and important.[119]

But the significance of the dum-dum declaration went much deeper than Britain's adherence to its limitation during the South African conflict. After the Boer War, in fact, there was no question that all exploding bullets were considered uncivilized. No 'civilized' state, then, could employ them as a military weapon without rebuke, not even in colonial warfare. Thus, when the British War Office reissued Mark V bullets during a spate of rebellions in Somaliland (Somalia) in 1903, a public outcry resulted, although some in Britain also defended the development.[120] Eight years later, when the *African Standard* discussed the Italo-Ottoman war in Tripoli, its journalist was incensed to find an Italian soldier with a dum-dum style bullet on him. His report is telling:

> By comparison with these [bullets], the old Dum-dum bullet, which in its time had been subject to so much condemnation, is a toy pellet . . . it is difficult to see what excuse the Italian Government can advance which will exonerate it from responsibility for it. The use of explosive bullets is distinctly forbidden in civilised warfare . . . Italy comes here upon a professedly civilizing mission. If for no other reason, therefore, how dare she stultify herself by resorting to such brutal and barbarous methods as this bullet betrays? The Arabs are perfectly aware that the

> use of such bullets is forbidden . . . Their only result is to add to the bitter hatred of the invaders which has been roused in them by the reports of the treatment of women, the massacres of men, women and children, the wanton destruction of gardens and other property, and by the use of bombs from airships, which the Arab places in the same category as the use of explosive bullets. If the Italians could only get out into the country now and poison a few wells, they would have left nothing undone to render a reconciliation impossible between them and the people with whom it is presumably their object to some day live in amity . . . Even if the Turks evacuated and handed over Tripoli to the Italians tomorrow, it is difficult to imagine they could ever conquer it. Their position is hopeless.[121]

Regardless of whether the Italians actually used dum-dums in Tripoli, the reference to exploding bullets offered a clear way to denounce Italy.

After 1899, the demonization of the dum-dum was near universal. Aside from the Somaliland situation noted above, the only defence of the dum-dum bullet found in the newspaper case studies undertaken for this chapter, appeared in the *Sumatra Post*, whose editor lambasted the Dutch General W.F.G. Snijders for suggesting the dum-dum was rarely cruel and, thus, particularly suited for police work.[122] The editor affirmed that dum-dums not only killed but also that all industrial warfare was cruel and that it was therefore hypocritical to single out the dum-dum for restriction using the rationale of cruelty.[123] The same editor also condemned the Dutch public for admonishing Britain's conduct in the Boer War while he had proof that hollow-nosed bullets were used in the colonial wars fought in the Dutch East Indies. He posited as an example that forty-six people died at Lho Trieng in Atcheh after the colonial authorities opened fire on them with hollow-nosed ammunition.[124] According to the *Sumatra Post* (and other colonial newspapers in the Indies), the Dutch government and press denied these claims and the Dutch public accepted their lies.[125] The *Post*'s perspective speaks volumes about the 'silencing' of state violence when it did not abide by public expectations. But it also highlights a creeping critique of imperialism and a growing awareness in the global press of some of the double standards that existed around the concept of 'civilization' (Figure 5.3). It clearly addressed what M. Ishay calls a rising awareness of 'social inequity' in the late-nineteenth- and early-twentieth-century European world and Joanna Bourke's assessment that by the late nineteenth century barbarism had 'taken residence in the house of the civilised' as a cultural and debated phenomenon.[126]

Significantly, after 1899, the dum-dum came to register a resolute standard of barbarism in public diplomacy. In the Russo-Japanese War, Japan alleged that the Russian army utilized dum-dum bullets alongside committing a host of other atrocities in contravention of the Hague protocols.[127] Unsurprisingly, Russia denied the claims and countered with similar accusations against Japan.[128] Russian propaganda also presented its war cause as Christian and civilized, conducted in defence against needless Japanese aggression.[129] In turn, the Japanese government commissioned three international lawyers to chart Japanese adherence to the international laws of war.[130] It also appointed the jurist Nagao Ariga as legal adviser to the commander-in-chief in

Figure 5.3 This scathing cartoon by Albert Hahn appeared in the Dutch socialist newspaper *Het Volk* on 3 September 1905. Captioned 'this is how murder is decorated', Hahn drew derisive attention to the violence committed by the Dutch colonial authorities in the Dutch East Indies (Albert Hahn [1877–1918] in *Het Volk* 3 September 1905, np, IISG PM BG1/29–62).

Manchuria.[131] Reports of dum-dums also circulated during the Balkan Wars (1912–13) and at the start of the First World War.[132]

In 1914, the German government offered all manner of evidence that the French and British used the ammunition on the western front. Exploded dum-dums were even put on display in a Berlin museum, while the German ambassador to the United States requested that the neutral Americans police their use (in the spirit of the Hague law).[133] For its part, a Russian commission of enquiry presented evidence of dum-dum use by enemy German and Austrian troops on the eastern front in an attempt to further barbarize the Central Powers in public perceptions as well.[134] Even at the end of this long and vicious war, the dum-dum remained a condemned weapon. In 1919, for example, the Loyalist League of Victoria (Australia) censured Sinn Fein's activities by arguing that the Irish nationalists fired 'brutal flat-nosed bullets which cause frightful wounds'. According to these Australian monarchists, 'these so-called dum-dum bullets, the use of which is tabooed in civilized warfare, and forbidden by the Hague Convention' clearly marked Sinn Fein out as a terrorist organization operating outside the norms of civilization.[135]

What a case study of dum-dums thus shows is that the act of regulation at The Hague had a significant impact. Not only did The Hague restrict the use of dum-dums in real terms, the ruling also normalized the idea that the dum-dum was an unconscionable weapon, regardless of circumstance. In similar ways, historians argue that the 1899 Hague prohibition on the use of chemical weapons helped to establish the principle that poison gas was an inhumane military weapon. Even though the First World War witnessed prolific employment of chemical weapons, the public discourse at the time and subsequently, did not affect its inhumane reputation.[136] In fact, after 1918, the notion that chemical warfare should be outlawed completely was firmly entrenched in international relations. Even today, its use is restricted to rogue states. Its regulation at The Hague mattered in real terms.[137]

Much the same can be said of the idea of arms limitation. While the 1899 Hague conference failed to establish any real parameters for disarmament or the restriction of armed force, it nevertheless validated the idea that states had a responsibility to manage their military expansion. While the arms race between the European great powers increased exponentially between 1899 and 1914, disarmament was considered a pressing and legitimate concern and was frequently raised in public diplomacy.[138] Furthermore, as Detlev Vagt shows, the Hague conventions of 1899 and the Martens Clause in particular established a moral basis for arms control in diplomacy that continues to have effect.[139] Andrew Webster's recent work also highlights how arms limitation became a justified part of international diplomacy after 1899, achieving its apex in the 1920s.[140]

The Hague conference's impact on the expansion of international arbitration, however, was even more pronounced. The Convention for the Pacific Settlement of International Disputes not only set up a mechanism (the PCA) to adjudicate arbitral procedures but it also triggered an explosion of arbitration treaties. Arbitration was a key feature of the nineteenth-century international system.[141] After 1899, arbitration became entrenched in international relations. From 1896 to 1916, no less than 326 bilateral arbitration agreements were signed by states within and outside Europe,[142] including one between France and Great Britain in 1903 (which offered a framework to enable the *Entente Cordiale* to be formalized the following year).[143] The smaller European neutrals, including the Netherlands, Belgium, Denmark, Portugal, Switzerland and Sweden-Norway, even considered a compulsory arbitration treaty to cover all their disputes in August 1899.[144] Most of these treaties proffered the PCA and the terms of the Hague convention as the means by which a conflict of interest could be resolved. These treaties indicated that the first Hague conference had legitimated arbitration as a valid international process. For legally minded internationalists the development was a magnificent step in the right direction. It affirmed their aspiration for the judicial organization of diplomatic affairs. The PCA intimated that 'peace through law' was an achievable goal.

That the value of arbitration and the 'peace through law' ideal permeated through the international press, however, made the concept of arbitration and the establishment of the PCA ('the Hague Court' as contemporaries called it) even more significant. The Hague Court featured prominently in contemporary press reporting. These newspapers offered up the PCA as a potential solution at almost every juncture of international crisis: from the Boer War and Boxer Rebellion to the outbreak of the Russo-Japanese War, from the Nanchang riots of 1906 and the controversy around the building of the Panama Canal in 1904 to the imposition of a sugar tax by Britain in 1902.[145] They also presented arbitral treaties as progressive developments in aid of stabilizing diplomatic relations.

In their public diplomacy, many governments referenced arbitration and its pacifying impact. The signing of the Anglo-French arbitration agreement in 1903 proves an excellent case in point.[146] Britain and France celebrated their new relationship in highly publicized ways including with an official visit of 200 British Members of Parliament to Paris in October 1903, which included a trip to the studios of artists M.M. Toché and Auguste Rodin to unveil a 'a great painting which is to commemorate the first conference of The Hague International Arbitration Court'.[147] The painting, 20 metres wide and 10 metres tall, was intended as a work of propaganda. It represented the *Huis ten Bosch*, the 110 delegates at the 1899 conference and the Tsar. Toché's ambition was for the painting to be reproduced as an etching and circulated around France and the world to educate rich and poor on the importance of The Hague.[148]

In the aftermath of the arbitration agreement, many newspapers also promoted Anglo-French cooperation in intervening in the Russo-Japanese war and utilizing the arbitration mechanisms of The Hague to bring it to a speedy close.[149] The allusions between peace, friendship and arbitration were fostered throughout the *Entente* years, including at the 1908 France-Britiain Expo held in London. At that show, the French Foreign Ministry's display included a massive coloured map highlighting the hundreds of arbitration treaties signed around the European continent, with the Anglo-French treaty holding pride of place.[150] Arbitration, then, sat at the heart of the public diplomacy circulating around the *Entente*. And The Hague sat at the heart of arbitration.

In similar ways, President Roosevelt's mediation of the Russo-Japanese War resulting in the signing of the Treaty of Portsmouth in 1905 was another signal of the pacifying effect of the Hague conventions in the public sphere. As the *Edinburgh Review* editorialized: The Hague gave Roosevelt the 'moral and express international right to intervene as a mediator in the conflict. This right is an immense gain to civilisation and must tend sometimes to prevent and sometimes to end wars'.[151] Even the *Japan Times* noted that Roosevelt's 'good offices' were a welcome development,[152] while the *Daily Express* in Britain commented that the American president's actions had a mollifying political impact: 'Mr Roosevelt has recently been accused by his political opponents of being a violent Jingo. His proposal [for peace] is evidently intended to counteract this influence.'[153] But Roosevelt was not the only head of state who understood the public power of The Hague. Russia's Count Mouravieff courted similar public favour when, in the midst of the Russo-Japanese War, he referred to the successful Venezuela arbitration concluded at the PCA in February 1904 as a signal that 'after the end of the war between a European and an Asiatic people, light would once more dawn, and

The Hague Arbitration Court would remain the bulwark of justice, truth, and reason, and the sublime hope of the future'.[154] Meanwhile, in the United States, Louis E. van Norman prophesied in the *American Monthly Review of Reviews* that the Portsmouth treaty signalled that 'Hague tribunals and peace treaties will be more plentiful than international wars and hatreds'.[155]

Despite the considerable number of arbitration agreements signed after 1899, only fourteen cases made it to the PCA before the outbreak of the First World War.[156] For some commentators the lack of use made of the PCA suggested the ineffectiveness of international arbitration. For others, it offered a reason to lament its financial expense.[157] To send a case to the PCA, governments carefully assessed the costs and benefits. Given that arbitral settlements were binding, states had good reasons to be wary of arbitration. They had equally good reason to consider the impact of an arbitral settlement on public perception. For example, when Scottish authorities impounded three Norwegian vessels for allegedly trawling British waters in February 1907, Norway suggested the PCA as a route for a solution. But as Edward Grey reminded the British prime minister: the PCA was not a solution Britain could entertain as the vessels had not actually violated British territorial waters and any case brought by the Norwegians would expose 'our violation of international law . . . before the whole world'.[158]

Nonetheless, the cases that were sent to the PCA were important.[159] The Pious Funds of the Californias case – presented at The Hague after Baron d'Estournelles persuaded President Theodore Roosevelt that the PCA needed a test case – ensured settlement of a long-existing dispute between the United States and Mexico over the latter's unwillingness to pay the Catholic Church in California for interest accrued on its capital holdings there.[160] The Venezuela arbitration of 1904 settled the claims of Germans, Italians and Britons for repayment of Venezuela's foreign debt and ended a tense blockade of the country that threatened US military involvement.[161] The Japanese government initiated what came to be called the Japan House Tax dispute to the PCA in 1902, questioning whether it could charge tax on foreign buildings built on tax-exempt land. The case was settled in 1905.

The newspaper reporting on these cases confirmed the value of arbitration as an internationalist ideal. For some, it indicated that The Hague's mechanisms were working to create a more peaceful and stable world. For others, it offered the possibility that warfare might be avoided altogether in the future. At the very least, as Britain's Attorney General Sir Robert Finlay suggested in response to the Venezuela arbitration in 1904, 'the task of the statesman is immensely facilitated if he finds ready to his hands the machinery for a peaceful settlement' as offered by the PCA.[162] Nevertheless, arbitration elicited its own share of controversy. For example, when the PCA settled against Japan in 1905, the Japanese press and government turned against the process.[163] Where the *Jiji* advocated that 'Japan should "gracefully" accept' the settlement, most other Japanese newspapers baulked at the result, including the *Asahi*, whose editors rebuked the 'preposterous' claims of the foreigners in strident terms.[164] Nevertheless, even these editors accepted that the arbitration settlement was binding.

The PCA's greatest success occurred in the Russo-Japanese War (1904–1905). When on its way to Japanese waters, the Russian High Seas Fleet intercepted a host of British fishing vessels in the North Sea, it mistook the ships for Japanese trawlers and engaged them, sinking one ship, damaging many others and killing three fishermen and two Russians (in the fog the Russian ships mistook each other for the enemy as well).[165] The Doggerbank incident, as it came to be known, incensed the British as much as it concerned the rest of the neutral world. After the event, Britain had every reason to declare war on Russia in support of its ally Japan. Yet it did not. Instead, in a brilliant diplomatic manoeuvre, the British and Russian governments agreed to have the PCA initiate a commission of inquiry, suggesting restitution for damage caused. The commission awarded Britain £60,000, which the Russians readily paid. The resolution of an international crisis involving national honour and prestige presented, as the American jurist John Bassettt Moore explained at the time, 'a striking exemplification of the restraining influence of a permanent arrangement for the peaceful settlement of international disputes'.[166] The world's media readily agreed.[167]

Well beyond the Doggerbank incident, however, the global newspaper commentary on the Russo-Japanese War illustrates how intimately the Hague conventions and ideals were integrated in popular understandings of war. The French *Pêle-Mêle* magazine, for example, presented the outbreak of the war as yet another failure of The Hague in a humorous cartoon in which a yawning caretaker surveyed the ruins of the unused 'conference room of the conference of peace', in which reigned a *tristesse profonde* (profound sadness), while rats gnawed on furnishings and cobwebs adorned cracked windows.[168] Throughout the conflict, the international press analysed the war's conduct in terms of The Hague: it described battlefronts, assessed levels of violence and ascertained how ably each side kept to The Hague's conventions. It asked whether Japan should have formally declared war on Russia before the attack on Port Arthur. It wondered whether the laying of sea mines was legal and whether Russia utilized dum-dums. It questioned the treatment of POWs by both sides, interrogated the conversion of Russian merchant vessels into warships on the open seas and investigated the cutting of telegraph cables.[169] Given that most of the world declared its neutrality in the war, the belligerents' conduct towards neutral countries, their territorial rights and their relationship to neutral merchants received particular scrutiny. The *North American Review* even published a study on the comparative neutrality needs of the United States, Great Britain, France and Germany co-authored by legal and naval experts from the four countries.[170] Furthermore, when Russia declared rice as contraband, sank British merchant ships for purportedly trading in contraband and boarded German mail carriers to requisition Japanese post, the neutral press roundly condemned these acts and questioned their legality in terms of The Hague.

Above all, the Russo-Japanese War confirmed the utility of a universal law of war, to which neutrals and belligerents could be held accountable. The ubiquity of this understanding is clear from the preface of the American political scientist Amos Hershey's popular book on the war, published in 1906:

> In view of the importance of the issues involved and the general interest manifested in the subject, perhaps no apology is needed for the appearance of a volume which aims to be a fairly complete history . . . International Law is in a state of constant

> growth and decay . . . The usages observed during the Russo-Japanese War . . . are an index to the present condition of international morality.[171]

The events of the war also suggested that the world could do with another Hague conference to advance the existing laws and improve their application. Others hoped that a second Hague conference might improve the working of the PCA so that international conflicts like this one might be avoided altogether. Such sentiments found favour in the press and among diplomats.[172] It is highly relevant then that President Roosevelt called for a second Hague peace conference within the context of the Russo-Japanese War. He did so voicing the concerns of the world watching the unfolding conflict, noting the desirability for certainty on the law of neutrality and proclaiming the beneficent work of the first Hague conference on arbitration and the laws of war.[173]

When considered together, the wars that erupted in the aftermath of the first Hague conference offer an important medium through which to gauge the conventions' impact. In media commentary, The Hague offered a language to assess the conduct of actual war. That language coexisted with a range of other ideas and representations of warfare: some of which exulted military action and heightened war and militarism as agents of national prestige, imperial pride and global power. If anything, an analysis of the ways in which the global media engaged and related to The Hague in wartime illustrates that war and state violence were complex ideas that mobilized and engaged individuals in variegated ways.

The media context of these wars also suggests a wider significance, namely, that the world's governments could not escape the consequences of having signed up to the conventions. Once the rules existed, they framed the understanding of warfare. Much like a rulebook in sports, The Hague represented the range of acceptable behaviour available to states. Even when they had not ratified a convention – as Britain had not with regards to the dum-dum bullet declaration – governments were nevertheless held accountable to the terms of the conventions. The 'rights' and 'wrongs' of their warmongering was considered in line with The Hague's rules universally applied. The rules created the realities. At one level, then, the Hague conventions enabled states as much as they constrained some of their activities. At another, it made the justification of war and state violence an essential part of any government's public diplomacy.

The Hague conventions certainly mattered to newspaper assessments of warfare. If anything, they brought the wartime conduct of 'civilized' states within and outside their empires into sharp relief. The significance of these assessments is well illustrated by the German repression of the Herero rebellion from 1904 on. When news of the declaration of a state of siege in South-West Africa reached the global press, it resulted in serious questions being asked of the origins of the uprising. The *Mafeking Mail*, for example, reminded its readers that the Herero had every reason to rebel for the German colonists had breached the terms of the Damaraland treaty signed in 1885. At the same time, the *Mail* also acknowledged that 'the atrocious crimes committed on the bodies of ill-fated settlers' by the Herero transcended the parameters of civilized violence.[174] The Germans responded with ferocious force, decimating the Herero in a concerted campaign of genocide that killed anywhere between 75 and 80 per cent of the population. The neighbouring Nama people witnessed a 45–50 per cent death toll.[175]

It would seem that the genocidal campaign launched by Governor Ludwig von Trotha was not fully sanctioned by the civilian government in Berlin, nor were the actions of the colonial forces fully supported by the German public.[176] The *Rhodesia Herald* for its part criticized the act of 'shoot[ing] down every Herero in the country' as unacceptable and cited an editorial in the mainstream German newspaper, the *Vossische Zeitung*, which asserted the action discredited Germany 'in the eyes of civilisation'.[177] While the historian Isabel Hull makes a persuasive case for the German state's (and certainly its military's) willingness to use the 'silences' of the Hague rules to allow Germany to launch a *Vernichtungs* policy in Africa in 1904, their actions did not escape condescension and critique at the time or after.[178]

The Herero situation proved a difficult public relations issue for the German government. How might it counter the anti-German rhetoric of the global press and of its own citizens? To this end, it mattered that the largely pro-colonial newspapers in New Zealand referenced the 'blood and iron' tactics of General von Trotha that so 'disgusted the German public'.[179] The populist *Sunday Sun* in Sydney reported on the 'absolutely rotten' German system of government in South-West Africa, which allowed German soldiers to *sjambok* (whip) Herero women even when they carried 'little children on their backs' and that the 'Hereros themselves . . . are being treated far worse than convicts'.[180] The *Japan Times* too commented on German public opinion with regards to the Herero rebellion, including a scathing attack by the head of the German socialist party (the SPD), August Bebel, that the Herero waged a 'desperate and heroic struggle against European usurers and bloodsuckers'.[181] If the hearts and minds of newspaper readers counted in shaping the public diplomacy of states, then events like the Herero genocide brought out how important the terms of reference to civilization and international law also were in those depictions. The normative value attached to The Hague and its conventions helped to set up those terms.

The Herero were not alone. As mentioned earlier, the colonial wars conducted in the Dutch East Indies offered instances of newspaper critiques, as did the Boxer Rebellion, the Congo horrors, the Armenian atrocities of 1904 and the Italo-Turkish War of 1911. Numerous voices came out in public and private to advocate for The Hague and the principles of civilized behaviour by 'civilized' states. In an editorial entitled 'A Question of Civilisation' published in 1900, the *Lagos Weekly Record* exclaimed its editor's disgust at the hypocrisy of the states represented at the Hague conference for continuing their oppression of native peoples.[182] In 1905, W.T. Stead crusaded for King Leopold II to be tried at the Hague court for the torture, murder and mutilation of women and children in the Belgian Congo.[183]

A year earlier, the International Eastern Question Association, whose membership included the Radical journalists H.W. Massingham, H.N. Brailsford and G.R. Malloch, organized an international conference to address the violence committed against Armenians in the Ottoman Empire. The conference invited 'the co-operation of all free peoples in the work of rescuing – irrespective of race or creed – the victims of Turkish misrule'.[184] In 1911, Edwin D. Mead urged the US secretary of state to condemn the

Italians for their military actions in a decisive tone: 'It seems to me that no government of a civilized people, no government that is a party of the Hague conventions of 1899 and 1907, should remain silent or inactive for a moment in the presence of what we are now witnessing in Tripoli.'[185] According to Mead, Italy had violated every Hague convention when it massacred the inhabitants of the city. Its behaviour represented the 'grossest international lawnessness', which the world's governments must protest otherwise 'their adoption of those great conventions becomes a mockery'. It left these states and the conventions themselves open to 'public irony and contempt'.[186] Baron d'Estournelles made a similar appeal to the French prime minister, who then publicly acknowledged he would utilize the mediation mechanisms provided by The Hague to intervene in the war.[187] In the aftermath of the Russian revolution of 1905, several Russian papers also called on the second Hague peace conference to extend the rules of war to instances of civil unrest. Interior insurrection should have rules like the wars waged between 'civilized' states. Such rules would enable the 'civilized world' to protect, as the *Vejstnik Jewrozy* argued, 'all humanity'.[188]

Altogether then, the first Hague conference inspired public dialogues about the value of war and militarism, the growth of industrial-military technology, the purpose of arms races and increased conscription quotas and the like. Given the contemporaneous context of the Boer War, Boxer Rebellion and the Dreyfus affair in France, the notion that the exercise of military power might need questioning was heightened in the aftermath of the 1899 Hague event. As the next chapter shows, internationalists and peace activists from the Inter-Parliamentary Union to the International Council of Women further exploited these international crises to advance the Hague rules and advocate for a future Hague conference.[189] The Hague continued to pervade the mainstream media after July 1899 as much as it did the public discourses of the world's governments. And so did the idea that warfare was inhumane. Significantly, when several monuments were erected to the British soldiers who served and died in the Boer War, the officials at the unveilings tended not to focus on the glory of war but on its 'inhumanity' and 'wickedness' or, as King Edward VII did in 1902, by honouring the thousands of Britons who opposed the war.[190] Perhaps the populist *Daily Mirror* summed up the value of such public sentiments best when in July 1906 it proclaimed that

> such speeches as have been delivered . . . in favour of arbitration and against war are not mere empty verbiage, as many think. They all help to alter public opinion. Public opinion not long ago said that it was nonsense to suppose the world could get along without war. Public opinion said exactly the same thing when it was first proposed to settle private quarrels by law instead of with meat-axes. Nevertheless[,] the meat-axe method has gone out of fashion. Now, by reason of Hague Conferences and Peace Congresses and continual speeches, public opinion is beginning to wonder whether war will not some day go out of fashion, too.[191]

Hope underwrote the pronouncement even if the cynical realities of the day denied its veracity.

6

A Holy Duty: Activists for The Hague

The sober-minded advocates of justice and righteousness will discover ample reason for the belief that international society has thrown up in the Hague Conference a most powerful organ, whose possibilities for good need to be developed by persistent efforts of every lover of his kind.

– T.J. Lawrence, 1908[1]

While he was in The Hague for the 1899 conference, the Austrian peace activist Alfred Fried authored the first instalment of *Die Friedens-Warte* (which loosely translates as 'the peace wait').[2] Fried hoped his journal would steer public opinion in German-speaking communities towards the issues prominently on display at the conference, namely: the advance of international law and arbitration, the avoidance of war and the regulation of armaments.[3] *Die Friedens-Warte* became an authoritative source for European peace activism in the early twentieth century.[4] It remains in print today. In September 1899, Fried wrote a lengthy editorial for the publication in which he relayed that on returning home from The Hague, he was repeatedly confronted with the question 'not much happened, did it?' He reminded his readers that such an attitude aimed at discrediting the conference. He condemned it as a perspective held only by philistines, who saw things not as they were but as they wanted them to be and who expended little thought on the serious implications of the 1899 Hague moment. Fried urged for accurate information about the Hague conference and conventions to circulate more widely. What was needed, he thought, was a concerted education campaign conducted through the daily press. He also argued that it was the 'holy duty' (*heilige Pflicht*) of all peace activists to set to work to publicize how The Hague represented progress, limited war and encouraged international conciliation. For Fried, promoting the work of The Hague encompassed the *grössten Kulturwerke aller Zeiten* ('the greatest work of civilization of all time').[5] After 1899, The Hague dominated Fried's public advocacy.[6]

The Inter-Parliamentary Union (IPU) was equally emphatic, if less oracular, about the utility of The Hague. Its members celebrated the success of the first Hague conference at the IPU convention held in Kristiania (Oslo) in August 1899.[7] As the *Advocate of Peace* noted, the IPU was an organization that had long promoted the establishment of a court of international arbitration. It now delighted that it could ratify the 'general features' of the Permanent Court of Arbitration (PCA) and 'lost no time . . . in extending its felicitations to the Emperor of Russia and to the sovereigns and governments represented at that Conference'. Still, the IPU convention also noted that the PCA was not a perfect institution and that while 'the first and most difficult step' had been taken in creating the court, which was of the 'greatest historic importance', much could be done to improve it and to mould public opinion in its favour. The IPU meeting also passed other Hague resolutions including the suggestion that future Hague conferences be held to advance arbitration and to progress 'the gradual constitution of a code of international law' that would fix the 'rights and duties of nations'.[8] After 1899, the IPU concentrated on advancing The Hague in all its activities.

Both Fried's and the IPU's positions highlight the extraordinary significance of the first Hague conference for peace activists and liberal internationalists alike.[9] The fact that a diplomatic conference was held at the behest of a major power to discuss key internationalist concerns – arbitration, disarmament and the international law of war – legitimized their 'peace through law' agenda. For these internationalists, the success of the 1899 event was not grounded in the content of the conventions as much as it was in the fact that any agreement was achieved at all on highly contentious subjects. The Hague confirmed that reform of the international system was possible, the regulation of international law was viable and the creation of international organizations was an attainable goal. The 1899 Hague conventions thus set a base line for future activism. The Hague offered them an unprecedented opportunity to take up Baron de Staal's pronouncement that 'the good seed is sown. Let the harvest come'.[10] They attended that harvest by publishing newspapers, journals, books and pamphlets and circulating them far and wide. They held public meetings and disseminated copies of their speeches. The most prominent among them launched international crusades propagating The Hague's causes. They sought widespread exposure for their ideas and for The Hague.

As this chapter shows, their activism helped to normalize the idea of 'The Hague' in public understanding. After 1899, the term 'The Hague' came to embody the ideas promoted by liberal internationalists, including the development of international governance, international justice and the regulation of war. While most activists for The Hague prioritized arbitration, their references to The Hague covered both generalities and specifics. They used The Hague to promote meaningful change on simultaneous fronts, including: the development and 'humanization' of the international law of war; the promotion of arbitration and mediation as suitable ways to resolve conflict; the expansion of a system of international courts; the promotion of neutrality as a means to alleviate international conflict; and the growth of public recognition that international relations may be better served by establishing more international institutions (like the PCA) and encouraging more multilateral forums (like the Hague conferences).[11] The Hague conventions offered these internationalists an accessible reference point that any newspaper reader would understand and a hopeful premise on which to build the future. After 1899, The Hague both offered a medium for liberal internationalists to improve the world according to these priorities and represented those priorities in the public sphere.

As such, The Hague presented a boundlessly optimistic concept, tendering up the possibility of righting great wrongs (like warfare and human suffering) and of making pragmatic improvements to the ways in which governments conducted their foreign affairs. As the American ambassador to the Netherlands David Jayne Hill explained to the readers of the *American Journal of International Law* in 1907: the first Hague conference had initiated a diplomatic process that enabled the alleviation and conciliation of conflict. That reality, according to Hill, offered the potential to advance social progress on a global scale.[12]

The British international lawyer T.J. Lawrence also presented the advantages of the Hague law in the newspaper media. His works included *War and Neutrality in the Far East* (1904), an exposé about the legal challenges posed by the Russo-Japanese War.[13] At the time of publication, the *New York Times* called it a 'remarkably pertinent book',[14] while the *Chicago Daily Tribune* explained that the volume answered 'questions which every reader of newspapers is now asking'.[15] The *Wairarapa Daily Times* in New Zealand described T.J. Lawrence as 'that well-known and entertaining publicist' as well as 'one of the leading authorities on International Law . . . anything he has to say . . . commands corresponding attention'.[16] In the preface of his 1908 textbook entitled *International Problem and Hague Conferences*, Lawrence explained:

> The aim of this book is twofold. It attempts to furnish students with an account of the Hague Conferences, considered not as isolated phenomena but as immensely important points in the evolution of international society, and it endeavours to place before thoughtful people who take an interest in the affairs of the world around them sound information about a series of events of which they have read in a desultory fashion in their newspapers . . . It is hoped that what suits the student . . . will also suit the intelligent citizen who wishes to do his duty by his age and country.[17]

After reading his book, Lawrence hoped that these 'intelligent citizens' would acknowledge that the Hague conferences were a 'powerful organ' endowed with the possibility to improve the 'society of states'.[18] For Lawrence, much like Jayne, Fried and the members of the IPU, The Hague offered an influential medium to advance international stability. It is significant then that Alfred Fried's study *Die zweite Haager Konferenz, ihre Arbeiten, ihre Ergebnisse und ihre Bedeutung* (The second Hague conference, its work, its results and its meaning), also published in 1908, went through sixty print runs within a few months. Twelve thousand copies of the book circulated in Germany, with another 6,000 in Austria and Switzerland.[19]

For the French international lawyers G. Lapradelle and A. Méringhac it was equally obvious that advocates of the 'peace through law' principle must attend to The Hague's harvest.[20] In a lengthy study published in 1900, Méringhac posited that the utility of The Hague to promote international stability was its most enduring legacy.[21] He also noted that even though the Hague conventions could not and did not prevent the violence of the age, that the 1899 conference nevertheless offered an ideal forum to advance public morality.[22] France's former prime minister and first delegate at the 1899 conference Léon Bourgeois authored the preface of Méringhac's work.[23] In the preface, Bourgeois indicated that due to the 'cruel' aftermath of the conference, as witnessed by the Boer War and Boxer rebellion, it was easy to consider The Hague a failure. But he agreed with the friends of peace and philanthropy that the achievements of the

Hague conventions were an incalculable extension of the international law of peace.[24] Bourgeois also suggested that future historians would recognize the civilizing forces at play at the conference.[25] Altogether, Bourgeois stressed that no one should approach The Hague with scepticism or impatience. The work of progress took time and careful thought.[26]

Count Albert Apponyi, one of Austria-Hungary's delegates at the first Hague conference, presented a similar argument when he addressed the Budapest Journalist Society in 1900 to advocate for the establishment of an international Peace Press Association (*Verbande der Presse im Dienste des Friedens*).[27] According to Apponyi, the very 'meaning of The Hague' was in play, which compelled the mobilization of the daily press behind hopeful messages for the progress of the world. As *Pester Lloyd*, the Budapest newspaper, reported: Apponyi began his speech by highlighting how the Hague peace conference offered both an opportunity and presented the 'absolute necessity' (*absolute Nothwendigkeit*) for the development of a press association aimed at the advancement of a practical 'peace through law' ideal. Given that the general populace was gaining influence and power, Apponyi was adamant that governments must listen to the popular voice raised against war. He described how before the Hague conference, many newspapers talked of the *Haager Fiasko* (Hague fiasco), asserting that it was sure to be a disaster but that this was 'absolutely not' the legacy of the event. Rather, the conference confirmed the importance of arbitration, sanctioned the work of internationalists and confirmed that they operated within the parameters of realistic politics (*realen Politik*). For Apponyi, the conference 'gives us an urgent task: we must breathe life into the work of The Hague'. It was the daily press (*Tagespresse*) that must be convinced and, according to Apponyi, it was the collective duty of all journalists to ensure that happened.[28]

Apponyi was not the first, nor would he be the last, person to suggest coordinating the press to influence public opinion in favour of peace and international organization. The *Association des journalists-amis de la paix* (Association of Journalist Friends of Peace), established in Paris in 1896, certainly preceded him.[29] Yet Apponyi's plan was significant and received global attention in 1900,[30] including in a scathing editorial published in the populist British *Daily Express*:

> The idea is both pathetic and humorous . . . [and] shows a lamentable ignorance of the size of editorial waste-paper baskets. The flood of gratis 'literature' which was poured into newspaper offices before and during the Peace Conference at The Hague, and later from the friends of the Boers in Holland, had, we are afraid, little influence on public opinion concerning war. Peace is a lovely thing, but the strongest International Peace Agency that could be formed would be powerless to secure its maintenance. War must always be one of the inevitable possibilities of life.[31]

Most internationalists did not agree with the *Daily Express*'s pronouncement of their insignificance. Élie Ducommun, for example, suggested in 1906 that public opinion against war was rising and that '[w]e are assisting at the awakening of the collective conscience among those classes that have never been consulted on questions affecting their most important interests . . . This expression of public sentiment has an increasing tendency to smother that of bellicose politicians'.[32] It is significant then that *The Times* published an editorial in 1913 that proclaimed:

> There is no great nation in Europe which today has the least desire that millions of men should be torn from their homes and flung headlong to destruction at the bidding of vain ambitions . . . Who then makes war? The answer is to be found in the Chancelleries of Europe, among the men who have too long played with human lives as pawns in a game of chess, who have become so enmeshed in formulas and the jargon of diplomacy that they have ceased to be conscious of the poignant realities with which they trifle. And thus will war continue to be made, until the great masses . . . say the word which shall bring, not eternal peace, for that is impossible but a determination that wars shall be fought only in a just and righteous and vital course.[33]

It is also significant that the Republican editor of the *Wyoming State Tribune*, W.C. Deming, editorialized that same year that the press had the means of 'arousing public opinion and wielding it in concrete form against evil or oppression' and that 'an agency, a world-wide instrument as the Press . . . which is able to provoke an unnecessary war [is] certainly potent enough to prevent one' too.[34]

Still in 1911, the renowned French pacifist Frédéric Passy presented the mainstream press as tendentious, ignorant of facts, judgemental, foolish (*trompée*), misleading (*trompeuse*) and unreflective. Yet he also acknowledged that the press was 'in large measure, the principal director of opinion, and, for better or worse, the accomplice or instigator of popular distractions and political and diplomatic intrigues'.[35] To that end, he supported Johan de Vries's suggestion that a universal newspaper be published, transcending national and local prejudices. Such a paper would be exacting in its journalism and ambitious in its impartiality, fostering mutual understanding and a communal domain. He furthered that 'what was not possible yesterday has become not only realisable but compellingly essential' today.[36] De Vries's compendium included letters in support of the idea from around the world, including from Andrew Carnegie.[37]

While a universal peace press was not established, its proposal should be considered as an example of a wider contemporary debate about the value of the global media and the responsibility of journalists in affecting public opinion.[38] While many populist editors seemed to care little about the veracity of their newspaper reports, most serious publications aimed at offering thoughtful and considered coverage of the news. If thoughtful analysis mattered to these editors, then so did the creation of a responsible editorial position. Even the editors of popular newspapers, like the British *Evening News* and *Daily Mail*, aimed at educating the masses on the affairs of the world.[39] If the jingo press readily advanced nationalism, xenophobia and militarism,[40] then the internationalists promoting The Hague were hopeful that the responsible press could (and, from their perspective, should) promote international arbitration, international law and international justice in their editorial positions. Judging from the quality and quantity of their reporting on these ideas, a remarkable number of newspaper editors agreed with this internationalist agenda, at least some of the time.

The rest of this chapter focuses on the advocacy work carried out by internationalists and peace activists in support of The Hague. Historians of peace tend to question the prevalence and relevance of peace activism in Anglo-European societies before the onset of the First World War.[41] Roger Chickering, for example, presents a stark case for pacifism barely registering in Wilhelmine Germany.[42] Sandi Cooper acknowledges that peace 'pricked at the public conscience' of Europeans; she also maintains that belligerent nationalism overwhelmed pacifist sentiment before 1914.[43] Martin Ceadel carefully argues that the acceptance of peace as an ideal made slow progress across the nineteenth century.[44] Merze Tate suggests that there is no evidence that the general public on either side of the Atlantic supported disarmament or the Hague conferences.[45] In turn, D.S. Patterson suggests that Progressive Era Americans happily embraced internationalism as a means of spreading American values globally, but that the American peace movement remained largely ineffective before 1914.[46] None of these perspectives hold up when considered in the context of The Hague's prevalence in the contemporary newspaper record.

When it came to The Hague, the advocacy of peace activists and other internationalists had considerable impact. The story of peace before the First World War, as C.J. Marchand also notes, was a story of international law, progressivism, international arbitration and international organization.[47] Between 1899 and 1914, all these concepts were firmly focused on The Hague. The political activity around them formed an essential part of what Glenda Sluga describes as the early-twentieth-century's 'internationalist turn', Cooper acknowledges as the 'final transformation of pacifism into internationalism' and James L. Tryon considers a 'tidal wave sweeping everything before it'.[48] The previous chapter emphasized the ways in which the Hague conventions were used as gauges to assess the conduct of war and state violence. This chapter argues that The Hague also captured the imagination of many newspaper editors and did so as an idea that promised improvement in international governance, in the advance of international law and in the promotion of international justice.[49] Newspapers were an important medium for advancing these liberal internationalist concepts.

This is not to say that The Hague was always approached in a positive manner in the press: cynicism abounded, particularly in 1907 at the time of the second conference. But such pessimism existed alongside equally reaffirming images and ideas. As an example, compare Albert Hahn's sardonic cartoon (Figure 6.1) with two images from the *Illustrated London News*, also from 1907, advocating for The Hague's peace appeal (Figures 6.2 and 6.3). The point is that The Hague brought out an array of perspectives and opinions in the media, among which those supported by liberal internationalists featured prominently. By 1907, then, The Hague was acknowledged as a core concept in international life that connected up a set of complex ideas relating to the conduct of war, the possibility of peace, the use of arbitration, the advance of international law and the creation of international governance mechanisms. Above all, when newspapers used the term 'The Hague', they used it to convey a sense of collective responsibility for international affairs. The internationalists who loudly and proudly advocated for The Hague from 1899 on played a key role in making that idea have depth and promise.

Figure 6.1 The Dutch cartoonist Albert Hahn presented a deeply cynical and despondent image of the promise of The Hague in this Christmas cartoon from 1907, published in the socialist newspaper *De Notenkraker*. The caption read: 'Peace: "Dear people. This time, I cannot come to earth. I am still undone by the mistreatment of the peace conference" ' (*De Notenkraker* 22 December 1907, front page, IISG BGC13/385).

That the newspapers of most industrializing states and their outposts included regular discussions and references to 'The Hague' between 1899 and 1914 is therefore vitally important. The existence of a multifaceted conceptualization of The Hague and its applications suggests that popular understandings of war and diplomacy were shaped by more than only national, imperial and religious ideas and impulses. They were also influenced by concepts of international law, humanitarianism and 'civilization'. The existence of the Hague conventions suggested that governments were

Figure 6.2 The *Illustrated London News* reprinted Henri Danger's famous 'Apostles of peace' painting on 22 June 1907, to celebrate the opening of the second Hague peace conference. The painting represented key delegates and an array of peace personages through the ages, including Confucius, Buddha, Plato, Erasmus, Baroness von Suttner and Alfred Nobel (*Illustrated London News* 22 June 1907, 960–61).

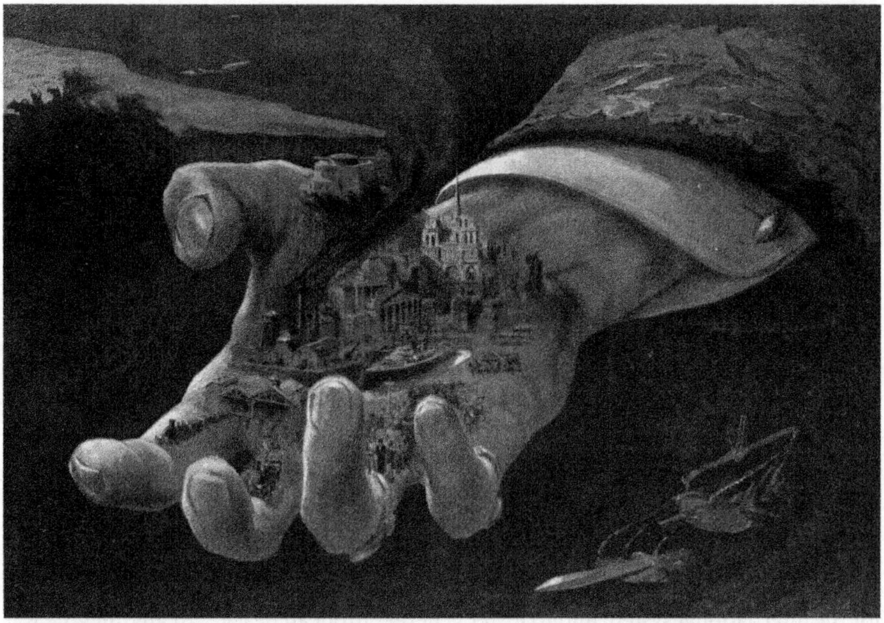

Figure 6.3 In August 1907, the *Illustrated London News* again reflected on the potential importance of the second Hague peace conference for stabilizing the world from war. This image reflects on the power of the state to force war on all classes of society from the church, to parliament, to the economy and to all people. If the conference could stay the hand of war, it would benefit them all (*Illustrated London News* 24 August 1907, 265).

willing to use international law to mould the international environment. That reality impacted how the press (and its readers) considered the conduct of international relations. The conventions also presented a set of rules by which the actions of states could be judged. After 1899, The Hague functioned as a reference point for a wide range of international interactions. The Hague offered solutions, promise, challenges and new ideas to consider international life writ large.

The delegates who attended the first Hague conference were the most obvious people to promote the conference's achievements. There were, in fact, a surprising number of delegates who publicly endorsed the utility of The Hague, including Léon Bourgeois and Count Apponyi.[50] They did so in part because they took pride in their work and in the achievements of the conference. They also did so because they believed in the importance of the Hague conventions. They were ideal figureheads to attend to Baron de Staal's 'harvest'. By and large, their assessments reinforced the internationalist and progressive appeal of The Hague.[51] Given that many of the delegates became minor celebrities due to their involvement in the first Hague conference, the media attention given to them ensured that their names lent esteem and honour to the internationalist ideas attached to The Hague and to the 'peace through law' cause more generally.

Of all delegates at the first Hague conference, the French aristocratic Baron Paul Henri d'Estournelles became the most important advocate for The Hague's ideas in its aftermath. Before 1899, d'Estournelles was a well-known French politician, diplomat and aristocrat who made no secret of his radical republican and internationalist views.[52] His profile recommended him to the French government as an ideal delegate for the conference, whose credentials for peace would stand up to any public scrutiny. D'Estournelles' advocacy for The Hague, however, was unparalleled. From the moment the conference closed its doors, d'Estournelles travelled around Europe and the United States utilizing his many high-powered contacts to influence official policy, to educate and persuade. At one public event in 1906 he described the purpose of his pro-Hague activism: 'Good example is contagious'. He further noted that while neither the Hague conference nor the recent French-British *Entente Cordiale* were able to prevent the outbreak of the Russo-Japanese War, to accept that there was a causal link between them was mere 'sophistry': 'Instead of recognising the good . . . we are called to account for the evils which they have not been able to prevent. . . . Would it not be more reasonable to rejoice at the ground we have gained?'[53] D'Estournelles waxed lyrical about the advantages of the *Entente Cordiale*. In 1910, he travelled to Russia to reaffirm the French-Russian friendship. By 1911, he was also a prolific promoter of a French-German *entente* to forego war.[54] He presented these 'friendships' as essential for the international system and to foster general European peace.[55] At all times, he was considered a representative of the French state as much as he was a private individual with a pronounced internationalist (and Hague-focused) agenda.[56]

Peace activists acclaimed d'Estournelles' activities, sought out his advice and promoted his presence at their events.[57] The IPU utilized d'Estournelles' fame and influence to advance their causes.[58] D'Estournelles was undoubtedly persuasive. The President of Columbia University Nicholas Murray Butler, for example, credited the French aristocrat and the 'stirring effects of the first Hague Conference' for reminding him that he should resume his annual visits to Europe to progress internationalism.[59] Even the French socialist Jean Jaurès accepted d'Estournelles' invitation to serve as the vice president of a non-partisan group in advance of international arbitration in 1903.[60] According to the rumours, it was also Baron d'Estournelles who convinced Andrew Carnegie to endow The Hague's peace palace. Furthermore, most historians credit d'Estournelles for convincing President Theodore Roosevelt to send the Pious Funds situation to the Permanent Court of Arbitration in 1902.[61] This development was more than a symbolic act: it ensured the PCA had its first case, thereby legitimizing the organization's existence. The Pious Funds case also established a powerful connection between Roosevelt and the liberal internationalist agenda.

More than anyone else alive at the time, d'Estournelles helped to keep The Hague in the news. The *New York Times* referred to d'Estournelles in 1904 as Europe's 'most illustrious exponent' of peace.[62] D'Estournelles promoted The Hague as a political priority, including at the 1911 First Universal Races Congress at which he proclaimed that '[t]he Hague conferences are only a first step' and that 'we must now pass on to a proclamation more international in kind . . . one day we shall begin to proclaim the Duties of Man' to all human beings in the spirit of the French revolution.[63] It was largely due to d'Estournelles' steadfast Hague advocacy and involvement as an official delegate for France in both Hague conferences that he was awarded the Nobel Peace Prize in 1909. D'Estournelles diplomacy for peace frequently featured in newspaper headlines. They quoted his speeches and noted his meetings with heads of state.[64] Some of his pronouncements were carefully timed and primed for the press, which was particularly true of his attempts in 1899 to promote France's ratification of the Hague conventions. But even in 1901, *The Times* headlined its Austro-Hungarian section with 'Baron d'Estournelles in Vienna' and offered an account of a lecture given 'before a large and distinguished audience', in which the 'well-known French diplomatist' discussed The Hague and the 'immense services which the new organization of the Court of Arbitration might render'. According to the account, d'Estournelles' speech 'was frequently interrupted by applause, and at the close . . . he was the object of quite an enthusiastic demonstration'.[65] When d'Estournelles visited the University of Georgia in 1911, the *Atlanta Constitution* lauded him as a 'far-seeing and patriotic' man, a 'distinguished disciple of peace'.[66]

While d'Estournelles was undoubtedly a leading figure in promoting The Hague in the public sphere, he was not alone. Like d'Estournelles, Frederick Holls, the secretary of the American delegation, used his connections in the United States and Germany to advance The Hague's cause. He published a book on the subject in 1900 and used every opportunity to make a case for The Hague's importance for American international life.[67] He sought out invitations to speak and gloried in his role as The Hague's foremost American sponsor.[68] For Holls, the 1899 conference was the 'most interesting and instructive experience of his life'.[69] He also embraced the notion that the conference 'provided the motor' for meaningful change in international affairs: 'the force of which is public opinion'.[70] To that end, Holls presented the 1899 conference as one conducted by experts and heightened the esteem and importance of The Hague through the quality of the participating delegations. In his words:

> To listen to the diplomatic wisdom of veteran statesmen like Baron de Staal, Count Nigra and Lord Pauncefote; to hear the profoundest problems of International Law debated thoroughly and most brilliantly by authorities like De Martens, Asser, Descamps, Lammasch and Zorn; to observe the noble idealism of Baron d'Estournelles, the sound judgment of M. de Basily and Jonkheer van Karnebeek, and the unerring prudence of Switzerland's efficient representative, M. Odier – and finally, to watch the perfection of decision and tact in the firm but most amiable management of all these various elements by the chairman [of the Third Commission], M. Bourgeois, – all of this would in itself be of sufficient general interest to deserve an enduring record.[71]

According to many who knew him, Holls was enamoured with his own sense of importance. His Hague accounts advanced his narcissism.[72] But they also heightened the public profile of the conferences and conventions in the United States. As the *American Monthly Review of Reviews* noted in 1900: 'an event like the great conference at The Hague usually lacks full contemporary appreciation'. This reality made Frederick Holls's book so significant and the man himself a prominent voice in the American media.[73] When Holls died in 1903, the *New York Times* headlined with 'Death of G. F.

W. Holls, Well-Known Lawyer Succumbs Suddenly to Heart Failure, Was Secretary of the United States Delegation to The Hague Conference'.[74] Even the *Manchester Guardian* noted his untimely demise, while *The Times* eulogized that 'Mr Holls's book on the Peace Conference ... is the most complete work of the kind that has appeared' and that 'Mr Holls may be considered to have saved The Hague meeting from shipwreck' given his intervention on behalf of arbitration in Germany at the time.[75]

Fyodor Martens, the Russian lawyer and key delegate at the first conference, was another prominent publicist for The Hague.[76] His published work on the subject sought to raise awareness of the conference and the application of its conventions.[77] Given his position as a foremost legal expert and his prominent role in shaping the Hague laws, Martens was an obvious Hague advocate. He certainly wrote numerous prefaces for other people's studies on the subject. One of these, a foreword for Méringhac's book on the laws and customs of war, praised the Hague conference for raising the 'practical value of international acts' and for advancing the 'peace through law' cause.[78] During a speech given in 1900 at a fundraising event for impoverished children, Martens presented the 1899 Hague conference as a civilizing moment. He further suggested that the growth in academic work on The Hague reflected the maturation of civilized society more generally.[79]

As Martens travelled around Europe and the United States, the press followed his movements and considered his pronouncements.[80] It is not surprising then to find the front page of the *Chicago Daily Tribune*'s 1903 Christmas issue reprinting quotations from the Berlin *Lokal Anzeiger*'s seasonal issue, including a quotation from Martens promoting 'real peace' through the 'rule of justice'.[81] Only a few months earlier Martens had been appointed, in the words of the *Washington Post*, as the 'distinguished lawyer' to sit on the Venezuelan Arbitration Commission.[82] Commentary on Martens was particularly prominent when the lawyer acted in an official capacity. Thus, during the negotiations of the Portsmouth Treaty in 1905, the *Atlanta Constitution* was pleased to report on Martens's approbation of the treaty and of the United States and its newspaper industry more generally.[83] The *Chicago Daily Tribune*, for its part, included a large photograph of Martens in its coverage of the peace negotiations and recommended him as an international lawyer of renown.[84] The newspaper had previously printed an article authored by Martens reflecting on the Boer War, Boxer Rebellion and the Hague conventions, along with another picture.[85]

In 1904, British newspapers equally prominently noted Martens's position on the PCA as a way of gauging the likelihood of a successful settlement of the Doggerbank incident.[86] Oxford University's Bodleian College bestowed an honorary doctorate on Martens in 1902; Yale had already done so the previous year. Both awards received mention in the local press.[87] On the earlier occasion, the *Washington Post* described Martens in its 'Men met in hotel lobbies' series.[88] Meanwhile, Edward Everett Hale used up an entire page of the *New York Times* in 1902 to laud the Pious Funds arbitration and Martens's chairmanship of the PCA's first case. According to Hale, Martens's role was of seminal importance, as the 'Chief Justice of Christendom' he initiated a beneficent 'omen of the civilization of the new century'.[89] Much like d'Estournelles, Holls, Apponyi and Bourgeois, Fyodor Martens personified the Hague ideal.

So did the German delegate and international lawyer Phillip Zorn. Unlike the other delegates noted above, however, Zorn was a reluctant convert to the liberal internationalist cause. Before 1899, in fact, he was not a strong advocate for the regulation of international law at all.[90] The experience of the conference fundamentally shifted Zorn's perspectives. After 1899, he published numerous studies on the Hague law and was quoted in newspapers within and outside Germany on Hague topics.[91] He represented Germany at the second Hague conference and suggested in 1908 that since the Hague conferences 'the development of international law has' evolved 'along the lines of modern organized pacifism'. He urged his fellow Germans to become more involved in that beneficial process.[92] Zorn also acknowledged that Germans, unlike the French and British, would never become peace idealists but that fact should not keep them from supporting the 'practical work' enabled by The Hague for developing 'international life' in general.[93] Even after the catastrophe of the First World War, as Zorn himself described that conflict in an oration at Tübingen University in 1924, he was convinced that the world must return to the 'spirit of the Hague peace conferences' to restore order to the international system.[94]

How prolific all these delegates' positions on The Hague and international law were in the public sphere is perhaps best illustrated by the way newspapers reported on their involvement in key internationalist events. For example, the *Institut de droit international*'s congress held in Edinburgh in September 1904 involved d'Estournelles, Martens as well as other prominent delegates from the 1899 Hague conference, including Belgium's Baron Descamps and Britain's John Ardagh. Newspaper reports on the event noted not only who was present – a list that included high-profile lawyers like Thomas Barclay and prominent British politicians and aristocrats – but also went into great detail about the content of their speeches and resolutions. Over the course of the conference, the *Manchester Guardian* presented a series of headlines, including 'Neutrals as Peacemakers', 'The Hague Court and Trade Matters', 'Russia and the Hague Conventions', 'Congress of Jurists, Lord Reay on Contraband Questions'. All of them spoke to the anxiety felt by many Britons about their neutral rights in the ongoing Russo-Japanese War.[95] Tellingly, the *Guardian* represented the *Institut*'s mission and the applications of the Hague law as essential and constructive to developing and stabilizing international relations. With a blazing 'Hope for Arbitration' headline, the *Washington Post* also reflected on Barclay's views on a potential British-American arbitration treaty, while the *New York Times* acknowledged that the key to Barclay's address lay in the fact that Canada was willing to accept such a bilateral arrangement.[96]

Beyond the official delegations to the Hague conferences, The Hague's internationalist causes were also kept firmly in the public sphere by the activism of peace campaigners. The novelist Baroness Bertha von Suttner (whom a Berlin newspaper called the most influential woman of all time in 1903),[97] journalist W.T. Stead, entrepreneur-cum-scholar Ivan Bloch, Dutch pacifist Waszklewicz van Schilfgaarde and the American peace couple Lucia Ames and Edwin Mead are all excellent examples of how well integrated peace activism and media representations of internationalist causes were in the aftermath of the 1899 conference. These peace activists focused on The Hague as the best medium to advance their message of peace. As Suttner explained it: 'I saw clearly what I had to do: it was to give as many of my fellow-countrymen as possible knowledge of the results of the [Hague] Conference, and I devoted myself diligently to this task.'[98] None of these individuals should be categorized as representatives of marginalized movements that had little to no impact on the assumptions of ordinary individuals. Each of them had prominent media profiles both within and outside their countries of residence. While the press commentary around their activism was never uniform, it is remarkable how often it lauded these individuals and their attempts at improving the world.[99] More often than not, the legitimacy of their activism was also founded on the notion that the Hague conventions improved international relations.

Take Ivan Bloch, for example: after 1899, he continued as a prominent campaigner for his *Is War Now Impossible?* publication. Wherever he went, he was fêted in the press.[100] In June 1902, Bloch opened a 'war and peace' museum in the Swiss town of Lucerne. The museum aimed to appeal to the public's 'practical rather than sentimental considerations' regarding war.[101] It did so by displaying weaponry, miniature battle scenes and sizeable graphs charting the destructive power of modern military equipment and the economic costs of warfare for neutrals and belligerents alike.[102] The museum displayed more than 4,000 objects.[103] By materializing warfare, Bloch hoped that visitors would be convinced by his thesis that an industrial war 'would ruin . . . belligerents, financially and economically, long before the end would have come in sight'.[104] The Hague was presented in the museum as a necessary process to enable states to prevent war.[105]

Bloch's museum caught the public's imagination. Many newspapers noted its opening, including the *Sumatra Post*, whose editor dedicated a large article to the subject, which included a potted biography of Bloch and an overview of his academic work.[106] The *Ohinemuri Gazette*, serving readers in the Coromandel region of New Zealand, explained in 1903 that the Lucerne museum, which immortalized Bloch's work, showed by means of 'modern science' just how expensive modern warfare was.[107] In 1905, a *Washington Post* special correspondent presented a review of the museum in a heavily illustrated article entitled 'The Horror of War Shown to Promote the Cause of Peace'.[108] By 1906, more than 300,000 visitors had passed through the museum's doors and the temporary structure in which the displays were located was in desperate need of repair.[109] In the end, Lucerne's war and peace museum did not survive the years of wear and tear. In 1909, *The Times* reported that the landmark, so beloved by tourists, would be replaced by a hotel.[110] Yet the museum's very existence spoke to the prominent public discourse that existed around the idea of war and the ideal of peace.

Another key signal of the normalization of the internationalist values attached to The Hague in the public sphere was the existence of a substantial body of academic work expressly focused on the subject. Hundreds of publications on the Hague conferences, the PCA and the international law of war appeared after 1899.[111] These publications, as Fried acknowledged, recognized the Hague conference as a key feature of contemporary international politics.[112] Fried described these academic works as the activism of 'neo-pacifists', whom he defined as scholars aiming to improve international relations along rational lines. Fried juxtaposed the work of neo-pacifists with that conducted by 'regular' pacifists, namely, the active members of organized peace societies. Neo-pacifists did not aspire to the generic peace of the world. Rather, they looked to stabilize international relations and institutionalize the international order through the regulation of international law.[113] According to Fried, neo-pacifism gained traction after 1899 and manifested itself in mainstream European politics, including in Germany.[114] Fried used the examples of Phillip Zorn and Christian Meurer to make his case. Like Zorn, Christian Meurer was a well-known German lawyer who advocated for The Hague in his academic work and in the public sphere. In 1903, he even presented a series of public addresses to celebrate the University of Würzburg's 321st anniversary. The lectures, entitled 'An Overview of the Work of The Hague', looked to replicate the success of a similar series given by d'Estournelles at the University of Lyon three years earlier.[115]

As with all things relating to The Hague, d'Estournelles, Zorn and Meurer were well supported. Numerous academics and international lawyers presented similar arguments relating to the widespread and global promise of the Hague conventions and the promotion of international law more generally, including the Germans Walther Schücking,[116] Otfried Nippold[117] and Hans Wehberg,[118] the British Thomas Barclay, T.E. Holland and T.J. Lawrence,[119] the French A. Méringhac and G. de Lapradelle, and the Italian economist Molinari.[120] Louis Renault, the French international lawyer, delegate at both Hague conferences and Nobel Peace Prize winner, was another prominent Hague commentator,[121] while in the United States James Scott Brown devoted his life to The Hague after 1907.[122] John W. Foster, the American diplomat and China's representative at the 1907 Hague conference, also became a proud Hague advocate.[123] Altogether, their work represented a vibrant slice of the *vie juridique internationale* ('international judicial life') as Frédéric Passy so eloquently noted, much of which focused on The Hague.[124] Books on The Hague tended to sell well in Europe, although not always as well as their authors might have hoped.[125]

It was in the United States, however, that the widespread adoption of internationalism was most pronounced in the press as an all-American value. The creation of the American International Law Association in 1906 highlights how well integrated concepts of internationalism, activism for The Hague and American progressivism were. The association's primary aim was to popularize international law and international justice and to make these ideas mainstream ones dominating the United States' foreign policy agenda.[126] Andrew Carnegie's Endowment for International Peace, established in 1911, likewise celebrated The Hague and international law more generally for acting as brakes on excessive state behaviour. The endowment, under the guidance of James Brown Scott who was a prominent delegate at the second Hague conference, published prolific amounts of Hague scholarship, much of which appeared during and in the immediate aftermath of the First World War.[127] As such, the Carnegie Endowment remained a loyal mouthpiece for Hague activism. Above all, however, the fact that many of the political elite who served the Roosevelt and Taft administrations were international lawyers and promoters of the 'peace through law' cause made the United States seem a beacon of peace and sensibility before 1914. As a result, The Hague featured prominently in these administrations' public diplomacy.[128]

The activism of these individuals, be they delegates, peace activists or scholars, existed alongside and was often undertaken on behalf of internationalist organizations, like the IPU, the *Institut de droit international* or the London Peace Society. From 1899 on, many of these organizations turned professional, reorganizing their policy objectives to augment the existing Hague conventions and build on the momentum of the first Hague conference. They mobilized their members to influence governments and the wider public about key Hague ideas. A case study of three such movements (out of hundreds) highlights the broad nature of their activism, namely, that of the IPU, the International Council of Women (ICW) and the '18 May' movement.[129]

The IPU was a long-standing elite organization made up of members of parliament from around the world who looked to improve parliamentary democracy and intergovernmental cooperation. After 1899, the IPU presented itself as The Hague's firmest and most steadfast proponent.[130] Its representatives included numerous official delegates to the first Hague conference and these proudly declared that the IPU's arbitration agenda had made an impact there.[131] Given that President Roosevelt called for a second Hague peace conference in 1904 after attendees at an IPU meeting in St Louis sent a telegram suggesting the idea to him, the causal link between the IPU and The Hague was firmly ensconced in the public sphere as well.[132]

The IPU remodelled its constitution after the first Hague conference. Its primary ambition from this point on was to advance the cause of arbitration by means of improving the PCA, working towards bilateral arbitration treaties between governments and educating the public regarding the content of the Hague conventions.[133] Its members raised these issues in parliamentary debates, by publishing pamphlets and books and by taking full advantage of newspaper coverage of their annual meetings. These meetings aimed at wide public exposure: they were held in prominent places and often overlapped with significant events. The St Louis meeting in 1904, for example, coincided with the St Louis World Fair, which brought more than nineteen million people to Missouri, and came in the same year as the Olympic Games were held in the city.[134] The IPU's meeting in 1900 concurred with the Paris Exposition. At that event, the membership resolved not only to advance the 'peace through law' agenda but also to promote the pacific quality of neutrality.[135] The meeting at Brussels in 1901 further sought to extend the Hague regulations to all warfare, including in instances involving states that had not signed up (or, in the case of South Africa, could not sign up) to the conventions.[136] By 1913, when the IPU's meeting was held in The Hague in conjunction with the inauguration of the Peace Palace, its list of priorities included: extending the Hague conventions to cover neutral canals; cooperating with other internationalist organizations to advance common goals; pushing governments for greater clarity on the agenda for the third Hague peace conference; and asking for effective sanctions to be established to punish states that breached the Hague conventions.[137] By this time, the IPU had numerous study committees in place to improve arbitration, the international law of war, the condition of neutrality and the permanent organization of the Hague conferences.[138]

Perhaps the most telling association between the IPU and the public appeal of The Hague as a concept that underwrote international stability came at the 1903 IPU convention held in Vienna. The official publication of the event opened with an overview of IPU achievements in relationship to arbitration, the Hague conventions and the PCA. It noted that 'public opinion increasingly supports arbitration' and that its own membership was growing (to 2,022 parliamentarians).[139] The publication went on to detail the speeches given and resolutions passed during the event, including from the Italian ambassador in Vienna who congratulated the IPU for 'germinating the seed of The Hague, which is starting to bear fruit'.[140] Vienna's outspoken populist mayor Karl Luegger welcomed attendees to Vienna, 'a city of peace' (*eine Stadt des Friedens*), while numerous delegates promoted improvements to the PCA and the Hague conventions more generally.[141] In the press, the 1903 conference received considerable coverage, including from the *Manchester Guardian* who acclaimed the event for fostering international friendships and advancing the cause of peace.[142] Many American newspapers were not only struck by the number of IPU delegates in attendance (600), the IPU's resolutions to expand arbitration treaties to all countries, but also by the agreement that the next IPU conference would be held on American soil for the first time, in St Louis.[143] The *Wiener Zeitung* for its part offered a blow-by-blow account of the conference's proceedings, taking up several pages of its early September issues.[144] Meanwhile, the *Interessante Blatt* offered photographs and anecdotes to lighten its readers' understanding of the IPU event.[145]

The ICW was another prominent pro-Hague society with exceptional transnational connections. In 1899, it organized a sizeable public movement in favour of the Tsar's rescript and the advance of the principle of international arbitration at the Hague conference.[146] As its president, Ishbel Aberdeen, explained at the ICW meeting held in London in June that year (which coincided with the Hague conference): 'all are unanimous in their opinion that this [arbitration] is a question which we may regard as having passed the controversial stage, and which the International Council should place in the foremost place on its programme'.[147] At the end of the conference, the ICW took on board the ideals of The Hague and integrated them fully into its organization. It established a separate executive committee to deal with the subject of 'Arbitration and Peace'.[148] From this point on, activism for The Hague sat alongside other key platforms, which included fostering transnational cooperation among women and promoting family health and positive education models. In 1899, the ICW included six million members from eleven different countries (including India, Persia, Argentina, Palestine, Japan and China).[149] By 1914, it counted twenty-six national affiliations.[150]

The ICW's quinquennial meetings gathered key representatives together and set priorities for the organization's future. The Hague featured prominently. For example, when the Hungarian representative Amelia Neumann explained to the 1904 quinquennial that the organization needed to make the press 'serve our purposes', she did so with an eye to developing an international petitioning movement to promote the cause of arbitration and influence the agenda of the next Hague peace conference.[151] At a 1908 meeting, the ICW's 'Peace and Arbitration' executive offered up four resolutions for approbation by the membership: the first to urge the third Hague peace conference to pass a 'general arbitration treaty'; the second to have all schools around the world celebrate the '18 May peace day' (see below); the third to push governments to advance disarmament; and the fourth to plan a massive public meeting on the subject of The Hague at the next quinquennial.[152] A year later, at the Toronto quinquennial, the ICW's leadership reiterated the organization's duty to The Hague: 'we consider it our business, by conferences, public meetings, essays, papers, resolutions, and by every other means we know of, to circulate a just, truthful and intelligent account of what has been accomplished by the first and second Hague Conferences'.[153]

The most impressive signal of the public power of women's agency for internationalist subjects surely was the ICW congress held in Berlin in June 1904.[154] While some in the ICW executive had reservations about holding an event in Germany, a country whose government made no secret of its disdain of arbitration and the peace movement in general, the event itself was a resounding success from the ICW's perspective.[155] According to *Die Friedens-Warte*, the Beethovensalle was packed to the rafters, the public spilled out into the streets surrounding the building, so much so that the Berlin police had trouble keeping order.[156] Lady Aberdeen later reminisced that she was overwhelmed by the thousands of German women in attendance.[157] May Wright Sewall recalled of the event that '[n]ever have I at any other Peace meeting [met with] such sympathy, such eagerness, such longing, as were expressed by that audience. Conspicuously feminine, it seemed an audience of the wives, daughters, and sweethearts of the [German] Empire's soldiery'.[158] Meanwhile, the speakers at the event, including Bertha von Suttner and Ishbel Aberdeen, received resounding cheers and applause. The meeting far extended its intended closing time of 11 p.m.[159]

In the English-language press, the Berlin quinquennial was roundly praised. New Zealand's ICW representative, Wilhemine Sheriff Bain, sent lengthy accounts which were published verbatim in a number of New Zealand papers.[160] The *New York Times* enthused that its American representatives received 'much attention and marked social favor' in a lengthy report.[161] The *Chicago Daily Tribune* and *Washington Post* both sent special correspondents and were equally effusive, the latter headlining with 'Women's New Victory. Peaceful Invasion and Conquest of Germany'.[162] The *Aberdeen Free Press* published an extensive account of the event, which was subsequently republished in pamphlet form.[163] The German press gave the event due recognition, including a leading article in the *Berliner Tageblatt*.[164] Meanwhile, the German ICW branch responsible for the event published an explosive seventy-two-page pamphlet that explained the importance of the peace crusade and the practical application of the Hague's conventions for German women.[165]

One of the ICW's platforms was the '18 May' movement.[166] The concept of an '18 May peace day' idea began with Selenka's initiative on 15 May 1899, which saw women's organizations around the world attending public meetings to approve and promote the upcoming Hague conference. In 1900, Selenka organized a remembrance celebration on 18 May, coinciding with the opening of the Hague conference the previous year.[167] According to Selenka, women should celebrate The Hague and work collectively towards advancing its cause: the first Hague conference had dawned 'a new era of right in human history'.[168] She proposed that they continue celebrating The Hague annually.[169] Her inspiration evolved into an enduring movement, which assigned the 18 May date as an international day of peace, during which pro-Hague and pro-peace activities were conducted.

The 18 May movement had extraordinary global uptake, especially among women's organizations, although they did not uniformly welcome the event at the outset. At the ICW's 1902 executive meeting, for example, the representatives from Argentina, Denmark, Germany, Sweden, Switzerland and Tasmania expressed their reservations.[170] Still, after 1903, the 18 May movement was firmly entrenched in the

ICW's international campaign schedule. But well beyond the ICW, 18 May became a significant date of global peace activism. The *Neue Hamburger Zeitung*, for example, noted in 1901 that 18 May was celebrated in The Hague, Kristiania, London and 'auch hier in Hamburg' (also here in Hamburg).[171] In the United States, the 18 May tradition really took off and was promoted by peace associations, women's groups and education commissions alike.[172] In 1907, the National Education Convention advocated for all American schools to take time to celebrate 18 May.[173] It did so after the International Congress of Public School Teachers promoted the idea to its constituents from across the Western world. By this stage, 15,000 French primary school teachers taught 'war against war' as part of their curriculum.[174] To sustain the 18 May curriculum in the United States, the American School Peace League was established in 1908. It also ran essay competitions for students about The Hague and published children's books explaining the importance of The Hague.[175] By this time, *Vogue* magazine acknowledged 18 May as 'Hague Day' and remarked how it was celebrated around the United States.[176] Lucia Ames Mead rather optimistically prophesized that 'one day the world will celebrate May 18 as we Americans celebrate July 4'.[177]

Across the British empire, the 18 May celebrations also thrived.[178] In the Netherlands, many groups promoted the 18 May movement, so much so that by 1907, it had become the most important peace celebration in the country, often attended by local officials and visiting dignitaries.[179] Even the Dutch minister of foreign affairs suggested to his internal affairs counterpart that since so many other countries were considering making 18 May an official day of commemoration, should the Netherlands not follow suit? Count Apponyi (who in 1907 was the Hungarian minister of education) was certainly making a staunch case for the importance of 18 May for his constituents.[180] The celebration of 18 May also extended to Japan: in 1907, the *Japan Times* reported on the enthusiastic uptake of residents in Tokyo, Kobe, Osaka and Kyoto.[181] Even the Bureau of Masonic Relations urged Freemason societies around the world to adopt 18 May as a gala day to commemorate the first Hague conference and in so doing 'associate universal Masonry with the work of peace and of arbitration'.[182]

In May 1914, the ICW's quinquennial meeting passed twenty-two resolutions to advance the 18 May concept and the general promotion of peace education. These included: programmes to limit war play at home; the revision of school history curricula; appeals to the 'press and pulpit' to establish a 'world festival' on 18 May; initiatives to push all schools to celebrate '18 May peace day'; an agenda to create a 'truer' conception of patriotism that aimed at non-violence; the circulation of encouraging editorials on all these subjects in mainstream newspapers; the aim to design and circulate peace calendars and postcards and to work on signing pro-Hague and pro-peace petitions; and a desire to establish peace essay prizes, to promote peace societies for youth and to establish peace libraries. Above all, the ICW resolved to advance the agenda of the third Hague peace conference with a particular focus on the topics of the immunity of private property at sea, the illegality of dropping bombs from airships, the need for an international judicial arbitration board and to advance disarmament.[183] There is no question that the ICW considered it had the platform to advance these ideas.

Most importantly, the ICW did not operate in a vacuum. It advocated so loudly and proudly for The Hague because its membership fervently believed that the Hague conferences offered a worthwhile and realistic forum to create meaningful change. They considered the successes of the first and second Hague conferences in real terms and considered them valid political programmes to underwrite their activism as women and as citizens of the world.

Significantly, The Hague also inspired organizations with only the faintest of connections to its internationalist platforms. Because of the perceived success of the Hague conferences and the general appeal of The Hague as a legitimate source for international cooperation, The Hague offered an excellent model for other transnational causes to emulate. To that end, The Hague was invoked by all manner of organizations to justify and promote their particular objectives. As an example, consider the fact that the First Universal Races Congress held in 1911 in London came out of meetings on the subject held in The Hague in 1907 while the peace conference sat.[184] The Zionists also organized their 1907 Congress in The Hague to coincide with the peace conference. Both initiatives made the association in part to attain additional press attention, which they received: a *Washington Post* article on 15 August 1907, for example, noted that the Hague conference could not achieve lasting peace without first obtaining justice for persecuted races.[185] It is entirely unsurprising then that the city of The Hague itself became recognized as a site of internationalist activism. When other conferences were held there, the connection to the peace conferences and to the wider meanings attached to The Hague in international relations was unavoidable.

The sheer volume of activism relating to The Hague's causes and the fact that much of it found its way into the daily press, particularly in the English-speaking world, speaks to the complex political environment of the time. The Hague certainly permeated mainstream reporting on all manner of issues: from the conduct of wars to the value of disarmament, to the possibility of establishing an international court of justice. These media representations suggest that contemporaries had access to a variety of sources to assess questions of international importance, the waging of war foremost among them. As a result, it is difficult to argue that thinking about peace was a marginal activity in the pre-1914 world. The fact that the main organ of the London Peace Society, the *Herald of Peace*, boasted mentions in more than 100 local and foreign newspapers in 1901 speaks to the ubiquity of the London Peace Society's wider activism.[186] Across the Atlantic, the American Association for International Conciliation noted in a June 1913 report that it had circulated 3,367,445 documents that year and that its membership now included individuals in Europe and the Asia Pacific, including the director of the Vatican Observatory, the secretary of the Chinese National Railway Corporation and a number of Australian high commissioners.[187] Both the American Association and the *Herald of Peace* were less-well-known examples of organizations that promoted The Hague. But much like their more prominent affiliations, the IPU, the ICW and the *Institut de droit international*, they all promoted The Hague as their *modus operandi* and their *modus vivendi*. They all flooded the public arena with information about The Hague.

It is therefore also significant that many of the newspapers used as sources for this book, from the *New York Times* to the *Vossische Zeitung*, from the *Japan Times* to the *Telegraaf*, from the *Manchester Guardian* to the *Australasian*, from the *Sumatra Post* to the *Hawera & Normanby Star*, repeatedly and loudly advocated in favour of the 'peace through law' cause. The *New York Times* even reported on the opening Peace Palace in The Hague in 1913 in terms of the building's potential as a powerful symbol for international peace making.[188] The Japanese newspaper *Yorodzu*, in turn, editorialized in April 1907 that it was the duty of its readers to interest themselves in the events developing at the second Hague conference. World events – in Morocco, with regards to Sino-French relations, the turmoil in South East Europe, Japan's struggle with China, and the relationship between Russia and the United States – all indicated to *Yorodzu*'s editors how important the global situation was to the lives of Japanese citizens. It advocated that 'more familiarity with foreign events and more liberal discussion of them is the only corrective'. Focusing on The Hague offered a good start.[189]

Of course, these internationalist readings of The Hague were not the only or necessarily the dominant way in which newspapers represented or interacted with the topic of warfare and international crisis. There is plenty of evidence to suggest that themes of patriotic nationalism and militarism abounded in the Anglo-European and American press of the time. The ever-critical editor of the *Sumatra Post* even admonished his colleagues in Britain and France on this point in 1906, when he assessed the Algeciras conference as a dangerous outcome of emotion-laden diplomacy filtered through an excitable press. Newspaper editors in Britain and France were to blame for trumping up the cause of war: if you make the suggestion, he furthered, the possibility of war becomes a reality. It did not help that, in his estimation, the year 1906 also witnessed a heightened interest in war fiction, especially in Germany where recent populist titles included: *Der deutsch englische Krieg, Vision eines Seefahrers* (The German-English war, visions of a seafarer), *Hamburg und Bremen in Gefahr!* (Hamburg and Bremen in danger!), Bise's *Kleine Garnison* (Small garrison) and Major a. D. Karl v. Bruchhausen's *Der kommende Krieg. Eine Studie über die militärische Lage Deutschlands* (The coming war. A study of the military position of Germany).[190] The point surely is that in the early twentieth century, internationalist readings of war and peace coexisted with militant and patriotic readings of war and peace. Even the 1910 German publication *Die Welt in hundert Jahren* (The world in 100 years) included a terrible vision of warfare involving motorized vehicles on land, sea and in the air alongside a chapter by Bertha von Suttner on the creation of a peace-loving cooperative world.[191] The pronounced contradiction between a vision of war and a vision of war's absence in this book was as stark as the discourses about the promise and reality of war and peace in their authors' present.

Yet despite the contradictions, which are more apparent than real, there is no question that after 1899 The Hague featured prominently in the international press as a concept that had widespread internationalist application. Indeed, it would have been surprising if people who were concerned about war and its legitimate use would not have been interested in the rightful choice of peace. Just how normalized this understanding of The Hague was can also be seen in the ways the media covered the annual Nobel Peace Prize award. Established in 1901 by Alfred Nobel, the inventor of dynamite, the Nobel Prize for Peace was awarded each year by the Norwegian Storting.[192] From the outset the announcement of the prize was a noted event, covered by most news publications.[193] The editor of New Zealand's *Hawke's Bay Herald*, for example, acknowledged in 1901 that 'the man who can qualify for a Nobel prize will have attained success'.[194] Another New Zealand paper noted in 1911 (the year the Dutch international lawyer and delegate of both Hague conferences, T.M.C. Asser, and pacifist and Hague promoter, Alfred Fried, shared the award) that '[t]he Nobel prize awards afford an opportunity of comparing the fertility of the nations in producing great men, and that fertility may be taken as a measure of the standard of civilisation reached by them'.[195]

As prominent peace campaigners, most Nobel Peace Prize winners before 1914 were either directly or indirectly connected to the Hague conferences. Many of them also referenced The Hague in their acceptance speeches.[196] When Baroness von Suttner received the award in 1906, some newspapers even credited her with inspiring Tsar Nicholas II's rescript.[197] The *Chicago Daily Tribune* ran a double-paged spread on her award with the headline 'Book That Inspired the Hague Peace Tribunal and Won the $40,000 Nobel Peace Prize'. The ensuing article called *Lay Down Your Arms* 'not a book, but an event' before précising its contents.[198] When Theodore Roosevelt received the prize for his work on bringing the Russo-Japanese War to a successful conclusion and having initiated the first case for the PCA, it was the Hague connection that he promoted most diligently.[199] In 1907, the French lawyer Louis Renault received the Nobel award for his work on international law and involvement in both Hague conferences.[200] He gave his acceptance speech on 18 May (the date was no coincidence) and entitled it 'The Work of The Hague in 1899 and 1907'.[201] Auguste Beernaert and Baron d'Estournelles shared the Nobel Prize in 1909 for similar reasons, while Elihu Root's award in 1912 included mention of his prominent work in the PCA.[202] At least before 1914, the Nobel Peace Prize and The Hague were largely synonymous terms in public understanding.

Well before the second Hague conference inaugurated in 1907, the phrase 'The Hague' had achieved widespread public significance and application. The Hague offered a lens through which to draw meaning out of global events and it contextualized contemporary debates and offered promise for those seeking pragmatic change in the international environment. It also influenced the public diplomacy of governments. It was with the public appeal of The Hague in mind that Theodore Roosevelt sent out his invitation in 1904 to hold another peace conference.

As the next chapter shows, the internationalist appeal of The Hague only grew as that event drew closer. This time, however, the governments in attendance were more alert to the public environment in which the peace conference took place. Their delegations came prepared not only to barter for the primary interests of their states but also to make the most of the media attention afforded to them by participating in the conference. In 1907, the *Realpolitik* of conference diplomacy clashed with the public idealism surrounding The Hague. Many came away from The Hague in 1907 despondent that more was not achieved. Yet even the second Hague conference, which was more globalized and sophisticated than its 1899 predecessor, made considerable headway on some key internationalist agendas. And those achievements spurred hope. As Joseph Choate, the US delegate at the 1907 conference, explained in his 1913 history on the topic:

The work of Peace is going on well, the conscience of the world is thoroughly aroused and determined [by The Hague], and perhaps thousands now living will see the day when war, as a means of settling international disputes, will be as generally condemned as the duel and slavery and the slave trade are to-day. Perhaps this also is another dream! But who can tell?[203]

7

When the World Showed Up: The Second Hague Conference, 1907

The world is becoming one in an altogether new sense . . . As the earth has narrowed through the new forces science has placed at our disposal . . . the movements of politics, of economics, and of thought, each of its regions, become more closely interwoven . . . Whatever happens in any part of the globe has now a significance for every other part. World History is tending to become One History.

– James Bryce, 1913[1]

Scanning the headlines of a singular French newspaper in 1907, a reader might be struck by the high degree of sensationalism presented. *Le Matin*, a popular Parisian daily with a circulation of 670,000, prided itself on reporting the latest news with flashy headlines and plenty of photographs.[2] If you read *Le Matin* in 1907, you were titillated by scandal, amazed by new discoveries, moralized about social inequity and kept abreast of the latest political news at a national and international level. A case study of its Thursday editions, for example, reveals a gaudy array of articles ranging from the tragic murders of children and jilted lovers to the orientalist attractions of the Peking-to-Paris automobile race. But it also regularly featured articles on the immigration status of Japanese subjects in the United States, the political tensions in Russia's Duma (which led to its dissolution by the Tsar in June), the actions of Britain's suffragettes, the nationalist uprisings in Bengal, concerns about the treatment of the people of the Congo and the development of a new cancer theory in Germany. Of greatest interest to *Le Matin*'s editors, however, was France's invasion of Morocco, which occurred in late July. The Casablanca campaign dominated the newspaper's pages, overriding all other news, including that relating to the second Hague peace conference, which met from 15 June to 18 October.

On the other side of the Atlantic Ocean, the *Washington Post*'s daily news did not differ in essentials from that of *Le Matin*. As the Capitol's most popular paper, the *Post* also thrived on sensationalized accounts.[3] Thus on Thursday 4 January 1907, its front-page headed with 'Dumb, Her Babe Dead', then teased out a story about a husband who came home to find his wife, unable to speak, carrying their murdered child in her arms. Other front-page articles that day included one about an actress in Paris mobbed at the Moulin Rouge and a lavish reception at the White House.[4] The paper's international coverage highlighted the German government's announcement that it would build a battleship larger than the *HMS Dreadnought*, Japan's willingness to send labourers to Hawai'i, Polish independence ambitions and the death of St Petersburg's Prefect.[5] Albeit less free with its illustrations as *Le Matin*, the *Washington Post* nevertheless offered its readers a similar range of tantalizing, informative and globally aware reports.[6] It also generously covered the second Hague conference.

In 1907, The Hague was omnipresent in the newspaper record. *Le Matin*, for example, regularly addressed the conference: it featured as headed page-3 news in seven Thursday editions before the conference opened. During the conference, and with the exception of the weeks in August and early September when the Casablanca offensive waged, it appeared as a headline in nine Thursday editions. Altogether, *Le Matin* made 244 references to 'La Haye' in 1907. Even at the height of the Casablanca campaign (in August), it referenced the conference repeatedly, albeit less prominently.[7] For *Le Matin*'s readers there was no escaping The Hague, even if they only skimmed the headlines. Nor could readers of the *Washington Post* avoid the topic. Throughout 1907, the *Post* made 611 mentions of 'The Hague', most of these in relation to the peace conference.

Similar numbers were repeated around the world. New Zealand's digitized newspaper database, for example, offers 4,738 results for 'The Hague' across 73 publications in 1907.[8] Australia's database of 240 titles references 7,858 articles on The Hague that same year, of which the Brisbane *Telegraph* was the most prolific (with 310 reports).[9] The London *Times* made 487 mentions of 'The Hague conference',[10] while the *Japan Times* did so on 537 occasions.[11] The Austrian newspaper index registers 298 results for 'Haag' in the *Wiener Zeitung*, closely followed by 243 in the Linzer *Tages-Post*, the *Neues Wiener Tageblatt* (234) and the *Neue Freie Presse* (212).[12] In Germany, the *Berliner Börsenzeitung* referred to 'Haag' 589 times that year with the *Berliner Tageblatt* offering 340 mentions, while the Dutch *Algemeen Handelsblad* referenced 'Den Haag' in combination with 'conferentie' on no less than 1,101 occasions.[13] Of course, the numbers tell us little more than that The Hague was considered newsworthy. Only by unpicking how these newspapers reported on The Hague is it obvious that in 1907, The Hague featured as an event worthy of editorial enquiry.

The existing historiography stresses how newspapers helped to augment national and military rivalries in Europe in the period before the outbreak of the First World War. From the Algeciras crisis of 1906 on, great power rivalry increased and popular fears of war were fuelled in the media.[14] William Mulligan also ascribes a shift in the public diplomacy of Europe's governments between the resolution of the Algeciras situation and the annexation of Bosnia-Herzegovina by Austria-Hungary in 1908.[15] He does so by drawing out the ways in which these governments mobilized the language of international law and teased out the concept of international obligation in their public statements, including in their advocacy for national interests. Mulligan makes an essential point: international norms mattered to contemporaries as much as national priorities and that, in many ways, national and international priorities were often aligned. The media's attention to the second Hague conference – which occurred between the Algeciras and Bosnia-Herzegovina crises – attests that they certainly read enough about such norms in the daily press.

That the second Hague conference occurred at this time of heightened great power tension is often left out of the origins of war narrative, however. Diplomatic historians tend to dismiss the 1907 conference like its 1899 predecessor as less than relevant to gauging European *Realpolitik* on the eve of the First World War. They often do so with an anachronistic bias: gauging the relevance of the conference in terms of what contemporaries could not have known was coming. In dismissing the 1907 conference, they also fail to register that a vociferous and public critique of 'old world' diplomacy, the arms race and secret diplomacy already existed on the eve of war, which was intimately bound to The Hague. For the public watching and reading about the 1907 conference in their newspapers it was obvious that The Hague mattered to shaping the dynamics of international relations. All forty-four governments that went to The Hague in 1907 understood that the conference could have a fundamental impact on their future. They would not have been there or expended as much energy as they did without that realization. In 1907, The Hague was a key site of international politics and a subject of in-depth editorial enquiry, which can tell us much about contemporary international values and politics.

In the eight years that passed between the two Hague conferences, the dynamics of international diplomacy had also changed, albeit subtly. In 1907, the European great powers no longer solved international crises by looking only to themselves. The concert of Europe's sway over diplomatic events was eroding, albeit ever so slowly.[16] Since 1899, the United States had grown as a great power: marked by its victory in the Spanish-American War, its acquisition of a Pacific empire, its exponential economic growth and Roosevelt's mediation of the Russo-Japanese War.[17] Japan also registered as a key diplomatic force. As victor of the Russo-Japanese War, it was busily expanding its own empire in the Asia-Pacific region.[18] With the growing prominence of these two non-European powers, the influence of other non-European states also gained purchase. The Latin American states, part of a formal Pan-American community, were of particular importance and China, too, remained significant. For the governments of these non-European states, the 1907 conference offered an opportunity to be recognized as having influence on the global stage. That forty-four governments sent their representatives to The Hague in 1907 ensured that the second Hague conference played out on a grander international stage than its predecessor.[19]

Given the stage, it is not surprising that media coverage of the second Hague conference reflected on a multitude of ideas and political priorities. What a newspaper reader was to make of The Hague's deliberations in 1907 was rarely straightforward, even if they read only one media source. For example, in the days leading up to the opening of the conference, *Le Matin* editorialized rather ambitiously that the conference would not spell the end of war but that the achievement of general peace may not be far off.[20] At conference end, the paper headlined optimistically that the 'Conference at The Hague Achieves Its Work', then highlighted the disappointment felt by many that more was not achieved for peace two days later.[21] A month on, the paper represented the conference in a different light again, relaying both Louis Renault and French Foreign Minister Stéphen Pichon's opinions that the conference tendered a moral victory for France and the world, by which they meant that the conference had advanced the 'peace through law' agenda.[22] *Le Matin* did not have a decided editorial opinion on The Hague in 1907, although it faithfully reported on conference developments, considered the importance of key conventions, applauded the internationalism of the Hague endeavour and praised the French delegation's role in the event.

The *Washington Post* also presented its readers with multiple lenses to assess the importance of the second Hague conference. On several occasions, its content offered conflicting representations. Thus on 30 August, it both described the 'Hague triumph' as 'ours' (as in, the United States') and headed an editorial with 'Humbug at The Hague'.[23] Three weeks later, it headlined with the Hague 'fiasco' on its front page, while several pages on it noted the conference as marking 'an epoch in history', again in a header.[24] At conference end, it described the conference once more as a 'humbug' and sensationalized its phenomenal cost in a bolded banner: 'Fiasco at The Hague . . . Expense Close to $3,000,000 of This Amount $526,600 Was Spent to Pay for 317 Dinners to Delegates'.[25] That same day, however, it also reported on Secretary of State Elihu Root's opinion that the conference achieved more than expected, a sentiment reinforced by the delegate Joseph Choate, who proclaimed that any one of the conventions agreed upon at The Hague justified the event (and, by implication, its expense).[26] By 29 December, the *Post* hailed the 'uplift year' of 1907 and isolated the Hague conference as a 'real advance for peace'.[27] It highlighted both John W. Foster's opinion that the conference was history's 'greatest event', which made the Magna Carta seem puny, and Root's representation of The Hague as 'foundational'.[28] Across 1907, the paper attached no singular narrative to The Hague, although its editors consistently presented the US government as a paragon of Hague idealism: as proud advocates of international law, arbitration, neutrality and peace. By implication, the *Post* upheld those same values as markers of positive change in the international arena.

The key point to make here is that on the one hand, *Le Matin* and the *Washington Post* presented the second Hague conference as a fraught diplomatic exercise pitting the sovereign interests of nations and great powers against each other, yet on the other, the conference also offered hopeful promise for the future of international organization. Both newspapers recognized that the Hague conference was a complex event with a massive agenda on which the achievement of universal consensus was next to impossible and acknowledged that the processes initiated at The Hague had value.

The obvious tensions that existed between government interest and international good were a repetitive theme in editorials and satire focused on The Hague in 1907. The *Auckland Star*, for example, recognized the complications when on 11 September 1907 it republished a cartoon from the *Spokane Spokesman Review* (Washington) entitled 'setting herself a hard task', which represented the conference as a peace dove sitting on a nest of unwieldy cannonballs (Figure 7.1).[29] The *Amsterdammer* journal repeatedly turned to the same subject in its weekly cartoons (Figures 7.2 and 7.3),[30] as did a cartoon entitled 'High jinks at The Hague' published in Melbourne's *Punch*, which portrayed the delegates at The Hague as drunk sailors boasting of their future endeavours and pitting the naval ambitions of Britain and Germany, Japan and the United States against each other. The sailors' sarcastic ditty finished with the line: 'Round let us bound, for 'tis Peace's holiday – Never we fight again – Hip, hip, hooray!'[31]

Of course, the idea that The Hague mattered needed no explanation to newspaper readers in 1907: they had encountered The Hague repeatedly since 1899. To that end,

Figure 7.1 This cartoon, republished from the *Spokane Spokesman Review* in the *Auckland Star* in September 1907, suggests that the delegates at the second Hague conference had a hard task bringing all their agenda items to fruition. It represented The Hague as a peace dove, unable to hatch her batch of cannonball eggs (*Auckland Star* 11 September 1907, 6).

Figure 7.2 This cartoon, originally published in the *Lustige Blätter*, appeared in the *Amsterdammer* weekly journal on 21 June 1907. It depicted the wives of the German, Russian, American, British, Japanese and French delegates at the conference dressed in national costume. Each woman's jewellery betrayed her country's real interests at The Hague: the protection of its armaments and military prowess (*Amsterdammer* 21 June 1907, 11).

Figure 7.3 Entitled 'In the international studio', this 1907 Johan Braakensiek cartoon depicted the powers at the second Hague conference, each painting the angel of peace in their own likeness and carrying their weapon of choice. The cartoon was published within and outside the Netherlands (*De Amsterdammer* 14 April 1907, IISG BG D23/630).

the media commentary around the second Hague conference was indicative of a wide range of political ideas in play that sometimes juxtaposed national with international interests, at others aimed at integrating them and sometimes promoted one without any reference to the other. The Hague was as much a subject of news reporting and editorial commentary as it remained a lens through which to ask questions of the world, its wars and the relationship between states. It certainly existed as a powerful internationalist idea, which appealed to many audiences.

Consider, for example, the political context in which the US President Theodore Roosevelt called for the second Hague conference in October 1904: he did so after the Inter-Parliamentary Union's (IPU) meeting in St Louis recommended that course of action to him.[32] Given that it was an election year, Roosevelt saw ample opportunity in promoting a popular internationalist cause, which played well with American voters and heightened his own international exposure.[33] As the Dutch Minister in Washington D.C. explained at the time: Roosevelt's invitation seized the imagination of the American press, 'as if the [Russo-Japanese] war in the far east could brought to a standstill through one word from the president'.[34] Roosevelt had nothing to lose by sending out the invitation, which he grounded in the need to improve the international law of neutrality (the Russo-Japanese War was wreaking havoc with world trade), the importance of negotiating the inviolability of private property at sea (a long-standing policy of the United States) and the desirability of regulating the naval bombardment of coastal towns (the Japanese bombing of Port Arthur rankled).[35] That Roosevelt's invitation appeared in the press on the same day as news of the Doggerbank incident broke was a coincidence, but it heightened the consequence of his call to The Hague.

The Russian naval attack on the neutral British fishing fleet was a particularly telling context in which to read Roosevelt's plea that '[t]he neutral is something more than an onlooker. His acts of omission or commission may have an influence – indirect, but tangible – on a war actually in progress; whilst on the other he may suffer from the exigencies of the belligerents. It is this phase of warfare which deeply concerns the world at large'.[36]

Beyond the opportunity to regulate the laws of neutrality, the long-term significance of holding another Hague conference was not lost on commentators either. As the New York journal, the *American*, editorialized: Roosevelt's invitation was even more important than the Tsar's original rescript as 'its purpose is to take up the work where The Hague of 1899 abandoned it and push it to its completion'.[37] The real importance of the 1907 event was, of course, that it institutionalized the Hague conferences. By dint of Roosevelt's request, The Hague now existed as a recurrent feature of international relations, rather than as a singular extraordinary event. This fact emboldened internationalists.[38] If the Hague machinery was regularized, then the 'peace through law' cause held genuine promise. Progress could be slow and measured, but the Hague conferences would ensure it occurred.

Nevertheless, the White House abandoned its Hague endeavour in December 1904, citing Roosevelt's role as one of initiative, not process. At this point, it suggested that the PCA's International Bureau might take up the responsibility of coordinating a second Hague conference without ongoing American involvement in the preparations.[39] The complications of organizing an international conference, which both annoyed the Russians and surprised the Dutch (neither government had been consulted in advance), effectively overwhelmed the Americans.[40]

That Tsar Nicholas II took up the Hague venture in September 1905, then, should also be read as an astute political move.[41] In the wake of Russia's disastrous loss in the Russo-Japanese War and amid the revolutionary struggles plaguing the tsarist regime, Nicholas II's renewed support for The Hague clearly aimed at resuscitating Russia's reputation as a civilized state attuned to international law and order.[42] And for some the connection was convincing: Bertha von Suttner reminded her readers in 1909 that while the Tsar was roundly criticized for his terrorism and oppression, he was also the Tsar of the peace conferences.[43] Others were less impressed (Figure 7.4).[44]

Much of what occurred in relation to the planning and course of the second Hague conference played out in the press and received critical attention.[45] At times, the issues involved caused serious diplomatic tensions. For example, when it came to the issue of arms limitation, the British and German governments would not agree. The Germans refused to allow the subject onto the conference agenda and did so mostly to avoid being cast as The Hague's villains, as they had in 1899. At the first conference, their representatives had rather bluntly argued that Germany's military strength protected its security and that therefore Germany need not discuss disarmament, a stand for which they were roundly critiqued. For its part, in 1906, the Liberal government in Britain had electioneered on the promise of disarmament and felt compelled to force The Hague's agenda in disarmament's favour. It even proclaimed that if The Hague allowed, the Royal Navy would reduce its *Dreadnought*-building programme.[46]

Figure 7.4 This powerful illustration by the Austrian artist Bertha Czegka juxtaposed the popular conception of Tsar Nicholas II as the 'Tsar of peace' and the Tsar responsible for a sea of violence: the Russo-Japanese War, the repression of uprisings and revolutions and the suppression of the *Duma* ('Der Friedenszar', c. 1914 [1907?], Mitchell Wolfson Jr. Collection, The Wolfsonian, 86.5.116).

By March 1907 when the Anglo-German disarmament controversy reached its zenith, the European arms race was in full swing.[47] The public debate was heated on both sides of the Channel,[48] and only heightened when the British Prime Minister Henry Campbell-Bannerman published an editorial in the newly established Radical newspaper, the *Nation*, in which he argued for the limitation of arms and a general acceptance of the principles of The Hague:

> Ever since the first Hague Conference was held, the points of disagreement between the Powers have become not more, but less acute; . . . the sentiment in favour of peace, so far as can be judged, has become incomparably stronger and more constant; and the idea of arbitration and the peaceful adjustment of international disputes has attained a practical potency and moral potency undreamt of in 1898.[49]

The public discussion that evolved in reaction to the editorial showed up the double-edged sword of The Hague's competing messages: while the Hague conventions had the potential to threaten the sovereign rights of states, the Hague conferences also promised the possibility for improving essential international laws, the practice of arbitration and the functions of international organization. The Hague inspired stability and peace. That the value of The Hague lay in the balancing act between state sovereignty and collective action was all too evident from these exchanges. Even W.T. Stead, who was a steadfast supporter of The Hague's internationalist mission, promoted the building of *Dreadnoughts*.[50] Roosevelt too founded his vision of the United States' global future on the dual platforms of naval strength and internationalist idealism.

It is not surprising then, that the governments who attended the 1907 Hague conference looked to the opportunism presented by the event to advance key interests and exhibit themselves in a favourable light. This time, the Germans were particularly well schooled in managing their Hague policies in public. Germany's Chancellor von Bülow, for example, defused the disarmament question when he gave an eloquent and measured speech in the *Reichstag* on 1 May 1907, commending the British government for its convictions. He explained that Germany too had 'pacific intentions' but did not consider it fair to commit to The Hague an agenda item that would not produce any practical result. Still, he promised that Germany would 'not make difficulties' or 'impede the work of the Conference'.[51] The speech was beautifully timed and spoke to the essence of The Hague's internationalism and public appeal.[52] It signalled above all that the German government was not going to be caught unprepared (as they had in 1899) to deal with the political complications of the conference agenda. In fact, the German Foreign Ministry prepared a thorough and thoughtful portfolio of policy priorities for their delegation, including an international prize court and the protection of the rights of neutral citizens residing in belligerent countries. It hoped to signal Germany's full cooperation with the spirit and practice of the Hague diplomacy and the advance of the Hague conventions.

The forty-four delegations that arrived in The Hague in June 1907 were carefully chosen by their governments.[53] They were prepared to work hard, albeit within the prescribed bounds of their government's instructions. Most of the participating governments expended an enormous amount of energy developing them.[54] Other than agreeing on the terms of the agenda, however, the delegations failed to effectively coordinate their policies before the conference met. The failure was mostly one of imagination rather than opportunity: the repeated delays in scheduling (the conference was initially planned for 1906)[55] would have made creating agreements entirely possible.[56] But the agenda was also massive. Released in April 1906, it covered four broad topics: the improvement of arbitration, commissions of enquiry and the PCA; the laws of war and neutrality on land; the laws of war and neutrality at sea (including private property); and the adaptation of the 1906 Geneva conventions to maritime warfare.[57] As Sir Edward Grey explained to Campbell-Bannerman: we cannot coordinate with the other states as 'we must first make up our own minds on these points'.[58] Many of them had dogged international relations for centuries.

Even after the Russian government sent Fyodor Martens on a tour of Europe in January 1907, the purpose of the highly publicized trip seemed to be more about avoiding a public relations disaster (particularly over the issue of disarmament) than affecting genuine multilateral agreement on the agenda.[59] Ultimately, the lack of pre-conference coordination precluded achievement on key issues, compulsory arbitration and the establishment of an international court of justice among them. All up, the conference was destined to become a drawn-out affair.

What struck contemporaries particularly about the 1907 conference, however, was its global reach. Almost every recognized nation-state participated. Never before had so many governments come together in one place to discuss a common agenda. With the advantage of hindsight, it is obvious that the second Hague conference signalled the advent of a new era of international diplomacy, expanding the reach of multilateral negotiations and collective security politics across the globe (rather than sustaining them within the Congress of Europe). At the time, commentators registered the key importance of expanding the voice and rights of small states (as opposed to those of the traditional European great powers) and noted that the new participants had to formally adhere to the 1899 Hague conventions before they could attend the 1907 conference. Widening the application of the Hague conventions to cover much of the world was, in itself, a revolutionary development.[60] It universalized the Hague laws and gave teeth to internationalists' claims that The Hague set the standard of 'civilization' for all to follow.

It is really not surprising then that many commentators focused on the progressive and global promise of The Hague. In a study of the 1899 conference published in 1907, the German legalist E. von Ullmann described the second Hague conference as an essential development guiding and steering international norms and reaffirming the power of collective action. According to Ullmann, The Hague helped to establish homogeneous cultural understandings and expectations.[61] The idea of a homogeneous global culture was, of course, not restricted to discourses about The Hague. The application of the idea in the Anglo-European world was amply illustrated by the address made by Britain's Ambassador to the United States James Bryce, at the 1913 International Congress of Historical Studies, in which he explained that the history of the world had become 'One history': where any event or development in one part of the world affected those of all the others.[62] Roosevelt invoked a similar theme in a speech given at the University of Berlin in 1910:

> This world movement of civilization, this movement which is now throbbing in every corner of the globe, should bind the nations of the world together . . . Under modern conditions the books we read, the news sent by telegraph to our newspapers, the strangers we meet, half of the things we hear and do each day, all tend to bring us into touch with other peoples. Each people can do justice to itself only if it does justice to others.[63]

Such assertions radiated with an arrogant confidence that the Anglo-European conception of 'civilization' would determine everyone's future.[64] The Hague was both a product of and motor for these ideas.[65]

The lengthy delay between the original call for a second conference (October 1904) and June 1907, when it opened, also ensured that The Hague remained in the newspaper spotlight. Often, media commentaries about current events, be it the Russo-Japanese War, the Algeciras crisis or the resolution of the PCA's arbitration decisions, were weaved together with reflections and analyses about the possibilities of the next Hague conference improving international affairs. For example, in June 1905, at the time the Japanese and Russians agreed to allow President Roosevelt to mediate their conflict, the *Japan Times* published a full-page article written by Theodore S. Woolsey, professor of law at Yale, which argued for a wide-ranging agenda at The Hague.[66] More whimsically in January 1907, the *Illustrated London News* reprinted a large photograph of an airship (the 'monster dirigible' *La Patrie*) under the headline 'Bombs from Balloons to Be Discouraged by the Next Hague Conference'.[67] Meanwhile, the *Cologne Gazette* mused on 3 April 1907 that the upcoming conference 'will give the Delegates of the Powers a great deal of work to do, and yet it cannot be said that there are any superfluous questions to be dealt with, as all those mentioned are of an eminently practical nature. Many of them refer to matters which caused difficulties . . . during the Russo-Japanese War'.[68]

The delay also ensured that internationalists, peace activists and other interested parties had ample time to mobilize public support. Much like in 1899, there was an extraordinary amount of public agitation in favour of the 1907 conference.[69] A considerable amount of it received press attention. W.T. Stead again occupied a prime place in these accounts, especially when he embarked on another peace pilgrimage in Europe and the United States in early 1907.[70] Stead resided in The Hague during the conference and published a daily newspaper, the *Courrier de la Conférence de la Paix*, reporting conference developments, profiling prominent delegates and advancing his own internationalist agenda.[71]

Ever since Andrew Carnegie had endowed The Hague's peace palace, his name too featured prominently in media reports on Hague matters. His participation in the National Arbitration and Peace Congress held in New York in May 1907 attracted a physical audience of thousands and a global newspaper audience of many thousands more.[72] Its resolutions were subsequently published in French and English for widespread circulation, including among the Hague delegations.[73] According to Warren Kuehl, the organizing committee of the New York Congress compiled a scrapbook of 32,977 newspaper clippings, weighing 250 pounds, all discussing the event.[74] How detailed some of these reports were is clear from coverage in *Current Literature* magazine, which included a fabulous cartoon depicting the angel of peace waylaid from arriving at the New York congress by a sea of cabs, noisy pedestrians, tunnel explosions and murders. Its caption read: 'this is the most unpeaceful place in the world to invite me'.[75] The journal also included a large photograph of the peace congress's speakers arrayed on a stage festooned with American flags and supported by a full orchestra.[76] The magazine's account finished with a five-page exposé on the building plans for the peace palace in The Hague, for which it richly commended Carnegie.[77]

As had happened in 1899, in 1907, many delegations at The Hague received an array of documents, petitions and letters from the wider public. The conference secretariat was inundated with such appeals.[78] It employed twenty-five secretaries to read through and reply to the flood of paper.[79] Recognition of the breadth of the public engagement was made at the plenary session of 20 June by the head of the correspondence commission, Willem de Beaufort. He explained how 'these telegrams, letters, petitions, books, pamphlets, etc., of which there are rather a large number, are naturally all inspired by the same principles': they sent their expressions of encouragement, professed their support for arbitration and looked to the delegates to accomplish a higher mission. Some also offered practical advice of how to achieve that mission.[80] Beaufort made particular mention of the 2 million signatures attached to a petition from the International Council of Women; the resolutions sent by 27,134 students and staff from twenty-three American colleges and universities[81]; the communications of church groups in Germany, Austria-Hungary, France, the Netherlands, Switzerland, Great Britain and the United States; and a manifestation signed by 15,000 Swedish citizens. He also enumerated the internationalist organizations that had formally petitioned The Hague and the great number of pamphlets, religious texts, poems, postcards, newspaper clippings, political treatises and books received, which were housed in the conference library for delegates to consult. That room came to be known as the 'curiosities chamber' (*curiositeiten-kamer*).[82]

At the final plenary session held in October, de Beaufort further recounted the best wishes from peace organizations in Japan and the petitions received in person and by mail from the International Red Cross Association, the International Peace and Arbitration Association in London, the American Humane Society, the Inter-Parliamentary Union, the inhabitants of Salem (Ohio) and the *Alianza Intelectual* society of Madrid (among many others). He reminded his audience that the only reply that could be sent to the many requests received from aggrieved individuals and maligned political causes was that the aim of the conference, as President Nelidov explained, was 'to study and establish the principles of international law, not to control its application to the international policy and the internal affairs of the various States'.[83] The Hague was not a catch-all event, although the hopes and fears of many seemed to ride on it being exactly that.

The 1907 Hague conference in fact attracted a range of political activists who bore little, if any, relationship to the content of the formal discussions. They looked to take advantage of the international attention focused on The Hague. The Zionists and the Subject Races Committee, for example, aligned their meetings to coincide with the conference.[84] Domela Nieuwenhuis organized a rally of 3,000 anarchist supporters to protest the conference's uselessness, an event reported on as far afield as the *Richmond River Express and Casino Kyogle Advertiser* in the Australian territory of New South Wales.[85] In August, an international conference of anarchists also met in nearby Amsterdam. The Dutch police utilized local and international resources to monitor the activities of these 'suspicious' and potentially dangerous individuals who might upset The Hague's proceedings.[86] That Karl Liebknecht's anti-militarist treatise *Militarismus und Antimilitarismus unter besonderer Berücklichtigung der internationalen Jugendbewegung* [Militarism and anti-militarism with a special focus on the international youth movement] appeared in 1907 was also no coincidence. Liebknecht drew his inspiration from the themes of peace, neutrality and war mongering discussed at The Hague.[87] But he was not alone. Several petitions were sent to The Hague in 1907 requesting that the powers gathered there organize an

International Opium Commission (in the end, an anti-Opium conference would be held in 1912 in The Hague and another in 1913).[88]

Aside from a bevy of peace activists, who congregated in The Hague in 1907 to affect conference negotiations, the most prominent activists at The Hague were those advocating for national and local grievances. Many of these groups, and some individuals, expected that the Hague conference would voice its united support for their cause and stand up for the rights of persecuted minorities and refugees. The conference organizers received such appeals from groups in India, Alsace-Lorraine, the Russian empire, the Balkans, Ireland, Latin America, Africa, the Mediterranean and the Middle East.[89] Some of the appellants came to The Hague to present their grievance in person. Of these, a Korean deputation maximized public attention when it appeared in the city touting their credentials as representatives of the Korean Emperor Kojong. The four Koreans were well schooled in Western protocols, international law and media management. They sought accreditation to the conference and, if that was refused, an audience with the delegations. Their ultimate aim was to achieve recognition of Korea's independence and the neutralization of the Korean peninsula.[90] They stayed at a prominent Hague hotel and proudly displayed the Korean flag in their window.[91]

The Korean situation required careful diplomatic handling. The Dutch government only met the Koreans in secret and the whole affair presented a public relations nightmare for the Japanese.[92] Japan's delegation argued that since Japan had annexed Korea, only the Japanese government could speak for Korea's interests. Inevitably, Korea was denied entry to the conference proper. But given that dozens of journalists were in The Hague, much was made of the Korean diversion.[93] Many nuanced and sensitive editorials appeared that carefully evaluated Korea's situation.[94] When one of Korea's representatives, the 22-year-old Yi Chun, died in his Hague hotel room in July, the media intrigue reached a crescendo.[95]

In response, the *Japan Times* offered a decisive editorial stand, namely, that all the powers in The Hague acknowledged Japan's protectorate over Korea, that the Korean emperor was playing games (the *Hochi* called the visit a 'mischievous intrigue') and that Japan should take a firm hand in dealing with the situation.[96] For his part, W.T. Stead invited the Koreans to speak at the headquarters of the *Fondation International*, which had set up its offices on the Prinsengracht as a space for delegates and internationalists to socialize.[97] The speech offered an informal forum for the Koreans to approach the delegations without offending the Japanese government. Stead offered up several pages of his conference newspaper to the Korean cause as well.[98] In the end, the Korean deputation failed to achieve any of its ambitious goals and only sped-up Japan's occupation of their country: including the forced abdication of Emperor Kojong on 18 July.[99]

Still, the Korean visit highlights how keenly aware the delegations were of the press attention given to the conference. Compared to 1899, the conference secretariat was much better prepared to deal with the press. It formally accredited journalists and issued tickets to the plenary sessions.[100] While the discussions held in the conference's four commissions occurred behind closed doors, the secretariat presented a bulletin of developments to journalists each day. As Nelidov explained: these accommodations were 'contrary to the precedent of 1899 as well as to the universally established usage for diplomatic assemblies' but the global interest in the conference recommended this course of action. He also asked delegates to keep secret those deliberations that were not public: 'We make no mystery of them . . . but we must guard against the false comments which communication to the public of disjointed items of news would undoubtedly involve. It is therefore essential that the full publicity of our labors be deferred until they shall be concluded. Until then discretion is the indispensable rule.'[101] Yet much like in 1899, journalists managed to obtain detailed information about the content of the daily negotiations, so much so that some of the delegates complained about their colleagues' lack of discretion.[102] On 20 July, Nelidov felt compelled to remind the delegations that they had pledged to keep confidence and to prevent conference documents from circulating in public.[103] It made little difference: the British delegation reported on 22 July that 'up to now – practically everything has been made public'.[104]

Nelidov's demand underscored the disconnect that existed between the range of public expectations attached to the Hague conference and the diplomatic realities within which the delegates at The Hague worked. That many of the great powers at The Hague had only limited ambitions for revising the Hague conventions is well illustrated by Nelidov's opening address, in which he cautioned:

> [L]et us not be too ambitious, gentlemen. Let us not forget that our means of action are limited . . . Above all, gentlemen, let us not forget that there is a whole series of cases, where honor, dignity, and essential interests are involved, where individuals are concerned as well as where nations are concerned, and in which neither, whatever may be the consequence, will recognize any other authority than that of their own judgment and personal feelings.[105]

Unlike his predecessor, Baron de Staal, who asked the delegations in 1899 to achieve something worthy in the name of peace and arbitration, Nelidov urged for internationalist ambition to be checked and for state sovereignty to dominate decision-making. Nelidov's hope for the conference was to improve the international institutions already in existence (in other words, the PCA) and to do whatever 'within the modest limit of our means' to lighten the 'burdens of war', for which humanity would be grateful.[106] The *Washington Post* reflected on Nelidov's speech with a figurative front-page headline: 'Bomb Jars Peace'.[107]

Regardless of Nelidov's intentions or the limited ambitions of any of the other governments at The Hague, the public power of The Hague's internationalist ideals nevertheless permeated the 1907 negotiations. They did so in part because everyone at The Hague was highly alert to the power of the press.[108] As the German delegate General Erich von Gündell noted in his diary: 'we must maintain good relations with the press'.[109] According to Heinrich Lammasch, at least, the Germans were largely successful in that mission.[110] The delegates that leaked documents, gave off-the-record interviews and made off-the-cuff remarks to journalists thus helped to keep the public informed of conference developments and allowed for an editorial commentary to appear around the event that privileged internationalism.

The 1907 conference also offered an extraordinary moment for the government of the Netherlands to present itself in a favourable light. Given the intense global interest in the proceedings at The Hague, the hosting responsibilities for the Netherlands were extensive. Not only did the city of The Hague have to find the means to accommodate the delegations and their staff, dozens of representatives of non-governmental organizations, journalists and gawking tourists, it also had to prove capable of feeding and entertaining them for months on end.[111] The House in the Woods proved too small to accommodate these numbers. Instead, the conference met in the medieval *Binnenhof* (inner court) of the Netherlands's parliamentary complex.[112]

The Dutch Foreign Ministry also looked to avoid public embarrassment. It even instructed delegates to wear 'gentlemen's attire' (*gekleede jas*) to the conference opening, barring military uniforms.[113] As the *South China Morning Post* editorialized: the Dutch government did not want a repeat of the levels of satire that accompanied the 1899 conference, which suggested it was a conference of war not peace. The editorial further commended 'these Dutch Carlyles' for 'preaching the gospel of clothes, and saying in effect, to the rest of the material universe – "strip off your feathers, and remember that you are men met to do men's work". That is exactly the right note and harmony may be thereby induced. Uniforms erect greater barriers between nations than any official frontier line'.[114]

Of course, the 1907 conference received due satirical attention. Dutch cartoonists were particularly adept at finding cause to laugh at The Hague. In a full-page drawing by Johan Braakensiek, for example, the angel of peace entered the *Ridderzaal* (Knights' Hall) where the peace conference was meeting. On confronting the delegates outfitted as soldiers, she asked 'am I in the right place'?[115] By conference end, Braakensiek drew the angel of peace mournfully hanging up her wings.[116] Louis Raemaekers was even more scathing. One of his cartoons portrayed two conference delegates – one with a black eye, another nursing a bloodied nose – splayed on the doorsteps of the *Binnenhof*. Its title read 'thrown-out diplomats'. In the caption, the first delegate exclaimed 'I proposed a limitation of armaments, but what did you suggest?' The second stammered his response: 'compulsory arbitration'.[117] Another Raemaeker cartoon with the title 'After 19 Centuries' pictured Jesus Christ denied entry to the conference because he was not dressed in military attire.[118]

Even the delegates themselves were not immune to the comedic value of the negotiations. The Argentine delegate Luis María Drago, for example, quipped that obligatory arbitration and the permanent court of justice suffered from the obligatory dinners and permanent servings of salmon.[119] T.M.C. Asser wrote to his family that one of his colleagues had sent two postcards home: one depicting four youthful Dutch women in traditional costumes, smiling, and another depicting three elderly Dutch women, also dressed in traditional garb but looking dour. He had invented his own captions for the pictures: 'the delegates before the conference' on the first card; 'the delegates after the conference (one has died!)' on the second.[120]

The Dutch certainly entertained their visitors. Queen Wilhelmina hosted a gala event at the opening of the conference and invited the delegations for a day-trip to Amsterdam, concluding with a banquet at her palace.[121] The minister of foreign affairs hosted a series of dinners, as did numerous delegates, prominent politicians and other public figures.[122] The Hague municipal authorities held a ball.[123] On 25 July, the government treated the delegations to a boating excursion along the Nieuwe Waterweg canal to the city of Rotterdam, replete with local exhibitions, children's choirs and folk dancing.[124] These activities aimed to promote The Hague and its environs as well as the Netherlands more generally as an attractive destination for tourists.[125] The Belgians too looked to capitalize on the proximity of the conference: the medieval town of Bruges invited the delegations and their families to visit on 29 July.[126] Within The Hague, local businesses made the most of the influx of foreigners.[127] The Norddeutscher Lloyd even set up a salon at the Twee Steden Hotel, equipped with newspapers, reading chairs, telegraph and telephone services, a currency exchange, ticket office and a pool of typists.[128] Not to be outdone, the North American Shipping Company hosted a 'festival for the press' on 24 July.[129]

The delegates attempted to maximize the opportunity presented by the conference to curry positive attention in the press as well. One of the more cooperative of these ventures came in the form of an embossed album collated to honour the Swedish King Oscar II, who had mediated a peaceful split between Sweden and Norway.[130] Other governments initiated important bilateral agreements while at The Hague, publicizing them in the plenary sessions. These included the signing of an arbitration treaty between Italy and Argentina in September and the Anglo-Russian *Entente* agreement on 31 August.[131]

The Latin American delegations were the most pronounced in their media liaison. Most of them came to The Hague determined to have their voices registered as influential.[132] As a result, they often presented long (and, in Ernest Satow's words, 'tedious') speeches.[133] The Brazilian representative Rui Barbosa was particularly adept at grand standing. He subsequently published a compendium of all his speeches and decisions, explaining their import.[134] Barbosa carved a lengthy political career out of his Hague experiences and remains, to this day, one of Brazil's most famous politicians.[135] But he was not alone: Columbia's delegates, Jorge Holguin and Marceliano Vargas, also published several pamphlets of conference addresses and Hague accounts, as did Cuba's Antonio S. de Bustamente y Sirven, whose compositions included a long yet erudite 780-page conference review.[136] The Argentinians were equally proud of Luis Drago.[137] Significantly, these men all received a considerable amount of global media attention in 1907. One of Rui Barbossa's biographers, for example, lists newspaper clippings from 239 newspapers on his Hague activities.[138]

For most delegates, however, the overriding impression of the conference was of fatigue. Sir Edward Fry described it as 'a weary business'.[139] Asser called it 'exhausting' (*afmattend*);[140] Lord Reay as 'arduous';[141] and Willem de Beaufort as 'annoying'.[142] Germany's Baron Marschal von Bieberstein explained that 'never since my examination for the bar have I worked as hard'.[143] The months of meetings, marred by lengthy speeches and the involvement of so many delegates, and the diplomacy of balancing small state with great power interests overwhelmed progress on many agenda items, as did the extensive list of bureaucratic formalities and array of compulsory social events.[144] Fyodor Martens spared no feeling when he described these impediments as a 'sorry fiasco'.[145]

But work they did.[146] The conference's tasks were divided into four commissions. Léon Bourgeois chaired the First Commission, which was responsible for revising the regulations relating to arbitration, mediation, commissions of enquiry and maritime prizes. Auguste Beernaert took charge of the Second Commission, which looked at the laws of warfare on land, the 1899 declarations, the rights and duties of neutrals on land and the opening of hostilities. Count Tornielli presided over the Third Commission, which negotiated the rules relating to the bombardment of towns and ports, the laying of sea mines, belligerent rights to access neutral ports and the extension of the 1906 Geneva Conventions to maritime warfare. Fyodor Martens chaired the Fourth Commission that had the unenviable task of negotiating the conversion of merchant vessels into warships on the open seas, private property at sea, the laws of neutrality at sea, blockade, contraband, neutral prizes and extending the provisions of land warfare to maritime warfare.

The conference's multiple volumes of proceedings speak to the incredible depth and range of discussions held by these commissions between 15 June and 18 October.[147] They dealt with some of the most complicated and controversial issues that had plagued international relations across the ages. In many respects, the mere fact that the world's governments willingly met to discuss these matters was one of The Hague's greatest achievements. It set a precedent for future multilateral forums and effectively signalled that no international question was too difficult for a conference setting. Still, the enduring impression of the conference was that many of the items on the agenda were too contentious to be resolved. The other enduring impression was that the conference made remarkable progress on them all.

The First Commission's primary achievement was the creation of an International Prize Court (IPC), the world's first appellate court to which neutral merchants unhappy with the prize-taking decisions of a belligerent power could take their complaints. The initiative behind the IPC lay with Germany and was broadly supported by Britain.[148] That almost all the governments at The Hague endorsed the court signalled, according to the French delegate Louis Renault, the 'beneficent influence' of the Hague environment: 'How many years of diplomatic negotiations would have been necessary to arrive at an agreement upon so difficult a subject when starting from positions so opposed! The Conference has changed years into weeks.'[149] The fifty-seven articles of the IPC regulations were substantive.[150] For the IPC to be able to function, however, it would need a uniform body of maritime law. Achieving conformity on that front, a task assigned to the Fourth Commission, was far more difficult.

The First Commission also undertook lengthy deliberations on the subject of arbitration, including improvements to the Permanent Court of Arbitration, the possibility of imposing compulsory arbitration mechanisms for differences where neither national honour nor a state's independence were at stake and the utility of establishing a Permanent Court of Arbitral Justice (PCAJ). The discussions about the PCA alone took up 116 pages of the commission's report.[151] As that report all too diplomatically noted, during the 'brilliant debates', the subject of arbitration 'was examined with care, studied with sincerely progressive and friendly mind, and gave rise to deep and thoughtful discussion'.[152] They certainly lasted for days on end. At the heart of the negotiations lay not only the issue of whether states could be compelled to arbitrate but also whether any universal obligation could be imposed upon them at all.[153] In the end, compulsory arbitration went nowhere. Nor was the PCAJ instituted. Where the commission met greater success was in adopting a revised version of the

Drago doctrine (named after Luis Drago, who had originally proposed it), which ruled that states could not use military force to recoup contract debts from other governments. These cases would be sent to the PCA.[154] The subject was of immense importance in Latin America, where the use of gunboat diplomacy had resulted in numerous international crises, the most significant of which involved a combined German-British-Italian blockade of Venezuela in 1902–1903.[155]

The Second Commission discussed the law of warfare on land. Some of its provisions, including those relating to the bombardment of undefended towns and the opening of hostilities, were passed with unanimity, albeit after extensive discussions.[156] Others were much more controversial. While the regulation of the law of neutrality on land was adopted 'without remark' at the plenary session,[157] many of the neutrality issues discussed during the commission's meetings failed to achieve consensus. Of these, the German government's proposal that neutral citizens residing in belligerent countries should receive preferential treatment was particularly complicated.[158] After weeks of discussion, the proposed regulations on the subject were jettisoned. As the Dutch military delegate Colonel Borel then reminded the other delegates: 'To admit that the Conference of 1907 is not able to regulate everything relating to neutrals is not to say that this important question should be considered as henceforth abandoned; it is rather to state that its subsequent solution, for the time being, should be sought and prepared in another way and by other means.'[159] To meet that brief, the conference adopted the *voeu* that civil and military authorities would do their utmost to protect peaceful relations between neutrals and belligerents and that individual states would seek bilateral agreements to make arrangements about their neutral citizens in case of war.[160]

The Second Commission also turned to the question of arms control, although the topic was not officially on the agenda. Fulfilling a pre-conference promise and all too conscious of the newspaper reports that would ensue, Britain's Sir Edward Fry announced that his government would now formally adhere to the 1899 dum-dum regulation.[161] He also reminded his audience that the Tsar called for the first Hague conference to discuss armaments, that the immense burden of military costs had not dissipated and that in 1906, it amounted to more than 320 million pounds. Fry proposed that this conference renew its support for the resolution included in the 1899 conventions that the limitation of arms remains a priority. The delegates from the United States, France and Spain chimed in their support, while Argentina and Chile announced they had just initiated a bilateral agreement to bring their naval arms race to a close.[162]

At this point, Nelidov explained why the question of disarmament was not on the agenda: he considered that the subject was 'not ripe for fruitful discussion' and that the Russian government had no wish to accentuate disagreement among the attending powers. He explained that the Russian delegation would not have taken part in such discussions and that he knew that many others would not either. Yet he also acknowledged that 'the seed sown at the time of the First Conference has germinated independently of the action of the Governments' and that the public today urged policies that governments were 'not in a position to satisfy'. Disarmament was one of them.[163] While the entire discussion lasted but a short time and was carefully stage-managed, the fact that it was held at all mattered well beyond Britain's face-saving measure.[164] It reaffirmed the precedent set by the 1899 conference that disarmament remained a legitimate topic of diplomatic negotiation, even if most governments were reluctant to acknowledge that reality.

Extending the 1906 Geneva Conventions to the war at sea was perhaps the simplest job of the conference, which fell to the Third Commission.[165] It took much longer for it to achieve any agreement on the question of the laying of sea mines, a highly complex subject that juxtaposed a belligerent's right of blockade and defence with a neutral's right to freely access the seas.[166] As happened in so many of the other commissions, the discussion on this subject also brought out the tensions that existed between humanitarian intent and national interest. Compare, for example, the exchange between Britain's delegate, Sir Ernest Satow, and Germany's representative, Baron Marschall von Bieberstein. Satow supported the regulation of sea mines in the most effusive terms:

> The high seas, gentlemen, form a great international highway. If the present state of international laws and customs, belligerents are permitted to fight out their quarrels upon the high seas, it is none the less incumbent upon them to do nothing which might, long after their departure from a particular place, render this highway dangerous for neutrals who are equally entitled to use it. We declare without hesitation that the right of the neutral to security of navigation on the high seas ought to come before the transitory right of the belligerent.[167]

Of course, Britain's blockading ambitions would be severely hampered if its enemy could protect its ports with floating mines. Britain stood most to gain from preventing the use of the new technology. In contrast, Germany would profit most from the mines. Thus, von Bieberstein invoked equally powerful humanitarian language to explain his government's position:

> No one will resort to this instrument of war [the mines] unless for military reasons of absolutely urgent character. But military acts are not solely governed by stipulations of international law. There are other factors: Conscience, good sense, and the sentiment of duty imposed by principles of humanity will be the surest guides for the conduct of sailors and will constitute the most effective guaranty [*sic*] against abuses. The officers of the German navy, I loudly proclaim it, will always fulfil in the strictest fashion the duties which emanate from the unwritten law of humanity and civilization.[168]

In the hands of these delegates, the language of 'civilization' had numerous applications and could underwrite ambitions for war and peace.[169]

The Fourth Commission had the most unenviable task: regulating the laws of maritime warfare. It took until 27 September for the commission to bring any recommendations to a plenary session. At that point, Nelidov reminded the delegations that the regulation of maritime relations between belligerents and neutrals was difficult, not least because there had never been universal agreement on the existing laws and agreements. Furthermore, it was nigh impossible to reconcile belligerent needs with neutral rights and to align the interests of the continental powers with those of the maritime nations.[170] He warned that the divergences were so great that he feared no agreement at all might ensue (which would also put the IPC in danger). But it was not for want of trying.

The Fourth Commission met thirty-two times and dealt with fifty-six proposals relating to a range of regulations, including: the conversion of merchant vessels into warships on the open seas (a major concern during the Russo-Japanese War, which threatened the reintroduction of privateering); the principle of 'free ships make free goods' (enemy property carried in neutral ships was exempt from capture); the exclusion of private property from capture at sea; the regulation of contraband (including Britain's radical suggestion that the concept of contraband should be abolished altogether); blockade; the destruction of neutral prizes (another legacy of the Russo-Japanese War); the laws of naval warfare; the protection of postal correspondence at sea (in the wake of Russia's capture of neutral postal ships during the 1904–1905 war); the capture of enemy merchant crews in neutral vessels; and the exemption from capture of enemy coastal fishing vessels.[171] In the end, it offered up laws to cover some of these subjects, but most remained unsolved.

To mitigate the inevitable disappointment that would be expressed in the press about the lack of unanimity on maritime issues, Nelidov reminded the plenary session how much had been achieved. They had made an all-important start.[172] The delegations then accepted a *voeu* that maritime law should be discussed at the next Hague conference.[173] In the end, Britain pre-empted those discussions by bringing the naval powers together in 1909 and designing a workable law of maritime warfare. That agreement – the Declaration of London – resolved most of the thorny questions that held up discussions at The Hague. The declaration also enabled the ratification of The Hague's IPC convention. It was a magnificent achievement. It was, then, rather ironic that the British House of Lords prevented ratification of the Declaration of London in 1911.[174]

Altogether, the 1907 Hague Conventions covered an exceptional array of laws and regulations, including: the Convention (I) for the Pacific Settlement of International Disputes; Convention (II) Respecting the Limitation of the Employment of Force for the Recovery of Contract Debts; Convention (III) Relative to the Opening of Hostilities; Convention (IV) Respecting the Laws and Customs of War on Land; Convention (V) Respecting the Rights and Duties of Neutral Powers and Persons in Case of War on Land; Convention (VI) Relative to the Status of Enemy Merchant Ships at the Outbreak of Hostilities; Convention (VII) Relating to the Conversion of Merchant Ships into War-Ships; Convention (VIII) Relative to the Laying of Automatic Submarine Contact Mines; Convention (IX) Concerning the Bombardment by Naval Forces in Time of War; Convention (X) for the Adaptation to Maritime Warfare of the Principles of the Geneva Convention; Convention (XI) Relative to Certain Restrictions with regard to the Exercise of the Right of Capture in Naval War; Convention (XII) Relative to the Creation of an International Prize Court; Convention (XIII) Concerning the Rights of Neutral Powers in Naval War. It also included the following *voeux* and declarations: Declaration (XIV) Prohibiting the Discharge of

Projectiles and Explosives from Balloons; a resolution relating to the 'limitation of military expenditure'; a recommendation to adopt a Court of Arbitral Justice; a wish for states to protect the commercial relationships between belligerents and neutrals in time of war; the desire to look after the military responsibilities of foreigners in belligerent countries; the desire to extend the laws of war on land to the laws of war at sea; and the desire to hold a third Hague conference.[175] This last *voeu* was particularly important. It foreshadowed the regular convocation of Hague conferences and put in place procedures so that those conferences could conduct their business 'with the necessary authority and expedition'.[176]

With the benefit of hindsight, it is difficult to understate the importance of these new Hague conventions. Legal historians today certainly invoke them as a 'point of origin' story and repeatedly tout what Randall Lesaffer calls Hague-iography in doing so.[177] The second Hague conference confirmed the importance of international law and legal discourse in twentieth-century international affairs. The era of 'peace through law' may not have arrived but the importance of law to international relations was confirmed by the 1907 Hague meeting.

Contemporaries were more nuanced in their responses to the conference. On the one hand, much of the media reception of the conventions and the lengthy deliberations that brought them into being was highly cynical and dismissive. The *Journal de St. Petersbourg* declared 'the conference is dead' in September.[178] *The Times* invoked a similar funerary theme to declare the Hague 'fiasco' a 'humiliation' and a 'sham' in October.[179] The *Natal Witness* opined in November that the conference was all 'gush and hypocrisy'.[180] The Radical journalist Henry Nevinson, who was in The Hague for the conference, was particularly derisive in his assessment that

> about 400 frock-coated, top-hatted gentlemen from various parts of the world . . . reared in the deadened circle of uniforms, decorations, and insincere courtesy, having no more knowledge of the people's desires than of the people's bacon, and instructed to maintain the cause of peace chiefly by safeguarding their country's military interests . . . [met in an] atmosphere of suspicion and secrecy . . . more dense than the fog of war.[181]

Other editorials dismissed the compromises made at The Hague as products of great power friction and wasteful procedures. The *Edinburgh Review*, for example, made much of the inability of the conference to make progress, describing the four months of negotiations as an 'unwieldy Hague machine' that failed to achieve 'effective compromise'.[182] Yet even this twenty-three-page review acknowledged that The Hague was now a permanent feature of the diplomatic arena and that as a result '"nationalism" and "internationalism" had every reason to join in an effort to rid the Hague institutions of its complexities and unrealities':

> A peace conference which is forbidden to discuss expenditure upon armaments . . . an assembly in which diplomacy and law confound each other, does not justify itself. It provides opportunities for political demonstrations, but to Powers which do not make use of those opportunities it brings little but

humiliations which are unrequited by any sense of lasting service done to the cause of peace.[183]

The key for the future, according to the *Review*, was to make the most of the Hague forum. Numerous German papers made a similar point: the *Berliner Tageblatt* lauded the conference as a diplomatic laboratory, the *Frankfurter Zeitung* recommended its practical work, while the *Vossische Zeitung* suggested the The Hague signalled the possibility of a future 'world parliament'.[184] The Hague machine, at any rate, was here to stay. That reality focused commentators on how it might be improved.

Paul S. Reinsch also offered an incisive perspective in the *American Political Science Review*, which explained that the second Hague was a diplomatic event that stymied legislation as delegates contended for tactical advantages, threw surprises and hampered their rivals' achievements for the sake of their own sovereign interests. As a result, the conference could not operate efficiently and only came up with a haphazard collection of new laws, all of which were significant but not cohesive. Yet Reinsch also noted how the conference 'added in many ways to our knowledge of the principles of international action'. While he admitted that the conference forum could not actually improve international relations, it could and did 'facilitate the creation of an international public opinion'. He reminded his readers that it was imperative that governments, leading politicians and public opinion should embrace the concept of international solidarity. The functioning of the international system of the future depended upon its success.[185]

Much like Reinsch, many internationalists were impressed by the institutionalization of the Hague conferences. That development ensured that the city of The Hague would continue as an important site for international diplomacy and confirmed its importance as a city of 'peace and law'. It also legitimized the 'peace through law' platform. The *Arbitrator* voiced its approbation by acclaiming that The Hague 'has come to stay. It has become a permanent institution. The Palace of Peace which Mr. Carnegie is building is not likely to want for tenants'.[186] After 1907, a third Hague conference was inevitable, as would a fourth, fifth and sixth one be (at least so everyone thought). The work of The Hague then, would be the work of generations, slowly but effectively building up the foundations of international order and regulation. For liberal internationalists, it was a hopeful development, promising the possibility of the federation of the world. After 1907, they mobilized their resources to maximize that promise.[187]

The German lawyer Walther Schücking expended an extraordinary amount of his energy on this ambition, publishing a book entitled *Das Werk vom Haag* in 1912.[188] Schücking's book was one of many published before the outbreak of the First World War, which explained the seminal importance of The Hague for improving international affairs.[189] Another, a lengthy article written by Raymond L. Bridgman, lauded the 1907 conference as a 'glorious success', 'so conspicuous that all its failures combined were merely an insignificant incident'.[190] The Hague continued to permeate media discussions around international events and crises after 1907 as well. Much of it was laudatory. Arthur Adler, for example, offered an overview of the Hague conventions in an accessible volume published in 1909. His foreword reminded readers of the importance of the Hague conventions for understanding the Balkan crises of that year (especially the annexation of Bosnia-Herzegovina by the Austro-Hungarian empire). His conclusion applauded the fact that future Hague conferences would be held, so that international relations would become more predictable.[191]

The global importance of the second Hague peace conference also continued to register in the press. Some of the more penetrating editorials even commented on how The Hague altered the effectiveness of the concert of Europe.[192] For old-style European diplomats, the rise of the 'new world' in The Hague only offered immense frustration.[193] They baulked at having to listen to and accept the validity of the concerns of the smaller states. They protested when these concerns upset their own negotiations and ambitions.[194] They also rejected many of the policy priorities advanced by the smaller states. Yet, the globality of the 1907 Hague meeting was a given.[195] For example, when Cuba's minister in Washington sent a copy of a new work he had written on the subject of arbitration to The Hague, Nelidov tabled it at a plenary session. He recommended that his colleagues pay 'attention to this interesting work . . . It testifies not only to the extended acceptance by the New World of this kind of solution for international disputes, but also to the lively interest taken in our work by its most eminent representatives'.[196]

Well before Paris 1919, then, The Hague offered an international forum for small states and non-European governments to voice their concerns and be heard.[197] Some commentators felt heartened by the shift.[198] Others less so.[199] An article written by Admiral Hoffmann in the *Vossische Zeitung* on the subject, which was subsequently republished in the *Manchester Guardian*, proclaimed:

> We living as we do in the heartland of Europe, can but with difficulty realise the point of view of the peoples beyond the sea. One must live for years away from Europe in order to understand how unimportant the balance of power – that is, the conflicts between the States of Europe – appear to the citizen of Sydney, Melbourne, Shanghai, and still more, to the inhabitants of some great American city . . . They understand but imperfectly when they are told that in the councils of the Great Powers of Europe, the fortunes even of the peoples living outside Europe are decided.[200]

Of course, the small states did not dominate the Hague negotiations, nor did they determine the conference's outcomes.[201] Until August 1914, at least, Europe continued to make the 'global weather'.[202] But the 1907 Hague conference did mark a subtle and important shift in the globalization of diplomacy and highlighted the potential ongoing tensions between national interests and the terms of the Hague conventions. In the British empire, for example, the shift was registered most clearly in the widening of self-governance offered to its Dominions, who in 1914 were offered a consultative voice in the British government's planning for the third Hague conference.[203]

The inherent tensions in the Hague agreements made the ratification process particularly fraught, however. This was best illustrated by the debate in Britain around the ratification of the 1909 Declaration of London. Fearing a loss of international prestige, the collapse of its naval power and with it the security of the British Isles and wider empire, conservatives in the House of Lords defeated the ratification bill in 1911.

The public debate on the issue juxtaposed the vital interests of Britain as a neutral and a belligerent. On one side, commentators like B.E. Monsell argued that the declaration risked England's 'life-blood'. If it was signed, 'streams of ships . . . disguised as peaceful merchantmen' would attack its mercantile trade, hampering the importation of food and resulting in 'starvation', which 'would probably mean . . . the end of our country and our Empire'.[204] On the other side, T.J. Lawrence argued that there was no need to be concerned about the impact of the declaration on wartime food supplies. In fact, the declaration protected Britain's merchant marine. He urged ratification as the most reasonable course of action and suggested that the declaration's critics enabled 'ignorance' to sit 'in judgment on knowledge': 'panic dictates to reason' every time.[205] The conservative interpretation prevailed in the House of Lords in 1911, but not without first arousing a fiery debate.

Britain's non-ratification of the Declaration of London had a number of decisive consequences. Most immediately, it complicated the country's diplomatic relationships with friends and rivals, all of whom had ratified.[206] It also prevented the establishment of the IPC, a court that would have been 'the first tribunal of a supra-national character' in existence.[207] In failing to set up the IPC, Britain denied neutrals a judicial means to protect their commercial rights in time of war.[208] The rights of belligerents won the day in Britain in 1911, where in 1907 at The Hague and in 1909 in London, those of neutrals had dominated.[209] That development had a direct bearing on the course of the First World War.[210]

From a 'peace through law' perspective, the British government's failure to ratify the Declaration of London should have been seen as highly distressing. At the time, however, most internationalists registered their disappointment but few felt disheartened. As James Brown Scott explained, even if the IPC failed, its regulation at The Hague nevertheless represented a key first step: the 'advantage of the first step is that you cannot retreat once you've taken it'.[211] At any rate, the third Hague conference would soon meet, offering the prospect of redress.

8

City of Peace: The Hague, 1907–15

Will coming generations make pilgrimages to thee?

– Baroness Bertha von Suttner, 7 July 1899[1]

The third Hague conference never met. The outbreak of the First World War in July 1914 prevented it from ever meeting. That war changed the fate of the world and with it altered the relative importance of The Hague to international politics. It did not, however, disassociate The Hague from the 'peace through law' agenda. The legacies of the Hague conferences lived on after 1918 in the international institutions situated in the city, in the longevity of the Hague laws, in the adoption of a multilateral conference model and in the development of international organization more generally. As most international lawyers today acknowledge, The Hague had multifarious legal and judicial applications after 1918 that continue to the present, not least in the International Court of Justice (ICJ) and International Criminal Court (ICC).[2] That the municipality of The Hague changed the city's motto to 'peace and justice' in 2012 speaks volumes about the ongoing public symbolism attached to these associations.

As this book has shown however, after 1899 and before the First World War, The Hague was a dynamic and multidimensional concept that stretched the boundaries of 'peace through law' in numerous global and normative directions. The institutionalization of the Hague conferences in 1907 only confirmed the importance of The Hague's multiple applications in international politics to contemporaries. In the period 1907–15, when a non-Dutch person spoke of The Hague, he or she could be referring to the rule of international law, the regulation of warfare, neutrality, arbitration and the working of the PCA or the concept of mediation. 'The Hague' also referenced international regulation, the institutionalization of global agencies in a world city, disarmament, 'peace through law' as well as the course and conduct of the two Hague conferences. If they were inclined to liberal internationalism or attracted to the idea of war avoidance, contemporaries might also have associated The Hague with a future in which warfare existed as an exceptional circumstance and the cooperation between states as the norm. Before July 1914, The Hague featured prominently as an international reality and as an internationalist ideal. It was also considered a promising platform for internationalization and as a subject and theme open to public discussion, criticism and debate. The outbreak of global war in 1914 only confirmed The Hague's importance as a lens through which contemporaries gauged the moral implications of war and state violence. It would take four years of total global war to alter The Hague's relative importance to their hopes and fears for the future.

Of course, The Hague was also an actual place: a city whose international importance shifted in the early twentieth century. Before the Tsar issued his rescript in 1898, The Hague was a quiet, unassuming town of well-to-do elites, odoriferous canals and a few diplomats. For most residents and visitors, the city's greatest attraction was its proximity to the seaside resort village of Scheveningen. After 1899, however, The Hague became a recognized site of diplomacy and internationalism. In the process, the city took on the symbolic power of the ideas and ideals that contemporaries attached to the phrase 'The Hague'. In institutionalizing the Hague conferences in 1907, The Hague as a 'city of peace' was also institutionalized. Coming generations did make pilgrimages 'to thee', as Bertha von Suttner mused they might in 1899.[3]

The opening of Andrew Carnegie's peace palace in 1913 offered a further manifestation of the permanence of The Hague as a symbolic presence in international life. Unsurprisingly, the associations also inspired a range of satirical commentary (Figure 8.1). Yet the importance of Andrew Carnegie's 1903 endowment of one and half million dollars to the Dutch government to build a 'palace of peace' cannot be overstated. Mark Mazower calls the gift the 'first significant influence of private philanthropic wealth on the emergent institutions of the new internationalism' and as

Figure 8.1 This *Puck* cartoon, published during the July crisis in 1914, highlights how integrated concepts of peace and The Hague were in American public understanding. It shows the angel of peace, 'Miss Peace of The Hague', blowing her horn while she hovers over the peace palace. Only war and discord come out the instrument, however. She laments: 'Ach! I blow it so sweet and it comes out so awful!' (*Puck* 75, 1950, 18 July 1914, centrefold, Library of Congress).

an 'act of faith in the future'.[4] Carnegie's vision was for a grand building to accommodate the Permanent Court of Arbitration, an international law library and any other Hague institutions that might be established in future. Carnegie aimed for the building to be palatial, a physical realization of the internationalist vision of a world working towards peaceful coexistence. Building the palace, however, was harder than he or anyone might have imagined.

The original idea for the peace palace came from a number of directions: W.T. Stead took credit, others attribute it to Baron d'Estournelles, Fyodor Martens, Frederick Holls and Andrew White.[5] For the Dutch government, Carnegie's offer came as a surprise. It took some doing before the cabinet would accept: it had to be sure the other powers were happy with Carnegie's proposal and that the country could support the longer-term costs and associated obligations.[6] At any rate, Carnegie never donated money unless he could guarantee a local commitment to the charitable enterprise.[7] His Hague palace required the donation of land and the establishment of a commission of oversight, authorized and recognized by the Dutch government, to run the day-to-day affairs of the building and its occupants.[8] In October 1903, the Carnegie Foundation (*Carnegie Stichting*) was established by government deed. Its regulations followed in May 1904.[9] Its first president was the Dutch politician and ex-minister of foreign affairs, Abraham Pieter Cornelis van Karnebeek. The Foundation still runs the peace palace today.[10]

From the outset, the peace palace project was mired in controversy – an 'embarrassing tale of pettiness' as the historian Arthur Eyffinger describes it – which came about in part because many Dutch politicians were not convinced of the long-terms gains for the Netherlands and worried about the extra costs it imposed on Dutch taxpayers.[11] Buy-in to Carnegie's plans was needed at a local, national and international level and took some time in coming. Critique and satirical commentary accompanied the ten-year building process not least because each stage of the project's realization bogged down: from where to erect the palace to who would design it and how it would be built. It took the second Hague conference of 1907 to turn some of that criticism around.

The question of where it would be built came down to a number of city sites: the public park of Malieveld, the Musschenberg dunes near Scheveningen and the royal woods at Zorgvliet among them.[12] In the end, the Zorgvliet site was approved amid an outpouring of local dismay.[13] At Carnegie's suggestion, the design for the palace was tendered to an international competition.[14] The move brought architects from around the world to The Hague.[15] But it also opened up the process to ridicule, which became especially strong when, out of 216 entries, the chosen design by the French architect Louis Marie Cordonnier failed to meet the competition's brief.[16] Cordonnier's palace was too big and too costly to build to specifications.[17] A barrage of protests followed, including from the well-known Dutch architect Hendrik Petrus Berlage, who lambasted the victorious design for ostentation and failing to keep to new developments in Dutch architecture.[18] Numerous editorials supported Berlage's claims, including one in the *Hamburger Nachrichten*, which called Cordonnier's design banal: a pompous building that did not represent the idea of peace.[19] Ultimately, to keep to budget, Cordonnier's ornate plans were sobered, but for many locals, even the toned-down building was an

Figure 8.2 French architect, Louis Cordonnier's prize-winning design for the peace palace in The Hague, 1906 (*Internationale prijsvraag der Carnegie-Stichting. Het vredespaleis te 's Gravenhage*. Amsterdam, Elsevier, 1906, np).

eyesore out of keeping with the sedate environment in which it gloried (Figures 8.2 and 8.3).[20]

These controversies nearly derailed the project.[21] The Dutch minister in Washington even met with Carnegie to offer his government's apologies for the delays, while cartoonists derided the lengthy enterprise.[22] In an attempt to counter the negative renderings, the Carnegie Foundation looked to make the most of the 1907 Hague conference. It planned an elaborate ceremony for the laying of the first stone on 30 July and enticed Andrew Carnegie to attend. Carnegie did come to The Hague in 1907, if reluctantly. He did not show up to the ceremony.[23] The Dutch Queen Wilhelmina was even more recalcitrant. She refused to participate in an event so distastefully soiled with intrigue, populism and outrage.[24]

Even without the queen or Carnegie attending, the organizers still pulled off a miracle. The press reported earnestly on the celebration. The erected tribunals were full, more than 1,000 people were reported to have witnessed the event.[25] The ceremony was solemn yet celebratory.[26] Even when tragedy struck the following morning when a grandstand collapsed, killing and injuring several workers, it did not mar the international attention given to the symbolic promise of the palace of peace.[27] In many respects, the stone-laying ceremony was a media highlight of the conference with similar significance as the United States' Grotius celebrations held in Delft on 4 July 1899: it reaffirmed the concept of global cooperation in the name of a

Figure 8.3 The peace palace in 1913 (F., *Een bezoek aan het vredespaleis.* The Hague, Luctor et Emergo, 1914, 2).

lofty international cause. Even Johan Braakensiek's satirical cartoon on the ceremony presented the event as a glorious success, requiring the angel of peace to explain that when she reascended to heaven, all she would leave behind on earth was the empty shell of the idea of peace.[28]

The importance of this press attention was recognized by all who had a stake in the success of the peace palace enterprise. In this context, a letter published by A. ten Bosch in March 1907 entitled 'The role of the Netherlands in the peace movement' presents a telling lens. In it, Ten Bosch argued that the only way to improve appreciation of the message of peace and international cooperation was to inspire journalists from different countries to learn from each other. The 1907 Hague conference offered an ideal opportunity to affect this kind of transnational discourse. To that end, it would be particularly useful for the Dutch to end their *kwade gedachten* (evil thoughts) about the peace palace.[29] The palace project heightened the international profile of the Netherlands and raised the value of The Hague's internationalist mission.

It was also with an eye to mobilizing the press in support of the palace venture that the Carnegie Foundation tried to effect buy-in from the delegates at the 1907 conference. D'Estournelles was particularly successful in making the case that each nation represented at the conference should contribute materials to the palace.[30] The advocacy worked. After 1907, the list of materials sourced from around the world to build and decorate the palace grew exponentially and included Norwegian granite, Belgian sandstone, Italian marble, French mosaics, American oak and Brazilian and Haitian hardwood.[31] German manufacturers crafted the palace's wrought-iron gates; Japan gifted tapestries; Russia, a priceless vase. Argentina presented a small-scale replica of its Christ of the Andes' statue, while Britain commissioned Douglas Strachan to fashion the stained-glass windows for the Hall of Justice. The Belgians carved the front door, the Danes gifted a fountain, while the Spanish and Australians donated inkwells.[32] Many of the gifts were reported on in the global press. Sometimes they evoked public debate, but most often they were lauded.[33] The palace's garden design competition, launched in 1908 and won by Thomas Mawson, was also generally praised.[34]

We should see the contributions made by the world's governments to the peace palace as a material realization of their acknowledged commitment to the Hague conferences. The peace palace stood as a symbolic manifestation of the Hague enterprise writ large and as a global and largely romantic initiative, which drew both praise and ire.[35] To that end, while Britain's secretary to the Office of Works considered the palace a 'monument of vulgarity', his government nevertheless accepted and promoted the symbolic importance of the palace and the need to be seen to endow it with a lavish and evocative gift.[36]

The palace's existence underwrote the equally powerful contemporary idea that The Hague had morphed into a city of peace, even a world city. Two Dutch entrepreneurs, Paul Horrix and P.H. Eijkman, brought this idea into fruition by committing time, energy and money to a realizing a 'world city' plan. From 1905 on, they conceived of The Hague as the heart of a global network of international institutions. They argued that if these institutions were to thrive they needed to be physically situated in the same place. Since The Hague was already the site of the Permanent Court of Arbitration, hosted the Hague conferences and would soon accommodate a peace palace, it presented an ideal space for global government to be realized. As the peace activist Richard Barthold described it, The Hague would become to the principle of international governance what the District of Columbia was to the United States.[37]

Horrix and Eijkman's plans were ambitious and wide ranging. The men set up the *Fondation International* (or, in the foundation's preferred language of Esperanto, the *Fondajo por Internacieco*) to promote their 'world city' concept as widely as possible.[38] The *Fondation* commissioned the architect A.K.P.C. de Bazel to redesign The Hague's municipal landscape, including coopting uninhabited land around the dunes of Scheveningen to form the hub of the world city.[39] A radial network of streets would emit from the peace palace (which they wished to have built there and not in Zorgvliet) to embrace a range of impressive buildings housing a number of institutions: from an International Tuberculosis Congress to an International Academy for Hygiene and a Royal Academy of Academic Research.[40] If Horrix and Eijkman had their way, The Hague would feature as the intellectual centre of the world as well as its judicial heart.[41]

Horrix and Eijkman's world city idea was influential. The press reported on it liberally, including during the 1907 Hague conference, when the men invited delegates and Dutch politicians to visit the proposed world city site.[42] But The Hague was not the only possible location for a world city. Internationalists in Belgium worked on an alternate base for world organization in Brussels. Geneva, Berne, Washington D.C. and Paris were also all mooted as better locations.[43] For Horrix and Eijkman, however, the international attention given to the 1907 conference offered an ideal forum to advance their Hague plans.

These plans were so influential that even Andrew Carnegie began asking questions whether the peace palace project should be integrated with Horrix and Eijkman's world city.[44] Berlage, furthermore, promoted the Horrix and Eijkman project in part to counter Cordonnier's palace but also to advance his role as the premier urban designer of the Netherlands.[45] W.T. Stead, too, was enamoured. During the 1907 conference, the *Fondation* rented space in The Hague, open to delegates and internationalists alike. It hosted Stead's weekly soirées and used its tea rooms to propagate a range of internationalist ideas.[46] The *Fondation* also published the *Review of Internationalism* magazine to draw even wider attention to the possibilities of world organization.[47]

In the end, the Carnegie Foundation made sure that the Dutch government did not consider an alternate to Cordonnier's palace built at Zorgvliet. For its part, the government kept a wary eye out on Horrix and Eijkman's world city idea, noting the moral prerogative asserted by the two founders and their 'fanciful' purpose to connect pedagogy with hygiene and economic reform in a global setting.[48] Yet the attention given to the enterprise within and outside the Netherlands spoke to a wider realization that the myriad international institutions that already existed could be streamlined better and that the creation of a space to focus on international organization might be helpful. The Hague offered an obvious focal point for these endeavours.

Significantly, the *Fondation* was not the only enterprise that aimed at capitalizing on The Hague's internationalist initiative. After 1899, other entrepreneurs also hoped to attract tourists and international visitors to the city. One such project was initiated by the *Internationale Vereeniging Vrede-Tentoonstelling* (International Association for a Peace Exhibition, IVVT), established in 1905 by a Dutch consortium of internationalists, politicians and entrepreneurs, which included A. ten Bosch.[49] The association proposed that The Hague host a colossal international fair to coincide with the opening of the peace palace. It looked to the example of the world fair held in Liège in 1905 – which attracted six million visitors – to show what might be achieved. It published an array of promotional pamphlets and sought subscriptions from all who could be persuaded.[50]

The IVVT presented a portfolio of carefully designed logistical plans to the Dutch Ministry of Agriculture, Industry and Trade in September 1907.[51] The plans included schemes for the purchase of vast tracts of land to host the many proposed exhibitions: from fields of flowers to working farms to ship-building factories, along with pavilions and entertainment spaces. The organizers also worked on improvements to transportation routes into and around the country. They envisaged a wide-ranging spectacle befitting a country situated at the centre of a global mission.[52] They expected that the world would want to come to the Netherlands in part because of the symbolic power of the peace palace to attract them.

The world fair idea received widespread public support and national press attention. The Dutch government also took notice. It invested in an ambitious range of public activities to mark the year 1913, which included many (but not all) of the IVVT's proposals.[53] Given the happy coincidence that 1913 was also the centennial of the country's independence from France, the nation had a double reason to celebrate. The government's 'Plan 1913' included a targeted campaign to entice foreigners to partake in the festivities. These were held around the country and included a large agricultural exhibition in Scheveningen.[54] The Hague hosted a 'Sport and Tourism' showcase and an art exhibition on the subject of peace curated by Jan ten Kate.[55] Amsterdam put on a 'Woman 1813–1913' expo, which attracted 300,000 visitors, along with a 'Home and Garden' fair.[56] The celebrations also covered more modest events, including civic parades, historical pageants, museum exhibitions, factory tours and sports competitions.[57] The crowning 1913 moment was the opening of the peace palace.[58]

The Dutch Ministry of Agriculture, Industry and Trade sent tens of thousands of posters, more than 205,000 brochures, 4 million bookmarks and 120,000 postcards to tourism operators, exchange bureaus, embassies, consulates and railway and shipping companies in Europe and the United States. All aimed at selling the Netherlands as an ideal destination for 1913.[59] It also forwarded brochures as inserts to foreign newspapers and commissioned dozens of illustrated articles on the subject, including six in the British *Graphic* magazine alone.[60] Hundreds of press reports appeared around the world about the country's 1913 festivities. Promoters also gave lantern slide lectures in Britain, Germany, Sweden and France.[61] According to all these depictions, the Netherlands was not only honouring its maturation as a monarchy in 1913, it also celebrated its international stature as a country of peace and internationalism. The city of The Hague was the nation's beating heart and the opening of the peace palace the main attraction (Figure 8.4, see also the poster on the cover of this book).[62] Above all, these messages seemed to confirm that the Dutch people wished to share their national achievements with the world.

The 1913 events certainly returned international attention to the Netherlands and The Hague. Hotels and transportation operators reported a bumper year.[63] The tram companies in Amsterdam, The Hague and Rotterdam accounted for an increase of 2 million passengers.[64] Nearly 50,000 people visited the peace palace in 1913, all paying an entry fee of 25 cents (in 1914 that number doubled to 100,000).[65] Still, the numbers were not overwhelming: Scheveningen's beach hotels noted increases of 200–400 guests in 1913 (as opposed to 1912) but none were full.[66] One hotel even complained it had 1,000 fewer lodgers and several restaurants in The Hague reported a downturn.[67] They determined that the reason was not due to the ineffectiveness of 'Plan 1913' to attract visitors but to the currency crisis in the United States, the Balkan Wars upsetting travel plans and persistently bad summer weather.[68]

Still, for the visitors that did come the associations between the Netherlands, The Hague and peace were solidified in 1913. Tourist publications and postcards certainly abounded with the message.[69] There is also evidence to suggest that the associations were formative. The memoirs of the American Elizabeth Enora Randall McCollester, for example, explain how her visit to The Hague in 1913 confirmed her perception that this place was 'so distinguished for its peaceful laws which have been made by a conclave of wise peacemakers, sent from all parts of the civilized world'.[70]

Figure 8.4 This tourism poster was one of many the Dutch government commissioned to entice foreign visitors to the Netherlands in 1913 to take part in its national celebrations. In this poster, the ease of travel to the Netherlands is stressed, as is the central focus on the opening of The Hague's peace palace (Centraal Bureau van Vreemdelingenverkeer, poster, 1913, Reclame Arsenaal).

The inauguration of the peace palace was particularly successful in confirming the message. More than 400 guests attended the formalities on 28 August, including Queen Wilhelmina, her mother, Andrew Carnegie and an array of international dignitaries.[71] The local and international press published photographs and joyous accounts foregrounding the palace's role as a 'laboratory for the regeneration of moral forces' (as the Dutch foreign minister, Renée de Marees van Swinderen, depicted it).[72] Meanwhile, cartoonists revelled in the ironies of the peace palace opening as the Balkan Wars raged. One such, published in the German *Lustige Blätter* magazine, depicted Andrew Carnegie shepherding a long procession of the maimed, wounded and displaced into the gates of the palace of peace, while war waged in the distance.[73] Another by Louis Raemaekers represented the angel of peace crucified rather graphically on the peace palace's front door.[74]

Still, for many internationalists the inauguration of the peace palace confirmed the attractions of The Hague as a city of peace. A vast array of internationalist organizations convened their conferences in The Hague in 1913, including the International Council of Women and the Inter-Parliamentary Union.[75] The 20th World Peace Congress was held there on the eve of the peace palace's opening.[76] They also published lavish documents in celebration, including a *festschrift* edited by the renowned international lawyers Josef Kohler (Berlin), Lassa Oppenheim (Cambridge) and Hans Wehberg (Düsseldorf).[77] Most of the discussions at their meetings focused on the agenda of the upcoming third Hague conference and on influencing public opinion in favour of The Hague mission more generally.[78]

With a similar ambition, the American peace activist Anna Eckstein came to The Hague in 1913 to find even more signatures for a monster petition, which urged that the third Hague conference consider compulsory arbitration, acknowledge war to be unlawful and accept the principle that any changes of a country's borders could only occur by agreement of all nations.[79] By July 1914, six million signatures appended the document from around Europe, the British empire and the United States.[80] The British Women's Suffrage Pilgrimage, based in London, also met in The Hague in August 1913 to underwrite their commitment to internationalism and women's suffrage. They planned a repeat event to coincide with the third Hague conference.[81] Although that conference never eventuated, the women still met in The Hague in 1915 (alongside a number of other women's groups), to advocate for a speedy resolution of the First World War and advance the cause of international cooperation.

But 1913 also brought less obviously peace-oriented international organizations to The Hague, including the International Tourism Congress, the second International Opium Congress, the International Lodging Congress, the International Pharmaceutical Congress, the International Conference of Master Cotton Spinners, an international chess tournament, the International Literature and Art Association conference, the International Congress for Children's Education and an International Students' Congress.[82] The Hague was an international destination of choice that year in large part because of 'Plan 1913' and the peace palace opening. In 1913, The Hague sat firmly at the centre of internationalism and was recognized as a world city dedicated to the message of global peace and international cooperation.

What these 1913 celebrations and events also suggest is how much had changed for the Dutch government in terms of international relations. From 1907 on, it was no longer the minor partner in conference planning. It took full responsibility for the Hague conferences and with it had to adapt its role in international affairs. That reality had a serious impact on its foreign policy.[83] Although no historian of Dutch neutrality or foreign policy has unpicked the importance of the shift, contemporary commentators were certainly cognisant of its importance and asked serious questions about the implications. The outspoken Dutch lawyer Cornelis van Vollenhoven, for example, expended much time and energy on the idea that the Netherlands should lead international affairs after 1907. As he explained it, the Dutch national mission should be internationalism. Its active neutrality should serve the peace of the world.[84]

Certainly, for the Dutch public, the year 1913 prompted a shift in self-perception. In part, the shift can be attributed to the nature of the centennial celebrations: they heightened patriotism, a love of monarchy and a sense of historical continuity.[85] The fact that the official celebrations also aimed at attracting foreigners led the Dutch to ask questions about how they should behave as international citizens. Newspapers considered whether locals should volunteer to be tour guides for the visitors and, if so, should the English, French and German language dominate the celebrations?[86] The press discourse around the 1913 events also focused on the implications of the Netherlands becoming a nation devoted to the 'peace through law' idea. They often did so with a cynical eye. The cartoonist Albert Hahn, for example, published a satirical cartoon in September depicting two Hague aristocrats in idle conversation: the lady asks: 'Baron, are you a pacifist too?' He responds: 'Yes, horse races easily bore, don't you agree?'[87] By implication, peace had become temporarily fashionable. Of course, peace had been fashionable in 1899 and 1907 as well.

Unsurprisingly, the Dutch peace organization *Vrede door Recht* revelled in the 'peace through law' association. Its annual report for 1913 argued that as a result of the peace palace inauguration, the Dutch public enmeshed nationalism with internationalism: Dutch patriotism was now imbued with the 'international character of modern civilization'. For these peace activists, 'civilization' implied national independence and a foreign policy based on neutrality and peaceful international cooperation. That the organization almost doubled its membership from 2,400 members to 4,500 in 1913 also spoke to its optimism for the future and the widespread adoption of their ideas.[88] In a similar vein, the University of Leiden used the context of the peace palace inauguration in 1913 to endow honorary degrees on leading internationalists including Elihu Root, Louis Renault, Alfred Fried and T.M.C. Asser.[89] This act of academic magnanimity spoke to the perceived national importance of these internationalists, all of whom were prominently associated with the Hague.

Van Vollenhoven too published a telling pamphlet in 1913. Dutch historians often quote from his *Het eendracht van het land* (The concord of the country) and argue that with this work van Vollenhoven redefined what 'being Dutch' meant.[90] Most contemporaries understood that van Vollenhoven's conceptualization of the Netherlands's national mission was driven by the internationalist promise he attached to The Hague.[91] By 1913 van Vollenhoven was a renowned and ardent promoter of an international police force aimed at enforcing the Hague conventions on the global stage.[92] Van Vollenhoven's enthusiasm for the link between the country's national and international missions was shared by other prominent academics, including H.T. Colenbrander and C. te Lintum, although not by the historians Hajo Brugman, Johan Huizinga and Johanna Naber, who all professed their unease at the patriotic overtones of the 1913 celebrations.[93]

The opening of the peace palace also reminded all that the third Hague conference was due to meet. The Dutch government worked hard on making that event happen without mishap. It established a commission of preparation and appointed Willem de Beaufort to lead it.[94] De Beaufort was well versed in the intricacies of Hague politics and logistics. He invited other leading Dutch dignitaries, including van Vollenhoven, T.M.C. Asser and J.A. Roëll, to be involved. The commission established an extensive but workable agenda for the new conference. It applied to the great powers for their commentary and made considerable progress on setting a date, aiming at the earliest for 1915 but (in December 1913) flagging the possibility of a postponement until 1916.[95]

By May 1914, the commission met weekly and was considering a range of subjects for the third Hague conference, including: the obligations of individuals to international law (private international law), the question of disarmament (because 'strong public opinion' demanded it),[96] the establishment of an International Court of Justice, the parameters of peaceful blockade, sea mines, aerial warfare, limits of territorial waters, the establishment of an international police force, punishment for the circulation of false and sensational messages that might endanger peace and the development of the Declaration of London.[97] The British government advocated adding the status of enemy and neutral subjects in belligerent territory to the agenda along with the question of the treatment of wounded animals in wartime.[98] Internationalist organizations around the world lobbied their governments and The Hague to have their agenda suggestions incorporated in planning for the forthcoming event as well. The *Institut de droit international*'s proposed agenda, for example, focused on the creation of a general arbitration treaty, the extension of the Hague conventions on the opening of hostilities, guidelines for military occupation, lighthouse operation in wartime, the jurisdiction of national tribunals to foreign states and diplomatic and consular privileges in time of war and peace.[99]

Importantly, the commission of preparation was highly alert to the need for the next conference to make effective progress. 'Fruitless' resolutions on disarmament and general internationalist principles would not assuage the general public and would lead, as a committee report of 27 March 1914 noted, to a 'painful impression' on the wider world.[100] What was needed was a serious commitment by the attending governments to the principles at hand as well as a well-crafted agenda so that the press could not take too much licence with uncontrolled ideas.[101] Certainly by mid-1914, most governments had set up preparatory commissions in response to the Dutch government's call for agenda items.[102] On 30 July, the same day Austria-Hungary bombed the Serbian capital of Belgrade and Russia mobilized fully for war, the United States Secretary of State W.J. Bryan was considering the implications of the proposed agenda, expecting to attend the third Hague conference in June 1915.[103] The following day, Germany declared war on Russia. The First World War had begun.

There is no question that on the eve of the First World War, The Hague was a serious and pervasive subject considered by governments, internationalists and a globalized newspaper-reading public. Their preoccupation with The Hague, however, did not detract from a range of coexisting forces that pushed the world over the brink of war in July 1914. That month, Europe's leading statesmen willingly dragged their countries and empires into a global war, neglecting the principles of restraint and moderation that had influenced the course of European relations since 1815. Despite some half-hearted attempts to utilize the mediation and arbitration mechanisms of the Hague conventions, The Hague barely featured in the calculations of these statesmen.[104] The Hague was not a brake on the July crisis.

Yet the First World War was The Hague's war. From the outset, contemporaries considered the course and conduct of the conflict in terms of The Hague's laws and regulations. Neutral governments invoked the rights and duties embedded in the Hague conventions to protect their sovereignty and non-belligerency and to present themselves as viable international agents. The belligerents also readily engaged with the Hague rules: both to assert their own virtue (when they abided by them) or to demonize their enemies and the occasional neutral (when they breached the conventions). In 1914, The Hague referenced the acceptable limits of 'civilized' wartime conduct.[105]

In the war of words that ensued, 'The Hague' was a powerful medium for condemnation and condescension. Both sets of belligerents presented the war as a conflict of primordial dimensions, pitting their civilization against a barbaric threat. They often defined 'barbarism' as the willingness of their enemies to breach the integrity of international law for personal gain. They greedily invoked the principles of The Hague to judge their enemies. As an example, the New Zealand newspaper database *Paperspast* registers 2,178 mentions of 'international law violations' in relationship to the war in eighty-one publications between 1 July and 31 December 1914, 309 of which directly referenced The Hague, almost all referred to Germany.[106] One of these, an editorial in the *New Zealand Times* on 26 August argued in support of French politician G. Hanotaux's assessment of the 'futility of The Hague'. It noted that because no great power existed to force compliance on Germany, The Hague had lost its potency. Germany was to blame, for it refused to keep to the rules.[107] It was Germany that willingly barbarized the conflict: by invading neutral Belgium, it rejected the precepts of treaty law and by ignoring The Hague, it rejected the premise of restraint. In another example, the *Timaru Herald*'s editor responded to the bombardment of the Tahitian port of Papeete by the German gunboat, *Zelee*, in early October. He ordained that the Hague conventions ruled the bombardment as illegal since Papeete was unfortified and undefended. He left his readers to ponder the horrifying implications, as all French and British port settlements in the Pacific region were now vulnerable to similar attacks. Germany's barbarism reached all too close to home for these civilian populations.[108]

In neutral countries too, The Hague was repeatedly used as a barometer to gauge the conduct and impact of the war. Thomas Munro's recent study on Anglo-American media during the war years, for example, highlights how prominent The Hague was as a lens of enquiry about the legitimacy of the conflict in the neutral United States and belligerent Great Britain.[109] The Hague preoccupied internationalists as well: consider the 1915 pamphlet published by the popular *Nederlands Anti-Oorlog Raad* (NAOR, Netherlands Anti-War Council), which debated the value of continuing the 18 May Hague tradition. In the pamphlet, the NAOR chair F.M. Knobel proffered two visions: one which privileged the reality of wartime violence and considered the palm tree planted in 1899 at The Hague as dead. The alternate vision was more propitious: it looked to the Hague conferences as the basis on which to grow a fruitful post-war peace. For Knobel, the latter vision was vital and presented a key reason why 18 May should continue to be celebrated.[110]

However, as the war lengthened and breaches of the Hague rules spiralled out of control, increasing numbers of contemporaries in belligerent and neutral countries registered their dismay (Figure 8.5). In 1916, the British author L.T. Hobhouse voiced his fears of the war's totalizing impact and described it as 'the break up of civilisation'. He lamented with palpable anguish: 'Don't you see that morals have come to an end'?[111] That same year, the German jurist Kohler, who had rejoiced at the opening of the peace palace in 1913, now lambasted the idea that international law could restrain violence. For Kohler, the peace palace had no future in a world dominated by U-boats, indiscriminate bombings and gas warfare.[112] By 1917, even Elihu Root acknowledged that the war had 'overtaken the slow growth of international law'.[113]

Figure 8.5 This 1917 cartoon by Louis Denis Valvérane in the French satirical magazine *Pêle-Mêle* suggests that the Hague conventions, the rights of neutrals and the neutrality of Belgium have all been rejected by Germany, thrown in the wastepaper basket of the German government at Potsdam (*Pêle-Mêle* 12 February 1917, 4).

Yet despite the existence of a growing despondency among some of The Hague's foremost pre-war proponents, other supporters of The Hague (including Root) held on to visions of a hopeful future.[114] As early as September 1914, the Radical English journalist H.N. Brailsford described that future as the realization of a federation of nations.[115] The Austrian jurist, Heinrich Lammasch made similar assertions in 1916.[116] In fact, many of the men and women who brought the League of Nations into being built that organization on the internationalist principles they advanced in relationship to The Hague before and during the war.[117] Many of them were also active members of the *Organisation centrale pour une paix durable* (Central Organization for Durable Peace, CODP), which was established in The Hague in 1915 under the auspices of the NAOR.[118] It met a fortnight before the International Women's Congress came to The Hague.[119] Both these 1915 events returned international attention to The Hague. Consequently, while the third Hague conference never met, 1915 remained a key Hague year. The agency of these non-governmental and transnationally aligned groups enabled The Hague to continue to matter in the international arena.

After 1915, the CODP attempted to influence belligerents and neutrals alike on the importance of the principles of international law and justice.[120] Of course, its members were all too aware that the war also brought out the weaknesses of The Hague's existing mechanisms and laws. As a result, they organized 'study conferences' in neutral countries and published voluminous tomes on how to improve international relations, ranging from a study on open-door diplomacy, to sanctions in international law, to the democratic control of foreign affairs, to the principle of the freedom of the seas, to the enforcement of peace, to the problem of armaments control.[121] They also advocated that a proper third Hague peace conference be held as soon as the war ended to establish a juridical basis for international organization.[122]

Of course, the COPD was not the only non-governmental organization to prioritize their plans for the post-war future. What the post-war international system would look like preoccupied belligerent and neutral governments as well. Increasingly, their plans avoided or negated The Hague. In 1916, the English author Maximilian Mügge presented one alternative: he warned that this 'terrible war' was proof that the Hague conferences failed to achieve their objectives, and that the future of peace relied on the 'juridical application of force on behalf of the whole Society of Nations'.[123] When President Wilson advanced his Fourteen Points later that year, they were not built on the precepts of The Hague. He, like Mügge, looked to the principle of collective security, which depended on mutual dependency between states rather than their mutual respect for international law.

Yet, The Hague's international and internationalist relevance did not end with the First World War. The pre-war Hague movement had numerous post-war legacies, including the enduring application of the Hague conventions. The Hague's juridical institutions continue to function today, augmented in 1923 by the establishment of the Permanent Court of International Justice (and after the Second World War, by the ICJ and ICC).[124] After 1918, then, The Hague remained a key site for international engagement, albeit more clearly constrained to the realm of international law. The Hague Academy of International Law, established in January 1914, also opened in 1923.[125] Despite the odd call to reinstitute the Hague conferences, after 1918, The

Hague no longer encapsulated the movement to bring international organizations together as it had before 1914.[126] The League of Nations' infrastructure was purposely housed elsewhere, in Geneva.

The First World War, then, interrupted and disrupted the history of The Hague as an internationalist idea as much as it interrupted and disrupted many other international developments that had defined the nineteenth-century world order. In the post-war world, The Hague retained an important role, but it did not define that world. After 1918, the internationalist ideals that contemporaries attached to The Hague in the pre-war era also receded from popular understanding. Still, they did not disappear. After 1918, the city of The Hague repeatedly commemorated the 1899, 1907 and 1915 Hague conferences.[127] It marked (and continues to mark) key anniversaries with public events. Today, The Hague formally acknowledges its status as a 'city of peace and law', even if historicized myths play an overly large role in presenting what that phrase means.[128]

The Hague's monumentality as a peace city came from the outside: from the world looking on and ascribing promise and expectation to The Hague in the period of the Hague conferences of 1899, 1907 and 1915. As a result of the Hague conferences, the city transformed into a place, space and concept that influenced the ways in which contemporaries considered warfare and the relationships of states. Between 1899 and 1915, The Hague helped to define international politics. The Hague permeated public discourses about the future of world organization, the role of international law in diplomatic affairs and the promise of conflict resolution. At the outbreak of the First World War, The Hague's normative appeal determined how contemporaries considered their world. It did not take the First World War for a politically engaged and globally alert newspaper-reading public to ask serious questions about the purpose and value of international organization and the power of collective action. They were already asking those questions before 1914. We must look for the origins of twentieth-century internationalism in the lead-up to the First World War. We can find them in The Hague between 1899 and 1915.

Notes

Introduction: For the Peace of the World

1 J. del Campo, *A history of the world for rebels and somnabulists*. London, Telegram, 2008, 21.
2 For an English translation: J.B. Scott, *The Hague peace conferences of 1899 and 1907. Volume 1. Part 1. A series of lectures delivered before the Johns Hopkins University in the year 1908*. Baltimore, Johns Hopkins UP, 1909, 41–42.
3 The rescript was released to the press on 28 August 1898: C.D. Davis, *The United States and the first Hague peace conference*. Ithaca, Cornell UP, 1962, 37–38.
4 *El Liberal de Reus* (Spain) 2, 415, 2 September 1898, np.
5 Cf. I. Clark, *International legitimacy and world society*. Oxford UP, 2007.
6 Cf. D. Hucker, 'International history and the study of public opinion. Towards methodological clarity' *International History Review* 34, 4, 2012, 775–794.
7 Cf. M. Krebs, *Gender, race and the writing of empire. Public discourse and the Boer War*. Cambridge UP, 1999, 36–37.
8 W.F. Kuehl, 'Concepts of internationalism in history' *Peace and Change* 11, 1, 1986, 1–10.
9 J. Osterhammel, 'Europe, the "West" and the civilizing mission' *German Historical Institute London. The 2005 annual lecture*. German Historical Institute London, 2005, 5–6.
10 S. Potter, *News and the British world. The emergence of an imperial press system 1876–1922*. Oxford UP, 2003; T. Ballentyne and A. Burton, *Empires and the reach of the global 1870–1945*. Cambridge, Bellknap, 2012.
11 A. Burton and I. Hofmeyr, 'Introduction. The spine of empire? Books and the making of an imperial commons' in A. Burton and I. Hofmeyer, eds, *Ten books that shaped the British empire. Creating an imperial commons*. Durham, Duke UP, 2014, 10.
12 J.A. Hobson, *Imperialism. A study*. London, James Nisbet, 1902, 181.
13 L. Hunt, *Inventing human rights. A history*. New York, W.W. Norton, 2007, 176.
14 E.D. Mead, 'International organization for inter-racial goodwill' in G. Spiller, ed., *Papers on inter-racial problems communicated to the First Universal Races Congress held at the University of London July 26–29, 1911*. London, P.S. King, 1911, 444 (in PCSC DG21).
15 D. Laqua, 'Alfred H. Fried and the challenges for "scientific pacifism" in the belle époque' in B. Rayward, ed., *Information beyond borders. International cultural and intellectual exchange in the belle époque*. London, Taylor & Francis, 2014, 183.
16 B.E. Vick, *The Congress of Vienna. Power and politics after Napoleon*. Cambridge, Harvard UP, 2014; H. McCarthy, *Women of the world. The rise of the female diplomat*. London, Bloomsbury, 2014, 4–5.
17 W.F. Kuehl, *Seeking world order. The United States and international organization to 1920*. Nashville, Vanderbilt UP, 1969, 48; M. Herren-Oesch and C. Knab, 'Die Zweite Haager Friedenskonferenz und die Liberalisierung des politischen

Informationsmarktes' *FW* 82, 4, 2007, 51–64; G.H. Aldrich and C.M. Chinkin, 'A century of achievement and unfinished work' *AJIL* 94, 1, 2000, 90–98.

18 McCarthy, *Women* 5; M. Glenny, *The Balkans 1804–1999. Nationalism, war and the great powers*. London, Penguin, 2000, 136–137.

19 Dutch Consul-General in St Petersburg to Dutch Minister of Foreign Affairs, 14 March 1871, in NA 2.05.19, 118.

20 L.M. Penson and H.W.V. Temperley, *A century of diplomatic blue books 1814–1914*. London, Routledge, 1966.

21 B.W. Tuchman, *The proud tower. A portrait of the world before the war 1890–1914*. New York, Ballantine Books, 1962 [1996], 257. Tuchman channelled Belgian delegate Auguste Beernaert's 1907 claim that 'to-day there is no assembly which must not sit with the widows opened, listening to the voices from outside' (in A. Eyffinger, *The 1899 Hague Peace Conference. The parliament of man, the federation of the world*. The Hague, Kluwer Law International, 1999, 342).

22 *Thames Star* (New Zealand) 24 October 1907, 2; Lord Ponsonby, *Democracy and foreign affairs*. np, 1912.

23 T.G. Otte, 'Old diplomacy. Reflections on the Foreign Office before 1914' in G. Johnson, ed., *The Foreign Office and British diplomacy in the twentieth century*. New York, Routledge, 2005, 43–56.

24 M. Tate, *The disarmament illusion. The movement for the limitation of armaments to 1907*. New York, MacMillan, 1942, 351.

25 S. Kern, *The culture of time and space 1880–1918*. Cambridge, Harvard UP, 1983, 230.

26 M. MacMillan, *The war that ended peace. How Europe abandoned peace for the First World War*. London, Profile Books, 2013, 284; R. Langhorne, *The collapse of the concert of Europe. International politics 1890–1914*. New York, St Martin's Press, 1981, 65; D. Hucker, 'British peace activism and "new" diplomacy. Revisiting the 1899 Hague Peace Conference' *Diplomacy & Statecraft* 26, 2015, 406; W. Langer, *The diplomacy of imperialism, 1890–1902*. New York, Knopf, 1951 [1935], 591.

27 S.R. Herman, *Eleven against war. Studies in American internationalist thought, 1898–1921*. Stanford, Hoover Institution Press, 1969, 18; Davis, *United States 1*, 213. Cf. C.D. Davis, *The United States and the second Hague Peace Conference. American diplomacy and international organization 1899–1914*. Durham, Duke UP, 1975.

28 N.J. Brailey, 'Sir Ernest Satow and the 1907 Second Hague Peace Conference' *Diplomacy & Statecraft* 13, 2, June 2002, 201.

29 A. Eyffinger, 'A highly critical moment. Role and record of the 1907 Hague Peace Conference' *Netherlands International Law Review* 54, 2007, 198. Cf. Eyffinger, *1899* 5.

30 G. Best, 'The restraint in war in historical and philosophical perspective' in A.J.M. Delissen and G.J. Tanja, eds, *Humanitarian law of armed conflict challenges ahead. Essays in honour of Frits Kalshoven*. Dordrecht, Martinus Nijhoff, 1991; G. Best, *Humanity in warfare. The modern history of the international law of armed conflict*. London, Methuen, 1983; I. Hueck, 'Peace, security and international organisations. The German international lawyers and the Hague conferences' in R. Lesaffer, ed., *Peace treaties and international law in European history. From the late Middle Ages to World War One*. Cambridge UP, 2004, 256; S. Rosenne, ed., *The Hague Peace Conferences of 1899 and 1907 and international arbitration. Reports and documents*. The Hague, T.M.C. Asser Press, 2001.

31 For good overview histories: Sandi Cooper, Martin Ceadel, Peter Brock and Verdiana Grossi.

32 I.L. Claude Jnr, *Swords into plowshares. The problems and progress of international organization*. New York, Random House, 1956, 34; Kuehl, *Seeking*; Clark, *International legitimacy*; G. Sluga, *Internationalism in the age of nationalism*. Philadelphia, University of Pennsylvania Press, 2013; M. Mazower, *Governing the world. The history of an idea, 1815 to the present*. London, Penguin, 2013.
33 J.C. Faries, *The rise of internationalism*. New York, np, 1915, 5.
34 In W. Schücking, *The international union of the Hague conferences*. Oxford, Clarendon Press, 1918 [1912], 37.
35 Cf. Claude, *Swords* 26.
36 Cf. T. Munro, 'The Hague's war, 1914–1918' PhD thesis, University of Auckland, forthcoming, 2018; I.V. Hull, *A scrap of paper. Breaking and making international law during the Great War*. Ithaca, Cornell UP, 2014; W. Mulligan, *The great war for peace*. New Haven, Yale UP, 2014; D.M. Segesser, 'Die Haager Landkriegsordnung in der internationalen wissenschaftlichen Debatte über Kriegsverbrechen im Ersten und Zweiten Weltkrieg' *FW* 82, 4, 2007, 65–82; A. Kramer, *Dynamic of destruction. Culture and mass killing in the First World War*. Oxford UP, 2007, 24–27.

1 How the Nineteenth Century Shaped the Hague Conferences

1 Scott, *Hague peace*, Volume 1, 738.
2 Scott, *Hague peace*, Volume 1, 738.
3 Cf. S. Pinker, *The better angels of our nature. A history of violence and humanity*. London, Penguin, 2011.
4 P.S. Reinsch, *Public international unions. Their word and organization*. Boston, Ginn, 1911, 1; B.C. Schmidt, 'Paul S. Reinsch and the study of imperialism and internationalism' in D. Long and B.C. Schmidt, eds, *Imperialism and internationalism in the discipline of international relations*. State University of New York Press, 2005, 66–67.
5 Reinsch, *Public* 1–3.
6 Reinsch, *Public* 3; emphasis in the original.
7 C. Kaul, 'Introductory Overview' in C. Kaul, ed., *Media and the British empire*. London, Palgrave, 2006, 4; Kern, *Culture* 7; M. Lake, 'Lowe Kong Meng appeals to international law. Transnational lives caught between empire and nation' in D. Deacon, P. Russell and A. Woollacott, eds, *Transnational lives. Biographies of global modernity 1700–present*. New York, Palgrave, 2010, 223–224.
8 D. Headrick, *The tools of empire. Technology and European imperialism in the nineteenth century*. Oxford University Press, 1981.
9 A. Hershey, 'International law since the Peace of Westphalia' *AJIL* 6, 1, January 1912, 54; Reinsch, *Public*; Faries, *Internationalism* 43–60, 73–98; N. Weiss, 'Institutionalised co-operation on international communication. The international administrative unions as a means of governing globalisation processes' in I. Löhr and R. Wenzlhuemer, eds, *The nation state and beyond. Governing globalization processes in the nineteenth and early twentieth centuries*. Heidelberg, Springer, 2013, 65–82.
10 Hershey, 'International law' 54; H.K. Meier, *The United States and Switzerland in the nineteenth century*. The Hague, Mouton, 1963, 145.
11 Hershey, 'International law' 54; *Archives Diplomatiques Recueil International de Diplomatie et d'Histoire*, Second series, 20, 1886, 162.

12 Kern, *Culture* 11–12; V. Ogle, *The global transformation of time 1870–1950*. Harvard UP, 2015.
13 Claude, *Swords* 32; Reinsch, *Public* 6.
14 Cf. I. Löhr and R. Wenzlhuemer, 'Introduction' in Löhr and Wenzlhuemer, eds, *Nation* 1–26; E.S. Rosenberg, ed., *A world connecting 1870–1945*. Cambridge, Harvard UP, 2012.
15 Cf. Burton and Hofmeyr, 'Introduction'.
16 Cf. S.A. Keefer, 'An obstacle though not a barrier. The role of international law in security planning during the *Pax Britannica*' *International History Review* 35, 5, 2013, 1045–1046.
17 E.Y.-J. Lee, 'Early development of modern international law in East Asia-with special reference to China, Japan and Korea' *Journal of the History of International Law* 4, 2002, 46–47.
18 J. MacKenzie, *The partition of Africa 1880–1900*. Third edition. London, Routledge, 2005, 22; A. Fitzmaurice, 'Liberalism and empire in nineteenth-century international law' *American Historical Review* 117, 1, 2012, 129–130; G.W. Gong, *The standard of 'civilization' in international society*. Oxford, Clarendon Press, 1984, 4.
19 K. Schlichtmann, 'Japan, Germany and the idea of the Hague peace conferences' *Journal of Peace Research* 40, 4, 2003, 378–380.
20 As examples: M. Lobban, 'English approaches to international law in the nineteenth century' in M. Craven, M. Fitzmaurice and M. Vogiatzi, eds, *Time, history and international law*. Leiden, Martinus Nijhoff, 2007, 72; M.S. Anderson, *The rise of modern diplomacy 1450–1919*. London, Longman, 1993, 113; F. Ito, 'One hundred years of international law studies in Japan' *Japanese Annual of International Law* 19, 1969, 19–26; V.E. Grabar, *The history of international law in Russia 1647–1917. A bio-bibliographical study*. Oxford, Clarendon Press, 1990.
21 Lee, 'Early' 47; H.-G. Sim, 'Brutal internal struggle against external imperialism. The initial phases in the reception of western law into Korean society in the 1890s' in M. Stolleis and M. Yanagihara, eds, *East Asian and European perspectives on international law*. Baden-Baden, Nomos, 2004, 22–39.
22 Cf. S. den Otter, '"A legislating empire". Victorian political theorists, codes of law and empire' in D. Bell, ed., *Victorian visions of global order. Empire and international relations in nineteenth-century political thought*. Cambridge UP, 2007, 89–112.
23 A.G. Genell, 'The well-defended domains. Eurocentric international law and the making of the Ottoman Office of Legal Counsel' *Journal of the Ottoman and Turkish Studies Association* 3, 2, November 2016, 256.
24 Cf. D. Kirkby and C. Coleborne, eds, *Law, history, colonialism. The reach of empire*. Manchester UP, 2001, 3; Lake, 'Lowe' 228–229.
25 A. Hutt, *Changing newspaper. Typographic trends in Britain and America 1622–1972*. London, Gordon Fraser, 1973, 68; K. Williams, *Read all about it! A history of the British newspaper*. London, Routledge, 2010, 125–148.
26 J.L. Huffman, *Creating a public. People and press in Meiji Japan*. Honolulu, University of Hawai'i Press, 1997, 224–270; X. Zang, *The origins of the modern Chinese press*. London, Routledge, 2007, 140–141.
27 M.B. Iwinsky in J.H. de Vries, *Pour la paix. Une presse mondiale*. Paris, Schleicher Frères, 1911, 131.
28 Cf. R. Ng, 'The *Yuandongbao*. A Chinese or a Russian newspaper?' in D. Ben-Canaan, F. Grüner and I. Prodöhl, eds, *The transcultural past of Northeast China*. Heidelberg, Springer, 2014, 101–118.

29 M. Czyzewska, *Der Allgemeine Deutsche Sprachverein und das Fremdwort*. Dresden, Neisse, 2008, 100–101.
30 Cf. Burton and Hofmeyr, 'Introduction' 14.
31 D. Read, *The power of news. The history of Reuters 1849–1989*. Oxford UP, 1992, 57; V. Barth, 'The formation of global news agencies, 1859–1914' in R.W. Boyd, ed., *Information beyond borders. International cultural and intellectual exchange in the belle époque*. London, Taylor & Francis, 2014, 36.
32 *Figaro* (Paris) 26 May 1904, 2.
33 *Figaro* 27 May 1904, 2.
34 *Indépendance Belge* 26 May 1904, 1; 27 May 1904, 4.
35 *NCH* 27 May 1904, 1086.
36 *TT* 25 May 1904, 10; *Nieuwe Tilburgsche Courant* 27 May 1904, 1; *Marlborough Express* 28 May 1904, 2; *Brisbane Courier* 27 May 1904, 5 *Nieuws van de Dag voor Nederlandsch-Indië* (Batavia) 24 June 1904, 6. So did Woolsey's opinions: *JT* 24 June 1905, 5.
37 MacMillan, *The war* 102; M.L. Roberts, 'Subversive copy. Feminist journalism in fin-de-siècle France' in D. de la Motte and J.M. Przyblyski, eds, *Making the news. Modernity and the mass press in nineteenth-century France*. Amherst, University of Massachusetts Press, 1999, 311–316.
38 *Evening Post* (Wellington, New Zealand) 4 May 1906, 5, in T. Fitzsimons, 'Wellington's newspaper space, 1896–1912' BA(Hons) dissertation, Victoria University of Wellington, 2012, 44.
39 Cf. I. Hofmeyr, *Ghandi's printing press*. Cambridge, Harvard UP, 2013, 8–11.
40 Cf. M. McLuhan, *Understanding media. The extensions of man*. London, Sphere Books, 1967.
41 H.N. Brailsford, *The war of steel and gold. The study of armed peace*. Sixth edition. London, G. Bell, 1916, 135.
42 M. Hampton, *Visions of the press in Britain 1850–1950*. Urbana, University of Illinois Press, 2004, 108–109.
43 Best, *Humanity* 139.
44 Mulligan, *Peace* 7–8; Hull, *Scrap*; N. Gullace, 'Sexual violence and family honor. British propaganda and international law during the First World War' *American Historical Review* June 1997, 715–742; T. Munro, 'The Hague as a framework for British and American newspapers' public presentations on the First World War' in M. Abbenhuis, C.E. Barber and A.R. Higgins, eds, *War, peace and international order. The legacies of the Hague conferences of 1899 and 1907*. New York, Routledge, 2017, 155–170.
45 For a similar argument applied to Germany: Czyzewska, *Allgemeine* 100–101.
46 Krebs, *Gender* 15–16. Cf. R.J. Goldstein, 'Introduction' in R.J. Goldstein, ed., *War for the public mind. Political censorship in nineteenth-century Europe*. Westport, Greenwood, 2000, 1–3.
47 Hampton, *Visions* 109–110.
48 Anderson, *Rise* 139; *La guerre et le militarisme*. Paris, Éditions des Annales de la Jeunesse Laique, 1899, 55.
49 MacMillan, *The war* 102; D. Geppert, 'The public challenge to diplomacy. German and British ways of dealing with the press 1890–1914' in M. Mösslang and T. Riotte, eds, *The diplomats' world. A cultural history of diplomacy 1815–1914*. Oxford UP, 2008, 139.
50 S. Hess, *The government/press connection. Press officers and their offices*. Washington D.C., Brookings Institute, 1984, 1; R.J. Young, *Marketing Marianne. French*

propaganda in America 1900–1940. New Brunswick, Rutgers UP, 2005, 14; P. Jackson, *Beyond the balance of power. France and the politics of national security in the era of the First World War*. Cambridge UP, 2013, 34; Potter, *News* 192; M. Palmer, 'The British press and international news 1851–99: of agencies and newspapers' in G. Boyce, J. Curran and P. Wingate, eds, *Newspaper history from the seventeenth century to the present day*. London, Constable, 1978, 210.

51 M. Schultz, '"A harmony of frenzy." Maori in Manhattan, 1909–10' *Theatre Studies* 67, 3, October 2015, 445–464.

52 Mazower, *Governing* 44; J. Burris, *Exhibiting religion. Colonialism and spectacle at international expositions 1851–1893*. Charlottesville, Virginia UP, 2001, xiii–xiv.

53 Faries, *Internationalism* 38.

54 G. Best, 'Peace conferences and the century of total war. The 1899 Hague Peace Conference and what came after' *International Affairs* 75, 3, 1999, 620; Kuehl, *Seeking* 48–49; R.W. Rydell, 'World's Columbian Exposition' *Encyclopedia of Chicago*. http://encyclopedia.chicagohistory.org/pages/1386.html (accessed March 2015).

55 R.K. Barney, 'The Olympic Games in modern times' in G. Schaus, ed., *Onward to the Olympics*. Waterloo, Wilfrid Laurier UP, 2007, 221–241; S. Widmalm, '"A superior type of universal civilisation". Science as politics in Sweden, 1917–1926' in R. Lettevall, G. Somsen and S. Widmalm, eds, *Neutrality in twentieth-century Europe. Intersections of science, culture, and politics after the First World War*. New York, Routledge, 2012, 68.

56 A. Schou, *Histoire de l'internationalisme. III Du Congres de Vienne jusqu'à la première guerre mondiale (1914)*. Oslo, H. Aschenhoug, 1963, 155–160.

57 Scott, *Hague peace*, Volume 1, 24; F.H. Hinsley, *Power and the pursuit of peace. Theory and practice in the history of relations between states*. Cambridge UP, 1963, 267; Faries, *Internationalism* 67–69.

58 Scott, *Hague peace*, Volume 1, 24.

59 Faries, *Internationalism*; C.L. Lange, *L'histoire de l'internationalism*. Volume 1, Kristiana, H. Aschehoug, 1919. On internationalism: C. Holbraad, *Internationalism and nationalism in European political thought*. London, Palgrave MacMillan, 2003; G. Schirbel, *Strukturen des Internationalismus. First Universal Races Congress London 1911*. Volume 1, Münster, Lit Verlag, 1991.

60 Davis, *United States 1* 9-10; Kuehl, *Seeking* 17; M. Ceadel, *The origins of war prevention. The British peace movement and international relations 1730–1854*. Oxford UP, 1996, 12; Mazower, *Governing* 31–32; P. Brock, *Twentieth-century pacifism*. New York, Van Nostrand Reinhold, 1970, 2.

61 S.E. Cooper, ed., *Internationalism in nineteenth-century Europe. The crisis of ideas and purpose*. New York, Garland, 1976, 247; S.E. Cooper, 'The origins and development of European peace movements. From Vienna to Frankfurt' *Wiener Beitrage zur Geschichte der Neuzeit* 11, 1984, 75; Kuehl, *Seeking* 38.

62 Kuehl, *Seeking* 20.

63 M. Ceadel, *Pacifism in Britain 1914–1945. The defining of a faith*. Oxford UP, 1979, 3; Cooper, ed., *Internationalism* 13. The word 'pacifism' was coined in 1899 by Emile Arnaud: B. Hamann, *Bertha von Suttner. A life for peace*. Syracuse UP, 1996, 153; Cooper, 'Origins' 75–76. The word 'pacifisist' was in use by 1907: G. Hanotaux in *American Review of Reviews* 36, July–December 1907, 227.

64 Kuehl, *Seeking* 39.

65 Scott, *Hague peace*, Volume 1, 523.

66 F. Trentmann, *Free trade nation*. Oxford UP, 2008.

67 Cf. G. Claeys, *Imperial sceptics. British critics of empire 1850–1920*. Cambridge UP, 2010.
68 Fitzmaurice, 'Liberalism' 123–124; Patterson, *Toward* 12–13.
69 G.H. Perris, *A short history of war and peace*. London, William and Norgate, [1911], 242; V. Enebakk, 'Nobel science of peace. Norwegian neutrality, internationalism, and the Nobel Peace Prize' in Letteval et al., eds, *Neutrality* 298.
70 Schou, *Histoire* 399–401.
71 *The Inter-Parliamentary Union from 1889–1930. A publication issued by the Inter-Parliamentary Union Bureau to commemorate the fiftieth anniversary of the union*. Lausanne, Payot, 1939; R. Uhlig, *Die Interparlementarische Union 1899–1914*. Wiesbaden, Franz Steiner, 1988.
72 A. Rolin, *Les origins de l'Institut de Droit International 1873–1923. Souvenirs d'un témoin*. np, 1923, 8–18, 30; M. Koskenniemi, *The gentle civilizer of nations. The rise and fall of international law 1870–1960*. Cambridge UP, 2001, 40.
73 J.B. Scott, *Resolutions of the Institute of International Law dealing with the law of nations with an historical introduction and explanatory notes*. New York, Oxford UP, 1916, viii–ix; J.B. Scott, 'The Institute of International Law' *AJIL* 21, 4, October 1927, 716; Schou, *Histoire* 311; I. Abrams, 'The emergence of the international law societies' *Review of Politics* 19, 3, July 1957, 363; Gong, *Standard* 14–15; C. Reeves, 'From red crosses to golden arches. China, the Red Cross, and The Hague Peace Conference, 1899–1900' in J.H. Bentley, R. Bridenthal and A.A. Yang, eds, *Interactions. Transregional perspectives on world history*. Honolulu, University of Hawai'i Press, 2005, 67–68.
74 Koskenniemi, *Gentle* 278.
75 D. Rodogno, 'European legal doctrines on intervention and the status of the Ottoman Empire within the "family of nations" throughout the nineteenth century' *Journal of the History of International Law* 18, 2016, 5–41.
76 M. Ryan, 'The price of legitimacy in humanitarian intervention. Britain, the right of search, and the abolition of the West African slave trade' and W. Mulligan, 'British anti-slave trade and anti-slavery policy in East Africa, Arabia and Turkey in the late nineteenth century' in B. Simms and D.J.B. Trim, eds, *Humanitarian intervention. A history*. Cambridge UP, 2011, 231–255, 256–280.
77 *War with China*. London, 1841, 17. J. Halcrow, 'Drugs, empire and international law. British debates over the First Opium War, 1839 – 1842' MA thesis, University of Auckland, 2017.
78 J.S. Mill as quoted by D.J.B. Trim and B. Simms, 'Towards a history of humanitarian intervention' in Simms and Trim, eds, *Humanitarian* 1.
79 J.F. Hutchinson, 'Rethinking the origins of the Red Cross' *Bulletin of the History of Medicine* 63, 4, 1989, 557–578.
80 J.F. Hutchinson, *Champions of charity. War and the rise of the Red Cross*. Boulder, Westview Press, 1996, 30–46; G. del Vecchio, 'On the history of the Red Cross' *Journal of the History of Ideas* 24, 4, 1963, 577–581; Best, *Humanity* 150.
81 Trim and Simms, 'Towards' 16–17. In the same volume: D. Rodogno, 'The "principles of humanity" and the European powers' intervention in Ottoman Lebanon and Syria in 1860–1861', 159–183.
82 M. Sewell, 'Humanitarian intervention, democracy, and imperialism. The American war with Spain, 1898, and after' in Simms and Trim, eds, *Humanitarian* 303–22; B. Miller, *From liberation to conquest. The visual and popular cultures of the Spanish-American War of 1898*. Amherst, University of Massachusetts Press, 2011.

83 Lord and Lady Aberdeen, *'We twa.' Reminiscences of Lord and Lady Aberdeen*. Volume 2, Glasgow, W. Collins, 1925, 296–7; L.J. Rupp, 'Constructing internationalism. The case of transnational women's organizations, 1888–1945' *American Historical Review* 99, 4, December 1994, 1571–1600; *Women in a changing world. The dynamic story of the International Council of Women since 1888*. London, Routledge and Kegan Paul, 1966, 15–16; M.J. Sewall, *Genesis of the International Council of Women and the story of its growth 1888–1893*. np, 1914.

84 H.H. Alonso, *Peace as a woman's issue. A history of the US movement for world peace and women's rights*. Syracuse UP, 1993, 49; Kuehl, *Seeking* 40; Davis, *United States 1* 11-12; S.E. Cooper, 'Women's participation in European peace movements. The struggle to prevent World War I' Unpublished, Berkshire Conference on the History of Women, June 1984 (National Library of Australia Microfiche); I. Tyrrell, 'The Woman's Christian Temperance Union and internationalism' *Women and Social Movements, International. 1840–Present*. Electronic database (accessed April 2016).

85 H.J. Forman, 'The progress of Esperanto' *North American Review* 186, 623, October 1907, 276; Mazower, *Governing* 112; Faries, *Internationalism* 115–116; M. Krajewski, 'Organizing a global idiom. Esperanto, Ido and the world auxiliary language movement before the First World War' in Boyd, ed., *Information* 97–122.

86 B. Schroeder-Gudehus, 'Probing the master narrative of scientific internationalism. Nationals and neutrals in the 1920s' in Letteval et al., eds, *Neutrality* 21; Faries, *Internationalism* 103–105; H. Ellis, 'National and transnational spaces. Academic networks and scholarly transfer between Britain and Germany in the nineteenth century' in Löhr and Wenzlhuemer, eds, *Nation* 127–148; C. van Praet and C. Verbruggen, '"Soldiers for a joint cause". A relational perspective on local and international educational leagues in the 1860s' *Low Countries Historical Review* 130, 1, 2015, 4–24.

87 Sluga, *Internationalism* 4; D. Laqua, *The age of internationalism and Belgium, 1880–1930. Peace, progress and prestige*. Manchester UP, 2015, 115–144.

88 Schou, *Histoire* 211–217, 222–227; V. Grossi, *Le pacifism européen 1889–1914*. Brussels, Bruylant, 1994, 13–15; J. Joll, *The second international 1889–1914*. Second edition. London, Routledge and Kegan Paul, 1974, 1–2.

89 Joll, *Second* 30; K. Callahan, '"Performing inter-nationalism" in Stuttgart in 1907. French and German socialist nationalism and the political culture of an international socialist congress' *International Review of Social History* 45, 2000, 52.

90 M. Sherwood, *Origins of Pan-Africanism. Henry Sylvester Williams, Africa and the African diaspora*. New York, Routledge, 2011, 45–48; F. Ugbaoaja Ohaegbulam, *West African responses to European imperialism in the nineteenth and twentieth centuries*. Lanham, UP of America, 1984, 239–267; Tabili, 'Race' 527–530.

91 Schou, *Histoire* 176–177.

92 N.F. Dryhurst, ed., *Nationalities and subject races. Report of conference held in Caxton Hall, Westminster June 28–30, 1910*. London, P.S. King, 1911, 175; Sluga, *Internationalism* 26.

93 Schirbel, *Strukturen*.

94 For the English version: I.S. Bloch, *Is war now impossible? Being an abridgment of 'The war of the future in its technical, economic and political relations*. London, Grant Richards, 1899; G. Dawson, 'Preventing "a great moral evil". Jean de Bloch's *The Future of War* as anti-revolutionary pacifism' *Journal of Contemporary History* 37, 1, 2002, 5–19.

95 P. Crook, *Darwinism, war and history*. Cambridge UP, 1994, 232.

96 Enebakk, 'Nobel' 299–300.

97 A. Wild, 'Frédéric Passy' in K. Holl and A.C. Kjelling, eds, *The Nobel Peace Prize and the laureates. The meaning and acceptance of the Nobel Peace Prize in the prize winners' countries*. Frankfurt, Peter Lang, 1994, 40–41.

98 A. Lysen, *A history of the Carnegie Foundation and the Peace Palace at The Hague*. Leiden, Brill, 1931; R. Lesaffer, 'The temple of peace. The Hague peace conferences, Andrew Carnegie and the building of the Peace Palace (1898–1913)' *Preadviezen. Mededelingen van de Koninklijke Nederlandse Vereniging voor Internationaal Recht* 140, November 2013, 1–38.

99 Reeves, 'Red crosses' 72; T. Hon, 'Global competition for power and wealth. The Chinese views of the world before and after the Great War' in T. Minohara, T. Hon and E. Dawley, eds, *The decade of the Great War. Japan and the wider world in the 1910s*. Leiden, Brill, 2014, 504; M. Dykstra and J. Wasserstrom, 'Did China have a *fin de siècle*?' in Saler, ed., *World*, 238–253.

100 J.L. Huffman, *Japan and imperialism 1853–1945*. Ann Arbor, Association for Asian Studies, 2010, 19; Y. Okamoto, 'Buddhism and the twenty-one demands. The politics behind the international movement of Japanese Buddhists' in Minohara et al., eds, *Decade* 394–414; K. Schlichtmann, *Japan in the world. Shidehara Kijūrō, pacifism, and the abolition of war*. Volume 1, Lanham, Rowman & Littlefield, 2009, 2–3, 5–6, 29, 38, 40.

101 C. Barber, 'The evolution of global politics and the pacific settlement of international disputes 1794–1907' PhD thesis, University of Auckland, 2017.

102 Cf. Rosenberg, *World*.

103 Gong, *Standard* 1, 4.

104 Cf. Reeves, 'Red crosses' 67.

105 S. Esenbel, 'Japan' in Saler, ed., *World* 254–255.

106 I choose not to make the distinction between foreign and domestic publics here, as people did not distinguish between the communications targeted at themselves as subjects and citizens of a state and those targeted at foreigners.

107 M. Baumont, 'L'Affaire Dreyfus dans la diplomatie française' in A.O. Sarkissian, ed., *Studies in diplomatic history and historiography in honour of G.P. Gooch*. London, Longmans, 1961, 26–47; Grossi, *Pacifism* 16.

108 I.F. Clarke, *Voices prophesying war 1763–1984*. Oxford UP, 1966, 64–65, 78–79, 131; G.R. Wilkinson, *Depictions and images of war in Edwardian newspapers, 1899–1914*. Houndsmills, Palgrave MacMillan, 2003, 54–57, 67–83.

109 Crook, *Darwinism*; Schou, *Histoire* 279–80.

110 Cf. Schulz, 'Norms'.

111 Cf. Sluga, *Internationalism* 2.

112 M. Ceadel, *Semi-detached idealists. The British peace movement and international relations 1854–1945*. Oxford UP, 2000, 164–165; Crook, *Darwinism* 100–101, 232; Clarke, *Voices* 79, 85, 89. Cf. D. Pick, *War machine. The rationalisation of slaughter in the modern age*. New Haven, Yale UP, 1996.

113 D.A. Bell, *The first total war. Napoleon's Europe and the birth of warfare as we know it*. Boston, Houghton Mifflin, 2007, 311; emphasis in the original.

114 Schou, *Histoire* 284; Ceadel, *Origins* 2–3.

115 G. Best, *War and law since 1945*. Oxford, Clarendon Press, 1994, 36; D.F. Segesser, *Recht statt Rache oder Rache durch Recht? Die Ahndung von Kriegsverbrechen in der internationalen wissenschaftlichen Debatte 1872–1945*. Paderborn, Ferdinand Schöningh, 1998. Cf. C.J. Bartlett, *Peace, war and the European powers, 1814–1914*. New York, St. Martin's Press, 1996, 68.

2 The Tsar, the Rescript and the World

1 In I.S. Rybachenok, *Rossiia i pervaia konferentsiia mira 1899 goda v Gaage*. Moscow, Russian Academy of Sciences, 2005, 195.
2 Dated according to the Gregorian calendar, not the Julian calendar in use in Russia at the time.
3 *Vaderlander* 28 January 1899, np, in NA 2.21.174, 4.
4 In NA 2.21.174, 4.
5 For example: Sir Charles Scott to the Marquis of Salisbury, 1 September 1898, PRO FO65/1555; Lord Arthur James Balfour to Sir Charles Scott, 30 August 1898, PRO FO65/1558; Mr Herbert H. D. Peirce, United States Minister in St Petersburg, to Secretary of State, John Hay, 9 November 1898, in United States Department of State, *Papers relating to the foreign relations of the United States, with the annual message of the President transmitted to Congress*. Washington D.C., United States Government Printing Office, 1898, 547.
6 In J. Sheehan, *Where have all the soldiers gone? The transformation of modern Europe*. Boston, Houghton Mifflin, 2008, 22.
7 Kaiser Wilhelm II to Tsar Nicholas II, 29 August 1898, in J. Dülffer, 'Citizens and diplomats. The debate on the First Hague Peace Conference (1899) in Germany' in C. Chatfield and P. van den Dungen, eds, *Voices prophesying war 1763–1984*. Knoxville, University of Tennessee Press, 1988, 23.
8 In Tuchman, *Proud* 239.
9 Alexander Izvol'skij, Russia's representative in Munich, in J. Dülffer, *Regeln gegen den Krieg. Die Haager Friedens-Konferenzen 1899 und 1907 in der internationalen Politik*. Berlin, Ulstein, 1980, 45; A. Yarmolinsky, ed., *The memoirs of Count Witte*. New York, Doubleday, 1921, 97.
10 Davis, *United States 1* 41.
11 W.R. Day, Department of State, to Mr Hitchcock, United States Ambassador in Russia, 14 September 1898, in United States, *Papers*, 1898, 545.
12 Dülffer, *Regeln* 166; French Minister of Foreign Affairs to French Ambassador in St Petersburg, 10 February 1899, in Ministère des Étrangères, *Documents diplomatiques. Conférence internationale de la paix 1899*. Paris, Imprimerie Nationale, 1900, 5–6.
13 Eyffinger, *1899* 29–30.
14 In Reeves, 'Red crosses' 72.
15 Cf. S.A. Keefer, 'Great Britain and naval arms control. International law and security 1898–1914' PhD, London School of Economics and Political Science, 2011.
16 Eyffinger, *1899* 36.
17 For the correspondence between Queen Wilhelmina and Tsar Nicholas II: Koninklijk Huisarchief, files A50-VIIb-r-01 and A50-VIIb-r-02.
18 G. Fonbelle, *Le Tsar et la paix*. Paris, L. Sauvaitre, 1899.
19 In L. Albertini, *The origins of the war of 1914*. Volume 1, Oxford UP, 1965, 108.
20 C. Andrew, *Théophile Delcassé and the making of the Entente Cordiale. A reappraisal of French foreign policy 1898–1905*. New York, St Martin's Press, 1968, 121; Dülffer, *Regeln* 167–168.
21 In *New England Magazine* 25, 5, January 1899, 583.
22 P. Blom, 'A trap of our own making: Mark Twain and the mechanized warfare of King Arthur's court' in S. Buttsworth and M. Abbenhuis, eds, *Wars, myths and fairy tales*. London, Palgrave Macmillan, 2017, 175–193; B. von Suttner, *Memoirs of Bertha von Suttner. The records of eventful lives*. Volume 2, New York, Ginn, 1910, 213.

23 *Press* (Christchurch, New Zealand) 4 March 1899, 6.
24 In B. Hamann, *Bertha von Suttner. A life for peace*. Syracuse UP, 1996, 140.
25 For example: S. Gustavo, 'En favour de la paz' *Suplemento a la Revista Blanca* 2, 1899, 2.
26 In *Herald of Peace* 590, 1 October 1898, 118.
27 In *Review of Reviews* October 1898, 368.
28 In 1901, the *Samoa Weekly Herald* would be rebranded the *Samoanische Zeitung* and be published in German, to reflect the change to the German administration of Samoa.
29 Accessed through: *Nineteenth-Century UK Periodicals Index*, *Paperspast*, *Gallica* and *Delpher*. I selected the newspapers at random. None of the papers stood out in terms of the number of references made to the Tsar or the upcoming conference. Because the first issues of the German-language colonial press in German-controlled Africa, China and Samoa did not appear until after the release of the rescript, they were left out of this case study: D.H.R. Spennemann, *The heritage of nineteenth-century Samoan newspapers. A bibliographical documentation*. Albury, Johnstone Centre, 2003.
30 *Friend* 1 September 1898, 4.
31 *Friend* 29 September 1898, 4.
32 *Friend* 29 September 1898, 6.
33 *Friend* 10 November 1898, 5, 6.
34 *Friend* 19 January 1899, 4.
35 L. Brake, M. Demoor, *Dictionary of nineteenth-century journalism in Great Britain and Ireland*. London, Academia Press, 2009, 236.
36 *Australasian* 3 September 1898, 542.
37 *Australasian* 3 September 1898, 542.
38 *Australasian* 11 March 1899, 537.
39 *Australasian* 11 March 1899, 537.
40 *SWH* 10 September 1898, 3.
41 *SWH* 10 September 1898, 2.
42 *SWH* 17 December 1898, 2.
43 *Courrier de Tlemcen* 9 September 1898, 2.
44 *Courrier de Tlemcen* 16 September 1898, 1.
45 *Courrier de Tlemcen* 26 May 1899, 1.
46 *Gazette Algerienne* 28 September 1898, 2.
47 *Gazette Algerienne* 15 March 1899, 1.
48 *Gazette Algerienne* 12 April 1899, 1.
49 *Surinamer* 22 September 1898, np.
50 Cf. T.J. Lawrence, 'The Tsar's rescript' *International Journal of Ethics* 9, 2, January 1899, 137.
51 Eyffinger, *1899*, 32–33, 67; Kuehl, *Seeking*, 44; A. Gestrich, 'Die Haager Friedenskonferenzen und die deutsche Presse' in C. Dipper, A. Gestrich and L. Raphael, eds, *Krieg, Frieden und Demokratie. Festschrift für Martin Vogt zum 65 Geburtstag*. Frankfurt, Peter Lang, 2001, 236–237, 241.
52 Dülffer, 'Citizens' 26.
53 Hamann, *Suttner* 142; Dülffer, 'Citizens' 28–29; D.J. Newton, *British labour, European socialism, and the struggle for peace 1889–1914*. Oxford UP, 1985, 64.
54 Suttner, *Memoirs*, Volume 2, 198.
55 A.H. Fried, *Was kann die Petersburger Friedenskonferenz erreichen?* Dresden, E. Pierson, 1899, 3.

56 *Herald of Peace* 598, 1 June 1899, 230.
57 K. von Stengel, *Der ewige Friede*. Paris, H. le Soudier, 1899; W. Killy, ed., *Dictionary of German Biography*. Volume 9, Munich, K.G. Saur, 2005, 521.
58 'Herr von Stengel und die Friedenskonferenz' *FW* 1, 10, September 1899, 53–55.
59 K. von Stengel, *Weltstaat und Friedensproblem*. Berlin, Reichl, 1909, viii. Cf. A.D. White, *The first Hague conference. Reprinted from Dr White's autobiography*. Boston, World Peace Foundation, 1912, 41–42.
60 For a Belgian example: L. Chomé, *Désarmer, c'est déchoir. La conference de la Haye*. Brussels, Imprimerie Gustave Deprez, 1899; H. Delbrück, *Zukunftskrieg und Zukunftsfriede*. np, 1899.
61 Marquis of Salisbury to the House of Commons, 7 February 1899, *HCPP* Fourth Series, Volume 66. For a cartoon: *Fun* 21 February 1899, 61.
62 Cf. Stengel, *Weltstaat* vii.
63 Ceadel, *Semi-detached* 152–153; P. Laity, *The British peace movement 1870–1914*. Oxford, Clarendon Press, 2001, 146; S. Barcroft, 'The Hague peace conference of 1899' *Irish Studies in International Affairs* 3, 1, 1989, 60; Hucker, 'British' 409.
64 *Arbitrator* December 1898.
65 *Herald of Peace* 598, 1 June 1899, 227.
66 These can be found in PRO FO83/1699, 1734, 1735, 1736, 1737, 1738, 1739; A.R. Higgins, 'Petitioning for peace. The British public movement in support of the proposed first Hague peace conference, 1898 – 1899' MA thesis, University of Auckland, 2016.
67 G. Eckley, *Maiden tribute. A life of W.T. Stead*. Philadelphia, Xlibris, 2007, 251.
68 *Concord* for 1898 and 1899.
69 In NA 2.21.174, 4.
70 *Herald of Peace* 598, 1 June 1899, 227; *The Tsar's rescript. A series of papers issued and circulated by the Peace Society*. London Peace Society, 1899, in NA 2.22.28, 228.
71 *AMRR* 19, March 1899, 339; *TT* Letters to the Editor, 23 December 1898, 24 December 1898, 27 December 1898, all on 8.
72 S. Low, 'The hypocrisies of the peace conference' *Nineteenth Century* 45, 267, May 1899, 689.
73 Cf. P. Fritzsche, 'The city and urban life' in Saler, ed., *World* 29–32.
74 *CDT* 29 August 1898, 1.
75 *CDT* 30 August 1898, 1.
76 *CDT* 30 August 1898, 3.
77 *CDT* 31 August 1898, 6; *NYT* 29 August 1898, 4.
78 *CDT* 31 August 1898, 6.
79 *CDT* 1 September 1898, 6.
80 *CDT* 1 September 1898, 7, 12.
81 *CDT* 3 September 1898, 6.
82 *CDT* 30 August 1898, 3.
83 Rybachenok, *Rossiia* 195.
84 This, and the below extracts, in *CDT* 30 August 1898, 3.
85 *NCH* 10 October 1898, 681.
86 *NCH* 12 December 1898, 1095.
87 *NCH* 12 December 1898, 1102.
88 *NCH* 17 October 1898, 728–729.
89 *Revista Moderna* (Brazil) 2, 23, August 1898, np.

90 *El Correo Español* 9 January 1899, 2.
91 *El Sol del Domingo* 11 September 1898, 1.
92 *Speaker* 14 January 1899, 48–49.
93 P. van den Dungen, 'The making of peace. Jean de Bloch and the first Hague peace conference' *Occasional Paper Series of the Center for the Study of Armament and Disarmament* 12, 1983, 8; *Black & White* (London) 17, 435, 3 June 1899, front page; Sir F. Lascelles to the Marquis of Salisbury, 22 December 1898, in PRO FO421, 65; S.J. Capper, *Translation into English of a speech delivered in German at the banquet at the Hotel National Lucerne 7 June 1902 on the occasion of the solemn inauguration of the Museum of Peace and War founded by the late Johann von Bloch, financier, economist and philanthropist whose work upon war led the Czar to issue HIS FAMOUS RESCRIPT which resulted in the CONGRESS AT THE HAGUE*. np, 1902 in PCSC 'Switzerland' CDGB.
94 J. de Bloch, 'The wars of the future' *Contemporary Review* 80, 1 July 1901, 312.
95 L. Tolstoy, *The way to peace and greetings to conscientious objectors*. Glasgow, Strickland Press, 1940 [1899]; L. Tolstoy, 'The Czar's peace proposal' *Independent* 5, 1, 1899, 997–1000.
96 *Spectator* 5 November 1898, 2.
97 *Herald of Peace* 595, 1 March 1899, 181.
98 'Count Tolstoy's opinion of the Peace Conference' *Advocate of Peace* 61, 5, May 1899, 115–116.
99 Rybachenok, *Rossiia* 251; *Herald of Peace* 594, 1 February 1899, 170.
100 *Liberty Review* 9, 15 September 1898, 198.
101 *Liberty Review* 9, 15 September 1898, 198.
102 Dülffer, *Regeln*, 19–33; Rybachenok, *Rossiia* Chapter 1.
103 T.K. Ford, 'The genesis of the first Hague Peace Conference' *Political Science Quarterly* 51, 3, September 1936, 381; D.L. Morrill, 'Nicholas II and the call for the first Hague conference' *Journal of Modern History* 46, 2, June 1974, 296–313.
104 S.A. Keefer, 'Building the palace of peace. The Hague Conference of 1899 and arms control in the progressive era' *Journal of the History of International Law* 8, 2006, 7–8; Tuchman, *Proud* 236–237; D. Bettez, 'Unfulfilled initiative. Disarmament negotiations and the Hague peace conferences of 1899 and 1907' *RUSI Journal* 133, 3, 1988, 57.
105 Eyffinger, *1899* 24; V.V. Pustogarov, *Our Martens. F.F. Martens international lawyer and architect of peace*. The Hague, Kluwer Law International, 2000, 158.
106 Davis, *United States 1* 44.
107 A. Roberts, 'Land warfare. From The Hague to Nuremberg' in M. Howard, G.G. Andreopoulos and M.R. Shulman, eds, *The laws of war. Constraints on warfare in the western world*. New Haven, Yale UP, 1994, 120; Dülffer, *Regeln* 26–27; D.F. Vagts, 'Hague conventions and arms control' *American Journal of International Law* 94, 4, 2000, 33; P. van den Dungen, 'Een interessante probleem: Jean Bloch en de eerste Haagse vredesconferentie' *Transaktie* 10, 1981, 189–214; P. van den Dungen, 'From St Petersburg to The Hague. Bloch and the first Hague peace conference (1899)' in G. Prins and H. Tromp, eds, *The future of war*. The Hague, Kluwer Law, 2000, 69–83.
108 Keefer, 'Building' 7–8.
109 Morrill, 'Nicholas II' 313.
110 *Advocate of Peace* 61, 2, February 1899, 29–31.
111 W.T. Stead in *AMRR* 19, January 1899, 43.

112 J.H. Choate, *The two Hague conferences*. Princeton UP, 1913, 4; H. Lammasch, 'Rückblicke auf die Haager Friedenskonferenzen' *Niemeyers Zeitschrift für Internationales Recht* 26, 1916, 154.
113 N. de Basily, *Memoirs. Diplomat of Imperial Russia 1903–1917*. Stanford, Hoover Institution Press, 1973, 11. A. Eyffinger, *The 1907 Hague Peace Conference. 'The conscience of the civilized world'*. The Hague, JudiCap, 2007, 14; Ford, 'Genesis' 360–361; Morrill, 'Nicholas II'.
114 A.C.F. Beales, *The history of peace. A short account of the organised movements for international peace*. London, G. Bell, 1931, 231; A.H. Fried, 'Baroness von Suttner' *The Peace Movement* 2, 6, 15 June 1913, 258.
115 E.D. Mead in W.E. Channing, *Discourses on war*. Boston, Ginn, 1903, xviii.
116 *Sunday Times* 28 December 1902, 2.
117 A. Upward, *Secret history of today. Being revelations of a diplomatic spy*. New York, G.P. Putnam, 1904, 117.
118 L. Appleton, *Fifty years historic record of the progress of European disarmament from 1849 to 1899*. London, British and Foreign Arbitration Association, 1899; Laity, *British* 103.
119 Appleton, *Fifty* 1–5.
120 N. Muir, *Dimitri Stancioff. Patriot and cosmopolitan 1864–1940*. London, John Murray, 1957, 83.
121 Muir, *Stancioff* 83.
122 Patterson, *Toward* 106–107; Davis, *United States 1* 56; Tate, *Disarmament* 215.
123 *Advocate of Peace* 60, 9, October 1898, 1.
124 *Guerre et le militarism*.
125 N. Notovitch, *Le pacification de l'Europe et Nicholas II*. Paris, Paul Ollendorff, 1899; D.T. McGetchin, *Indology, Indomania and orientalism. Ancient India's rebirth in modern Germany*. Madison, Fairleigh Dickinson UP, 2009, 133.
126 Suttner, *Memoirs*, Volume 2, 197–199. For an excellent compendium: S. Cooper, *Arbitration or war? Contemporary reactions to the Hague peace conference of 1899*. New York, Garland, 1972.
127 R. Kipling, 'The truce of the bear' 1898, poetryloverspage.com (accessed April 2015); italics in original.
128 Barcroft, 'Hague' 60.
129 C. Guieysse, *La France et la paix armée. La conference de la Haye*. Paris, Pages Libres, 1905.
130 J. Braakensiek, *Het jaar 1899*. Amsterdam, np, 1900.
131 *De vredes-conferentie. Prentenboek voor oud en jong*. Amsterdam, H. Gerlings, 1899, 49 (published in German as *Abrüstungs-Bilderbuch. Die Friedenskonferenz in der Karikatur aller Völker*. Berlin, Dr Eysler, 1899).
132 *Vredes-conferentie* 47.
133 *Vredes-conferentie* 37.
134 Hamann, *Suttner* 140.
135 Henri Dunant to Bertha von Suttner, 21 September 1898, in Suttner, *Memoirs*, Volume 2, 196; Hamann, *Suttner* 139.
136 Bjørnstjerne Bjørnson to Bertha von Suttner, 30 August 1898, in Suttner, *Memoirs*, Volume 2, 193.
137 *Advocate of Peace* 60, 8, August–September 1898, 176 (cites full text of the rescript on 191).

138 Clarke, *Voices* 131; B. Bond, *War and society in Europe 1870–1970*. Gloucestershire, Sutton, 1984 [1998], 26.
139 Cf. Patterson, *Toward* 99; Davis, *United States 1* 61.
140 H. Wehberg, *Deutschland und die Friedensbewegung*. Berlin, Deutsche Verlagsgesellschaft für Politik und Geschichte, 1924, 7.
141 *Hawke's Bay Herald* (New Zealand) 24 March 1899, 2.
142 Barber, 'Evolution'.
143 V. Genin, 'La diplomatie belge et le droit international face à la Conférence de la Paix de la Haye en 1899. Attraits et méfiances' Unpublished, 'International Law and Arbitration from the Hague conferences to the League of Nations' seminar, University of Antwerp, 2 June 2015, 4. Cf. R. Verwaest, *Van Den Haag tot Genève. België en het internationale oorlogsrecht (1874–1950)*. Brugge, Die Keure, 2011.
144 Genin, 'Diplomatie' 2.
145 Stengel, *Weltstaat* ix. Chomé, *Désarmer* 33.
146 *AMRR* 19, January 1899, 113.
147 E.M. Bliss in *AMRR* 19, April 1899, 434.
148 *AMRR* 19, March 1899, 337.
149 *Journal des Économistes* 35, September 1898, 465.
150 *Journal des Économistes* 36, May 1899, 169. Cf. L. Courtney, 'The approaching conference' *Contemporary Review* 75, January 1899, 609–619.
151 P. Fiore, 'The Czar of Russia and the peace conference. Translated for "The Chautauquan" from the Italian "Nuova Antologia"' *Chautauquan* 29, 1899, 242–246.

3 A *Coram Publies*: Planning the First Hague Conference, 1899

1 *Poverty Bay Herald* (New Zealand) 26, 8512, 9 May 1899, 3.
2 Sir H. Rumbold to the Marquis of Salisbury, 14 September 1898, in G.P. Gooch and H. Temperley, eds, *British Documents on the Origins of the War 1898–1914*. Volume 1. London, His Majesty's Stationery Office, 1927, 219.
3 Imperial rescript, 12/24 August 1898: Scott, *Hague peace*, Volume 1, 41–42.
4 *Journal de St-Petersbourg* 28 August 1898, front page, and special bulletin; Davis, *United States 1*, 38; J. Mack, 'Nicholas II and the rescript for peace of 1898. Apostle of peace or shrewd politician?' *Russian History* 31, 1–2, 2004, 84–90.
5 Morrill, 'Nicholas II' 308; Rybachenok, *Rossiia*.
6 Cf. K. Hamilton, 'Britain and the Hague peace conference of 1899' in K. Hamilton and E. Johnson, eds, *Arms and disarmament in diplomacy*. London, Vallentine Mitchell, 2008, 9–32; Hucker, 'British' 409; Hamilton, 'Britain'.
7 Cooper, ed., *Arbitration* 13.
8 Rybachenok, *Rossiia*. Cf. J.B. Scott, ed., *Proceedings of the international peace conference. The Hague, May 18–July 29, 1899*. New edition. Washington D.C., Carnegie Endowment for International Peace, 1920, 17.
9 C.W. Porter, *The career of Théophile Delcassé*. Philadelphia, University of Pennsylvania Press, 1936, 208–209.
10 Porter, *Delcassé* 210.

11 For example: Italy's Minister in Vienna to Italy's Foreign Minister, 4 February 1899, in Ministero degli affair esteri, *I documenti diplomatici italiani.* Series III, Volume III. Rome, Libreria dello stato, 1962, 91; Dutch Minister of Foreign Affairs to Dutch Minister in Berlin, 20 May 1899, in C. Smit, ed., *Bescheiden betreffende de buitenlandsche politiek van Nederland 1848–1919. Derde period 1899–1919.* Volume 1, 1964, 65–66; Dülffer, *Regeln* 126.
12 British Minister in St Petersburg, Charles S. Scott, to the Marquis of Salisbury, 1 September 1898, PRO FO65, 1555.
13 A.N. Kuropatkin, 22 September 1898, in Pustogarov, *Martens* 157.
14 US Ambassador in St Petersburg, H.D. Peirce, to Secretary of State, John Hay, 9 November 1898, in United States, *Papers*, 1898, 546–547.
15 In Schlichtmann, 'Japan' 382.
16 Henry Howard to the Marquis of Salisbury, 23 February 1899 in PRO FO421, 65.
17 PRO FO421, 65.
18 Dutch Minister of Foreign Affairs, Willem de Beaufort, to Dutch Minister in Berlin, Tets van Goudriaan, 24 February 1899, in Smit, ed., *Bescheiden.* Volume 1, 24; Draft dispatch from the Marquis of Salisbury to Charles Scott, October 1898, PRO CAB37/48/73; Marquis of Salisbury to Sir C. Scott, 24 October 1898, in Gooch, Temperley, eds, *Origins.* Volume 1, 220–221.
19 Marquis of Salisbury, House of Commons Sitting, 7 February 1899, in *HCPP* 4th Series, Volume 66.
20 *Hawke's Bay Herald* 1 September 1898, 3; *Thames Star* 3 September 1898, 4; *Star* (Christchurch) 5 September 1898, 4; *Otago Witness* 8 September 1898, 16; *Wanganui Chronicle* 2 September 1898, 2; *Thames Advertiser* 2 September 1898, 2.
21 *Auckland Star* 5 October 1898, 5.
22 M. Hutching, '"Turn back this tide of barbarism". New Zealand women who were opposed to war, 1896–1919' MA thesis, University of Auckland, 1990, 17–29.
23 *Evening Post* 12 November 1898, 2.
24 *Thames Advertiser* 19 October 1898, 2.
25 *New Zealand Herald* 19 December 1898, 5; *Wanganui Herald* 6 January 1899, 2.
26 *Evening Star* (Dunedin) 8 February 1899, 4.
27 *Hawke's Bay Herald* 3 March 1899, 3.
28 Rybachenok, *Rossiia* 135.
29 Cf. Clark, *International legitimacy.*
30 B.J.M.C. Waszclewicz-van Schilfgaarde, *Internationale ontwapening. Een vrouwenzaak en een vrouwenbelang.* Amsterdam, W. Verslys, 1899, esp. 22–25, in PCSC 'Netherlands' CDGB; *Guerre et le militarism* 250–253.
31 NA 2.21.174, 2; *Vrede door Recht* May 1901, 82–83 in NA 2.21.174, 3; B.J.M.C. Wasklewicz-van Schilfgaarde, *Open brief aan Felix Ortt. Een word tot de Tolstoïanen en Christelijk-Anarchisten.* Amsterdam, W. Versluys, 1899; *Nederlandsche Vredebond Jaarboek* 1900, 6–8, in PCSC, 'Nederlandsche Vredesbond' CDGB.
32 For a compilation: NA2.21.174, 4, 5.
33 *International Council of Women. Report* 1900, 242–243; *Bredasche Courant* 25 February 1899, np, in NA 2.21.174, 4.
34 *Nederlandsche Dagblad* 14 April 1899, np, in NA 2.21.74, 4.
35 Baroness Johanna Waszklewicz van Schilfgaarde's report to the Executive Committee of the Nederlandse Vrouwenbond ter Internationale Ontwapening, 14 April 1899, in NA 2.21.174, 2.
36 *Echo* 5 April 1899, np, in NA 2.21.174, 4.

37 *Hollandia* 22 April 1899, np, in NA 2.21.174, 4.
38 *Amsterdammer* 6 March 1899, in NA 2.21.174, 4; B. van der Schuyt, *De 's Gravenlandseweg en zijn bewoners*. Hilversum, Verloren, 2005, 288–289.
39 *Centrum* 24 March 1899, np, in NA 2.21.174, 4.
40 *Tijd* 26 January 1899, np, in NA 2.21.174, 4.
41 *Familie Blad* 25 January 1899, np, in NA 2.21.174, 4.
42 *Nederlandsche Dagblad* 26 January 1899, in NA 2.21.174, 4.
43 N.I. Agøy, 'It will serve to increase our Union difficulties. Norway, Sweden and the Hague peace conference of 1899' *Historisk tidsskirft* 79, 2000, 181–208; A. Rindfleisch, 'The question of Danish neutrality' in M. Epkenhans and G.P. Gross, eds, *The Danish straits and German naval power 1905–1918*. Potsdam, Militärgeschichtliches Forschungsamt, 2010, 63–74; P. Luntinen, 'Neutrality in northern Europe before the First World War' in J. Nevakivi, ed., *Neutrality in history. Proceedings of the conference on the history of neutrality organized in Helsinki 9–12 September 1992 under the auspices of the Commission of History of International Relations*. Helsinki, Finnish Historical Society, 1993, 107–114.
44 NA 2.05.03, 524.
45 Mr Fane to the Marquis of Salisbury, 4 May 1899, in PRO FO421, 65.
46 Sir F. Pakenham to the Marquis of Salisbury, 6 March 1899; Mr Fane to the Marquis of Salisbury, 4 May 1899, both in PRO FO421, 65.
47 Belgique Croisade de la Paix Statistique, 1899, in NA 2.05.03, 528.
48 NA 2.05.03, 526.
49 A. von Siebold, *Der ewige Krieg und die Friedenskonferenz*. Munich, August Schupp, 1899; Dülffer, 'Citizens' 29–30; Davis, *United States 1* 86; E. Loewenthal, *Grunzüge zur Reform und Codification des Völkerrechts*. Berlin, Otto Dreyer, 1898; H.O. Kats, *Sonnenaufgang. Ein Gespräch über die Friedens-Conferenz im Haag*. Munich, August Schupp, [1899]; A. Kirchhoff, ed., *Männer der Wissenschaft über die Friedens-Konferenz*. Berlin Stankiewicz, 1899.
50 Dülffer, 'Citizens' 31–32.
51 J.B.B., 'De vredesconferentie te Turijn' *Nederlandsch Vredesbond Jaarboek* 1899, 60–65, in PCSC 'Netherlands Vredesbond'.
52 *Pax! Ricordo del 29 settembre 1898 Il Congressisti della Pace à Torre Pellice*. Tore Pelicce, Fipografia Alpina, 1899, in NA 2.22.28, 271.
53 Kirchhoff, *Männer*.
54 *Evening Post* 3 January 1899, 5.
55 May Wright Sewall, letter to the Secretariat of the Hague Peace Conference, 19 May 1899, in NA 2.05.03, 528; *Addresses of the New York State Bar Association to His Imperial Majesty, Nicholas II, Emperor of all the Russias and to the President of the United States, on the occasion and in commendation of the peace congress at The Hague and recommending the creation of an international court*. New York, np, 1899.
56 Alonso, *Peace* 52.
57 *The peace crusade. A record of the peace conference at The Hague. May 18 to July 29 1899*. Boston, Lend a Hand Society, 1899, in PCSC, DG21, Reel 78.1, Box 2; *War Against War* January–March 1899.
58 Davis, *United States 1* 101.
59 Patterson, *Toward* 105–106.
60 W.S. Robinson, *Muckraker. The scandalous life and times of W.T. Stead, Britain's first investigative journalist*. London, Biteback, 2012.

61 Hampton, *Visions* 112; H. Wyndham, *Victorian sensations*. London, Jarrolds, 1933, 122–153.
62 Cf. Miller, *Liberation* 4.
63 W.T. Stead, *The united states of Europe on the eve of the parliament of peace*. London, np, 1899, 123.
64 Stead, *United*; F. Whyte, *The life of W.T. Stead*. Volume 2, London, Jonathan Cape, 1925, 129–146.
65 Stead, *United*.
66 Ford, 'Genesis' 354; Foreign Office report, 11 February 1907, in PRO FO372/65; Davis, *United States 1* 60; Tuchman, *Proud* 248; A. Balfour to W.T. Stead, 20 June 1899, in CAC STED1/4. Cf. A. Meyerdorff, *Correspondance diplomatique du Baron de Staal (1884–1900)*. Volume 2, Paris, Marcel Rivière, 1929, 407.
67 *Advocate of Peace* 61, 1, January 1899, 6; Eckley, *Maiden* 247.
68 Edwin H. Stout to W.T. Stead, 16 November 1899 and W.H. Smith & Son to W.T. Stead, 18 January 1899, both in CAC STED1/68.
69 *Herald of Peace* 596, 1 April 1899, 200.
70 The phrase 'W.T. Stead' occurs 645 times in a digital search of 40 New Zealand newspapers between 1898 and 1899 (*Papers Past*, January 2016); 219 times in Dutch-language newspapers in the same period (*Delpher*, March 2016); 1,058 times in the *Chicago Tribune*, 627 times in the *Washington Post* and 46 times in the *Irish Times* for the same period (*ProQuest Historical Newspapers* database, March 2016).
71 *JT* 17 July 1907, 5; J. Nerone, K. Barnhurst, 'Stead in America' in L. Brake, E. King, R. Luckhurst and J. Mussell, eds, *W.T. Stead. Newspaper revolutionary*. London, British Library, 2013, 98–114.
72 W.T. Stead, ed., *The M.P. for Russia. Reminiscences and correspondence of Madame Olga Novikoff*. Volume 2, London, Andrew Melrose, 1909, 405–406; *JT* 17 July 1907, 5; C.P. Scott to W.T. Stead, 10 August 1899, CAC STED1/64.
73 *Wairarapa Daily Times* 17 May 1899, 2; *Auckland Star* 18 March 1899, 1; *Daily Telegraph* 16 December 1898, 3.
74 *Spectator* 24 December 1898, 7.
75 Higgins, 'Petitioning'.
76 Higgins, 'Petitioning'; A.R. Higgins, 'Writing for peace. The British public peace petitioning movement's historical legacies after 1898' in Abbenhuis et al., eds, *War*, 138–154.
77 Sir U. Kay Shuttlesworth, House of Commons, 13 March 1899, *HCPP*, Fourth Series, Volume 66.
78 In NA 2.05.03, 528.
79 White, *Hague* 3.
80 Davis, *United States 1* 102.
81 'Suggestions sur le meilleurs moyens d'assurer la paix générale' in Cooper, ed., *Arbitration* 25.
82 Other examples: L. le Foyer, *Lettre à MM. les membres de la conférence de la paix de la Haye. Le droit des peuples*. Paris, V. Giard & E. Brière, 1899; NA 2.05.03, 528.
83 Dülffer, 'Citizens' 30; *International Council of Women*, 1909, Volume 2, 132–133; *Advocate of Peace* 60, 9, October 1898, 197.
84 For example: J.A. Davy, 'Pacifist thought and gender ideology in political biographies of women peace activists in Germany 1899–1970' *Journal of Women's History* 13, 3, 2001, 35–36.
85 Hodgson Pratt to Albert Gobat, 3 February 1899, IPUA Box 20.

86 H. Wehberg, 'The Inter-Parliamentary Union and the development of international organization' and L. Quidde, 'The creation of the Inter-Parliamentary Union' both in *Inter-Parliamentary Union* 35, 39–60.
87 U. Kätzel, 'A radical women's rights and peace activist. Margarethe Lenore Selenka, initiator of the first worldwide women's peace demonstration in 1899' *Journal of Women's History* 13, 3, Autumn 2001, 46–69.
88 *International Council of Women*, 1899, 232; M. Selenka, *Die internationale Kundgebung der Frauen zur Friedens-Konferenz vom 15 mai 1899*. Munich, August Schripp, 1900, VII.
89 *Advocate of Peace* 63, 6, June 1901, 128; *Woman's Exponent* (Salt Lake City) 15 May 1899, 1. The *Los Angeles Times* reported sixty-eight meetings across thirteen American states, with an attendance of 27,482 women and representing a constituency of 85,561 women (18 May 1899, 2). On 21 May, it reported 90,000 women were represented across the United States at the 18 May celebrations (A4).
90 *International Council of Women*, 1900, 232; *Die deutsche Frau in der Friedensbewegung*. Second edition. Munich, J.F. Lehmann, 1900.
91 In NA 2.05.03, 545; Selenka, *Internationale*.
92 *International Council of Women*, 1904, Volume 2, 134.
93 Selenka, *Internationale* V, 128; Kätzel, 'Radical' 51–52.
94 Selenka, *Internationale* IV, 120.
95 In Selenka, *Internationale* 50–52.
96 *Kobe Weekly Chronicle* 28 June 1899, 521, in Schlichtmann, 'Japan' 383.
97 G. Nishi to Waszcklewicz von Schilfgaarde, 31 July 1899, NA 2.21.174, 5.
98 Selenka, *Internationale* IV; Hutching, 'Turn' 49–50.
99 *International Council of Women*, 1899, 213; P. Gordon, ed., *Politics and society. The journals of Lady Knightley of Fawsley 1885–1913*. London, Routledge, 2016, np [Tuesday 27 June].
100 Cooper, 'Women' 22; Tuchman, *Proud* 257.
101 British Minister in St Petersburg, Sir Charles Scott, to the Marquis of Salisbury, 31 October 1898, in PRO FO65/1555; Dülffer, *Regeln* 48–49.
102 Pustogarov, *Martens*; Eyffinger, *1899*; H. Wehberg, 'Friedrich v. Martens und die Haager Friedenskonferenzen' *Zeitschrift für internationales Recht* 10, 1910, 343–357.
103 In Hamann, *Suttner* 143; emphasis in the original.
104 *Journal de St-Petersbourg* 18 May 1899, 2.
105 Dutch Minister of Foreign Affairs, Willem de Beaufort, to Dutch Minister in St Petersburg, Wttewaal van Stoetwegen, 24 January 1899, in Smit, ed., *Bescheiden*, Volume 1, 2.
106 French Minister of Foreign Affairs to the French Ambassador in St Petersburg, 10 February 1899, in Ministère des Éstrangères, *Conférence 1899* 5-6.
107 Dülffer, *Regeln* 173–174.
108 Second circular 30 December 1898/11 January 1899, in Scott, *Hague peace*, Volume 1, 45.
109 Hamann, *Suttner* 144–145.
110 Sir Charles Scott to Arthur Balfour, 3 September 1898, in Gooch and Temperley, eds, *Origins*, Volume 1, 217; Mr Hitchcock to Mr Day, 3 September 1898, in United States, *Papers*, 1899, 542–543; Dülffer, *Regeln* 167.
111 Cf. Andrew, *Delcassé* 121.
112 Sir Charles Scott to the Marquis of Salisbury, 5 October 1898, in PRO FO65, 1555.

113 For example: W.J. Stillman, 'The peace of Europe' *Contemporary Review* 1 January 1899, 311–322.
114 *Jugend* 4, 31, 29 July 1899, front cover. Art by Arpad Schmidhammer.
115 *Mataura Ensign* 21 January 1899, 4.
116 *Evening Post* 17 January 1899, 2.
117 Marquis of Salisbury to Charles S. Scott, 1 March 1899, in BL Add MS52297.
118 *TT* 9 March 1899, 9. House of Commons, 9 March 1899, *HCPP*, Fourth Series, Volume 68.
119 First Lord of the Admiralty, G.J. Goschen, House of Commons, 9 March 1899, *HCPP*, Fourth Series, Volume 68.
120 Hamilton, 'Britain' 11–14.
121 Mr Labouchère, House of Commons, 24 February 1899, *HCPP*, Fourth Series, Volume 67.
122 Sir U. Kay Shuttlesworth, House of Commons, 13 March 1899, *HCPP*, Fourth Series, Volume 68.
123 PRO FO83, 1700.
124 Dülffer, *Regeln* 122–123.
125 Dülffer, *Regeln* 45, 50.
126 Dutch Minister in St Petersburg to Dutch Minister of Foreign Affairs, 12 January 1899, in Smit, ed., *Bescheiden*, Volume 1, 1.
127 Eyffinger, *1899* 40; *Tilburgsche Courant* 15 June 1899, np.
128 A. Eyffinger, 'Living up to a tradition' in P.J. van Krieken and D. McKay, eds, *The Hague. Legal capital of the world*. The Hague, T.M.C. Asser Press, 2005, 33.
129 Eyffinger, *1899* 30.
130 Dutch Minister in St Petersburg to Dutch Minister of Foreign Affairs, 25 January 1899, in Smit, ed., *Bescheiden*, Volume 1, 3.
131 C. Fasseur, *Wilhelmina. De jonge koningin*. Amsterdam, Balans, 1998, 393–395; G. Somsen, '"Holland's calling". Dutch scientists' self-fashioning as international mediators' in Letteval et al., eds, *Neutrality* 47; A. Eyffinger, *De hele wereld bijeen. De eerste Haagse vredesconferentie van 1899. Mesdagkwartier lezing III*. np, 1995, 14; Wilhelmina, *Eenzaam maar niet alleen*. np, W. ten Have, 1959, 92.
132 *Lustige Blätter* 14 May 1899; Eyffinger, *1899* 100. Also: *Der Floh* (Vienna) 21, 31, 1899, front page.
133 *Tilburgsche Courant* 23 March 1899, np; HGA 0353-01; Davis, *United States 1* 91.
134 *Poverty Bay Herald* 9 May 1899, 3. Cf. E. Lecky, 'The house in the wood' *Nineteenth Century* 45, 267, May 1899, 795–801.
135 For which: correspondence between the Netherlands and Russia, February to May 1899: Smit, ed., *Bescheiden*, Volume 1.
136 A. Lanza, *La santa sede e le conferenz della pace dell'aja del 1899 e 1907*. Rome, Lateran UP, 2002.
137 Dutch Minister in St Petersburg to Minister Foreign Affairs, 15 February 1899, in Smit, ed., *Bescheiden*, Volume 1, 16–17.
138 Italy's Foreign Minister to Italy's Minister in Vienna, 4 February 1899, in Ministero, *I documenti*, Series III, Volume III, 90–92.
139 Dutch Minister of Foreign Affairs to Dutch Minister in Berlin, 22 February 1899, in Smit, ed., *Bescheiden*, Volume 1, 22–23.
140 P. Villiot, *Le recours au siege apostolique et la première conférence international de la paix. Les enseignments des archives du Quai d'Orsay*. Paris, Collection Archétypes

Contemporaines, 1999; D. Alvarez, 'The Holy See and the first Hague peace conference (1899)' *Archivum Historiae Pontificiae* 26, 1988, 431–438.

141 In *North Queensland Register* 6 March 1899, 4.
142 *Catholic World* 119, April–December 1899, 128, 280.
143 *Tijd* 20 April 1899, np.
144 Davis, *United States 1* 87; Fasseur, *Wilhelmina* 341; Scott, *Proceedings 1899* 222–223.
145 *Venloosche Bode* 4 August 1907, 1, in NA 2.21.290, 86.
146 Dutch Minister in Berlin to Dutch Foreign Minister, 25 February 1899, in Smit, ed., *Bescheiden*, Volume 1, 25–26.
147 In PRO DO119, 546 and FO83, 1700.
148 *Herald of Peace* 598, 1 June 1899, 231.
149 J.P. de Valk, M. van Fassen, eds, *Dagboeken en aantekeningen van Willem Hendrik de Beaufort*. Volume 2, The Hague, ING, 1993, 52; Henry Howard to Marquis of Salisbury, 18 July 1899, in PRO FO37/825.
150 Dutch Minister of Foreign Affairs to Dutch Minister in St Petersburg, 28 February 1899, in Smit, ed., *Bescheiden*, Volume 1, 29.
151 Valk and Fassen, eds, *Beaufort*, Volume 1, 54.
152 Sir Henry Howard to the Marquis of Salisbury, 14 April 1899, in PRO FO421, 65.
153 Lord Fisher, *Records by Admiral of the Fleet Lord Fisher*. London, Hodder and Stoughton, 1919, 55.
154 Hamilton, 'Britain' 13–14.
155 D. Steele, *Lord Salisbury. A political biography*. London, University College London Press, 1999, 329–330.
156 *AMRR* 19 May 1899, 545; *New York Tribune* in PRO FO421, 65.
157 *NYT* 4 May 1899, 4.
158 Davis, *United States 1* 75.
159 Davis, *United States 1* 85.
160 Koskenniemi, *Gentle* 208, 211.
161 In a cartoon, the *Lustige Blätter* depicted Professor Stengel as a goat eating the 'peace flowers' of The Hague (in W.T. Stead, *La chronique de la conference de la Haye 1899. Accompagné du texte des conventions*. The Hague, J. Hoekstra, 1899, 118).
162 Wickham Stead to W.T. Stead, 11 May 1899, in CAC STED1/66.
163 M. Lammasch and H. Sperl, eds, *Heinrich Lammasch. Seine Aufzeichnungen, sein Wirken und seine Politik*. Vienna, Franz Deuticke, 1922.
164 H. Lammasch, 'Aus meinem Leben' in Lammasch and Sperl, eds, *Heinrich* 18.
165 Dungen, 'Making' 15.
166 Davis, *United States 1* 88.
167 Pustogarov, *Martens* 171.
168 Davis, *United States 1* 77–80.
169 Hamilton, 'Britain' 12–15.
170 Hamilton, 'Britain' 16.
171 Albertini, *Origins*, Volume 1, 109. Cf. Wehberg, *Deutschland* 8.
172 G.A. Finch, *Adventures in internationalism. A biography of James Brown Scott*. Clark, Lawbook Exchange, 2012, 102.
173 Dülffer, *Regeln* 188–189.
174 Dutch Minister of Foreign Affairs to Dutch Minister in Berlin, 9 February 1899, in Smit, ed., *Bescheiden*, Volume 1, 10–11.
175 Ivan Bloch to Bertha von Suttner, 8 April 1899, in Suttner, *Memoirs*, Volume 2, 236.

176 Davis, *United States 1* 100.
177 Davis, *United States 1* 101.
178 *Telegraaf* 18 May 1899, 4.
179 A. Gall, Fabriek van Pyr Decoratien in Rotterdam to Dutch Minister of Foreign Affairs, 3 May 1899, in NA 2.05.03, 519.
180 *Telegraaf* 19 May 1899, np.
181 *Vrede door Recht* February 1900, 11; May 1901, 85; P. van den Dungen, 'Preventing catastrophe. The world's first peace museum' *Ritsumeikan Kokusai Kenkyu* 18, 3, March 2006, 449–462. For a catalogue: J. Ten Kate, *In the cause of humanity*. London, Doré Gallery, nd, and *Notes sur le peintre hollandaise Jan ten Kate et sur ses tableaux pour l'humanité*. Antwerp, Georges Meyer, nd [1902], in NA 2.06.001, 5259.
182 NA 2.05.03, 519.

4 It Is Not Enough! The First Hague Conference, 1899

1 G. de Lapradelle, *La conférence de la paix (La Haye, 18 mai-29 juillet) par la Revue Générale de Droit International Public*. Paris, A. Pedone, 1900, 8.
2 *Australasian* 27 May 1899, 1153.
3 In R. Hough, *First Sea Lord. An authorized biography of Admiral Lord Fisher*. London, George Allen and Unwin, 1969, 114.
4 Cecil Fisher to John Fisher, 16 May 1899, in CAC FISR 1/ 4.
5 White, *Hague* 8; Davis, *United States 1* 89–90.
6 White, *Hague* 8.
7 British Ambassador to Vienna, Sir H. Rumbold, to the Marquis of Salisbury, 13 April 1899, in PRO FO421, 65.
8 British Minister in Vienna, Ralph Milbanks, to the Marquis of Salisbury, 12 May 1899, in PRO FO83, 1700; Count Münster in R. Cortissoz, *The life of Whitelaw Reid*. Volume 2, New York, Charles Scribner's Sons, 1921, 258.
9 R.M. Ogden, ed., *The diaries of Andrew D. White*. Ithaca, Cornell University Library, 1959, 357; Davis, *United States 1* 73.
10 In Muir, *Stancioff* 86.
11 *Journal de St-Petersbourg* 18 May 1899, 2.
12 For example: *Telegraaf* 2 June 1899, 2.
13 *Dagblad van Zuid-Holland en 's Gravenhage* 19 May 1899, np, in NA 2.21.290, 84.
14 Dutch Minister of War to Local Commander in The Hague, 16 May 1899, in NA 2.05.03, 519.
15 For examples: NA 2.05.03, 519.
16 *Telegraaf* 18 May 1899, 6; Eyffinger, *1899* 109–110.
17 *Matin* 25 September 1899, 2.
18 The *Los Angeles Times* referenced 'The Hague' 118 times between 18 May and 1 August 1898, including in a number of lengthy editorials. In the same period, the *Telegraaf* referred to the conference (*vredesconferentie*) in 233 articles, *Le Matin* made 201 references to 'La Haye', while 64 out of a total of 74 issues of the *Wiener Zeitung* discussed the conference, often at great length. The *Japan Times* presented several columns on news from The Hague in sizeable editorial comments every two or three days. These newspapers were selected at random from the dozens available in the following digital newspaper archives: *ProQuest*, *Delpher*, *Gallica*, *Anno* and the *Japan Times Digital Archive*. In searching for the term 'La Haye', 'vredesconferentie',

'The Hague' and 'Haag' in these archives, none of the papers selected here were extraordinary in terms of the quantity of their references to the conference or in the quality of their editorial content.

19 NA 2.21.018; NA 2.21.290, 284.
20 *LAT* 18 May 1899, 2.
21 *LAT* 19 May 1899, 2.
22 *LAT* 20 May 1899, 1.
23 *LAT* 21 May 1899, 2.
24 *LAT* 23 May 1899, 1; 24 May 1899, 2.
25 *Friend* 6 July 1899, 6.
26 *LAT* 23 June 1899, 8.
27 Davis, *United States 1* 103; Beales, *History* 233; Tate, *Disarmament* 351.
28 Perris, *History* 29; B. von Suttner, *Die Haager Friedenskonferenz. Tagebuchblätter.* Dresden, E. Pierson, 1901, 88–89, 91, 100; F. Holls, 'Reminiscenses of the peace conference at The Hague, 1899' in HLH, Ms Am 1308, 364; Laity, *British* 151.
29 *Telegraaf* 29 May 1899, 3.
30 Davis, *United States 1*; Dülffer, *Regeln*; Eyffinger, *1899*; Hamilton, 'Britain'; Keefer, 'Building'.
31 N. Wylie, 'Muddied waters. The influence of the first Hague conference on the evolution of the Geneva conventions of 1864 and 1906' in Abbenhuis et al., eds, *War* 52–68.
32 Lapradelle, *Conférence* 8.
33 W.E. Darby, *The peace conference at The Hague. Its history, work and results.* London, Peace Society, [1900], 54.
34 Eyffinger counts thirty-seven newspapers represented (Eyffinger, *1899* 346); A. Gestrich suggests forty ('Haager' 233).
35 Scott, *Proceedings 1899* 20–21; Davis, *United States 1* 94.
36 NA 2.05.03, 518–531.
37 Cf. R. Sharwood, 'Princes and peacemakers. The story of the Hague peace conference of 1899' in Rosenne, ed., *Hague* 455.
38 *LAT* 21 May 1899, A4; 23 May 1899, 2; Rybachenok, *Rossiia* 133–134, 251; NA 2.21.018, 314; NA2.05.03, 519.
39 *LAT* 25 May 1899, 8.
40 In *LAT* 4 June 1899, 2.
41 Scott, *Proceedings 1899* 20; Scott, *Hague peace*, Volume 1, 54. R.P. Maxwell to British Foreign Office, 30 May 1899, in PRO FO83, 1700.
42 For example: Frederick Holls to Bertha von Suttner in Suttner, *Memoirs*, Volume 2, 272–273.
43 Scott, *Proceedings 1899* 582; White, *Hague* 18; Holls, 'Reminiscenses'.
44 Suttner, *Memoirs*, Volume 2, 258.
45 Suttner, *Memoirs*, Volume 2, 266, 277, 279, 291; White, *Hague* 68.
46 Suttner, *Memoirs*, Volume 2, 291.
47 Scott, *Proceedings 1899* 586.
48 In *Telegraaf* 5 June 1899, 2.
49 Baron de Staal in Scott, *Proceedings 1899* 17; italics in original. The official reports of the first Hague peace conference were published in French: *Conférence internationale de la paix. La Haye 18 mai-29 juillet 1899.* The Hague, Imprimerie Nationale, 1899. I have used the English translation: Scott, *Proceedings 1899.*
50 Cf. Schücking, *International union* 23, 64–65.

51 Baron de Staal in Scott, *Proceedings 1899* 19.
52 W.E. Darby in *Herald of Peace* 599, 1 July 1899, 245.
53 White, *Hague* 11.
54 The *Nieuws van de Dag* advertised the compendium (20 May 1899, 3); A. van Daehne van Varick, *Documents relations to the program of the First Hague Peace Conference laid before the conference by the Netherlands government. Translation*. Oxford, Clarendon Press, 1899 [1921].
55 *Journal de St-Petersbourg* 24 May 1899, 2; *Standard* 20 May 1899, 7; *Locomotief* (Samarang) 16 June 1899, np; *Middelbursche Courant* 19 May 1899, np; *Telegraaf* 18 May 1899, 1; *Matin* 22 May 1899, 2.
56 For example: E. Castelar, 'Revue politique: le congrès de la paix' *La nouvelle revue internationale* 31, 10, 1 June 1899, 771–781.
57 Suttner, *Memoirs*, Volume 2, 281–284, 293; Dungen, 'Making' 22–23.
58 *Telegraaf* 19 May 1899, 3; 23 June 1899, 2.
59 W.H. Fremantle, *Patriotism and cosmopolitanism. A sermon for the peace conference, preaches in the English Church at The Hague on Sunday May 28th 1899*. Ripon, Thirlway, 1899, 13; *NYT* 22 May 1899 in Davis, *United States 1* 97; *Old and new. Sermons by Henry Scott Holland of St. Paul's*. London, S.T. Freemantle, 1900.
60 *Telegraaf* 4 June 1899, 1.
61 White, *Hague* 25; Eyffinger, *1899* 337–340; *Telegraaf* 3 June 1899, 3.
62 White, *Hague* 29; *Journal de St-Petersbourg* 1 June 1899, 2; HGA 0353-01, 1132.
63 White, *Hague* 46–47.
64 Julian Pauncefote to Foreign Office, 26 May 1899, in PRO FO83, 1695.
65 White, *Hague* 95; Julian Pauncefote, 8 July 1899, in PRO FO83, 1696.
66 White, *Hague* 77.
67 NA 2.21.290, 284; Valk and Fassen, eds, *Beaufort*, Volume 1, 56; Suttner, *Haager* 24–25; Holls, 'Reminiscenses'.
68 *Daily News* 29 June 1899, np, in CAC FISR, 8/38; Lammasch, 'Aus meinem' 12–19; Cecil Delves Braighton to Lady Fisher, 22 June 1899, in CAC FISR, 2/1; A. Marder, ed., *Fear God and dread nought. The correspondence of Admiral of the Fleet Lord Fisher of Kilverstone*. Volume 2, London, Jonathan Cape, 1952, 141–143; NA 2.21.018, 314.
69 In Muir, *Stancioff* 84.
70 Muir, *Stancioff* 84.
71 *Daily News* 29 June 1899, np, in CAC FISR, 8/38; S.M Ardagh, *The life of Major-General Sir John Ardagh*. London, John Murray, 1909, 371; Tuchman, *Proud* 259.
72 O. van Berensteyn, 'Binnenland', 5 June 1899, in NA 2.18.018, 314.
73 White, *Hague* 26.
74 R.B. Mowat, *The life of Lord Pauncefote. First Ambassador to the United States*. London, Constable, 1928, 244.
75 Theodor Herzl in Hamann, *Suttner* 150. Cf. Suttner, *Memoirs*, Volume 2, 255; 'Die Haager Tagebuch der Baronin von Suttner' *FW* 2, 25, June 1900, 100.
76 NA 2.21.018, 314. The *Graphic* (London) magazine had a special artist in The Hague: 3 June 1899, 699–700.
77 Lammasch, 'Rückblicke' 179. The conference secretariat thought the photographs might placate the press: NA 2.05.03, 528.
78 *Telegraaf* 7 June 1899, 3, 4; *Utrechtse Courant* 20 May 1899, np, in NA 2.21.290, 84.
79 *Telegraaf* 23 June 1899, 3; *La conférence de la paix. La Haye 1899*. The Hague, np, 1899, in PPL 'Carnegie Stichting Collection'; NA 2.05.03, 519.
80 Letter to the editor, *Tijd* 31 December 1899, np.

81 *Nieuws van de Dag* 3 August 1899, np.
82 *Proceedings at the laying of a wreath on the tomb of Hugo Grotius in the Nieuwe Kerk, in the city of Delft, July 4th 1899 by the Commission of the United States of America to the International Peace Conference of The Hague*. The Hague, Martinus Nijhoff, 1899.
83 White, *Hague* 91–92.
84 Holls, 'Reminiscenses'.
85 According to *Le Temps* it lasted forty-five minutes (6 July 1899, 2).
86 Andrew D. White's speech, 4 July 1899, in *Proceedings at the laying of a wreath* 14; NA 2.21.014, 287.
87 White in *Proceedings at the laying of a wreath* 15–16.
88 Davis, *United States 1* 77–80.
89 Cf. A. Mamolea, 'The United States and the Hague tradition. Myth and reality', Unpublished paper, University of Auckland, 19 April 2016.
90 *Guardian* 6 July 1899, 4.
91 *Revue de Droit International et de Legislation Comparée* 1899, 37; *Journal des Débats Politiques et Littéraires* 10 August 1899, np.
92 *LAT* 5 July 1899, 1.
93 *CDT* 9 July 1899, 10.
94 *NYT* 26 July 1899, 6.
95 *NYT* 26 July 1899, 6.
96 White, *Hague* 94–95, 96.
97 Suttner, *Memoirs*, Volume 2, 260, 289.
98 Theodor Herzl to Bertha von Suttner, 12 December 1899, in UNOG IPM/FS/BvS/20/243-3/5.
99 White, *Hague* 13; *JT* 15 June 1899, 4; NA 2.05.03, 528; *The cause of Poland in reference to the International Peace Conference to be held at The Hague, Europe*. Chicago, Zgoda, 1899.
100 'Rapport adressé au Ministre des Affaires Étrangères par MM. Léon Bourgeois, G. Bihourd et d'Estournelles de Constant, délégues de la République Française à la Conférence internationale de la paix (31 December 1899)' in Ministère des Éstrangères, *Conférence 1899* 10; E. Turpin, *Requête à messieurs les presidents et membres de la conférence de la paix à la Haye*. Paris, Chaix, 1899; H.L. Boyle, *Plan for an international insurance to prevent wars*. np, 1898; NA 2.05.03, 528; Dutch Ministry of Foreign Affairs, 29 May 1899, in NA 2.05.19, 519.
101 Assistant Secretary to the Hague conference, Arthur Raffalovich, to the President of the Hague conference, Baron von Staal, 21 May 1899, in NA 2.05.03, 528.
102 White, *Hague* 46; Sir Henry Howard, Minister in The Hague, to the Marquis of Salisbury, 28 June 1899 in PRO FO421, 65.
103 *LAT* 20 May 1899, 1; NA 2.05.03, 528.
104 Eyffinger, *1899* 349–351. *De Telegraaf* noted the *Daily News*' commentary on the Tcheraz affair on 31 May 1899, 3, and returned to it repeatedly.
105 Sir Henry Howard to the Marquis of Salisbury, 28 June 1899, in PRO FO421, 65; Rybachenok, *Rossiia* 251;Valk and Fassen, eds, *Beaufort*, Volume 1, 59–66.
106 *Telegraaf* 2 June 1899, 2; 5 July 1899, 1; NA 2.21.018, 314.
107 *Telegraaf* 12 July 1899, 1.
108 *Telegraaf* 22 June 1899, 2.
109 Sir Julian Pauncefote to the Marquis of Salisbury, 31 July 1899, in PRO FO83, 1697.
110 Wylie, 'Muddied'; K. Nabulsi, *Traditions of war. Occupation, resistance and the law*. Oxford UP, 1999, 5.

111 Lammasch, 'Aus meinein' 14–15; Lesaffer, 'Temple' 25.
112 A.M. Anderson, '"Jacky Fisher" and the 1899 Hague conference. A reassessment' *New Zealand Journal of Research on Europe* 11, 1, March 2017, 54–92; 'Sir John Fisher. A study in the personality of the First Sea Lord of the Admiralty' *London Magazine* nd, 673–680 in CAC FISR, 11/11; R.F. Mackay, *Fisher of Kilverstone*. Oxford, Clarendon Press, 1973, 219–220.
113 Mackay, *Fisher* 220.
114 Scott, *Proceedings 1899* 272.
115 Scott, *Proceedings 1899* 301.
116 Scott, *Proceedings 1899* 301–302.
117 Scott, *Proceedings 1899* 302.
118 Scott, *Proceedings 1899* 303.
119 Scott, *Proceedings 1899* 309.
120 Scott, *Proceedings 1899* 311.
121 Scott, *Proceedings 1899* 317.
122 Suttner, *Memoirs*, Volume 2, 312; A. Méringhac, *La conférence internationale de la paix. Étude historique, exégétique et critique des travaux et des resolutions de la conference de la Haye de 1899*. Paris, Arthur Rousseau, 1900, 67.
123 Scott, *Proceedings 1899* 318.
124 Scott, *Proceedings 1899* 90.
125 A. Webster, 'Reconsidering disarmament and the Hague peace conference of 1899, and after' in Abbenhuis et al., eds, *War* 69–85.
126 Scott, *Proceedings 1899* 89, 331–382; PRO FO83, 1695, 1696 and 1697.
127 Scott, *Proceedings 1899* 79–90.
128 Scott, *Proceedings 1899* 79.
129 Scott, *Proceedings 1899* 79.
130 Scott, *Proceedings 1899* 272–279; E.M. Spiers, 'The use of the dum dum bullet in colonial warfare' *Journal of Commonwealth and Imperial History* 4, 1, 1975 1–14; S.A. Keefer, 'Explosive missals. International law, technology and security in nineteenth-century disarmament conferences' *War in History* 21, 4, 2014, 445–464.
131 Scott, *Proceedings 1899* 286.
132 Evan MacGregor, British Admiralty, to British Under-Secretary of State, 16 May 1899, in PRO FO83, 1702.
133 Scott, *Proceedings 1899* 287.
134 Preamble to the St Petersburg Declaration 1868, in 'Treaties, State Parties and Commentaries' *International Committee of the Red Cross* website https://www.icrc.org/applic/ihl/ihl.nsf/Article.xsp?action=openDocument&documentId=568842C2B90F4A29C12563CD0051547C (accessed May 2016).
135 J.B. Scott, ed., *Instructions to the American delegates to the Hague peace conferences and their official reports*. New York, Oxford UP, 1916, 33.
136 Scott, *Proceedings 1899* 82; Julian Pauncefote and Sir John Ardagh, 8 July 1899, in PRO FO83, 1696.
137 William R. Crozier to General Corbin, 19 July 1899, in Davis, *United States 1* 136.
138 In Scott, *Proceedings 1899* 51, also 416–417.
139 Scott, *Proceedings 1899* 52; italics in original.
140 Scott, *Proceedings 1899* 31–44.
141 Scott, *Proceedings 1899* 32.
142 The Geneva Conventions would be reworked in 1906.
143 Wylie, 'Muddied'.

144 Scott, *Proceedings 1899* 50–78.
145 I.V. Hull, '"Military necessity" and the laws of war in Imperial Germany' in S.N. Kalyva, I. Shapiro and T. Masoud, eds, *Order, conflict and violence*. Cambridge UP, 2008, 352–377.
146 Hull, 'Military necessity' 358.
147 Scott, *Proceedings 1899* 53.
148 Hull, *Scrap* 73–75.
149 Scott, *Proceedings 1899* 45–46.
150 Scott, *Proceedings 1899* 208.
151 J. Sarkin, 'The historical origins, convergence and interrelationship of international human rights law, international humanitarian law, international criminal law and public international law and their application since the nineteenth century' *Human Rights and International Legal Discourse* 125, 2007, 125–172; T. Meron, 'The Martens Clause, principles of humanity, and dictates of public conscience' *AJIL* 94, 1, January 2000, 78–89; R. Schircks, *Die Martens'sche Klause. Rezeption und Rechtsqualität*. Baden-Baden, Nomos, nd; Verwaest, *Den Haag* 32–35.
152 Cf. Hull, *Scrap* 74–76.
153 Cf. 'Explanatory Note Concerning Article 5 of the Russian Draft' in Scott, *Proceedings 1899* 170.
154 Barber, 'Empire'.
155 Hamilton, 'Britain' 15–16.
156 Scott, *Proceedings 1899* 126.
157 Scott, *Proceedings 1899* 597–598.
158 Scott, *Proceedings 1899* 123.
159 Scott, *Proceedings 1899* 125.
160 Koskenniemi, *Gentle* 212; Lammasch and Sperl, eds, *Heinrich* 17; P. Zorn to Friedrich Holstein, 13 June 1899, in N. Rich and M.H. Fisher, eds, *The Holstein Papers*. Volume 4, Cambridge UP, 1963, 123.
161 N.M. Butler, *Across the busy years. Recollections and reflections*. Volume 1, New York, Charles Scribner's Sons, 1939; Davis, *United States 1* 69, 142, 193.
162 White, *Hague* 61–77; Holls, 'Reminiscenses'.
163 Dülffer, *Regeln* 93.
164 In CAC NBKR, 8/20/3.
165 Scott, *Proceedings 1899* 92.
166 Scott, *Proceedings 1899* 93.
167 Scott, *Proceedings 1899* 137; italics in original.
168 Scott, *Proceedings 1899* 91.
169 Scott, *Proceedings 1899* 91.
170 Scott, *Proceedings 1899* 129.
171 Basily, *Memoirs* 12; Hamilton, 'Britain' 19.
172 R. Lesaffer, 'Peace through law. The Hague peace conference and the rise of the *ius contra bellum*' in Abbenhuis et al., eds, *War* 31–51.
173 Dülffer, 'Citizens' 24–25.
174 Dutch Minister in Berlin to Dutch Minister Foreign Affairs, 10 June 1899, in Smit, ed., *Bescheiden*, Volume 1, 73–75.
175 Count Münster to Friedrich Holstein, 14 June 1899, in Rich and Fisher, eds, *Holstein* 19.
176 Dutch Minister in Berlin to Dutch Minister of Foreign Affairs, 8 June 1899, in Smit, ed., *Bescheiden*, Volume 1, 72.

177 Cf. G. Cavallar, 'Eye-deep in hell. Heinrich Lammasch, the confederation of neutral states, and Austrian neutrality 1899–1920' in Lettevall et al., eds, *Neutrality* 275; Dülffer, *Regeln* 130.
178 Hamilton, 'Britain' 18–19.
179 Cf. Dülffer, *Regeln* 131–137; C.S. Campbell Jnr, *Anglo-American understanding 1898–1903*. Baltimore, Johns Hopkins Press, 1957, 158.
180 Dülffer, 'Citizens' 25; White, *Hague* 65; Mowat, *Pauncefote* 234–235; Count Nigra to Visconti Venosta, 24 June 1899, in Ministero, *Documenti*, Series III, Volume III, 180.
181 Including *NHZ* 19 June 1899, 1.
182 *JT* 19 August 1899, 4.
183 *LAT* 11 June 1899, B1; 12 June 1899, 2; 13 June 1899, 8; 14 June 1899, 8; 17 June 1899, 2; 18 June 1899, A2; 19 June 1899, 2; 21 June 1899, 3; 22 June 1899, 2; 24 June 1899, 2; 26 June 1899, 1.
184 *LAT* 13 June 1899, 8.
185 *Friend* 22 June 1899, 20–21.
186 Scott, *Proceedings 1899* 226.
187 Cortissoz, *Reid*, Volume 2, 259; italics in original.
188 Scott, *Proceedings 1899* 102–104.
189 For example: British Minister in St Petersburg to the Marquis of Salisbury, 24 July 1899; British Minister in Vienna to the Marquis of Salisbury, 31 July 1899, both in PRO FO83, 1701.
190 Muir, *Stancioff* 85.
191 Muir, *Stancioff* 85.
192 In Koskenniemi, *Gentle* 284.
193 Lammasch and Sperl, eds, *Heinrich* 10; Cavallar, 'Eye-deep' 275.
194 Koskenniemi, *Gentle* 275; Cavallar, 'Eye-deep' 274.
195 In Pustogarov, *Martens* 178.
196 Sir John Ardagh to Sir James Gowar, 29 July 1899, in Ardagh, *Ardagh* 324.
197 Suttner, *Memoirs*, Volume 2, 318.
198 In Suttner, *Memoirs*, Volume 2, 273–274.
199 *Wahre Jacob* 338, 4 July 1899, 3019.
200 White, *Hague* 100; *Anglo-Saxon Review* September 1899, 260.
201 *Friend* 3 August 1899, 1.
202 *Blackwood's Edinburgh Magazine* July 1899, 139–142.
203 *Grazer Tageblatt* 30 July 1899, np.
204 British Minister in Vienna to the Marquis of Salisbury, 31 July 1899, in PRO FO83, 1701.
205 *JT* 9 September 1899 2.
206 *LAT* 27 June 1899 8.
207 *LAT* 29 June 1899 8.
208 M. Batilliat, *Paul Adam*. Paris, 1903.
209 Although Passy was unable to attend the conference itself, due to a medical condition.
210 *Telegraaf* 19 May 1899, 3; Suttner, *Haager* 20; Tuchman, *Proud* 263.
211 P. Adam, *Les impérialismes et la morale des peuples*. Paris, Furne, 1908.
212 Suttner, *Memoirs*, Volume 2, 327.
213 *JT* 31 August 1899, 4.
214 'Arthur Desjardins über die Haager Konferenz' *FW* 1, 13, September 1899, 78–79.
215 *LAT* 16 July 1899, A2; 30 July 1899, 2.

216 *Berliner Tageblatt* 23 July 1899, 1.
217 In *NHZ* 6 August 1899, 4.
218 *Economist* 15 July 1899, 1007.
219 *Church Times* (London) 8 August 1899, 129.
220 *Leeuwarder Courant* 8 August 1899, np.
221 P.v.D., 'De uitkomsten der vredesconferentie' *Elseviers Geillustreerd Maandschrift* 1899, 284, in NA 2.21.014, 236.
222 *Algemeen Handelsblad* 24 July 1899, 3.
223 In *Herald of Peace* 560, 1 August 1899, 258.
224 Ogden, ed., *White* 358.
225 White, *Hague* 102; *Advocate of Peace* 61, 8, September 1899, 176.
226 P. Zorn, 'Pour apprécier la conférence de la Haye' *Revue de Droit Public et de la Science Politique en France et à l'Étranger* 11, 21, 1904, 241; 'Die völkerrechtlichen Ergebnisse der haager Conferenz' *Deutsche Rundschau* January–March 1900, 208–225.
227 For Apponyi: Suttner, *Memoirs*, Volume 2, 338. For d'Estournelles: *Temps* 4 November 1899, 1; *Les résultats de la conférence de la Haye. Conférence faite devant la Société des Amis de l'Université de Lyon 14 janvier 1900.* Paris, A. Storck, 1900; 'Vorwort' in A.H. Fried, *Die Haager Conferenz. Ihre Bedeutung und ihre Ergebnisse.* Berlin, Hugo Bermüler, 1900; 'Die Haager Konferenz und der Transvaalkrieg' *FW* 1, 20, November 1899, 125–128. For Martens: *La conférence de la paix à la Haye. Etude d'histoire contemporaine.* Paris, Arthur Rousseau, 1900; *FW* 1, 19, November 1899, 122. For White: *Hague.* For Nigra: *FW* 1, 12, September 1899, 71; Suttner, *Haager* iv. For Holls: *The Hague Peace conference and international law.* London, MacMillan, 1900; Frederick Holls to T.M.C. Asser, 16 October 1900, in NA 2.21.014, 286; Davis, *United States 1* 193. For Bourgeois: Suttner, *Haager* iv; Koskenniemi, *Gentle* 286; J. Dülffer and C. Haas, 'Léon Bourgeois' in Holl and Kjelling, eds, *Nobel* 137; 'Preface' in Méringhac, *Conférence*; 'Eine Rede Bourgeois' über die Bedeutung der Haager Konvention' *FW* 4, 2, January 1902 14–16. For Low: 'The international conference of peace' *North American Review* 169, 516, November 1899, 625–639. For Arthur Raffalovich: *Mémoires sur la conférence de la paix.* Paris, np, 1899. Alfred Mahan and Karl von Stengel also published commentaries on The Hague, albeit with a more critical eye: A.T. Mahan, *Lessons of the war with Spain and other articles.* Boston, Little, Brown and Company, 1899, 207–238; A.T. Mahan, *Some neglected aspects of war.* London, Sampson, Low, Marston and Company, 1907; A.T. Mahan, *Armaments and arbitration or the place of force in the international relations of states.* New York, Harper Brothers, 1912; K. von Stengel, 'Die Haager Friedenskonferenz und das Völkerrecht' *Archiv für öffentliches Recht* 15, 1900, 139–201.
228 Dülffer, *Regeln* 71; 'The peace conference. Its possible practical results by a Diplomatist at The Hague' *North American Review* 168, 511, June 1899, 771–778.
229 J.H. Vickery, 'The conference at the Hague, and its results' *Independent* 51, 21 September 1899, 2533.
230 J.H. Vickery, 'International law and the peace conference' *Popular Science Monthly* 57, 1900, 76–86.
231 In *Journal de St-Petersbourg* 31 July 1899, 2.
232 Sir Julian Pauncefote to the Marquis of Salisbury, 31 July 1899, in Gooch and Temperley, eds, *Origins*, Volume 1, 1927, 232–233; 'Rapport adressé au Ministre des Affaires Étrangères par MM. Léon Bourgeois, G. Bihourd et d'Estournelles de Constant, délégues de la République Française à la Conférence internationale de la

paix (31 December 1899)' in Ministère des Éstrangères, *Conférence 1899* esp. 47; 'Report to the Secretary of State of the delegates to the First Hague Conference' 31 July 1899, in Scott, ed., *Instructions* 17–58.

233 In *FW* 1, 14, 2 October 1899, 81.

234 'Die Haager Konferenz im Deutschen Reichstag' *FW* 2, 11–12, March 1900, 38–40.

235 In Suttner, *Memoirs*, Volume 2, 338.

236 Low, 'International conference' 638–639; J.B. Moore, 'What the arbitration treaty is and is not' *AMRR* 21, January–July 1900, 50–51.

237 *Daily Mail* 20 September 1899, 3; *Guardian* 20 September 1899, 6.

238 *Signatures, ratifications, adhesions and reservations to the conventions and declarations of the first and second Hague peace conferences.* Washington D.C., Carnegie Endowment for International Peace, 1914.

239 PRO FO421, 65; FO 83, 1701; Hamilton, 'Britain'; Agøy, 'It will serve' 203–205; *Matin* 9 July 1899, 3; Genin, 'Diplomatie' 12–13.

240 Only Turkey and China had not ratified any of the conventions by 1904: Zorn, 'Pour apprécier' 241.

5 Civilization at War, 1899–1906

1 Darby, *Peace conference* 59.

2 The first Anglo-Boer War occurred in 1880–81.

3 K. Wilson, ed., *The international impact of the Boer War*. Chesham, Acumen, 2001; Krebs, *Gender*; M.J. Douma, 'Ethnic identities in a transnational context: The Dutch American reaction to the Anglo-Boer War 1899–1902' *South African Historical Journal* 65, 4, 2013, 481–503; S.E. Knee, 'Anglo-American understanding and the Boer War' *Australian Journal of Politics and History* 30, 2, 1984, 196–199; Claeys, *Imperial* 4. Cf. Cooper, ed., *Internationalism* 495.

4 *JT* 5 December 1900, 3; A. du Toit, 'Victims of "British justice"? A *Century of Wrong* as anti-imperial tract, core narrative of the Afrikaner "nation", and victim-based solidarity-building discourse' in Burton and Hofmeyr, *Ten* 112–130; Verwaest, *Den Haag* 61.

5 *AMRR* 21, January–July 1900, 343; *Telegraaf* 26 June 1899, 1; *NHZ* 14 October 1899, 1.

6 *SP* 16 February 1900, 1; *Gunten's Magazine* 17, July–December 1899, 258.

7 Imperial rescript, 12/24 August 1898, in Scott, *Hague peace*, Volume 1, 41–42.

8 W.M. Kennedy, 'The imperialism of internment. Boer prisoners of war in India and civic reconstruction in Southern Africa, 1899–1905' *Journal of Imperial and Commonwealth History* 44, 3, 2016, 423–208.

9 W. Mommsen, 'Introduction' in Wilson, ed., *Boer War* 1; A.K. Ebergardt, 'The Russian Red Cross in the Anglo-Boer War 1899–1902' *Historia* 22, 1977, 112.

10 D. Spring, 'Russian foreign policy and the Boer War' in Wilson, ed., *Boer War* 57.

11 Krebs, *Gender*; P. Bridgen, *The Labour Party and the politics of war and peace 1900–1924*. Woodbridge, Boydell Press, 2009, 23, 35–36; A.F. Havighurst, *Radical journalist. H.W. Massingham (1860–1924)*. Cambridge UP, 1974, 104, 107; Suttner, *Memoirs*, Volume 2, 343, 345; Claeys, *Imperial* 282, 284.

12 C.L. von Bar, *Der Burenkrieg, die Russificierung Finnlands, die Haager Friedenskonferenz und die Errichtung einer internationalen Academie zur Ausgleichung von Streitigkeiten der Staaten*. Hannover, Helwingsche Verlagsbuchhandlung, 1900.

13 Darby, *Peace conference* 59.

14 Cf. Osterhammel, 'Europe', esp. 20–25; M. Duranti, *The conservative human rights revolution. European identity, transnational politics, and the origins of the European Convention*. Oxford UP, 2017, 23–26.
15 Gong, *Standard.*
16 T.J. Lawrence, *International problems and Hague conferences*. London, J.M. Dent, 1908, 34.
17 Cf. M. Kingsberg, *Moral nation. Modern Japan and narcotics in global history*. Berkeley, University of California Press, 2014, 1; Lee, 'Early' 42.
18 P. Maguire, *Law and war. International law and American history*. Revised edition, New York, Columbia UP, 2010, 49.
19 Cf. D. Bell, 'Race, utopia, perpetual peace. Andrew Carnegie's dreamworld' in J.-F. Drolet, J. Dunkerley, eds, *American foreign policy. Studies in intellectual history*. Manchester UP, 2017.
20 Cf. Segesser, *Recht* 31.
21 J. Bourke, *Deep violence. Military violence, war play and the social life of weapons*. Berkeley, Counterpoint, 2015; Hull, *Scrap*; C. af Jochnick, R. Normand, 'The legitimation of violence. A critical history of the laws of war' *Harvard International Law Journal* 35, 1, 1994, 49–95.
22 Bourke, *Deep*.
23 Hull, *Scrap.*
24 Bourke, *Deep*.
25 Cf. Bourke, *Deep* 70.
26 Evan MacGregor, British Admiralty, to British Under-Secretary of State, 16 May 1899 in PRO FO83, 1702.
27 This chapter analyses newspaper reports between October 1899 and December 1905 including in the: *Daily Mail* (London), *Irish Times* (Dublin), *Neue Hamburger Zeitung*, *African-American* (Baltimore), *Sumatra Post*, *Le Gaulois* (Paris), *Edmonton Bulletin* (Canada) and *Calgary Weekly News* (Canada).
28 Transvaal was not allowed to take part in the 1899 Hague conference and could, therefore, not accede to them and Britain did not ratify the Hague conventions until 1900. Cf. Segesser, *Recht* 129–140.
29 Dutch Minister in Stockholm to Dutch Foreign Minister, 12 March 1900, in Smit, ed., *Bescheiden*. Volume 1, 181–183.
30 *AMRR* 23, January–June 1901, 3; *SP* 17 January 1901, 1; *JT* 24 May 1900, 4.
31 P. Venier, 'French Foreign Policy and the Boer War' in Wilson, ed., *Boer War* 72–74.
32 Bar, *Burenkrieg* 56.
33 Bar, *Burenkrieg* 5–7. Cf. Martens, *Conférence* 34–43; Clark, *International legitimacy*.
34 In d'Estournelles, 'Transvaalkrieg' 127.
35 See Chapter 4.
36 W. Lippmann, *Public opinion*. New York, Harcourt, Brace, 1922. Cf. Krebs, *Gender* esp. 35.
37 *Vogue* 31 January 1901, 66.
38 D.M. Segesser, '"Unlawful warfare is uncivilised". The international debate on the punishment of war crimes, 1872–1918' *European Review of History* 14, 2, 2007, esp. 218–219; W. Mulligan, 'Justifying military action. International law, The Hague and diplomacy before 1914' in Abbenhuis, *War* 12–30; S. Wank, 'The Austrian peace movement and the Habsburg ruling elite' in Chatfield and van den Dungen, eds, *Voices* 40–64; MacMillan, *The war* 102; Sheehan, *Where?* 26.
39 *DM* 2 September 1899, np.

40 *DM* 7 October 1899, 5. Campbell-Bannerman's Liberal party lost the 'khaki election' of 1900: P. Readman, 'The Conservative Party, patriotism and British politics. The case of the general election of 1900' *Journal of British Studies* 40, 1, 2001, 107–145.
41 As examples: *NHZ* 20 September 1899, 7; *Calgary Weekly Herald* 2 November 1899, 6; *Matin* 4 November 1899, 1; *IT* 23 November 1901, 8.
42 *Gaulois* 21 October 1900, 2.
43 *SP* 12 April 1901, 2.
44 R.D. Story, *Arbitration or war? A view of the Transvaal question with a glance at arbitration in politics generally*. London, F. Parker, 1899.
45 John Dillon in House of Commons, 17 October 1899, *HCPP*, Fourth Series, 77.
46 *DM* 22 September 1899, 5.
47 *NHZ* 28 November 1900, 2.
48 *The International Union: what it is, what it wants to do, how it tries to do it*. London, Office of the British Centre of the International Union, 1901, 24, in NA 2.21.174, 5.
49 *Gaulois* 25 December 1900, 5.
50 *Weekly Mail* (Cardiff) 2 December 1899, 8.
51 *DM* 16 September 1899, 5; 19 September 1899, 5; 10 October 1899, 3.
52 Cf. S.P. Spies, 'Die Haagse Konvensie van 1899 en die Boererepublieke' in F. Pretorius, ed., *Verskroeide aarde*. Capetown, Human & Rousseau, 2001, 168–177.
53 A.J. van der Peet, *Belangen en prestige. Nederlandse* gunboat diplomacy *omstreeks 1900*. Amsterdam, De Bataafsche Leeuw, 1999, 42–49.
54 Grossi, *Pacifism* 228; Wascklewicz van Schilfgaarde, 'Plea for the grant of a neutral territory for the Boer women and children' The Hague, 15 April 1901, in NA 2.21.174, 5.
55 Krebs, *Gender* 32; D. Mutch, '"Are we Christians?" W.T. Stead, Keir Hardie and the Boer War' in Brake et al., eds, *Stead* 134.
56 Krebs, *Gender* 33. Cf. Australian Peace Humanity and Arbitration Society, 1902, in PCSC, 'Australia' CDGB.
57 *Rhodesia Herald* 2 December 1899, 5; A. Griffiths, 'Winston Churchill, the *Morning Post* and end of the imperial romance' *Victorian Periodicals Review* 46, 2, 2013, 163–183; Eckley, *Maiden* 263.
58 W.T. Stead, *Methods of barbarism. War is war and war is hell. The case for intervention*. London, Mowbray House, 1901; I. Hanson, '"God'll send the bill to you". The costs of war and the God who counts in W.T. Stead's pro-Boer peace campaign' *Journal of Victorian Culture* 20, 2, 2015, 168–185; S.J. Potter, 'W.T. Stead, imperial federation and the South African War' in Brake et al., eds, *Stead* 115–132.
59 Stead, *Methods* 3.
60 Stead, *Methods* 4.
61 Stead, *Methods* 4–5.
62 Stead, *Methods* 12.
63 Krebs, *Gender* 82–83.
64 Krebs, *Gender* 82–83; J.O. Baylen, A. Conan Doyle, 'Sir Arthur Conan Doyle and W.T. Stead. The novelist and the journalist' *Albion* 2, 1, 1970, 3–16; E. Bradlow, 'Idealism and realism. Conan Doyle, imperialism and the Anglo-Boer War' *Kleio* 35, 1, 2003, 19–40.
65 A. Conan Doyle, *The war in South Africa. Its cause and conduct*. London, Smith Elder, 1902.
66 Conan Doyle, *South Africa* np.
67 Kennedy, 'Imperialism'.

68 Bradlow, 'Idealism' 33.
69 *CDT* 15 February 1902, 9.
70 *Het Volk* 4 May 1902, np.
71 *Algemeen Dagblad* 23 February 1902, 1.
72 *Soerabaijasch Handelsblad* 27 March 1902, 1.
73 There are 593 references to 'W.T. Stead' and 'Transvaal' in the Dutch-language newspaper archive (*Delpher*) for the period 11 October 1899–December 1902, which covers thirty-eight different titles (accessed September 2016). A search for 'Conan Doyle' and 'Transvaal' offers 106 results for the same period.
74 *Star* (Christchurch), 21 October 1901, np.
75 *Star* 21 October 1901, np.
76 *NHZ* 2 September 1901, 1.
77 *NHZ* 14 September 1901, 2.
78 *DE* 20 February 1902, 1.
79 *SP* 21 September 1901, 1.
80 B.E. Elleman, *Modern Chinese warfare 1795–1989*. London, Routledge, 2002, 123–124, 131–132; R. Bickers and R.G. Tiedemann, eds, *The Boxers, China and the world*. Lanham, Rowman and Littlefield, 2007; Peet, *Belangen* 62.
81 William McKinley, 3 December 1900, in United States, *Papers*, 1900, xvi; Pustogarov, *Martens* 138. The idea was reported on around the world: *Sierra Leone Weekly News* (Freetown) 1 June 1901, 5; *Gaulois* 13 November 1900, 2.
82 *NHZ* 19 September 1900, 4.
83 *Church Times* 2 November 1900, 494.
84 *Calgary Weekly Herald* 16 November 1899, 4. Cf. Mutch, 'Christians' 140–141.
85 *International Union* 37; *NHZ* 22 August 1900, 1; *TT* 22 February 1901, 5; *Evening Star* 5 June 1907, 3.
86 In *AMRR* 23, January–June 1901, 220–223; *JT* 21 April 1901, 4.
87 House of Commons, 11 March 1901 and 3 May 1901, *HCPP*, Fourth Series, 90.
88 *Matin* 26 October 1899, 2; *SP* 21 September 1901, 1.
89 *SP* 9 July 1900, 1; italics in original.
90 *SP* 5 August 1899, 1.
91 *SP* 1 August 1900, 1.
92 St Petersburg Declaration, 1868, *The Avalon Project*, http://avalon.law.yale.edu/19th_century/decpeter.asp (accessed October 2016).
93 *British Medical Journal* 11 June 1898, 1559; 29 July 1899, 278–281.
94 Scott, *Proceedings 1899* 272–279.
95 *Journal de Débats* in *DM* 8 September 1899, 4.
96 *Bulletin du Photo-club de Paris* 1898, 136–139.
97 *Otago Witness* 26 October 1899, 61; *Friend* 13 July 1899, 2.
98 Bourke, *Deep* 21–22, 44, 67, 72.
99 Bourke, *Deep* 74.
100 Keefer, 'Explosive'; Keefer, 'Great Britain' 110–112.
101 Jochnick and Normand, 'Legitimation' 52–53.
102 Jochnick and Normand, 'Legitimation' 50, 77; Bourke, *Deep* 67.
103 Spiers, 'Dum dum' 12.
104 Sir H. Brackenbury to the Marquis of Lansdowne, 22 June 1899, and Sir John Ardagh to Sir Thomas Sanderson, 27 June 1899, both in PRO FO83, 1700.
105 Spiers, 'Dum dum' 11; Report by the War Office to the Foreign Office, 7 October 1899, in PRO FO83, 1701.

106 British Minister in The Hague, Henry Howard, to the Marquis of Salisbury, 18 July 1899, in PRO FO37, 825.
107 All the non-British newspapers surveyed here reported on the war and dum-dum bullets at least once. Many of the pro-British press reported on the Afrikaners using dum-dum bullets as well.
108 Other French examples: *Journal Pour Tous* 10 August 1899, 9; *Rire* 23 November 1899, 6.
109 Spiers, 'Dum dum' 12; E.M. Spiers, *The Victorian soldier in Africa*. Manchester UP, 2004, 145.
110 *DM* 1 September 1897, 3; 15 December 1897, 5; 28 April 1898, 7; 28 June 1898, 3; 20 September 1898, 7.
111 *DM* 8 November 1898, 4; 12 November 1898, 4; 25 February 1898, 3; 26 February 1898, 5; 12 March 1898, 5; 16 March 1898, 5; 3 January 1899, 5.
112 *DM* 2 June 1899, 4–5; 12 June 1899, 4; 23 June 1899, 7; 13 July 1899, 3; 25 July 1899, 4.
113 *DM* 25 January 1900, 7.
114 *DM* 27 November 1899, 5; 17 January 1900, np. Also: *DE* 26 July 1900, 7.
115 *DM* 17 November 1900, 3.
116 *DM* 16 January 1902, 4.
117 C. Dupuis, A. Desjardins, *La conférence de la Haye a-t-elle donné des résultats appréciables?* Paris, Secrétariat de la Société d'Economie Sociale, 1900, 26, in NA 2.22.28, 232.
118 Dupuis and Desjardins, *Conférence* 36.
119 W.D. Thomson, 'Some notes on the peace convention held at The Hague in May 1899, with its resultant effect on "custom of war"' *Journal of the Military Services Institution of the United States* 28, May 1901, 404–417, quotations on 408–409, 416, 417.
120 For critiques: *TT* 1 May 1903, 7. In defense: Infantryman, letter to the editor, *TT* 2 May 1903, 4.
121 *African Standard* (Mombasa) 25 May 1911, 25; *SP* 27 July 1912, 2.
122 *SP* 1 September 1899, 1.
123 *SP* 1 September 1899, 1.
124 *SP* 4 October 1899, 1; 29 January 1906, 2.
125 *SP* 4 October 1899, 1.
126 M. Ishay, *The history of human rights from ancient times to the globalisation era*. Berkeley, University of California Press, 2004, 118; J. Bourke, 'Barbarization vs civilization in time of war' in G. Kassimeris, ed., *The barbarization of warfare*. New York UP, 2006, 19–38. Cf. Laqua, *Age* 68; U. Pallua, *Eurocentrism, racism, colonialism in the Victorian and Edwardian age*. Heidelberg, Winter, 2005, esp. 59–60; Claeys, *Imperial*, esp. 2–8.
127 *JT* 19 July 1904, 2; 12 September 1905, 2.
128 *Journal* (Grahamstown) 17 September 1904, 7.
129 F. Martens, 'Preface' in J.A. Jacobsen, *Le premier grand proces internationale à la cour de la Haye*. Paris, V. Giard & E. Brière, 1904, vi–viii; *DM* 30 April 1904, 4; *IT* 30 March 1904, 5.
130 S. Takahashi, *International law applied to the Russo-Japanese War with the decisions of the Japanese prize courts*. London, Stevens, 1908, esp. v–vi.
131 *JT* 5 July 1904, 3.
132 For examples: *Rhodesia Herald* 21 March 1913, 22. There are 114 mentions of dum-dum bullets in the *IT* in 1914 alone.

133 G.K. Chesteron, *The appetite of tyranny. Including letters to an old Garibaldian.* New York, Dodd and Mead, 1915, 34; C. Weber, *Kriegspatronen und Dum-Dum Geschosse*. Stuttgart, J.E.G. Wegner, 1914.

134 C. Parker, *German barbarities in Russia. The evidence illustrated.* Melbourne, 1916; *German atrocities. Germany and inhumanity versus humanity and Christianity issued by the Director-General of Recruiting*. Melbourne, Director-General of Recruiting, 1917.

135 A. Leeper, *The true story of Sinn Fein. A lecture*. Melbourne, Loyalist League of Victoria, 1919, 18.

136 P. van den Dungen, 'Civil resistance to chemical warfare in the First World War' and J.P. Zanders, 'The road to Geneva' in J.P. Zanders, ed., *Innocence slaughtered. Gas and the transformation of warfare and society*. London, Uniform Press, 2015, 190–211, 238–267; N.J. McCamley, *Secret history of chemical warfare*. Barnsley, Penn & Sword, 2006, 1.

137 M. Girard Dorsey, 'More than just a taboo. The legacy of the chemical warfare prohibitions of the 1899 and 1907 Hague conferences' in Abbenhuis et al., eds, *War* 86–102.

138 P.J. Noel-Baker, *Disarmament*. Second edition, London, Hogarth Press, 1927.

139 Vagts, 'Hague'.

140 Webster, 'Reconsidering'.

141 Barber, 'Evolution'; Best, 'Restraint' 12–13.

142 Bureau International de la Cour Permanente Arbitrage, *Exposé de quelques traits d'arbitrage*. The Hague, 1905, and *Relevé general de clauses arbitrages communiqués au Bureau International*. Np, 1906, both in PCSC, 'Netherlands. Bureau International de la Cour d'Arbitrage' CDGB. J.B. Scott, *The exhibit on friendship between nations sesqui-centennial exposition*. Philadelphia, np, 1926, 13; H.L. Boyle, *History of peace*. Grand Rapids, History of Peace, 1902 [1905], appendices.

143 R.R. Doerries, 'From neutrality to war. Woodrow Wilson and the German challenge' in W.N. Tilchin, C.E. Neu, eds, *Artists of power. Theodore Roosevelt, Woodrow Wilson and their enduring impact on US foreign policy*. Westport, Praeger Security International, 2006, 26–32.

144 Dutch Minister of Foreign Affairs to Dutch Minister in Stockholm, 16 August 1899, in Smit, ed., *Bescheiden*. Volume 1, 85–86.

145 For the Boxer Rebellion: *AMRR* 22, July–December 1900, 278, 450. For the Russo-Japanese War: *JT* 11 June 1904, 6; *DE* 26 December 1903, 1; 29 December 1903, 1; 7 January 1904, 4. For the Nanchang affair: *JT* 6 March 1906, 2. For the Panama Canal: *AMRR* 29, January–June 1904, 143. For Britain's sugar tax: *JT* 2 December 1902, 3.

146 R. Beazly, 'Campbell Bannerman and peace opportunities in 1905–1907' *Berliner Monatshefte* 14, April 1936, 268.

147 *DE* 28 October 1903 1. Also: *FW* 5, 23–24 December 1903, 185–186.

148 *SP* 20 May 1902, 1; *SP* 23 April 1906, 1.

149 *IT* 15 January 1904, 5.

150 Ministère d'Affaires Étrangeres, 'Progrès de l'arbitrage obligatoire de 1903 à 1908' map, in *Revue de la Paix* October 1908; *TT* 22 July 1908, 12.

151 *Edinburgh Review* April 1906, 483.

152 *JT* 8 November 1904, 5.

153 *DE* 26 September 1904, 1.

154 In *DE* 23 February 1904, 1.

155 L.E. van Norman, 'The making of a modern peace treaty' *AMRR* 32, July–December 1905, 418.
156 Beales, *History* 237; W.E. Darby, *The arrested development of international arbitration*. London, Richard Flint, 1912.
157 *IT* 21 January 1903, 5. Cf. *DE* 12 March 1903, 5.
158 Edward Grey to Henry Campbell-Bannerman, 9 February 1907, in BL Add MS 52514.
159 PCSC, Bureau.
160 Eyffinger, *1907* 37; Kuehl, *Seeking* 59–60.
161 T. Dennett, *John Hay. From poetry to politics*. New York, Dodd and Mead, 1934 346; A. Gaché, *Le conflit Vénézuélien et l'arbitrage de la Haye*. Paris, np, 1904; Campbell, *Anglo-American* 269–285.
162 Reported in numerous newspapers including: *DE* 18 November 1904, 5 (quoted here) and *IT* 22 Jan 1904, 5.
163 S. Murase, 'The most-favored nation treatment in Japan's treaty practice during the period 1854–1905' *AJIL* 70, 2, April 1976, 88.
164 In *JT* 25 May 1905, 2; 2 June 1905, 6.
165 PRO BT13/39.
166 J.B. Moore, *The collected papers of John Bassett Moore*. Volume 3, New Haven, Yale UP, 1944, 196–197; Pustogarov, *Martens* 185.
167 *IT* 7 November 1904, 6; 24 November 1904, 5; 28 February 1905, 5; *DE* 29 October 1904, 1; J. Macdonnell, 'The future Hague conference' *Contemporary Review* 1 July 1905, 848.
168 Espagnat, 'Document de l'histoire de la guerre actuelle' *Pêle-Mêle* 20 March 1904, 1–2.
169 M. Abbenhuis, *Age of neutrals. Great power politics 1815–1914*. Cambridge UP, 2014, 178–218; J.N. Westwood, *Russia against Japan 1904–1905. A new look at the Russo-Japanese War*. State University of New York Press, 1986; E.R. Scidmore, *As The Hague ordains. Journal of a Russian prisoner's wife in Japan*. London, Henry Holt, 1914 [1907].
170 H. Taylor, C. Bellairs, C. Dupuis and Commander von Uslar, 'National maritime rights and responsibilities in time of war' *North American Review* 585, August 1905, 161–190; Hershey, *Russo-Japanese*; T.J. Lawrence, 'Problems of neutrality connected with the Russo-Japanese War' *RUSI Journal* 48, 318, 1904, 915–937; E.J. Dillon, 'The first period of the Russo-Japanese campaign' *Contemporary Review* 86, 1 July 1904, 743–754.
171 A.S. Hershey, *The international law and diplomacy of the Russo-Japanese War*. London, MacMillan, 1906, vii–viii.
172 *IT* 21 April 1905, 5.
173 Scott, *Hague peace* Volume 2, 52–53.
174 *Mafeking Mail* 12 October 1904, 4.
175 I.V. Hull, 'Military culture and the production of "final solutions" in the colonies. The example of Wilhelmine Germany' in R. Gellately and B. Kiernan, eds, *The spectre of genocide. Mass murder in historical perspective*. Cambridge UP, 2003, 144; D.J. Schaller, 'The genocide of the Herero and Nama in German South-West Africa 1904–1907' in S. Totten and W.S. Parsons, eds, *Centuries of genocide. Essays and eyewitness accounts*. Fourth edition, New York, Routledge, 2013, 90; B. Kiernan, *Blood and soil. A world history of genocide and extermination from Sparta to Darfur*. New Haven, Yale UP, 2007, 382–387.

176 Hull, 'Military necessity' 145; D.J. Schaller, '"Every Herero will be shot": genocide, concentration camps and slave labor in German South-West Africa' in R. Lemarchand, ed., *Forgotten genocides. Oblivion, denial and memory*. University of Pennsylvania Press, 2011, 65–66; Kiernan, *Blood* 387; J. Sarkin, *Germany's genocide of the Herero. Kaiser Wilhelm II, his generals, his settlers, his soldiers*. Cape Town, UCT, 2011.
177 *Rhodesia Herald* 24 August 1905, 6.
178 Hull, 'Military culture' 141–162; D. Stone, 'White men and low moral standards? German anthropology and the Herero genocide' in D. Moses and D. Stone, eds, *Colonialism and genocide*. New York, Routledge, 2007, 181–194; Sarkin, *Herero* 30–32.
179 *Evening Post* 7 October 1905, 9.
180 *Sunday Sun* (Sydney) 1 May 1904, 5.
181 *JT* 20 May 1904, 5.
182 *Lagos Weekly Herald* 17 March 1900, 5.
183 *Daily Mirror* 9 September 1905, 4.
184 *Report of the international conference on the situation in the Near East. Held in London on 29 June 1904*. London Office of 'Pro Armenia', 1904, in PCSC 'Great Britain' CDGB.
185 Edwin D. Mead to Philander C. Knox, 7 November 1911, in PCSC MEAD Reel 78:1, Box 1.
186 Edwin D. Mead to Philander C. Knox, 7 November 1911 in PCSC MEAD Reel 78:1, Box 1. Cf. T.W. Childs, *Italo-Turkish diplomacy and the war over Libya 1911–1912*. Leiden, Brill, 1990, 36–42, 86; E. Salerno, *Genocidio in Libia. Le atrocità nacoste dell'avventura colonial 1911–1933*. Milan, Sugarco Edizione, 1979, 20.
187 *TT* 5 October 1911, 3; *Wanganui Herald* 12 May 1911, 4.
188 *JT* 27 February 1906, 4.
189 Cf. Claeys *Imperial* 26–27.
190 *Daily Mirror* 28 August 1905, 7; *SP* 6 June 1902, 1.
191 *Daily Mirror* 28 July 1906, 7.

6 A Holy Duty: Activists for The Hague

1 Lawrence, *International problems* vi.
2 D. Porsch, 'Die *Friedens-Warte* zwischen Friedensbewegung und Wissenschaft' *FW* 74, 1–2, 1999, 39–40, 42; W. Göhring, *Verdrängt und vergessen. Friedensnobelpreisträger Alfred Hermann Fried*. Vienna, Kremayr & Scheriau, 2006, 47–56, 84, 87; D. Laqua, 'Alfred H. Fried and the challenges for "scientific pacifism" in the *belle époque*' in Boyd, ed., *Information* 181–199.
3 Porsch, 'Friedens-Warte' 42–43.
4 T. Gray, *Champions of peace. The story of Alfred Nobel, the peace prize and the laureates*. Birmingham, Paddington, 1976, 111.
5 Alfred Fried in *FW* September 1899, 73–75, quotation on 75. Cf. *Herald of Peace* 600, 1 August 1899, 258.
6 Göhring, *Verdrängt* 90, 112–114; Fried, *Conferenz*.
7 Agøy, 'It will serve' 200–201.
8 *Advocate of Peace* 61, 9, October 1899, 220.

9 Also: F.W. Fox, *Some historical incidents in connexion with the establishment of the International Tribunal of Arbitration at The Hague in 1899 and international arbitration*. London, West Newman, 1901, in PCSC Box 4.
10 Scott, *Proceedings 1899* 226.
11 A.H. Fried, *Die moderne Friedensbewegung*. Leipzig, B.G. Teubner, 1907.
12 D.J. Hill, 'The second peace conference at the Hague' *AJIL* 1, 3, January–April 1907, 671–691.
13 T.J. Lawrence, *War and neutrality in the far east*. London, MacMillan, 1904. Also: Lawrence, 'Problems'; T.J. Lawrence, *The principles of international law*. Boston, D.C. Heath, 1913 [1910].
14 *NYT* 30 July 1904, BR512.
15 *CDT* 25 July 1904, 6.
16 *Wairarapa Daily Times* 21 May 1913, 4.
17 Lawrence, *International problems* v.
18 Lawrence, *International problems* vi.
19 According to *FW* 10, April 1908, 72. According to WorldCat (worldcat.org), 241 research libraries have a copy of Lawrence's *International problems and Hague conferences* including Melbourne, Negiri Sembilan, Tokyo, Buenos Aires, Waco, Pretoria and Groningen.
20 Lapradelle, *Conférence* 200. Also: C. Giovannini, *I grandi stati, la guistizia e la pace (a proposito della conferenza dell'aia)*. Rome, G. Mariette, 1899, 5.
21 Méringhac, *Conférence* 396–398.
22 Méringhac, *Conférence* 399.
23 Koskenniemi, *Gentle* 286–288; 'Léon Bourgeois' in *Les Hommes du Jour* 30 March 1912, np; R. Jacomet, *La guerre et les traités. Étude de droit international et d'histoire diplomatique*. Paris, Henri Charles-Lavauzelle, nd.
24 L. Bourgeois, 'Preface' in Méringhac, *Conférence* v–vi.
25 Bourgeois, 'Preface' vi–vii.
26 Bourgeois, 'Preface' viii. Also: H.C.C.J. van der Mandere [E. de Melville], *De Haagsche overeenkomst betreffende de vreedzame beslechting van internationale geschillen en het Permanente Hof van Arbitrage*. Rhenen, B. van de Watering, 1907, xii; A. DeLourne, *Les lois de la guerre contemporaine à l'occasion du livre de M. Méringhac sur la conference d la paix*. Toulouse, Lagarde et Sebille, 1901, in NA 2.22.28, 231.
27 *FW* 2, April 1900, 52–55.
28 *FW* 2, April 1900, 54.
29 *FW* 2, April 1900, 52. Also: *Herald of Peace* 590, 1 October 1898, 121.
30 There were thirty-one mentions of Apponyi in the Dutch-language press in 1900, of which sixteen referenced his proposal for the international peace press (*Delpher*). The *Sumatra Post* returned to Apponyi's idea in 1905: 15 September 1905, 1.
31 *DE* 3 August 1900, 7.
32 É. Ducommun, *The probable consequences of a European war*. London, International Arbitration and Peace Association, 1906, 4, in PCSC, 'Great Britain.'
33 *American Association for International Conciliation* 1913, 1–10.
34 W.C. Deming, 'The opportunity and duty of the press in relation to world peace' *American Association for International Conciliation* 1913, 3; T.A. Larson, *History of Wyoming*. Second edition, University of Nebraska Press, 1990, 387.
35 F. Passy, 'Preface' in Vries, *Pour* 9.
36 Passy, 'Preface' 9.

37 Vries, *Pour* 13–14.
38 Herman, *Eleven* 41; Geppert, 'Public' 133–164; Best, *Humanity* 139.
39 Palmer, 'British' 216–217; Kern, *Culture* 231.
40 Cf. Potter, *News* 40.
41 Cf. Winter, *Dreams*.
42 R. Chickering, 'War, peace and social mobilization in Imperial Germany. Patriotic societies, the peace movement and socialist labor' in Chatfield and van den Dungen, eds, *Voices*.
43 Cooper, ed., *Internationalism* 11; S.E. Cooper, *Patriotic pacifism. Waging war on war in Europe 1815–1914*. New York, Oxford UP, 1991.
44 Ceadel, *Semi-detached*.
45 Tate, *Disarmament* 215.
46 Patterson, *Toward* vii–viii. Cf. Marchand, *American* 5, 10, 23; Kuehl, *Seeking* 75–76; C.E. Neu, *The troubled encounter. The United States and Japan*. New York, John Wiley, 1975, 37–38.
47 Marchand, *American* 41.
48 Sluga, *Internationalism* 16; Cooper, ed., *Internationalism* 249; James L. Tryon (1919) in Marchand, *American* 10.
49 Cf. Sluga, *Internationalism* 2.
50 Including Prince Mirza Rhiza Khan: A.-du-D. M. Riza Khan, *Échos de la conference de la Haye*. Constantinople, np, 1903.
51 D.D. Caron, 'War and international adjudication. Reflections on the 1899 peace conference' *AJIL* 94, 4, 2000, 13.
52 A. Wild, *Baron d'Estournelles de Constant (1852–1914)*. Hamburg, Europa-Kolleg, 1973; A. Wild, 'Paul Henri d'Estournelles de Constant' in Holl and Kjelling, eds, *Nobel*; Eyffinger, *1907* 204–205.
53 *International peace. Speeches delivered by Baron d'Estournelles de Constant and others*. Edinburgh, np, 1906, 6, 8. *TT* 5 November 1906, 14.
54 Wild, *Estournelles*.
55 As examples: *Grazer Volksblatt*. 2 April 1903, 14; *NYT* 29 October 1903, 5; *Bludenzer Anzeiger* 17 April 1909, 3; *Bush Advocate* 8 May 1909, 3; *Russische Rundschau* (Berlin) 23 February 1910, 3; *Southland Times* (New Zealand) 6 March 1911, 5; *NYT* 7 October 1912, 5; *Manawatu Times* 30 December 1913, 5.
56 Jackson, *Beyond* esp. 77.
57 As examples: *Nederlandsche Vredesbond Jaarboek 1900* 4, in PCSC 'Nederlandsche Vredesbond'; P.H.B. d'Estournelles de Constant, 'Woman and the cause of peace' *American Association for International Conciliation* 1911, 5–17; E.D. Mead, 'Baron d'Estournelles in America' *Unity* 6 April 1911, 93–94 in PCSC MEAD, Reel 78:2, Box 3; *FW* 4, 6, March 1902, 46; F. Passy, *Pour la paix. Notes et documents*. Paris, Bibliothèque-Charpentier, 1909, 170–172.
58 P.H.B. d'Estournelles de Constant, *Limitation des charges navales et militaires*. Brussels, Misch and Thron, 1912, in PCSC IPU, Box 2; *Herald of Peace* 688, December 1906, 301.
59 Butler, *Across* 15, 55–56.
60 Wild, 'Paul' 73.
61 Gray, *Champions* 101; Tuchman, *Proud* 273; *Hastings Times* (New Zealand) 17 February 1903, 4.
62 *NYT* 2 June 1904, 2.

63 D'Estournelles de Constant in Spiller, *Papers* 384.

64 *The Times* referenced d'Estournelles 210 times between 1 July 1899 and 1 July 1914. The *New York Times* made 178 references to d'Estournelles across that same period. He received 45 mentions in the Finnish newspaper the *Hufvudstadsbladet* and 49 in the *Berliner Tageblatt*.

65 *TT* 26 April 1901, 5; *Neue Freie Presse* 18 March 1901, 3; *Wiener Salonblatt* 14 April 1901, 7; *Matin* 23 April 1901, 3; *Temps* 24 April 1901, 2; *Croix* 27 April 1901, 3.

66 *Atlanta Constitution* 14 March 1911, 8.

67 F. Holls, *The peace conference at The Hague and its bearings on international law and policy*. New York, MacMillan, 1900; *Herald of Peace* 611, July 1900, 88–89; F. Holls to T.M.C. Asser, 16 October 1900, in NA 2.21.014, 286.

68 *WP* 6 February 1900, 2; *CDT* 29 April 1900, 2; *NYT* 22 November 1900, 7; Suttner, *Memoirs*, Volume 2, 371.

69 Holls, 'Reminiscenses'.

70 In Boyle, *History* 169.

71 Holls, *Hague* 172–173.

72 *TT* 1 January 1901, 10; G. Rümelin, *Politics and the moral law*. New York, MacMillan, 1901, 128.

73 *AMRR* 22, December 1900, 643; *Harper's Weekly* 30 December 1899, 1315; *LAT* 7 September 1899, 2; *NYT* 14 August 1901, 3; 16 October 1910, 43; *WP* 16 December 1899, 7; 12 December 1900, 3; 16 June 1901, 3; 18 September 1901, 3; *CDT* 4 November 1899, 12; 16 June 1901, 10; 14 August 1901, 5; *Atlanta Constitution* 14 August 1901, 4.

74 *NYT* 24 July 1903, 3. Also: *CDT* 24 July 1903, 4; *Atlanta Constitution* 24 July 1903, 3.

75 *Guardian* 24 July 1903, 10; *TT* 27 July 1902, 6.

76 Pustogarov, *Martens*; Grabar, *History* 381–387.

77 Including: *Results of the Hague conference*. New York, North American Review, 1899; *La paix et la guerre*. Paris, Arthur Rousseau, 1901; *Étude de F. de Martens, membre de la cour permanente d'arbitrage de la Haye*. Paris, H. Charles-Lavauzelle, 1906; *Tratado de derecho internacional. La paz y la guerra apéndice*. Madrid, España Moderna, 1905; *Hacia la paz por la justicia*. Mexico, Tipografia Económica, 1911; *Kokusaiho*. Tokyo, Hatsubaimoto Hakubunkan, 1900; F. de Martens, *Par la justice vers la paix*. Paris, Henri Charles-Lavauzelle, 1902.

78 F. Martens, 'Preface' in A. Méringhac, *Les lois et coutumes de la guerre sure terre d'apres le droit international moderne et la codification de la conférence de la Haye de 1899*. Paris, Marescq Ainé, 1903, v–vii, quotation on v.

79 Martens, *Conférence* 8–9, 34; Pustogarov, *Martens* 51–52, 133–134.

80 As examples: *NYT* 5 June 1902, 3; 20 October 1901, 4; *Guardian* 29 September 1904, 12; *LAT* 29 September 1904, 5. *The Times* referenced Martens 264 times between 1 August 1899 and 1914, the *New York Times* 130 times, with the *Hufvudstadsbladet* registering his name 22 times. The *Berliner Tageblatt* made 255 references to 'Martens' and 'Haag' in the same time period.

81 *CDT* 25 December 1903, 1.

82 *WP* 27 September 1903, 3.

83 *Atlanta Constitution* 27 November 1905, 4; *Afro-American* 2 September 1905, 2.

84 *CDT* 17 June 1905, 4.

85 F. de Martens, 'Europe, China and the Hague conference' *CDT* 28 October 1900, 41. The *NYT* (page 2), *LAT* (3) and *Guardian* (7) had similar reports on 17 November 1899.

86 *Guardian* 2 November 1904, 6.
87 *Guardian* 8 October 1902, 9.
88 *WP* 8 August 1902, 7.
89 E.E. Hale in *NYT* 31 August 1902, 25.
90 M. Lachs, *The teacher in international law. Teaches and teaching*. Second revised edition. The Hague, Martinus Nijhoff, 1987, 73.
91 Including: *Die Fortschritte des Seekriegsrechtes durch die zweite Haager Friedenskonferenz*. Tübingen, J.C.B. Mohr, 1908; *Die Ergebnisse der Haager Konferenzen das Kriegsverhütungsrecht*. Stuttgart, W. Kohlhammer, 1915; *Weltunionen, Haager Friedenskonferenzen und Völkerbund*. Berlin, Ferd. Dümmlers, 1925; P. Zorn, 'Zur Erinnerung an die erste Friedenskonferenz' in W. Schücking, ed., *Das Werk vom Haag. Zweite Serie. Die gerichtlichen Entscheidungen*. Volume 1, Leipzig, Duncker und Humblot, 1917 [1912], 1–42; *AMRR* 21, January–July 1900.
92 Schücking, *International union* 8, fn 2; F.A. Schmidt, *Von den Haager Friedensabkommen bis zum Kellogg-Pakt*. np, 1931, 1, 28–29.
93 P. Zorn, 'Friedensbewegung und Haager Konferenz' *Deutsche Revue* 31, 1906 132–134. Zorn received less attention in the English-language press. Still, *The Times* mentioned 'Zorn' and 'Hague' on 14 occasions between 1 August 1899 and 1 July 1914, while the *New York Times* did so 17 times. It was near impossible to isolate a search for Phillip Zorn in the available German-language press databases (in large part because the noun 'Zorn' in German means 'anger') although a search for 'Zorn' and 'Haag' came up with an unlikely 1,540 results in the *Berliner Tageblatt*, many of which had nothing to do with either the peace conference or Phillip Zorn, although a surprising number did.
94 Zorn, *Weltunionen* 10.
95 *Guardian* 23 September 1904, 5; 24 September 1904, 9; 27 September 1904, 4; 28 September 1904, 5; 29 September 1904, 12.
96 *WP* 24 September 1904, 4; *NYT* 24 September 1904, 5.
97 *Otago Witness* 16 September 1903, 69.
98 Suttner, *Memoirs*, Volume 2, 339.
99 Between 1 July 1899 and 1 July 1914, Bertha von Suttner was mentioned 15 times in the *The Times*, 81 times in the *New York Times*, no less than 94 times by the *Hufvudstadsbladet* and 236 times by the *Berliner Tageblatt*. The Austrian satirical magazine *Kikeriki*, for its part, dedicated 114 jokes to Suttner between 1899 and 1913. W.T. Stead received similar attention: 273 times in *The Times*, 94 times (with 'Hague') in the *New York Times*, 75 times (with 'Haag') in the *Hufvudstadsbladet* and 80 times (with 'Haag') in the *Berliner Tageblatt*. Wasczklewicz van Schilfgaarde was less-well-known in the foreign press, although she received considerable attention in the Dutch press: with 17 mentions in the *Algemeen Handelsblad* and 14 in the *Nieuws van de Dag*. The *Manchester Guardian* discussed her twice in relationship to the Boer War (3 January 1900, 10; 17 June 1901, 5) and the *Berliner Tageblatt* once (2 December 1901, 2). The Meads were frequently mentioned in the North American press: 'Edwin Mead' and 'peace' appears 112 times in the *New York Times*, 'Lucy Mead' and 'peace' another 37 times. *The Times* referred to Edwin Mead 4 times, reserving no mentions for his wife. The *Berlin Tageblatt* makes 11 mentions of Edwin, none of Lucy.
100 *JT* 17 March 1900, 4; *AMRR* 22, July-December 1900, 475; *Star* (Christchurch) 5 August 1901, 2; *Taranaki Herald* 20 August 1900, 1; *Grey River Argus* 19 September 1901, 4; *Poverty Bay Herald* 28 March 1903, 2.

101 G.H. Perris, *Jean de Bloch and the museum of war and peace*. London, International Arbitration Association, 1902, 4, in PCSC 'Switzerland'.
102 *Catalogue of the international war and peace museum in Lucerne, 1903*. Lucerne, Genossenschafts Buchdruckerei, 1903 in PCSC 'Switzerland'.
103 'Museum of peace and war in Lucerne', report, nd, in PCSC 'Switzerland'.
104 Bloch, 'Wars' 306.
105 *Catalogue of the international war and peace museum* 40.
106 *SP* 30 July 1902, 1; *WP* 14 September 1902, 14; *NYT* 29 June 1902, 32; *Guardian* 10 June 1902, 12; *Illustrierte Sontagsblat* (*Pusterhaler Boter*, Italy) 1 August 1902, 244; 'M. Bloch's great war museum at Lucerne' *AMRR* 26, July–December 1902, 174–176; E.D. Mead, *Jean de Bloch and 'future of war'*. Boston, International Union, 1904.
107 *Ohinemuri Gazette* 24 April 1903, 2.
108 *WP* 19 March 1905, 2.
109 'Museum of peace and war in Lucerne'.
110 *TT* 29 March 1909, 10.
111 Grabar lists thirteen Russian lawyers who published on The Hague before 1914 (*History* 527).
112 A.H. Fried, 'Neo-Pacifisten' *FW* 5, 13, July 1903, 85–89. Cf. C. Richet, 'Pacifisme, antimilitarisme, internationalisme' *Revue de la Paix* 11, 12, December 1906, 316–325.
113 Cf. H. Wehberg, 'Max Huber im Zeitalter der Haager Friedenskonferenzen' *FW* 44, 6, 1944, 432; Sewall, 'New' 22–23.
114 Cf. Schücking, *International union* 24; Göhring, *Verdrängt* 92.
115 Fried, 'Neo-Pacifisten'; C. Meurer, *Übersicht über die Arbeiten der Haager Friedenskonferenz inbesondere das Abkommen zur friedlichen Erledigung international Streitfälle vom 29 juli 1899*. Munich, J. Schweiter, 1903; *FW* 5, 11–12, June 1903, 83; C. Meurer, *Das Friedensrecht der Haager Konferenz*. Munich, J. Schweitzer Verlag, 1905; C. Meurer, *Das Kriegsrecht der Haager Konferenz*. Munich, J. Schweitzer, 1907; P.H.B. d'Estournelles de Constant, *Les résultats de la conférence de la paix*. Lyon, A. Storck, 1900. Also: *FW* 3, 21–22, June 1901, 81–82; J.P. Suijling, *The Hague peace conferences of 1899 and 1907*. The Hague, Martinus Nijhoff, 1910.
116 Schücking's work on The Hague is voluminous.
117 O. Nippold, *Die Fortbildung des Verfahrens in völkerrechtlichen Streitigkeiten. Ein völkerrechliches Problem der Gegenwart speziell im Hinblick auf die Haager Friedenskonferenzen*. Leipzig, Duncker & Humblot, 1907.
118 Wehberg even produced a pocketbook on The Hague: *Der Abkommen der Haager Friedenskonferenzen, der Londoner Seekriegskonferenz nebst Genfer Konvention*. Berlin, J. Guttentag, 1910; *Capture in war on land and sea*. London, S. King, 1911.
119 T.E. Holland to Lord Sanderson, 9 January 1906, in PRO FO372, 38; Thomas Barclay to Inter-Departmental Committee organizing the second Hague conference, 13 May 1906, in PRO CAB17, 85. Also PRO FO372, 23.
120 G. de Molinari, *The society of tomorrow*. London, T. Fisher Unwin, 1904.
121 Gray, *Champions* 94–95.
122 C.R. Rossi, *Broken chain of being. James Brown Scott and the origins of modern international law*. The Hague, Kluwer Law International, 1998, 4–9; Finch, *Adventures*.
123 C. Landauer, 'The ambivalence of power. Launching the *American Journal of International Law* in an era of empire and globalisation' *Leiden Journal of International Law* 20, 2, June 2007, 325–358.
124 Passy, *Pour* 175.

125 Lapradelle, *Conférence*; *FW* August 1901, 111–112; *The Friend* 49, 3 December 1909, v; A.P. Higgins, *The Hague conference and other international conferences concerning the laws and usages of war*. London, Stevens, 1904. Cf. Hamann, *Suttner* 158.
126 F.A. Boyle, *Foundations of world order. The legalist approach to international relations (1898–1922)*. Durham, Duke UP, 1999, 12, 18; Herman, *Eleven* 23; Landauer, 'Ambivalence' 327–329; D.J. Bederman, 'Appreciating a century of scholarship in the *American Journal of International Law*' *AJIL* 100, 2006, 22; Kuehl, *Seeking* 78; E. Root, 'The need of popular understanding of international law' *AJIL* 1, 1, January 1907, 1–3; Finch, *Adventures* xv.
127 A.R. Higgins, 'Law not war. James Brown Scott's interest in and representation of the 1899 and 1907 Hague peace conferences' Summer Scholar Research Essay, University of Auckland, 2014. Cf. J. Hepp, 'James Brown Scott and the rise of public international law' *Journal of the Gilded Age and Progressive Era* 7, 2, April 2008, 151–179.
128 Kuehl, *Seeking* 47–48.
129 A.H. Fried, *Handbuch der Friedensbewegung*. Vienna, Oesterreichischen Friedensgesellschaft, 1905, 350.
130 'Procès-verbaux des réunions de Comité executive créé par decision de la Conférence de Berlin, Septembre 1908' 11 January 1910, in IPU Box 254. Cf. *The international union. What it is, what it wants to do, how it tries to do it*. London, Office of the British Centre of the International Union, 1901, in NA 2.21.174, 5; Uhlig, *Interparlamentarische Union*.
131 Wehberg, 'Inter-Parliamentary' 39, 41, 60; C. Lange, *L'arbitrage obligatoire en 1913*. Brussels, Misch & Thron, 1914.
132 Scott, *Hague peace*, Volume 1, 90–91; IPU to President Roosevelt, 13 September 1904, RSC, TRP, Series 1, Reel 47; H. Davis, ed., *Among the world's peacemakers*. New York, Progressive, 1907.
133 IPU, *Actes essentiels premier supplément des 'resolutions votées par les huit premières conférences interparlementaires*. Berne, K.J. Wyss, 1902, in PCSC IPU Box 2.
134 *World Fair's Bulletin* 5, 12, October 1904, 25–26.
135 IPU, *Actes* 25–27.
136 IPU, *Actes* 30–31.
137 IPU, *XVIIIe conférence, La Haye, 3–5 Septembre, 1913. Résolutions adoptées et nominations faites par la conférence*. Brussels, Bureau Interparlementaire, 1913.
138 Available at the IPU Archives, Geneva.
139 IPU, *Session de 1903 compte rendu de la XIe conférence tenue à Vienne, Palais du Reichsrat du 7 au 9 septembre 1903*. Vienna, Otto Maass, 1903, v.
140 IPU, *Session de 1903* 20.
141 IPU, *Session de 1903* 21.
142 *Guardian*. 15 July 1903, 5; 10 September 1903, 7.
143 *NYT* 7 September 1903, 2; 8 September 1903, 6; 9 September 1903, 6; *LAT* 29 September 1903, 3.
144 *Wiener Zeitung* 7 September 1903, 2–5; 8 September 1903, 2; 9 September 1903, 2–4, 10 September 1903, 3–6.
145 *Interessante Blatt* (Vienna) 10 September 1903, 4. Also: IPU Box 194, 254.
146 International Council of Women, *1899* esp. 6, 33.
147 Ishbel Aberdeen, public address, 26 June 1899 in International Council of Women, *1899* 48.
148 International Council of Women, *1904*, Volume 1.

149 Alonso, *Peace* 54; International Council of Women, *1899* 70.
150 E. Gubin, L. van Molle, eds, *Women changing the world. A history of the International Council of Women*. Brussels, Racine, 2005, 19.
151 International Council of Women, *1904*, Volume 2, 134.
152 International Council of Women, *1908* 37–39.
153 International Council of Women, *1909* 241; AVG-CARHIF ICW, 205.
154 LSE 51CW/B04 Box 12.
155 International Council of Women, *1904*, Volume 2, 107–108.
156 *FW* 6, 6, June 1904, 109–110.
157 Lord and Lady Aberdeen, *'We twa'. Reminiscences of Lord and Lady Aberdeen*. Volume 2, Glasgow, W. Collins, 1925, 301–302.
158 In International Council of Women, *1904*, Volume 2, 109; *Address of the President of the International Council of Women by May Wright Sewall at the opening of its third quinquennial in Berlin June 8 1904*. Berlin, Kitzler & Hampel, 1904, in LSE 51CW/BO4 Box 12.
159 International Council of Women, *1904*, Volume 2, 109–117.
160 *Star* (Christchurch) 17 September 1904, 3.
161 *NYT* 7 August 1904, 4.
162 *CDT* 19 July 1904, 6; *WP* 3 July 1904, E2.
163 O. Gordon, *The International Council of Women and the meetings of the International Congress of Women in Berlin 1904. Letters by Mrs Ogilvie Gordon*. np, 1904, in LSE 51CW/B04 Box 12.
164 *Berliner Tageblatt* 3 June 1904, 1; 5 June 1904, 29; *NHZ* 13 June 1904, 2.
165 *Frau von Suttner, der Frauenweltbund und der Krieg*. Berlin, Vossische Buchhandlung, 1905.
166 International Council of Women, *1908* 37.
167 International Council of Women, *1904*, Volume 1, 53.
168 Selenka, *Internationale* xix.
169 Selenka, *Internationale* xxi–xxiii.
170 International Council of Women, *1904*, Volume 1, 70–74.
171 *NHZ* 18 May 1901, 3; *SP* 20 June 1901, 1; *FW* 3 June 1901, 77–79.
172 *Advocate for Peace* 63, 6, June 1901, 127–128; *NYT* 19 May 1905, 4.
173 E.D. Mead, 'America at The Hague. The duty of the hour' speech, 20 July 1907, in PCSC MEAD Reel 78:1, Box 2; NA 2.05.03, 544.
174 E.D. Mead, 'Peace teachings in schools' *Journal of Education* 25 January 1906, 89, in PCSC MEAD Reel 78:1, Box 2; 'L'Anniversaire de la conférence de la Haye' *Revue de la Paix* 10, 5–6, May-June 1905, 160–165.
175 Kuehl, *Seeking* 109; W.I. Hull, *The two Hague conferences and their contributions to international law*. Boston, Ginn, 1908, v; P. Filene, 'The world peace foundation and progressivism, 1910–1919' *New England Quarterly* 36, 4, December 1963, 478–501.
176 *Vogue* 31 December 1908, 1096.
177 L.A. Mead, 'The Czar's rescript and Jean de Bloch' np, 1904, in PCSC MEAD Reel 78:10, Box 14; *Neues Wiener Tageblatt* 8 September 1911, 10; 12 September 1911, 10; 17 September 1911, 8.
178 Melbourne Peace Society, 'The new patriotism and the 18th of May' nd [1907], in PCSC 'Australia'.
179 Vrede door Recht, *Waarom wij 18 mei vieren*. The Hague, Vrede door Recht, 1914, in HGA Lf4; *Vrede door Recht* reports 1901–1907, in NA 2.21.174, 3; *18 Mei. Leidraad*

voor de 18 Mei-viering of de scholen. The Hague, Vrede door Recht, 1914, in PCSC 'Vrede door Recht'.

180 Dutch Minister of Foreign Affairs to Dutch Minister of Internal Affairs, 3 June 1907, in NA 2.05.03, 536.

181 *JT* 2 May 1907, 3; 15 May 1907, 6; 21 May 1907, 2; 22 May 1907, 2; 23 May 1907, 6.

182 N. Lubelski-Bernard, 'Freemasonry and peace in Europe, 1867–1914' in Chatfield and van den Dungen, eds, *Voices* 87.

183 International Council of Women, *1914* 409–415.

184 NA 2.05.03, 544.

185 *WP* 15 August 1907, np.

186 *Herald of Peace* 622, June 1901, 68.

187 American Association for International Conciliation (New York), Quarterly report to the Council of Direction, June 1913, in PCSC CDGA.

188 *NYT* 31 August 1913, 10.

189 *JT* 2 April 1907, 6.

190 *SP* 4 May 1906, 1–2.

191 A. Brehmer, ed., *Die Welt in hundert Jahren*. Berlin, Verlagsanstalt Buntdruck, 1910.

192 Gray, *Champions* 64.

193 N. Lubelski-Bernard, 'The Institute of International Law, Auguste Beernaert and Henri la Fontaine' in Holl and Kjellings, eds, *Nobel* 109–134; Wild, 'Passy' 40–41; G. Lundestad, 'The meaning of the Nobel Peace Prize' in Holl and Kjelling, eds, *Nobel* 9; Hamann, *Suttner* 85, 88. New Zealand's *Paperspast* notes 693 records on the Nobel Peace Prize award between 1901 and 1913.

194 *Hawke's Bay Herald* 5 June 1901, 2.

195 *Hawera & Normanby Star* 8 March 1911, 3.

196 F.W. Haberman, ed., *Nobel lectures including presentation speeches and laureates' biographies. Peace 1901–1925*. Singapore, World Scientific, 1972.

197 *Poverty Bay Herald* 23 January 1903, 4; I. Abrams, 'Bertha von Suttner and the Nobel Peace Prize' *Journal of Central European Affairs* 22, 1962–63, 286–307.

198 *CDT* 17 December 1905, B1.

199 T. Roosevelt, *African and European addresses*. New York, G.P. Putnam, 1910, 78; E.P. Trani, D.E. Davis, 'End of an era. Theodore Roosevelt and the Treaty of Portsmouth' in S. Ricard, ed., *A companion to Theodore Roosevelt*. London, Blackwell, 2011, 368–390.

200 Koskeniemmi, *Gentle* 278.

201 L. Renault, *L'oeuvre de la Haye en 1899 et en 1907*. Stockholm, P.A. Norstedt, 1908, in NA 2.22.28, 255.

202 *New Zealand Herald* 12 December 1913, 7; 'Senator Root and the Nobel Peace Prize' *AJIL* 8, 1, January 1914, 133–137.

203 Choate, *Two* 44.

7 When the World Showed Up: The Second Hague Conference, 1907

1 In F.S. Marvin, *The living past. A sketch of western progress*. Oxford, Clarendon Press, 1913, vi–vii; italics in original.

2 C. Belanger, J.G. Guiral and F. Terrou, eds, *L'histoire générale de la presse française*. Volume 3, Paris, Presses Universitaires de France, 1972, 296, 311.

3 C.M. Roberts, *The Washington Post. The first 100 years*. Boston, Houghton Mifflin, 1977, 87, 89–90.
4 *WP* 4 January 1907, 1.
5 *WP* 4 January 1907, 3.
6 Roberts, *Washington* 90–91.
7 *Matin* 1 August 1907, 3; 2 August 1907, 3; 7 August 1907, 3; 11 August 1907, 3; 13 August 1907, 3; 14 August 1907, 3; 19 August 1907, 3; 22 August 1907, 3; 23 August 1907, 3; 28 August 1907, 3; 30 August 1907, 3.
8 *Paperspast* (June 2017).
9 *Trove* (June 2017).
10 *Times* digital archive (June 2017).
11 *Japan Times* database (June 2017).
12 *Anno* (June 2017).
13 *Delpher* (June 2017).
14 J. Rüger, *The great naval game. Britain and Germany in the age of empire*. Cambridge UP, 2007; Wilkinson, *Depictions*; M. Paris, *Warrior nation. Images of war in British popular culture*. London, Reaktion, 2002; M. Martin, *Images at war. Illustrated periodicals and constructed nations*. Toronto, University of Toronto Press, 2006, esp. 245–246; T. Scheer, 'The Habsburg Empire's German-speaking public sphere and the first Balkan War' in D. Geppert, W. Mulligan and A. Rose, eds, *The wars before the Great War. Conflict and international politics before the outbreak of the First World War*. Cambridge UP, 2015, 301–319.
15 Mulligan, 'Justifying'.
16 Mulligan, *Peace* 12.
17 Landauer, 'Ambivalences' 348–349.
18 Ito, 'One hundred' 22–24; T. Minohara, T. Hon and E. Dawley, 'Introduction' in Minohara et al., eds, *Decade*, 2.
19 Cf. T.F. McGann, *Argentina, the United States and the inter-American system 1880–1914*. Cambridge, Harvard UP, 1957, 265.
20 *Matin* 14 June 1907, 3.
21 *Matin* 19 October 1907, 3; 21 October 1907, 3.
22 *Matin* 15 November 1907, 2.
23 *WP* 30 August 1907, 4, 6.
24 *WP* 22 September 1907, 1, 11.
25 *WP* 18 October 1907, 6; 22 October 1907, 12.
26 *WP* 22 October 1907, 4; 6 November 1907, 4; W.A. Rogers, cartoon, Library of Congress, DCL/PP-192:0042, www.loc.gov/pictures/item/2010717678 (accessed August 2017).
27 *WP* 29 December 1907, SM2.
28 *WP* 16 November 1907, 6; 22 November 1907, 4; 22 December 1907, E4; J.W. Foster, *Diplomatic memoirs*. Volume 2. Boston, Houghton Mifflin, 1909, 212–213, 240–241.
29 Also: 'Disarmament' cartoon, *New Zealand Herald* 5 June 1907, 9.
30 Also: *AMRR* 35, April 1907, 532.
31 *Punch* (Melbourne) 31 October 1907, 7. Also: 'Es klapper die Mühle . . .!' poem in *Glühlichter* 28 August 1907, 3; 'De conferentie hurah! hurah! hurah!' cartoon in *Algemeen Handelsblad* 31 July 1907, 5.
32 United States Minister in The Hague to Dutch Minister of Foreign Affairs, 4 November 1904, in Smit, *Bescheiden*, Volume 3, 319–321; Scott, *Hague peace*, Volume 2, 89–90.

33 As examples: Theodore Roosevelt to Elihu Root, 2 June 1904, and to Joseph Gunney Cannon, 12 September 1904, both in E.E. Morison, ed., *The letters of Theodore Roosevelt*. Cambridge, Harvard UP, 1951, 810–812, 923; Theodore Roosevelt, address, 26 April 1907, in RSC TRP Series 5C, Reel 427; M. Koskenniemi, 'The ideology of international adjudication at the 1907 Hague conference' in Y. Daudet, ed., *Actualité de la conférence de la Haye de 1907, deuxième conférence de la paix*. The Hague, Martinus Nijhoff, 2008, 137.
34 Dutch Minister in Washington D.C. to Dutch Minister of Foreign Affairs, 28 September 1904, in NA 2.05.03, 532.
35 Scott, *Hague peace*, Volume 1, 92.
36 J. Hay, 'Proposal for second Hague conference', 21 October 1904, in NA 2.05.03, 532; Eyffinger, *1907* 66.
37 In Davis, *Among* 83.
38 *FW* October 1907, 182.
39 United States Minister in The Hague to Dutch Minister of Foreign Affairs, 27 December 1904; Dutch Minister in Washington D.C. to Dutch Minister of Foreign Affairs, 8 December 1904, both in NA2.05.03, 532.
40 Director of the Cabinet of Queen Wilhelmina to Dutch Minister of Foreign Affairs, 22 November 1904, in NA 2.05.03, 532; Smit, *Bescheiden*, Volume 3, Part 2, 297, 317–319, 329–330.
41 Smit, *Bescheiden*, Volume 3, Part 2, 514; Pustogarov, *Martens* 298–299. Cf. S. Schattenberg, 'The diplomat "as actor on a great stage before all the people"? A cultural history of diplomacy and the Portsmouth peace negotiations of 1905' in Mösslang and Riotte, eds, *Diplomats* 190; Dülffer, *Regeln* 280.
42 P. Holquist, 'Dilemmas of an "official with progressive views". Baron Boris Nolde' *Baltic Yearbook of International Law* 7, 2007, 211–249.
43 In *FW* 11, July 1909, 130.
44 Including Alfred Fried: *FW* 10, 7, October 1905, 185.
45 As an example: *Soerabaiasch-Handelsblad* 22 May 1906, 1.
46 A.W. Ward, G.P. Gooch, *Cambridge history of British foreign policy, 1783–1919*. Volume 3, Cambridge UP, 1923, 351; J. Wilson, *CB. A life of Sir Henry Campbell-Bannerman*. London, Constable, 1973, 534; Excubitor, 'The peace conference and the navy' *Fortnightly Review* 81, 485, May 1907, 843–856.
47 S.A. Keefer, 'Building the palace of peace. The Hague conference of 1899 and arms control in the progressive era' *Journal of the History of International Law* 8, 2006, 1–17; J.A. Grant, *Rulers, guns and money. The global arms trade in the age of imperialism*. Cambridge, Harvard UP, 2007.
48 G.H. Perris, *For an arrest of armaments. A note for the second Hague conference*. London, Caxton House, 1906; E. Halévy, *The rule of democracy 1905–1914*. London, Ernest Benn, 1961, 222–224.
49 C.B., 'The Hague conference and the limitation of armaments' *Nation* 1, 1. J.A. Spender, *The life of the Right Hon. Sir Henry Campbell-Bannerman*. Volume 2, London, Hodder & Stoughton, nd, 328–330; *TT* 15 March 1907, 5; 1 May 1907, 5; F.M. Leventhal, *The last dissenter. H.N. Brailsford and his world*. Oxford, Clarendon Press, 1985, 61; Wilson, *CB* 540; Havighurst, *Massingham* 144.
50 W.T. Stead to Sir John Fisher, 12 June 1907, in CHAR FISR8/25; H.W. Nevinson, *Fire of life*. London, James Nesbit, 1935, 219.
51 Sir Edward Grey to A. Nicolson, 1 May 1907, in PRO FO800/72; *TT* 1 May 1907, 5, 3 May 1907, 5; Bülow, *Memoirs* 290.

52 Cf. *TT* 16 May 1907, 5; 20 May 1907, 3–4.
53 J.B. Scott, ed., *The proceedings of the Hague peace conferences. Translated of the official texts. The conference of 1907.* Volume 1, New York, Oxford UP, 1920, 2–15; Smit, *Bescheiden*, Volume 3, Part 2, 546–547, 583–587, 564–566, 693–695; *AJIL* January 1908, 14.
54 Scott, ed., *Instructions* esp. 69–85; Scott, *Hague peace*, Volume 1, 95–106; Davis, *United States 2*; Coogan, *End* 69, 72–73, 82–84; PRO CAB17/85, CAB38/11/20, CAB38/11/17, CAB38/10/76, CAB38/12/33, MT9/805, BT13/19, FO372/65–66; B. Semmel, *Liberalism and naval strategy. Ideology, interest and sea power during the Pax Britannica.* Boston, Allen & Unwin, 1986, 101–103; NA 2.05.03, 534, 536, 540, 549; NA 2.21.315, 87; NA 2.21.014, 312.
55 There were numerous reasons why the conference was repeatedly delayed, most of which had to do with the Geneva and Pan-American Congresses held in 1906: Scott, *Hague peace*, Volume 1, 96. The Algeciras crisis caused further delays.
56 Lord Reay to Henry Campbell-Bannerman, 21 July 1907, in BL MS 52514; Sir Edward Grey, 16 February 1907, in PRO FO372/65; T. Barclay, *The second Hague peace conference.* London, np, 1906, 552–555.
57 Scott, *Proceedings 1907*, Volume 1, 1.
58 Edward Grey to Henry Campbell-Bannerman, 20 August 1906, BL MS 41218.
59 *TT* 23 January 1907, 3; British Foreign Office memorandum, 19 January 1907, in PRO FO372/65; Dutch Minister of Foreign Affairs to Queen Wilhelmina, 11 February 1907, in NA 2.05.03, 536; Pustogarov, *Martens* 8, 312.
60 Scott, *Hague peace*, Volume 1, Part 1, 97–100; Smit, *Bescheiden*, Volume 3, Part 2, 263–264; NA 2.05.03, 518.
61 E. von Ullmann, *Die Haager Konferenz von 1899 und die Weiterbildung der Völkerrechts.* Tübingen, J.C.B. Mohr, 1907, quotation on 2.
62 James Bryce, 1913, in Marvin, *Living* vi–vii.
63 In Roosevelt, *African* 138.
64 Kingsberg, *Moral* esp. 1–2; Schlichtman, 'Japan'; Schirbel, *Strukturen*, Volume 1, 237–245; XYZ Suisse, *Discours nécessaires à la conférence de la Haye.* Paris, Génerale Lahure, 1906.
65 Cf. C. Veeser, 'A forgotten instrument of global capitalism?' *International History Review* 35, 5, 2013, 1142.
66 *JT* 24 June 1905, 5.
67 *Illustrated London News* 26 January 1907, 145.
68 *Cologne Gazette* 3 April 1907, np, in PRO FO372/66.
69 For example: *Deuxième conférence de la Haye. Opinions, projets, propositions diverses.* Paris, Institut International de la Paix, 1907 (also available in Esperanto: PCSC Box 4); Barclay, *Second.*
70 *FW* February 1907, 22–25.
71 *Courrier de la Conférence de la Paix* 15 June–20 October 1907, in PPL; C. Knab, 'Civil society diplomacy? W.T. Stead, world peace and transgressive journalism' *Comparativ* 23, 6, 2013, 22–51; W.T. Stead, *Le parlement de l'humanité 1907. Biographies et photographies.* Amsterdam, Maas van Suchtelen, 1907.
72 NA 2.05.03, 541; *AJIL* 1, 3, July 1907, 727–729; *NYT* 20 January 1907, 4.
73 *Résultats du congrès pour l'arbitrage et la paix tenu à New York en Avril 1907 par Andrew Carnegie.* np, 1907, in NA 2.05.03, 544; A. Carnegie, *Results of the National Arbitration and Peace Congress.* New York, American Branch of the Association for International Arbitration Council, 1907.

74 Kuehl, *Seeking* 96.
75 *Current Literature* 42, January–June 1907, 486.
76 *Current Literature* 42, January–June 1907, 487.
77 *Current Literature* 42, January–June 1907, 488–493.
78 In NA 2.05.03, 534–545.
79 Eyffinger, *1907* 93.
80 Scott, *Proceedings 1907*, Volume 1, 60.
81 Hull, *Two* 26–27.
82 Scott, *Proceedings 1907*, Volume 1, 60–61; O. van Beresteijn, 'De curiositeiten-kamer' *Nieuw van de Dag* 26 October 1907, 1, in NA 2.21.018, 322.
83 Scott, *Proceedings 1907*, Volume 1, 578.
84 A. Johns, *War, journalism and the shaping of the twentieth century*. London, I.B. Tauris, 2006, 74–75.
85 Dutch Minister of Internal Affairs to Dutch Minister of Justice, 24 May 1907, in NA 2.05.03, 191; *Richmond River Express and Casino Kyogle Advertiser* 21 June 1907, 4.
86 HGA 0432-01, 6038; NA2.09.05, 6650; Dutch Minister in Berlin to Dutch Minister of Foreign Affairs, 13 June 1907, in NA 2.05.03, 191.
87 K. Liebknecht, *Militarismus und Antimilitarismus unter besonderer Berücklichtigung der internationalen Jugendbewegung*. Leipzig, np, 1907, esp. 100–101.
88 Telegram from Monsieur Dubosc to Secretary Morley, India Office, 29 June 1907, in PRO FO372/68; Nanking Viceroy Tuan Fan to Hague Peace Conference secretariat, 1907; China Centenary Missionary Conference to Hague Peace Conference secretariat, 13 July 1907, both in NA 2.05.03, 545; *Matin* 26 July 1907, 3.
89 NA 2.05.03, 534, 537, 540, 544, 545; NA 2.21.290, 300.
90 K. de Ceuster, 'The third man. Yi Wijong and the Korean mission to the 1907 Hague peace conference' in M. Prost, ed., *Mélanges offerts à Marc Orange et Alexandre Guillemoz*. Paris, Collège de France, 2010, 131–142; S. Murase, '1907nen hāgu heiwakaigi saihō: kankoku kōtei no shōsetsu' *Gaiko Forum* 6, 227, 2007, 56–63.
91 S. Murase, 'The presence of Asia at the Hague peace conference of 1907' *Colloquium. Topicality of the Hague peace conference of 1907*. The Hague, Martinus Nijhoff, 2007, 92.
92 V.T.o.g., in NA 2.05.03, 535; NA 2.21.290, 300.
93 Eyffinger, *1907* 88; NA 2.05.03, 540; *Courrier de la Conférence de la Paix* 22 September 1907, 1.
94 As examples: *New York Herald* 5 July 1907, np, in RSC TRP Series 15, Reel 469; *WP* 30 June 1907, 1; *Observer* 7 July 1907, 5.
95 Ceuster, 'Third' 132, 138.
96 *JT* 14 July 1907, 2.
97 Ceuster, 'Third' 136; 'Le cercle international' *Courrier de la Conférence* 15 June 1907, 5.
98 Murase, 'Presence' 95–96.
99 Ceuster, 'Third' 138.
100 Scott, *Proceedings 1907*, Volume 1, 53; NA 2.05.03, 540.
101 Scott, *Proceedings 1907*, Volume 1, 57.
102 *TT* 1 June 1907, 9; 4 June 1907, 5.
103 Scott, *Proceedings 1907*, Volume 1, 66.
104 In PRO FO372/69.
105 Scott, *Proceedings 1907*, Volume 1, 48–49.
106 Scott, *Proceedings 1907*, Volume 1, 49.

107 *WP* 16 June 1907, 1–2.
108 P.C. Jessup, *Elihu Root*. New York, Dodd & Mead, 1938, 82; Dutch Minister in Berlin to Dutch Minister of Foreign Affairs, 9 February 1907, in NA 2.05.03, 536.
109 W. Obkircher, ed., *General Erich von Gündell. Aus seinen Tagebüchen*. Hamburg, Hanseatische Verlagsanstalt, 1939, 80.
110 Lammasch, 'Rückblicke' 170.
111 NA 2.05.03, 536; NA 2.09.05, 6650.
112 HGA 0432-01, 6038.
113 14 June 1907, in NA 2.05.03, 540.
114 *South China Morning Post* 26 June 1907, 6, in NA 2.05.03, 534. An example: C. Hassmann, cartoon, *Puck* 58, 1497, 8 November 1905, centrefold.
115 *Amsterdammer* 2 June 1907, 12.
116 *Amsterdammer* 27 October 1907, 12.
117 'Eruitgesmeten diplomaten' in L. Raemaekers, *Ha! Ha! Ha! Alweer een vredesconferentie*. Amsterdam, Koster, 1907, np.
118 'Na 19 eeuwen' in Raemaekers, *Ha!* np.
119 Lammasch, 'Rückblicke' 182. Also: *Notenkraker* 11 August 1907, front page; 2 September 1907, 4.
120 T.M.C. Asser, 'De tweede vredes-conferentie. Een terugblik' *Tijdspiegel* 1908, 1–16.
121 NA 2.05.03, 535; Choate, *Two* 89; Eyffinger, *1907* 132.
122 NA2.05.03, 542; V.C. Lacerda, *Rui Barbosa em Haia*. Rio de Janiero, Casa de Rui Barbosa, 1957; Eyffinger, *1907* 132; Foster, *Memoirs*, Volume 2, 230–231; *WP* 6 October 1907, E9.
123 Choate, *Two* 89.
124 NA 2.05.03, 542; Eyffinger, *1907* 133–135; *Wereldkroniek* 14, 18, 3 August 1907, 277–280.
125 Dutch Minister of Foreign Affairs to Queen Wilhelmina, letters, August 1907, NA 2.05.03, 542.
126 Scott, *Proceedings 1907*, Volume 1, 66; Choate, *Two* 89.
127 NA 2.05.03, 535. Many advertised in the *Courrier de la Conférence*.
128 Norddeutscher Lloyd advertising pamphlet, 25 July 1907, HGA 0432-01, 6038; Eyffinger, *1907* 143–145.
129 NA 2.05.03, 542.
130 *Album d'hommage à son Majesté Oscar II*. The Hague, np, 1908, in PPL.
131 Scott, *Proceedings 1907*, Volume 1, 162, 173–175; Havighurst, *Massingham* 179.
132 A.A.C. Trindade, 'The presence and participation of Latin America at the second Hague peace conference of 1907' in Daudet, ed., *Actualité* 51–84; K. Wolfke, *Great and small powers in international law from 1814 to 1920*. Wroclaw, np, 1961, 61–63.
133 I.C. Ruxton, ed., *The diaries and letters of Sir Ernest Satow (1843–1929)*. Lewiston, Edwin Mellen, 1998, 359; Edward Fry to Edward Grey, 6 July 1907, in PRO FO800/929.
134 R. Barbosa, *Deuxième conférence de la paix. Actes et discours*. The Hague, W.P. van Stockum, 1907. Also: R. Barbosa, *O Brasil e a nações Latin-Americanas em Haya*. Rio de Janiero, Imprensa Nacional, 1908.
135 M. de Lima Barbosa, *Ruy Barbosa de la conférence de la Haye à la guerre des nations*. Paris, Garnier, 1917; L.A. Silva, *O discurso modernizador de Rui Barbosa (1879–1923)*. np, Universidade Federal de Juiz de Fora, 2009. Cf. H. Accioly, 'O barão do Rio Branco e a 2a conferência de Haia' *Revista do Instituto Histórico e Geográfico*

Brasileiro 187, 1945, 61–104; C.V. Laidler, *A segunda conferência sa paz de Haia 1907*. Rio de Janiero, Casa de Rui Barbosa, 2010, 77; Lacerda, *Rui*; P.P. da Cunha, *A diplomacia da paz. Rui Barbosa em Haia*. Rio de Janiero, Ministério da Educaçao e Cultura, 1977.

136 J. Holguin, *L'arbitrage*, and *La doctrine de la Drago*, np, 1907, in NA 2.22.28, 249; J. Holguin, *Segunda conferencia internacional de la Haya*. Bogota, Imprenta Nacional, 1908; *Informes y notas de la delegación de Columbia en la segunda conferencia de la paz de la Haya*. Rotterdam, M. Wyt, 1908; M. Vargas, *Recuerdos intimos. Conferencia internacional de la paz en la Haya*. Bogota, El Correo Nacional, 1908; A.S. Bustamente Y Sirven, *La seconde conférence de la paix. Réunie à la Haye en 1907*. Paris, L. Larose & L. Tenin, 1909; A.S. de Bustamente, 'The Hague convention concerning the rights and duties of neutral powers and persons in land warfare' *AJIL* 95, 1908, 95–120; F.S. de Fuentes, A.S. de Bustamente and M.S. Gonzola de Quesada, *Informe relativo a la segunda conferencia internacional de la paz reunida en el Haye en 1907*. Two volumes, Habana, La Moderna Poesia, 1908; F.H. y Carvajal, *Memoria que los señores Dr. Francisco Henriquez y Carvajal y Lic Apolinar Tejera, delegados plenipotenciarios de la Republica Dominicana en la segunda conferencia internacional de la paz*. Santo Domingo, J.R. Vda. Garcia, 1908; A.N. Léger, *La doctrine Drago et la deuxième conférence de la paix*. Port au Prince, Matin, 1915.

137 McGann, *Argentina* 219; C.A. Becu, *La neutralidad segun las conveniones de la Haya*. Buenos Aires, Arnoldo Moen Y Hermano, 1908.

138 Lacerda, *Rui* 136–163.

139 A. Fry, ed., *A memoir of the Right Honourable Sir Edward Fry G.C.B. 1827–1918*. Oxford UP, 1921, 209; *WP* 20 July 1907, 13.

140 Asser, 'Tweede' 1.

141 Lord Reay to Henry Campbell-Bannerman, 21 July 1907, in BL MS 52514.

142 Eyffinger, *1907* 85.

143 In Tuchman, *Proud* 286.

144 Asser, 'Tweede' 1; Fry, *Memoir* 210; Lammasch,'Rückblicke' 180; Dülffer, *Regeln* 300.

145 In Pustogarov, *Martens* 325. Cf. Coogan, *End* 100.

146 The best overview history is: Dülffer, *Regeln* 302–327.

147 Scott, *Proceedings 1907*, Three volumes.

148 Scott, *Proceedings 1907*, Volume 1, 165.

149 Scott, *Proceedings 1907*, Volume 1, 165.

150 Scott, *Proceedings 1907*, Volume 1, 215–225.

151 Scott, *Proceedings 1907*, Volume 1, 341–457.

152 Scott, *Proceedings 1907*, Volume 1, 457–537 quotations on 458 and 457.

153 Scott, *Proceedings 1907*, Volume 1, 513.

154 McGann, *Argentina* 241–242, 266; Trindade, 'Presence' 54–55; L.M. Drago, 'State loans in their relation to international policy' *AJIL* 1, 3, July 1907, 692–726.

155 McGann, *Argentina* 218–226.

156 Scott, *Proceedings 1907*, Volume 1, 111–119.

157 Scott, *Proceedings 1907*, Volume 1, 125.

158 Scott, *Proceedings 1907*, Volume 1, 125.

159 Scott, *Proceedings 1907*, Volume 1, 163.

160 Scott, *Proceedings 1907*, Volume 1, 164.

161 Scott, *Proceedings 1907*, Volume 1, 86.

162 Scott, *Proceedings 1907*, Volume 1, 88-92, 120–123.

163 Scott, *Proceedings 1907*, Volume 1, 92.
164 Tuchman, *Proud* 285.
165 Scott, *Proceedings 1907*, Volume 1, 67–82.
166 Scott, *Proceedings 1907*, Volume 1, 272.
167 Scott, *Proceedings 1907*, Volume 1, 275.
168 Scott, *Proceedings 1907*, Volume 1, 275.
169 Cf. Sir E. Fry to Sir E. Grey, 16 October 1907, in PRO FO412/90.
170 Scott, *Proceedings 1907*, Volume 1, 227–228.
171 Scott, *Proceedings 1907*, Volume 1, 231.
172 Scott, *Proceedings 1907*, Volume 1, 228; italics in original.
173 Scott, *Proceedings 1907*, Volume 1, 232.
174 Semmel, *Liberalism* 116–117. Cf. E. Root, 'The real significance of the Declaration of London' in J.B. Scott, *The Declaration of London February 26, 1909*. New York, Oxford UP, 1919 [1912], 1–12.
175 For the full conventions: Scott, *Proceedings 1907*, Volume 1, 599–696.
176 Scott, *Proceedings 1907*, Volume 1,169.
177 Lesaffer, 'Temple'.
178 *Journal de St Petersbourg* 13/26 September 1907, np, in NA 2.05.03, 534.
179 *TT* 19 October 1907, 9; Brailey, 'Satow' 215.
180 *Natal Witness* 21 November 1907, 4.
181 H.W. Nevinson, *Peace and war in the balance*. London, Watts, 1911, 26–27. Also: 'Lettre de la Haye: à la conférence' *Le Censeur* 27, 2, 6 July 1907, 293–294, in NA 2.22.28, 240.
182 'Art. X-The second Hague conference' *Edinburgh Review* 207, 423, January 1908, 224–247, quotation on 242.
183 'Art. X' 247.
184 *FW* November 1907, 215; Gestrich, 'Haager' 241.
185 P.S. Reinsch, 'Failures and successes at the second Hague conference' *American Political Science Review* 2, 2, February 1908, 204–220, quotations on 217.
186 *Arbitrator* 350, April 1908, 139.
187 M.J. de Sillac, 'Periodical peace conferences' *AJIL* 5, 4, 1911, 968–986.
188 Schücking, *Werk*; Schücking, *International union*.
189 For other examples: A.H. Fried, *Die zweite Haager Konferenz. Ihre Arbeiten, ihre Ergebnisse und ihre Bedeutung*. Leipzig, B. Elischer Nachfolger, 1907; *Ergebnisse der zweiten Haager Friedenskonferenz*. Berlin, Ernst Siegfried Mittler, 1908; O. Nippold, *Die zweite Haager Friedenskonferenz*. Leipzig, Von Duncker & Humblot, 1908; General Pédoya, *Les conférences de la Haye. Arbitrage et désarmement*. Paris, J. Rueff, 1907; Choate, *Two*; Barclay, *Second*; J.C.C. den Beer van Poortugael, *Oorlogs- en neutraliteitsrecht op de grondslag van de conferentie van Genève in 1906 en de twee Haagsche vredes-conferentiën*. The Hague, Van Cleef, 1907; Groupe Parlementaire Français de l'Arbitrage International, *La deuxième conférence de la Haye*. Paris, Delagrave, 1907; A. Tetterborn, *Das Haager Schiedsgericht*. Bonn, Carl Georgi, 1911; E.D. de Medina, *La segunda conferencia de la Haya y la América Latina*. La Paz, Impresión Artística Ayacucho, 1908; Wehberg, *Abkommen*; J. Beinhauer, *Die Kriegsgefangenschaft nach den Bestimmungen der Haager Friedenskonferenzen von 1899 und 1907*. Koblenz, Heinr. L. Scheid, 1908; O. Nippold, 'Das Deutsches Reich und die zweite Haager Friedenskonferenz' *Deutsche Revue* 33, 1908 169–174; E. Lémonon, *La second conférence de la paix. La Haye (Juin–Octobre 1907)*. Paris, Librairie Générale de Droit et de Jurisprudence, 1908; A. Mérignhac, *La deuxième*

conférence internationale de la paix. Conférence de la Haye de 1907. Paris, Henri Charles-Lavauzelle, 1908; H.L. van Oordt, 'De tweede vredesconferentie' *Orgaan ter Beoefening van de Krijgswetenschap* 5, 1908–1909, 229–364. I could find very few anti-Hague publications published after 1907, although there was plenty of anti-Hague rhetoric in the newspapers of the time.

190 R.L. Bridgman, 'Success at The Hague' *Inter-nation* January 1908, 29–44, quotations on 29 and 41, in NA 2.22.28, 243.

191 A. Adler, *Die Haager Friedenskonferenz des Jahres 1907 und die Fortbilding des Völkerrechtes*. Berlin, Puttkammer & Mühlbrecht, 1909, introduction and 67.

192 Cf. Claude, *Swords* 25; 'The great powers. Which are they, and for how long?' *Harper's Weekly* 21 March 1908, 6; R. Teixeira Mendes, *La diplomatie et la régéneration sociale*. Rio de Janiero, Temple de l'Humanité, 1907.

193 F.C. Hicks, 'The equality of states and the Hague conferences' *AJIL* 2, 3, July 1908, 530–561; *WP* 15 October 1907, 4.

194 Cf. G.H. Aldrich, 'The laws of war on land' *AJIL* 94, 4, 2000, 44; Jessup, *Root* 78.

195 W.I. Hull, 'The United States and Latin America at The Hague' *American Association for International Conciliation* 1911, 3–13.

196 Scott, *Proceedings 1907*, Volume 1, 271.

197 Cf. Eyffinger, 'Caught' 7.

198 H. la Fontaine, *La conférence de la paix. Extrait de la Revue Belgique*. Brussels, M. Weissenbruch, 1908, 100–101; Cf. I. Chiba, 'From cooperation to conflict. Japanese-Russian relations from the formation of the Russo-Japanese entente to the Siberian intervention' in Minohara et al., eds, *Decade* 135.

199 For example: 'La Suisse à la Haye' *Journal de Genève* 22 October 1905, np, in NA 2.05.03, 541.

200 *Guardian* 17 December 1912, 11.

201 Dülffer, *Regeln* 187, 331.

202 D. Geppert, W. Mulligan and A. Rose, 'Introduction' in D. Geppert, W. Mulligan, and A. Rose, eds, *The wars before the Great War. Conflict and international politics before the outbreak of the First World War*. Cambridge UP, 2015, 4.

203 British Secretary of State for the Colonies to the Governor-General of Australia, 17 July 1914, in NAA A11804, 1914/55.

204 B.E. Monsell, 'The Declaration of London' *Fortnightly Review* 89, 1911, 263.

205 T.J. Lawrence, 'The Declaration of London and foodstuffs' *Contemporary Review* 99, 1 January 1911, 348–356, quotations on 355 and 356. Also: N. Bentwich, 'The Declaration of London' *Fortnightly Review* 88, 524, August 1910, 327–339; 'Art. VII.- International prize law and the Declaration of London' *Edinburgh Review* 210, 429, July 1909, 162–178.

206 J.B. Scott, 'The International Court of Prize' *AJIL* 5, 2, 1911, 302–324; Coogan, *End* 125–147; A. Rindfleisch, 'Das Seekriegsrecht und die "Zivilisierung der Menschheit". Debatten zur zweiten Haager Friedenskonferenz und ihre Folgen' *FW* 82, 2007, 83–95.

207 M. Erzberger, *The league of nations. The way to the world's peace*. New York, Henry Holt, 1919, 134.

208 Scott, *Hague peace*, Volume 1, 466–467.

209 Cf. Inter-Department Committee memo, 1906, in PRO CAB17/85.

210 C. Parry, 'Foreign policy and international law' in F.H. Hinsley, ed., *British foreign policy under Sir Edward Grey*. Cambridge UP, 1977, 103.

211 Scott, *Proceedings 1907*, Volume 1, 465.

8 City of Peace: The Hague, 1907–15

1 Suttner, *Memoirs* 320.
2 Abbenhuis et al., eds, *War*.
3 Suttner, *Memoirs* 320.
4 Mazower, *Governing* 82, 83.
5 Eyffinger, *1899* 447–450; Kuehl, *Seeking* 77; Lesaffer, 'Temple' 26; J.H. Attana to W.T. Stead, 19 January 1903, in CAC STED 1/1; A.D. White, 'Zur Vorgeschichte des Haager Friedenspalast' *FW* 15, 8, August 1913, 281–285; Lysen, *History* 2–62.
6 NA 2.05.08, 600.
7 Dutch Minister in Washington D.C. to Dutch Minister of Foreign Affairs, 10 February 1903, 25 May 1903 and 12 October 1903, in NA 2.05.18, 600.
8 Dutch Minister in Washington D.C. to Andrew Carnegie, 16 April 1903, in NA 2.16.19.34, 1.
9 Lysen, *History* 65–69; NA 2.05.18, 600.
10 A. Eyffinger, *The trusteeship of an ideal. The Carnegie Foundation, vignettes of a century*. Amsterdam, Joh. Enschede, 2004.
11 Eyffinger, *1907* 50; Lesaffer, 'Temple' 30–31.
12 Minister of Water Management, Trade and Industry to Queen Wilhelmina, 14 November 1904, in NA 2.05.18, 600; Lysen, *History* 79–90.
13 *Judgments of the Dutch experts on the location of the peace palace in Zorgvliet*. np, 1905.
14 Dutch Minister in Washington D.C. to Dutch Minister of Foreign Affairs, 25 May 1903, in NA 2.05.18, 600; HGA 4.CLF.
15 M.W. Waller, *Through the gates of the Netherlands*. Boston, Little Brown, 1907.
16 Eyffinger, *1907* 56–60.
17 J. Sluyters, 'Het einde van een internationale wedstrijd' cartoon, 1907, HGA kl. B4445.
18 Jan F. Groll to A.F. Savornin Lohman, 9 October 1903, in NA 2.05.18, 600; *Adres aan de tweede kamer der Staten-Generaal inzake het vredespaleis*. Amsterdam, np, 1907; A. Eyffinger, 'Den Haag. Het vredespaleis' in J. Bank, M. Mathijsen, eds, *Plaatsen van herinnering. Nederland in de negentiende eeuw*. Amsterdam, Bert Bakker, 2006, 519–520; Thomas Collcutt to British Foreign Office, 25 May 1906, PRO FO371/97; *Pétition à la seconde chambre des etats généraux au sujet de palais de la paix*. np, 1907, in NA 2.22.28, 264.
19 *Hamburger Nachrichten* 8 June 1906, np, in NA 2.05.18, 600.
20 Eyffinger, *1907* 137.
21 NA 2.18.12, 414–422.
22 Dutch Minister in Washington D.C. to Dutch Minister of Foreign Affairs, 8 December 1904, in NA 2.05.03, 532; Johan Braakensiek, 'De bekroning van het ontwerp-Cordonnier voor een vredespaleis' cartoon, 1906, in HGA Tc45.
23 Eyffinger, *1907* 136; *WP* 26 June 1907, 3.
24 Eyffinger, *1907* 137; *WP* 31 July 1907, 3; Fasseur, *Wilhelmina* 396.
25 *WP* 31 July 1907, 3.
26 *Het vredespaleis. Gedenkboek*. The Hague, Belifante, 1913, 11, 15; A. van Karnebeek, *Discours du président du comité des directeurs de la Fondation Carnegie à l'occasion de la pose de la première pierre du palais de la paix, 30 juillet 1907*. The Hague, np, 1907.
27 Sir Edward Fry to Sir Edward Grey, 26 August 1907, PRO FO372, 72; Eyffinger, 'Den Haag' 515–516; NA 2.05.03, 542.

28 J. Braakensiek, 'Eerste steen-legging van het vredespaleis' cartoon, September 1913, in HGA kl. B4450.
29 A. ten Bosch N. Jzn., 11 March 1907, in NA 2.05.03, 534
30 British Foreign Office memo, 17 October 1907, PRO FO372/75.
31 Eyffinger, 'Den Haag' 522.
32 Wilhelmina, *Eenzaam* 113–114; PRO WORK 10/45/1; NA 2.05.03, 176; Bureau International de la Cour Permanente d'Arbitrage, *Rapport du conseil administratif de la Cour Permanente d'Arbitrage 1913.* The Hague, Van Langehuysen, 1914, 19–20.
33 As examples: L.A. Mead, 'Our gift to the peace palace' *Evening Post* nd, in PCSC Mead, Reel 78:10, Box 14; *LAT* 20 August 1913, 6; *Guardian* 22 August 1913, 8; *Observer* 24 August 1913, 7; *Guardian* 28 August 1913, 7; *NYT* 29 August 1913, 4.
34 E.D. Leeuwin, 'The arts of peace. Thomas H. Mawson's gardens at the peace palace, The Hague' *Garden History Society*. 28, 2, Winter 2000, 264.
35 Cf. Duranti, *Conservative* 32–33.
36 Lionel Earle to Douglas Strachan, 29 July 1913, PRO WORK 10/45/1.
37 *Algemeen Handelsblad* 10 September 1907, np, in NA 2.06.001, 5259.
38 Somsen, 'Holland'; G. Somsen, 'Global government through science. Pieter Eijkman's plan for a world capital' in Rayward, ed., *Information* 201–220.
39 A.W. Reinink, *K.P.C. de Bazel.* Amsterdam, J.M. Meulenhoff, 1965, 9; A.K.P.C. de Bazel in Eyffinger, *Trusteeship* 54–64.
40 Fondajo por Internacieco, *Internationalisme en de wereld-hoofstad. (Intellectueel weredcentrum).* The Hague, Stichting van Internationalisme, 1906, in NA 2.06.001, 5259.
41 'Confidential list in alphabetical order of the members of the preliminary world committee of the Foundation of Internationalism' 10 June 1907 (2nd edition), 27 August 1907 (3rd edition) in PCSC Netherlands CDGB; P.H. Eijkman, *L'Internationalisme scientifique*. The Hague, W.P. van Stockum, 1911; G. Somsen, 'Science, medicine and arbitration. Pieter Eijkman's world capital in The Hague' in M. Kemperink, L. Vermeer, eds, *Utopianism and the sciences 1880–1930*. Leuven, Peeters, 2010, 125–146; P.H. Eijkman, *Over internationalisme*. The Hague, Stichting voor Internationalisme, 1908.
42 For example: *Algemeen Handelsblad* 10 September 1907, np, in NA 2.06.001, 5259; *American Review of Reviews* 3, January–June 1906, 610–611; *NYT* 22 May 1910, SM12; P. Brooshooft, 'Scheveningen wereld-centrum?' *De Beweging*. 2, 1906, 172–194; PPL Y3643.
43 S.E. Cooper, ed., *Peace activities in Belgium and the Netherlands*. New York, Garland, 1972, 14–15; L.A. Mead, 'Geneva as world capital', 1907, in PCSC Mead, Reel 78:10, Box 14; Kern, *Culture* 232; Somsen, 'Science' 126, 132; *WP* 4 June 1905, F7; *CDT* 21 May 1913, 15.
44 Eyffinger, 'Den Haag' 520–521; W.J. Bartnett, *The federation of the world.* San Francisco, Murdock, 1906, esp. 14.
45 Reinink, *Bazel* 9.
46 P.H. Eijkman, P. Horrix, letter to Dutch Minister of Foreign Affairs, 8 January 1908, in NA 2.05.03, 548.
47 *Review of Internationalism* in PCSC Netherlands CDGB.
48 NA 2.16.19.34, 6.
49 NA 2.06.001, 5259
50 K.H.H. van Bennekom, *De vredetentoonstelling*. The Hague, np, 1906, and A. ten Bosch N. Jzn., *Wat wil de Internationale Vereeninging Vrede-tentoonstelling.*

Rotterdam, np, 1906, both in NA 2.06.001, 5259; A. ten Bosch N. Jzn., *Wat willen de pacifisten? Waartoe een vrede-tentoonstelling*. Rotterdam, Nijgh & van Ditmar, 1905, in PCSC Netherlands ANB; PPL 71A20.

51 Proposal, September 1907, NA 2.06.001, 5259.

52 NA 2.06.001, 5259.

53 Dutch Minister of Agriculture, Industry and Trade to Cabinet, 11 May 1906, and 'Rapport van de Commissie voor Voorbereiding Tentoonstelling Huldiging Paleis van Arbitrage' September 1907, both in NA 2.06.001, 5259; *Verslag betreffende de handelingen der centrale commissie voor Plan 1913*. Utrecht, J. van Boekhoven, 1914, in NA 2.06.001, 5255.

54 *Catalogus van de nationale en internationale landbouw tentoonstelling te 's Gravenhage 29 August–15 September 1913*. np, 1913, in HGA CO2.

55 'Sport en Tourisme' poster, 1913, *Reclame Arsenaal* BG E17/485; NA 2.06.001, 5258; Dutch Minister of Economic Affairs to Dutch Minister of Internal Affairs, 11 June 1912, in NA 2.06.001, 5259.

56 'Tentoonstelling *De Vrouw 1813–1913*' in *Atria. Kennisinstituut voor Emancipatie en Vrouwengeschiedienis* 2015, https://www.atria.nl/nl/publicatie/tentoonstelling-de-vrouw-1813–1913 (accessed October 2016).

57 *Verslag betreffende de handelingen der centrale commissie voor Plan 1913*. Utrecht, J. van Boekhoven, 1914, Bijlage X, XIII, and *Official programme issued by the committee 1913*. 7, 18 July 1913, both in NA 2.06.001, 5255; Tourism brochures, 1913, in NA 2.06.001, 5258; M.M. Knijn, 'Het "Plan 1913". Idealisme en winstbejag' in J. de Vries, ed., *Nederland 1913. Een reconstructive van het culturele leven*. Meulenhoff, Landshof, 1988, 71–80.

58 Cf. Knijn, '1913' 69.

59 *Verslag* 17–19.

60 *Verslag* 29–66; NA 2.06.001, 5256; PPL Y3475.

61 *Verslag* 53.

62 *Amsterdammer* 2 February 1913, 6; NA 2.06.001, 5256.

63 *Verslag* 67–76.

64 *Verslag* 76.

65 Bureau International de la Cour Permanente d'Arbitrage, *Rapport 1913*, 20; Bureau International de la Cour Permanente d'Arbitrage, *Rapport du conseil administratif de la Cour Permanente d'Arbitrage 1914*. The Hague, Van Langehuysen, 1915, 18.

66 *Verslag* 70–71.

67 *Verslag* Bijlage IX; Postcard W.P. Byler to E.D. Mead, September 1913, PCSC Mead Reel 78:1, Box 1.

68 *Verslag* Bijlage IX.

69 For example: *Notes on four stained glass windows in the Great Court of Justice at the Palace of Peace in The Hague*. np, 1913, in HGA Tc45; J.H. Gore, *Holland. The home of peace. 1813–1913 Commemorating the centenary celebration of the Kingdom of the Netherlands and the dedication of the peace palace*. New York, Holland America Line, 1913; 'Si vi pacem, cole justitiam' postcard, 1913, in PCSC Mead Reel 78:1, Box 1.

70 S.H. McCollester, *Memorial of Elizabeth Elnora Randall McCollester*. Malboro, Rumford, 1913, 239.

71 Lesaffer, 'Temple' 5–6.

72 As examples: HGA Tc45; 'Peace Palace opening 1913' youtube, https://www.youtube.com/watch?v=ULCrzpruEXQ (accessed October 2017); *Guardian* 29 August 1913,

7; *IT* 29 August 1913, 7; *NYT* 29 August 1913, 4; *Globe* (Canada) 29 August 1913, 2; *CDT* 29 August 1913, 2; *WP* 29 August 1913, 2; *LAT* 29 August 1913, 11.

73 HGA Tc45.

74 L. Raemaekers, 'Axioma's' cartoon, 1913, in IISG BG C18/13.

75 IPUA Box 233.

76 *Bulletin official du XXe congrès universel de la paix tenu à la Haye 1913*. Berne, Bureau International de la Paix, 1913.

77 Vrede door Recht, *Le palais de la paix*. The Hague, Belinfante, 1913; *Zeitschrift für Völkerrecht* 7, 3, 1913, whole issue; Koskenniemi, *Gentle* 213–214.

78 'Procès-verbaux du Comité Exécutif d l'Union Interparlementaire' 18 March 1913, in IPUA Box 254; Vrede door Recht, *Jaarverslag over het jaar 1913*. np, 1914, in PCSC Netherlands ANB.

79 Grossi, *Pacifism* 337–339; Petition, in PCSC Box 5; PCSC Eckstein, 2.

80 Grossi, *Pacifism* 339; 'Pétition universelle en faveur du règlement sans guerre des conflits entre les états' 1912 and A. Eckstein, 'Commentary to the world petition submitting a plan to prevent all war to the high signatories of the Briand-Kellogg General Pacts for the Renunciation of War', 1928, both in PCSC Eckstein, 2.

81 *Women's Leader and the Common Cause* 230, 5 September 1913, 369.

82 NA 2.06.001, 5256; *Verslag* Bijlage XIV.

83 Dutch Minister of Foreign Affairs to Willem de Beaufort, 1914, in NA 2.05.40, 7. Also: NA 2.05.03, 540.

84 Somsen, 'Holland' 48–49.

85 J. Bank, M. van Buuren, *Dutch culture in a European perspective. Volume 3. 1900 the age of bourgeois culture*. Assen, Royal van Gorcum, 2004, 72–75.

86 'English spoken – en parle français!' *Kampioen*, nd, 93–94, in NA 2.06.001, 5255. Cf. Somsen, 'Science' 133.

87 Albert Hahn, cartoon, 6 September 1913, in IISG BG C6/31.

88 Vrede door Recht, *Jaarverslag over het jaar 1913*. np, 1914, in PCSC Netherlands ANB.

89 *WP* 15 August 1913, 6.

90 Bank and van Buuren, *Dutch* 76; H.W. von der Dunk, 'Negentiendertien. Verhinderde kentering' in de Vries, ed., *Nederland* 17–21.

91 L.P.A. van der Brandeler, *Eendracht van het land. Open brief aan het hoofdbestuur en alle leden van den Alg. N. Bond 'Vrede door Recht' naar aanleiding van Prof. Mr. C. van Vollenhoven*. Leiden, S.C. van Doesburgh, 1913; B. de Jong van Beek en Donk, *The history of the peace movement in the Netherlands*. The Hague, PPIE, 1915, 21–24.

92 NA 2.21.169, 36; H. te Velde, 'Van grondwet naar grondwet. Oefenen met parlement, partij en schaalvergroting' in R. Aerts, H. de Liagre Böhl, P. de Rooij, H. te Velde, eds, *Land van kleine gebaren. Een politieke geschiedenis van Nederland 1780–1990*. Nijmegen, SUN, 1999, 167–169; Cooper, *Peace* 12; *Guardian* 22 August 1913, 8.

93 H.T.Colenbrander, 'Nederland en de derde vredesconferentie' *Gids* 4, 1911, np, in NA 2.22.28, 273; P.B.M. Blaas, *Geschiedenis en nostalgie. De historiografie van een kleine natie met cen groot verleden*. Hilversum, Verloren, 2000, 129; Bank and van Buuren, *Dutch* 77–78.

94 Dutch Minister of Foreign Affairs to J.A. Roëll, 14 July 1911, in NA 2.21.315, 89.

95 Commission of Preparation for the Third Peace Conference, 10 December 1913, in NA 2.05.40, 6.

96 W.J.M. van Eijsinga, 'Eenige punten, meer en minder belangrijk, dooreen die ter sprake zouden kunnen komen in de commissie tot voorbereiding der derde vredesconference' 1911 in NA 2.21.315, 89.

97 NA 2.21.169, 37; NA 2.05.03, 560.
98 British Secretary of State for the Colonies to Governor-General of Australia, 17 July 1914, in NAA A11804, 1914/55.
99 British Secretary of State for the Colonies to Governor-General of Australia, 17 July 1914, in NAA A11804, 1914/55; PRO FO 881/10567X.
100 Subcommission report, 27 March 1914, in NA 2.21.169, 37.
101 Meeting of the Commission of Preparation for the Third Peace Conference, 7 February 1914, in NA 2.05.40, 7.
102 J. Dülffer, 'Chances and limits of armament control 1898–1914' in H. Afflerbach, D. Stevenson, eds, *An improbable war. The outbreak of World War I and European political culture before 1914*. New York, Berghahn, 2007, 109–110; NA 2.05.03, 561.
103 Finch, *Adventures* 124.
104 Basily, *Memoirs* 97.
105 Segesser, 'Haager'.
106 *Paperspast*, database search, November 2017.
107 *New Zealand Times* 26 August 1914, 4.
108 *Timaru Herald* 7 October 1914, 6.
109 Munro, 'The Hague's war'.
110 *De beteekenis van den arbeid der vredesconferenties gezien in het licht van en in verband met de oorlog*. The Hague, J. Morks, 1915, in PCSC Netherlands ANB.
111 L.T. Hobhouse, *Questions of war and peace*. London, T. Fisher Unwin, 1916, 10.
112 Koskenniemi, *Gentle* 215. Cf. Hull, *Scrap* 77–78.
113 Herman, *Eleven* 45. Cf. W.C. Widenor, *Henry Cabot Lodge and the search for an American foreign policy*. Berkeley, University of California Press, 1980, 352.
114 J.B. Scott, 'Should there be a third Hague peace conference?' *Advocate of Peace through Justice*. 87, 1, 1925, 27–37; T. Barclay, *New methods of adjusting international disputes and the future*. London, Constable, 1917; F.H. Stead, *To abolish war at the third Hague conference. An appeal to the peoples*. Letchworth, Garden City Press, 1916.
115 Brailsford, *War* 283–284, 287, 308.
116 Lammasch, 'Rückblicke' 183.
117 D. Acker, *Walther Schücking*. Münster, Aschendroffsche Verlagsbuchhandlung, 1970, 65. Cf. M. Ceadel, 'Enforced pacific settlement or guaranteed mutual defence? British and US approaches to collective security in the eclectic covenant of the League of Nations' *International History Review* 35, 5, 2013, 1001; J. Addams, *Peace and bread in time of war*. Champaign, University of Illinois Press, 2002 [1922], 24–27.
118 C.L. Lange, *Développement de l'oeuvre de la Haye. Organisation de la conférence de la paix*. The Hague, Organisation pour une Paix Durable, 1917; PCSC CODP Box 1.
119 Beek en Donk, *History* 46.
120 *Friedenskonferenzen nach dem Kriege? Zur Errinnerung en die Eröffnunf der ersten Friedenskonferenz 1899 – den 18ten Mai – 1916*. Leiden, A.W. Sijthoff, 1916.
121 PCSC Netherlands COPD 2.
122 PCSC Netherlands CODP 1.
123 M.A. Mügge, *The parliament of man*. London, C.W. Daniel, 1916, 10.
124 Finch, *Adventures* 84–85; M. Koskenniemi, 'The ideology of international adjudication and the 1907 Hague conference' and R. Higgins, 'The 1907 Hague peace conference as a milestone in the development of international law' both in Daudet, ed., *Actualité* 127–129, 29–40.

125 *Académie de droit international de la Haye établie avec le concours de la dotation Carnegie pour la paix internationale, 1923*. Bulletin, in NA 2.05.03, 151; Eyffinger, *1907* 150.

126 *H.J. Res. 221. Hearings before the Committee on Foreign Affairs. House of Representatives*. Washington D.C., Government Printing Office, 1926; Scott, 'Should'; Nederlandsch Comité te Totstandkoming eener Internationale Vredesconferentie in Den Haag, petition, August 1939, in PPL C58-1.

127 PPL Y3466.

128 Cf. P. van Krieken, D. McKay, 'Introduction' and A. Eyffinger, 'Living up to a tradition' both in Krieken and McKay, eds, *The Hague* 3–28, 29–44; Lesaffer, 'Temple' 6–7; Somsen, 'Holland' 47; A. Eyffinger, *The Hague. International centre of justice and peace*. The Hague, Jongbloed Law, 2003; V. Mamadouh, A. Meijer, J.D. Sidway, H. van der Wusten, 'Toward an urban geography of diplomacy. Lessons from The Hague' *Professional Geographer*. 2015, doi: 10.1080/00330124.2014.987184, 2.

Bibliography

Primary

Archives

Archief- en Onderzoekcentrum voor Vrouwengeschiedenis, Brussels [AVG-CARHIF]

- AVG-CARHIF, 'International Council of Women Archive' ICW

British Library Manuscript Collections, British Library, London [BL]

- BL, 'Campbell-Bannerman Papers' Add MS52514, MS 41218
- BL, 'Scott Papers. Vols II-IV. Correspondence of Scott with Foreign Secretaries; 1866–1904' Add MS52295-52297

Churchill Archives Centre, Churchill College, Cambridge University [CAC]

- CAC, 'The Papers of 1st Lord Fisher of Kilverstone' GBR/0014/FISR
- CAC, 'The Papers of Baron Noel-Baker' GBR/0014/NBKR
- CAC, 'The Papers of William T. Stead' GBR/0014/STED

Haags Gemeentearchief, The Hague [HGA]

- HGA, 'Gemeentebestuur van 's-Gravenhage 1851–1936' 0353-01
- HGA, 'Gemeentepolitie, 1827–1994' 0432-01
- HGA Lf4
- HGA 4.CLF
- HGA kl. B4445
- HGA Tc45
- HGA CO2

Houghton Library, Harvard University [HLH]

- HLH, 'Frederick William Holls papers, 1879–1938' Ms Am 1308

Instituut van Sociale Geschiedenis, Amsterdam [IISG]

- IISG, 'F. Domela Nieuwenhuis Archief' BG C18/13
- IISG, 'Albert Hahn Archief' BG C6/31

Inter-Parliamentary Union Archives, Geneva [IPUA]

Koninklijk Huisarchief, The Hague

London School of Economics Women's Archive [LSE]

- LSE, 'International Council of Women Archive'

Nationaal Archief, The Hague [NA]

- NA, 'Ministerie van Buitenlandse Zaken. A-dossiers, 1815–1940' 2.05.03
- NA, 'Ministerie van Buitenlandse Zaken. Tractaten' 2.05.08
- NA, 'Ministerie van Buitenlandse Zaken. Kabinetsarchief' 2.05.18
- NA, 'Ministerie van Buitenlandse Zaken. Geheime Rapporten en Kabinetsrapporten, 1868–1940' 2.05.19
- NA, 'Ministerie van Buitenlandse Zaken. Commissie van Advies voor Volkenrechtelijke Vraagstukken [tot 1920]' 2.05.40
- NA, 'Ministerie van Economische Zaken. Directie van Handel en Nijverheid' 2.06.001

- NA, 'Justitie, 1876–1914' 2.09.05
- NA, 'Ministerie van Verkeer en Waterstaat. Raad van Toezich Carnegie-Stichting, 1903–1953' 2.16.19.34
- NA, 'H. van Poelgeest, Zakelijke Archieven' 2.18.12
- NA, 'Collectie 238 Familiearchief Asser' 2.21.014
- NA, 'Collectie 197 Familiearchief Van Beresteyn' 2.21.018
- NA, 'A.P. van Schilfgaarde' 2.21.174
- NA, 'Collectie 319 C. van Vollenhoven' 2.21.169
- NA, 'Collectie 343 De Beaufort' 2.21.290
- NA, 'Collection 233 Familie Roëll' 2.21.315
- NA, 'De Beaufort/verzameling brochures' 2.22.28

National Archives of Australia, Canberra [NAA]

National Archives, London [PRO]

- PRO, 'Board of Trade and successors. Correspondence and papers, 1905' BT13
- PRO 'Committee of Imperial Defence. Miscellaneous correspondence and memoranda' CAB17
- PRO, 'Cabinet Office. Photographic copies of Cabinet papers, c1880–1916' CAB37
- PRO, 'Committee of Imperial Defence. Photographic copies of minutes and memoranda' CAB38
- PRO, 'Dominions Office. Drafts of telegrams about negotiations with South African Republic (1899)' DO119
- PRO 'Foreign Office. General Correspondence before 1906, Holland (later Netherlands)' FO37
- PRO, 'Foreign Office. General correspondence before 1906, Russian Empire. Diplomatic' FO65
- PRO, 'Foreign Office. General correspondence before 1906, Great Britain and General' FO83
- PRO, 'Foreign Office. General correspondence from 1906–1966' FO371
- PRO, 'Foreign Office. General correspondence from 1906. Netherlands' FO372
- PRO, 'Foreign Office. Second peace conference at The Hague' FO412
- PRO, 'Foreign Office Confidential Print. South East Europe. Affairs of South-Eastern Europe' FO421
- PRO, 'Foreign Office. Confidential Print' FO881
- PRO, 'Board of Trade and Ministry of Transport and successors. Russo-Japanese War. Hague Conference and matters arising' MT9/805
- PRO 'Office of Woods, Forests, Land Revenues, Works and Buildings. The Hague' WORK 10/45/1

Peace Palace Library, The Hague [PPL]

- PPL, 'Carnegie Stichting Collection'
- PPL, 'Collection de document divers, dactylographiés et imprimés relatifs à la deuxième conférence de la paix réunie par W.J.M. van Eysinga, 1906–1907' 14A17
- PPL, 'Document relatifs aux projets de fondation d'une association internationale pour l'organisation d'une exposition pacifiste mondiale à l'occasion d'ouverture du palais de la paix' 71A20
- PPL, 'Collection de photographies, de brochures etc. relatives à l'exposition en l'honneur d'André Carnegie au palais du paix, 25 novembre-15 décembre 1935' Y3466
- PPL, 'Collection de photographies, de caricatures, de brochures, de découpures etc. relatives à la fondation du palais de la paix, 1903-' Y3475

- PPL, 'Collection de brochures, d'extraits et de découpures relatives aux de P.H. Eijkman et de P.P. Horrix d'une fondation pour l'internationalisme à la Haye, 1905–1929' Y3643
- PPL, 'Collection de documents divers manuscripts, dactylographiés et imprimés, relatifs à la conference de la paix, La Hay 1899 réunie par J. C.C. den Beer Poortugael' Y3961

Roosevelt Study Centre, Middelburg [RSC]

- RSC, 'Theodore Roosevelt Paper' Library of Congress, TRP

Swarthmore College Peace Collection, Swarthmore, Pennsylvania [PCSC]

- PCSC, 'Australia, Collective Box' CDGB
- PCSC, 'CDGA Collective Box' CDGA
- PCSC, 'Germany. Eckstein, Anna B'
- PCSC, 'Great Britain. Collective box' CDGB
- PCSC, 'Mead, Edwin D., & Lucia Ames' DG21
- PCSC, 'Nederlandsche Vredesbond' CDGB
- PCSC, 'Netherlands. Bureau International de la Cour d'Arbitrage' CDGB
- PCSC, 'Netherlands. Central Organisation for Durable Peace' CODP
- PCSC, 'Netherlands. Collective Box' CDGB
- PCSC, 'Nethlerlands. Algemeene Nederlandsche Vredesbond "Vrede door Recht" ' CDGB ANB
- PCSC, 'Society of Friends' DG-33
- PCSC, 'Switzerland. Collective Box' CDGB

United Nations Office at Geneva Archives, Geneva [UNOG]

- UNOG, 'Bertha von Suttner Papers (1843–1914)' IPM/FS/BvS

Digital databases and archives

African Newspapers. World Newspaper Archive, Center for Research Libraries

Anno. Historische österreichische Zeitungen und Zeitschriften. Österreichische Nationalbibliothek

Archives Unbound. Gale Publishing

Avalon Project. Documents in Law, History and Diplomacy. www.avalon.law.yale.edu

Belgica. Bibliotheque Numerique de la Bibliotheque Royale de Belge

Biblioteca Nacional de Portugal.

Biblioteca Virtual de Prensa Histórica. Ministerio de Educación, Cultura y Deporte, Spain

British Library Newspapers. Gale Publishing

Compact Memory. Goethe University Library, Frankfurt am Main

Daily Mail Historical Archive. Gale Cengage

Delpher. Koninklijke Bibliotheek van Nederland

Economist Historical Archive. Gale Cengage

European Library. www.europeanlibrary.org

Freiburger Zeitung Digital.

Gallica. Bibliotheque Nationale de la France

Geheugen van Nederland. www.geheugenvannederland.nl

Groene Amsterdammer Historisch Archief. historisch.groene.nl

Haagsche Beeldbank. Haags Gemeentearchief

Harper's Weekly Archive. HarpWeek

HeinOnline.

Hemerotica Digital. Biblioteca Nacional de España
History of Feminism. Routledge
History of Mass Tourism. Adam Matthew
House of Commons. Parliamentary Papers. Proquest [*HCPP*]
Illustrated London News Historical Archive.
Internet Archive. internetarchive.org
Japan Times Digital Archive.
J-STOR. Ithaca
Library of Congress Digital Collections. www.loc.gov
Making of the Modern World. Gale Cengage
Mormon Publications. 19th and 20th Centuries. Brigham Young University
Nineteenth-Century Index. Proquest
Nineteenth-Century UK Periodicals. Gale Cengage
North China Herald Online. Brill
Papers Past. National Library of New Zealand
Peel's Prairie Provinces. University of Alberta Libraries
Proquest Historical Newspapers. Proquest
Spectator Archive. archive.spectator.co.uk
Sunday Times Digital Archive. Gale Cengage
Time Machine. New York Times Database
The Times Digital Archive. Gale Cengage
Trove. National Library of Australia
UK Press Online. www.ukpressonline.co.uk
Victorian Popular Culture. Adam Matthew
Vogue Archive. Proquest
Welsh Newspapers Online. National Library of Wales
World's Fairs. A Global History of Expositions. Adam Matthew

Contemporary newspapers, magazines and journals

Algeria
    Courrier de Tlemcen
    Gazette Algerienne, La
Argentina
    El Sol del Domingo
Australia
    Australasian
    Brisbane Courier
    Bush Advocate
    North Queensland Register
    Punch (Melbourne)
    Richmond River Express and Casino Kyogle Advertiser
    Sunday Sun (Sydney)
Austria-Hungary
    Bludenzer Anzeiger
    Floh, Der (Vienna)
    Glühlichter, Die
    Grazer Tageblatt

Grazer Volksblatt
Interessante Blatt, Das (Vienna)
Kikeriki
Neue Freie Presse
Neues Wiener Tageblatt
Wiener Salonblatt
Wiener Zeitung
Belgium
Indépendance Belge, L'
Brazil
Revista Moderna
British East Africa (Kenya)
African Standard (Mombasa)
Canada
Calgary Weekly Herald
Calgary Weekly News
Edmonton Bulletin
Globe
China
North China Herald [*NCH*]
Finland
Hufvudstadsbladet
France
Archives Diplomatiques Recueil International de Diplomatie et d'Histoire
Bulletin du Photo-club de Paris
Caricature, La
Croix, La
Figaro, Le
Gaulois, Le
Hommes du Jour, Les
Journal de Débats. Politiques et Littéraires
Journal des Économistes
Journal Pour Tous, Le
Matin, Le
Nouvelle Revue Internationale, La
Pêle-Mêle, Le
Revue de Droit International et de Legislation Comparée
Revue de Droit Public et de la Science Politique en France et à l'Étranger
Revue de la Paix
Rire, Le
Temps, Le
Vie Illustrée, La
Germany
Archiv für öffentliches Recht
Berliner Monatshefte
Berliner Tageblatt
Deutsche Revue
Friedens-Warte, Die [*FW*]
Jugend

Lustige Blätter
Neue Hamburger Zeitung [NHZ]
Niemeyers Zeitschrift für Internationales Recht
Russische Rundschau (Berlin)
Wahre Jacob, Die
Zeitschrift für Internationales Recht
Zeitschrift für Völkerrecht

Great Britain, including Ireland

Anglo-Saxon Review
Arbitrator, The
Black & White (London)
Blackwood's Edinburgh Magazine
British Medical Journal
Church Times (London)
Concord. The Journal of the International Arbitration and Peace Association
Contemporary Review
Daily Express [*DE*]
Daily Mail [*DM*]
Daily Mirror
Daily Telegraph
Economist
Edinburgh Review
Fortnightly Review
Fun
Graphic
Gunten's Magazine
Herald of Peace and International Arbitration [*Herald of Peace*]
Illustrated London News
International Journal of Ethics
Irish Times [*IT*]
Liberty Review
Manchester Guardian [*Guardian*]
Nineteenth Century
Observer, The
Punch
Review of Reviews
Royal United Services Institution Journal
Speaker, The
Spectator
Standard
Sunday Times
The Times [*TT*]
War Against War. A Chronicle of the International Crusade of Peace
Weekly Mail (Cardiff)
Women's Leader and the Common Cause

India

Friend of India & Statesman [*Friend*]

Italy

Illustrierte Sontagsblat (*Pusterhaler Boter*)

Japan
Japan Times [*JT*]
Mexico
El Correo Español
Netherlands and the Dutch Empire
Algemeen Dagblad
Algemeen Handelsblad
Amsterdammer, De
Courrier de la Conférence de la Paix
Dagblad van Zuid-Holland en 's Gravenhage
Java Bode
Leeuwarder Courant
Locomotief (Samarang)
Middelbursche Courant
Nederlandsche Vredesbond Jaarboek
Nieuwe Tilbursche Courant
Nieuws van de Dag
Nieuws van de Dag voor Nederlandsch-Indië (Batavia)
Notenkraker, De
Orgaan ter Beoefening van de Krijgswetenschap
Soerabaijasch Handelsblad
Sumatra Post [*SP*]
Surinamer (Paramaribo)
Telegraaf, De
Tijd, De
Tijdspiegel
Tilburgsche Courant
Vaderlander
Volk, Het
Vragen van de Dag
Vrede door Recht
Wereldkroniek
New Zealand
Auckland Star
Evening Post (Wellington)
Evening Star (Dunedin)
Grey River Argus
Hastings Times
Hawera & Normanby Star
Hawke's Bay Herald
Manawatu Times
Marlborough Express
Mataura Ensign
New Zealand Herald (Auckland)
Ohinemuri Gazette
Otago Witness
Poverty Bay Herald
Press, The (Christchurch)
Southland Times

Star, The (Christchurch)
Taranaki Herald
Thames Advertiser
Thames Star
Wairarapa Daily Times
Wanganui Chronicle
Wanganui Herald

Nigeria
Lagos Weekly Herald

Rhodesia
Rhodesia Herald

Russia
Journal de St-Petersbourg

Samoa
Samoan Weekly Herald [*SWH*]

Sierra Leone
Sierra Leone Weekly News

South Africa (Transvaal, Orange Free State)
Journal (Grahamstown)
Mafeking Mail
Natal Witness

Spain
El Correo Español
El Liberal de Reus
Suplemento a la Revista Blanca

United States of America
Advocate of Peace [*through Justice*]
Afro-American
American Association for International Conciliation
American Journal of International Law [*AJIL*]
American Monthly Review of Reviews [*AMRR*]
American Political Science Review
Atlanta Constitution
Catholic World
Chautauquan
Chicago Daily Tribune [*CDT*]
Current Literature
Harper's Weekly
Independent
Inter-Nation
Journal of the Military Services Institution of the United States
Los Angeles Times [*LAT*]
New England Magazine
New York Herald
New York Times [*NYT*]
North American Review
Peace Movement, The
Popular Science Monthly
Puck

Vogue
Washington Post [*WP*]
Woman's Exponent (Salt Lake City)
World's Fair Bulletin (St Louis)

Published

Aberdeen, Lord and Lady, *'We twa.' Reminiscences of Lord and Lady Aberdeen*. Two volumes, Glasgow, W. Collins, 1925

Abrüstungs-Bilderbuch. Die Friedenskonferenz in der Karikatur aller Völker. Berlin, Dr Eysler, 1899

Adam, P., *Les impérialismes et la morale des peuples*. Paris, Furne, 1908

Addams, J., *Peace and bread in time of war*. Champaign, University of Illinois Press, 2002 [1922]

Addresses of the New York State Bar Association to His Imperial Majesty, Nicholas II, Emperor of all the Russias and to the President of the United States, on the occasion and in commendation of the peace congress at The Hague and recommending the creation of an international court. New York, np, 1899

Adler, A. *Die Haager Friedenskonferenz des Jahres 1907 und die Fortbilding des Völkerrechtes*. Berlin, Puttkammer & Mühlbrecht, 1909.

Adres aan de tweede kamer der Staten-Generaal inzake het vredespaleis. Amsterdam, np, 1907

Album d'hommage à son Majesté Oscar II. The Hague, np, 1908

Appleton, L., *Fifty years historic record of the progress of European disarmament from 1849 to 1899*. London, British and Foreign Arbitration Association, 1899

Ardagh, S.M., *The life of Major-General Sir John Ardagh*. London, John Murray, 1909

Bacon, R.H., *The life of Lord Fisher of Kilverstone. Admiral of the Fleet*. London, Hodder and Stoughton, 1929

Baily, H.L., *Grotius. A study from the seventeenth century*. Richmond, Peace Association of Friends in America, 1906

Bar, L. von, *Der Burenkrieg, die Russificierung Finnlands, die Haager Friedenskonferenz und die Errichtung einer internationalen Academie zur Ausgleichung von Streitigkeiten der Staaten*. Hannover, Helwingsche Verlagsbuchhandlung, 1900

Barbosa, R., *Deuxieème conference de la paix. Actes et discours*. The Hague, W.P. van Stockum, 1907

Barbosa, R., *O Brasil e a nações Latin-Americanas em Haya*. Rio de Janiero, Imprensa Nacional, 1908

Barclay, T., *New methods of adjusting international disputes and the future*. London, Constable, 1917

Barclay, T., *The second Hague peace conference*. London, np, 1906

Bartnett, W.J., *The federation of the world*. San Francisco, Murdock, 1906

Basily, N., *Memoirs. Diplomat of Imperial Russia 1903–1917*. Stanford, Hoover Institution Press, 1973

Batilliat, M., *Paul Adam*. Paris, 1903

Beales, A.C.F., *The history of peace. A short account of the organised movements for international peace*. London, G. Bell, 1931

Becu, C.A., *La neutralidad segun las convenciones de la Haya*. Buenos Aires, Arnoldo Moen Y Hermano, 1908

Beek en Donk, B. de Jong van, *The history of the peace movement in the Netherlands*. The Hague, PPIE, 1915

Beer van Poortugael, J.C.C. den, *Oorlogs- en neutraliteitsrecht op de grondslag van de conferentie van Genève en de twee Haagsche vredesconferentiën*. The Hague, Van Cleef, 1907

Beinhauer, J., *Die Kriegsgefangenschaft nach den Bestimmungen der Haager Friedenskonferenzen von 1899 und 1907*. Koblenz, Heinr. L. Scheid, 1908

Billard de Saint-Laumer, J., *Droit de guerre sur terre d'après la conférence de la Haye de 1907*. Paris, Jouve, 1910

Bloch, I.S., *Is war now impossible? Being an abridgment of 'The war of the future in its technical, economic and political relations*. London, Grant Richards, 1899

Boyle, H.L., *History of peace*. Grand Rapids, History of Peace, 1902 [1905]

Boyle, H.L., *Plan for an international insurance to prevent wars*. np, 1898

Braakensiek, J., *Het jaar 1899*. Amsterdam, np, 1900

Brailsford, H.N., *The war of steel and gold. The study of armed peace*. Sixth edition. London, G. Bell, 1916

Brandeler, L.P.A. van der, *Eendracht van het land. Open brief aan het hoofdbestuur en alle leden van den Alg. N. Bond 'Vrede door Recht' naar aanleiding van Prof. Mr. C. van Vollenhoven*. Leiden, S.C. van Doesburgh, 1913

Brehmer, A., ed., *Die Welt in hundert Jahren*. Berlin, Verlagsanstalt Buntdruck, 1910

Brooshooft, P., 'Scheveningen wereld-centrum?' *De Beweging* 2, 1906, 172–194

Bulletin official du XXe congrès universel de la paix tenu à la Haye 1913. Berne, Bureau International de la Paix, 1913

Bülow, Prince von, *Memoirs 1903–1909*. London, Putnam, 1931

Bureau International de la Cour Permanente d'Arbitrage, *Rapport du conseil administratif de la Cour Permanente d'Arbitrage 1913 [1914]*. The Hague, Van Langehuysen, 1914 [1915]

Bustamente y Sirven, A.S., *La seconde conference de la paiz. Réunie à la Haye en 1907*. Paris, L. Larose & L. Tenin, 1909

Butler, N.M., *Across the busy years. Recollections and reflections*. Two volumes, New York, Charles Scribner's Sons, 1939

Capper, S.J., *Translation into English of a speech delivered in German at the banquet at the Hotel National Lucerne 7 June 1902 on the occasion of the solemn inauguration of the Museum of Peace and War founded by the late Johann von Bloch, financier, economist and philanthropist whose work upon war led the Czar to issue HIS FAMOUS RESCRIPT which resulted in the CONGRESS AT THE HAGUE*. np, 1902

Carnegie, A., *The autobiography of Andrew Carnegie*. Boston, Houghton Mifflin, 1924

Carnegie, A., *Results of the National Arbitration and Peace Congress*. New York, American Branch of the Association for International Arbitration Council, 1907

Carvahal, F.H. y, *Memoria que los señores Dr. Francisco Henriquez y Lic Apolinar Tejera, delegados plenipotenciarios de la Republica Dominicana en la segunda conferencia internacional de la paz*. Santo Domingo, J.R. Vda. Garcia, 1908

Catalogue of the international war and peace museum in Lucerne, 1903. Lucerne, Genossenschafts Buchdruckerei, 1902

The cause of Poland in reference to the International Peace Conference to be held at The Hague, Europe. Chicago, Zgoda, 1899

Channing, W.E., *Discourses on war*. Boston, Ginn, 1903

Chesteron, G.K., *The appetite of tyranny. Including letters to an old Garibaldian*. New York, Dodd and Mead, 1915

Choate, J.H., *The two Hague conferences*. Princeton UP, 1913

Chomé, L., *Désarmer, c'est déchoir. La conference de la Haye*. Brussels, Imprimerie Gustave Deprez, 1899
Conan Doyle, A., *The war in South Africa. Its cause and conduct*. London, Smith Elder, 1902
Conférence international de la paix. La Haye 18 mai-29 juillet 1899. The Hague, Imprimerie Nationale, 1899
Cortissoz, R., *The life of Whitelaw Reid*. Two volumes, New York, Charles Scribner's Sons, 1921
Daehne van Varick, A. van, *Documents relations to the program of the First Hague Peace Conference laid before the conference by the Netherlands government. Translation*. Oxford, Clarendon Press, 1899 [1921]
Darby, W.E., *The arrested development of international arbitration*. London, Richard Flint, 1912
Darby, W.E., *International tribunals. A collection of various schemes which have been propounded; and of instances since 1815*. Third edition, London, J.M. Dent, 1900
Darby, W.E., *The peace conference at The Hague. Its history, work and results*. London, Peace Society, [1900]
Davis, H., *Among the world's peacemakers*. New York, Progressive, 1907
Delbrück, H., *Zukunftskrieg und Zukunftsfriede*. np, 1899
DeLourne, A., *Les lois de la guerre contemporaine à l'occasion du livre de M. Méringhac sur la conference de la paix*. Toulouse, Lagarde et Sebille, 1901
Dennett, T., *John Hay. From poetry to politics*. New York, Dodd and Mead, 1934
Deuxième conférence de la Haye. Opinions, projets, propositions diverses. Paris, Institut de la Paix, 1907
Die deutsche Frau in der Friedensbewegung. Second edition. Munich, J.F. Lehmann, 1900
Dryhurst, N.F., ed., *Nationalities and subject races. Report of conference held in Caxton Hall, Westminster June 28–30, 1910*. London, P.S. King, 1911
Ducommun, É., *The probable consequences of a European war*. London, International Arbitration and Peace Association, 1906
Dupuis, C., A. Desjardins, *La conférence de la Haye a-t-elle donné des résultats appréciables?* Paris, Secrétariat de la Société d'Economie Sociale, 1900
Ebergardt, A.K., 'The Russian Red Cross in the Anglo-Boer War 1899–1902. The report of a Russian doctor translated by C. Moody' *Historia* 22, 1977, 112–129
Eijkman, P.H., *L'Internationalisme scientifique*. The Hague, W.P. van Stockum, 1911
Eijkman, P.H., *Over internationalisme*. The Hague, Stichting voor Internationalisme, 1908
Erzberger, M., *The league of nations. The way to the world's peace*. New York, Henry Holt, 1919
Estournelles de Constant, P.H.B. de, *International peace. Speeches delivered by Baron d'Estournelles de Constant and others*. Edinburgh, np, 1906
Estournelles de Constant, P.H.B. de, *Limitation des charges navales et militaires*. Brussels, Misch and Thron, 1912
Estournelles de Constant, P.H.B. de, *Les résultats de la conférence de la paix*. Lyon, A. Storck, 1900
F., *Een bezoek aan het vredespaleis*. The Hague, Luctor et Emergo, 1914
Faries, J.C., *The rise of internationalism*. New York, np, 1915
Fisher, Lord, *Records by Admiral of the Fleet Lord Fisher*. London, Hodder and Stoughton, 1919
Fonbelle, G., *Le Tsar et la paix*. Paris, L. Sauvaitre, 1899

Fontaine, H. la, *La conférence de la paiz. Extrait de la Revue Belgique*. Brussels, M. Weissenbruch, 1907
Foster, J.W., *Diplomatic memoirs*. Two volumes, Boston, Houghton Mifflin, 1909
Fox, F.W., *Some historical incidents in connexion with the establishment of the International Tribunal of Arbitration at The Hague in 1899 and international arbitration*. London, West Newman, 1901
Foyer, L. le, *Lettre à MM. les membres de la conférence de la paix de la Haye. Le droit des peuples*. Paris, V. Giard & E. Brière, 1899
Frau von Suttner, der Frauenweltbund und der Krieg. Berlin, Vossische Buchhandlung, 1905
Fremantle, W.H., *Patriotism and cosmopolitanism. A sermon for the peace conference, preaches in the English Church at The Hague on Sunday May 28th 1899*. Ripon, Thirlway, 1899
Fried, A.H., *Ergebnisse der zweiten Haager Friedenskonferenz*. Berlin, Ernst Siegfried Mittler, 1908
Fried, A.H., *Die Haager Conferenz. Ihre Bedeutung und ihre Ergebnisse*. Berlin, Hugo Bermüler, 1900
Fried, A.H., *Handbuch der Friedensbewegung*. Vienna, Oesterreichischen Friedensgesellschaft, 1905
Fried, A.H., *Die moderne Friedensbewegung*. Leipzig, B.G. Teubner, 1907
Fried, A.H., *Was kann die Petersburger Friedenskonferenz erreichen?* Dresden, E. Pierson, 1899
Fried, A.H., *Die zweite Haager Konferenz. Ihre Arbeiten, ihre Ergebnisse und ihre Bedeutung*. Leipzig, B. Elischer Nachfolger, 1907
Friedenskonferenzen nach dem Kriege? Zur Errinnerung en die Eröffnunf der ersten Friedenskonferenz 1899 – den 18ten Mai – 1916. Leiden, A.W. Sijthoff, 1916
Fry, A., ed., *A memoir of the Right Honourable Sir Edward Fry G.C.B. 1827–1918*. Oxford UP, 1921
Fuentes, F.S. de, A.S. de Bustamente, M.S. Gonzola de Quesada, *Informe relativo a la segunda conferencia internacional de la paz reunida en el Haye en 1907*. Two volumes, Habana, La Moderna Poesia, 1908
Gaché, A., *Le conflit Vénézuélien et l'arbitrage de la Haye*. Paris, np, 1904
German atrocities. Germany and inhumanity versus humanity and Christianity issued by the Director-General of Recruiting. Melbourne, Director-General of Recruiting, 1917
Giovannini, C., *I grandi stati, la guistizia e la pace (a proposito della conferenza dell'aia)*. Rome, G. Mariette, 1899
Gooch, G.P., H. Temperley, eds, *British Documents on the Origins of the War 1898–1914*. Volume 1. London, His Majesty's Stationery Office, 1927
Gordon, P., ed., *Politics and society. The journals of Lady Knightley of Fawsley 1885–1913*. London, Routledge, 2016
Gore, J.H., *Holland. The home of peace. 1813–1913 Commemorating the centenary celebration of the Kingdom of the Netherlands and the dedication of the peace palace*. New York, Holland America Line, 1913
Groupe Parlementaire Français de l'arbitrage International, *La deuxième conférence de la Haye*. Paris, Delagrave, 1907
La guerre et le militarisme. Paris, Éditions des Annales de la Jeunesse Laique, 1899
Guieysse, C., *La France et la paix armée. La conference de la Haye*. Paris, Pages Libres, 1905
Haberman, F.W., ed., *Nobel lectures including presentation speeches and laureates' biographies. Peace 1901–1925*. Singapore, World Scientific, 1972

Hemery de Goascaradec, A., *De l'évolution de la notion de contrabande de guerre.* Rennes, Eugène Prost, 1910

Hershey, A., *The international law and diplomacy of the Russo-Japanese War.* London, MacMillan, 1906

Higgins, A.P., *The Hague conferences and other international conferences concerning the laws and usages of war.* London, Stevens, 1904

H.J. Res. 221. Hearings before the Committee on Foreign Affairs. House of Representatives. Washington D.C., Government Printing Office, 1926

Hobhouse, L.T., *Questions of war and peace.* London, T. Fisher Unwin, 1916

Hobson, J.A., *Imperialism. A study.* London, James Nisbet, 1902

Holguin, J., *Informes y notas de la delegación de Columbia en la segunda conferencia de la paz da la Haya.* Rotterdam, M. Wyt, 1908

Holguin, J. *Segunda conferencia internacional de la Haya.* Botoga, Imprenta Nacional, 1908

Holland, T.E., *The laws of war on land (written and unwritten).* Oxford, Clarendon Press, 1908

Holls, F.W., *The Hague Peace conference and international law.* London, MacMillan, 1900

Holls, F.W. *The peace conference at The Hague and its bearings on international law and policy.* New York, MacMillan, 1900

Hull, W.I., *The two Hague conferences and their contributions to international law.* Boston, Ginn, 1908

International Council of Women. Reports. Various publishers, 1899–1914

Internationale prijsvraag der Carnegie-Stichting. Het vredespaleis te 's Gravenhage. Amsterdam, Elsevier, 1906

The International Union: what it is, what it wants to do, how it tries to do it. London, Office of the British Centre of the International Union, 1901

The Inter-Parliamentary Union from 1889–1930. A publication issued by the Inter-Parliamentary Union Bureau to commemorate the fiftieth anniversary of the union. Lausanne, Payot, 1939

Inter-Parliamentary Union, *Actes essentiels premier supplement de 'resolutions votées par les huit premières conferences interparlementaires.* Berne, K.J. Wyss, 1902

Inter-Parliamentary Union, *Session de 1903 compte rendu de la XIe conférence tenue à Veinne, Palais du Reichsrat du 7 au 9 septembre 1903.* Vienna, Otto Maass, 1903

Inter-Parliamentary Union, *XVIIIe conférence, La Haye, 3–5 Septembre 1913. Résolutions adoptées et nominations faites par la conférence.* Brussels, Bureau Interparlementaire, 1913

Jacobsen, J.A., *Le premier grand proces international à la cour de la Haye.* Paris, V. Giard & E. Brière, 1904

Jacomet, R., *La guerre et let traités. Étude de droit international et d'histoire diplomatique.* Paris, Henri Charles-Lavauzelle, nd

Jessup, P.C., *Elihu Root.* New York, Dodd & Mead, 1938

Judgments of the Dutch experts on the location of the peace palace in Zorgvliet. np, 1905

Karnebeek, A. van, *Discours du président du comité des directeurs de la Fondation Carnegie à l'occasion de la pose de la première pierre du palais de la paix, 30 juillet 1907.* The Hague, np, 1907

Kats, H.O., *Sonnenaufgang. Ein Gespräch über die Friedens-Conferenz im Haag.* Munich, August Schupp, [1899]

Kellermann, O., *La guerre et la paix. Etude moral dédiée aux membres de la conférence de la Haye.* Paris, M. Vasseur, 1900

Kipling, R., *100 poems old and new*. Cambridge UP, 2013
Kipling, R., 'The truce of the bear' 1898, poetryloverspage.com (accessed April 2015)
Kirchhoff, A., ed., *Männer der Wissenschaft über die Friedens-Konferenz*. Berlin, P. Stankiewicz, 1899
Lacerda, V.C., *Rui Barbosa em Haia*. Rio de Janiero, Casa de Ruis Barbosa, 1957
Lammasch, M., H. Sperl, eds, *Heinrich Lammasch. Seine Aufzeichnungen, sein Wirken und seine Politik*. Vienna, Franz Deuticke, 1922
Lange, C.L., *L'arbitrage obligatoire en 1913*. Brussels, Misch & Thron, 1914
Lange, C.L., *Développement de l'oeuvre de la Haye. Organisation de la conférence de la paix*. The Hague, Organisation pour une Paix Durable, 1917
Lange, C.L., *L'histoire de l'internationalism*. Volume 1, Kristiana, H. Aschehoug, 1919
Lapradelle, G. de, *La conférence de la paix (La Haye, 18 mai-29 juillet) par la Revue Générale de Droit International Public*. Paris, A. Pedone, 1900
Lawrence, T.J., 'The Hague conference and naval war' 52, 362, 1908, 479–509
Lawrence, T.J., *International problems and Hague conferences*. London, J.M. Dent, 1908
Lawrence, T.J., *The principles of international law*. Boston, D.C. Heath, 1914
Lawrence, T.J., *War and neutrality in the far east*. London, MacMillan, 1904
Leeper, A., *The true story of Sinn Fein. A lecture*. Melbourne, Loyalist League of Victoria, 1919
Léger, A.N., *La doctrine Drago et la deuxième conference de la paix*. Port au Prince, Matin, 1915
Lémonon, E., *La second conférence de la paiz. Conférence de la Haye de 1907*. Paris, Henri Charles-Lavauzelle, 1908
Liebknecht, K. von, *Militarismus und Antimilitarismus unter besonderer Berücktlichtigung der internationalen Jugendbewegung*. Leipzig, np, 1907
Lima Barbosa, M. de, *Ruy Barbosa de la conference de la Haye à la guerre des nations*. Paris, Garnier, 1917
Lippmann, W., *Public Opinion*. New York, Harcourt, Brace and Company, 1922
Loewenthal, E., *Grunzüge zur Reform und Codification des Völkerrechts*. Berlin, Otto Dreyer, 1898
Lysen, A., *A history of the Carnegie Foundation and the Peace Palace at The Hague*. Leiden, Brill, 1931
Magnier, A., *Paix et désarmement avec un apercu sur la conference de la Haye*. Paris, Bibliothèque de l'Association, 1899
Mahan, A.T., *Armaments and arbitration or the place of force in the international relations of states*. New York, Harper Brothers, 1912
Mahan, A.T., *The influence of sea power upon history 1660–1783*. Boston, Little Brown, 1898 [1890]
Mahan, A.T., *Lessons of the war with Spain and other articles*. Boston, Little, Brown and Company, 1899
Mahan, A.T., *Some neglected aspects of war*. London, Sampson, Low, Marston and Company, 1907
Mandere, H.C.C.J. van der [E. de Melville], *De Haagsche overeenkomst betreffende de vreedzame beslechting van internationale geschillen en het Permanente Hof van Arbitrage*. Rhenen, B. van de Watering, 1907
Marder, A., ed., *Fear God and dread nought. The correspondence of Admiral of the Fleet Lord Fisher of Kilverstone*. Two volumes, London, Jonathan Cape, 1952
Martens, F., *La conférence de la paix à la Haye. Etude d'histoire contemporaine*. Paris, Arthur Rousseau, 1900

Martens, F., *Étude de F. de Martens, membre de la cour permanente d'arbitrage de la Haye*. Paris, H. Charles-Lavauzell, 1906
Martens, F., *Hacia la paz por la justicia*. Mexico, Tipografia Económica, 1911
Martens, F., *Kokusaiho*. Tokyo, Hatsubaimoto Hakubunkan, 1900
Martens, F., *La paix et la guerre*. Paris, Arthur Roussea, 1901
Martens, F., *Par la justice vers la paix*. Paris, Henri Charles-Lavauzelle, 1902
Martens, F., *Tratado de derecho internacional. La paz y la Guerra apéndice*. Madrid, España Moderna, 1905
Marvin, F.S., *The living past. A sketch of westen progress*. Oxford, Clarendon Press, 1913
McCollester, S.H., *Memorial of Elizabeth Elnora Randall McCollester*. Malboro, Rumford, 1913
Mead, E.D., *Jean de Bloch and the 'future of war'*. Boston, International Union, 1904
Medina, E.D. de, *La segunda conferencia de la Haya y la Améric Latina*. La Paz, Impresión Artística Ayacucho, 1908
Méringhac, A., *La conférence international de la paix. Étude historique, exégétique et critique des travaux et des resolutions de la conference de la Haye de 1899*. Paris, Arthur Rousseau, 1900
Méringhac, A., *Les lois et coutumes de la guerre sur terre d'apres le droit international moderne et la codification de la conférence de la Haye de 1899*. Paris, Marescq Ainé, 1903
Meurer, C., *Das Kriegsrecht der Haager Konferenz*. Munich, J. Schweitzer, 1907
Meurer, C., *Übersicht über die Arbeiten der Haager Friedenskonferenz inbesondere das Abkommen zur friedlichen Erledigung international Streitfälle vom 29 juli 1899*. Munich, J. Schweiter, 1903
Meyerdorff, A., *Correspondance diplomatique du Baron de Staal (1884–1900)*. Two volumes, Paris, Marcel Rivière, 1929
Ministère des Étrangères, *Documents diplomatiques. Conférence internationale de la paix 1899*. Paris, Imprimerie Nationale, 1900
Ministero degli affair esteri, *I documenti diplomatici italiani*. Series III, Volume III, Rome, Libreria dello stato, 1962
Molinari, G. de, *The society of tomorrow*. London, T. Fisher Unwin, 1904
Moore, J.B., *The collected papers of John Bassett Moore*. Seven volumes, New Haven, Yale UP, 1944
Morison, E.E., ed., *The letters of Theodore Roosevelt*. Cambridge, Harvard UP, 1951
Mowat, R.B., *The life of Lord Pauncefote. First Ambassador to the United States*. London, Constable, 1928
Nevinson, H.W., *Fire of life*. London, James Nesbit, 1935
Nevinson, H.W., *Peace and war in the balance*. London, Watts, 1911
Nippold, O., *Die Fortbildung der Verfahrens in völkerrechtlichen Streitigkeiten. Ein völkerrechtliches Problem der Gegenwart speziell im Hinblick auf die Haager Friedenskonferenzen*. Leipzig, Duncker & Humblot, 1907
Nippold, O., *Die zweite Haager Friedenskonferenz*. Leipzig, Von Duncker & Humblot, 1908
Noel-Baker, P.J., *Disarmament*. Second edition, London, Hogarth Press, 1927
Notovitch, N., *Le pacification de l'Europe et Nicholas II*. Paris, Paul Ollendorff, 1899
Obkircher, W., ed., *General Erich von Gündell. Aus seinen Tagebüchen*. Hamburg, Hanseatischen Verlagsanstalt, 1939
Ogden, R.M., ed., *The diaries of Andrew D. White*. Ithaca, Cornell University Library, 1959
Old and new. Sermons by Henry Scott Holland of St. Paul's. London, S.T. Freemantle, 1900

Oliveira, A. d', *Memória da vida diplomática. Portugal na conferência de Haia em 1907.* Paris, Livrarias Aillaud e Bertrand, 1926
Parker, C., *German barbarities in Russia. The evidence illustrated.* Melbourne, 1916
Passy, F. de, *Pour la paix. Notes et documents.* Paris, Bibliothèque-Charpentier, 1909
Pax! Ricordo del 29 settembre 1898 Il Congressisti della Pace à Torre Pellice. Tore Pelicce, Fipografia Alpina, 1899
The peace crusade. A record of the peace conference at The Hague. May 18 to July 29 1899. Boston, Lend a Hand Society, 1899
Pédoya, General, *Les conferences de la Haye. Arbitrage et désarmement.* Paris, J. Rueff, 1907
Perris, G.H., *For an arrest of armaments. A note for the second Hague conference.* London, Caxton House, 1906
Perris, G.H., *Jean de Bloch and the museum of war and peace.* London, International Arbitration Association, 1902
Perris, G.H., *A short history of war and peace.* London, William and Norgate, [1911]
Ponsonby, Lord, *Democracy and foreign affairs.* np, 1912
Porter, C.W., *The career of Théophile Delcassé.* Philadelphia, University of Pennsylvania Press, 1936
Proceedings at the laying of a wreath on the tomb of Hugo Grotius in the Nieuwe Kerk, in the city of Delft, July 4th 1899 by the Commission of the United States of America to the International Peace Conference of The Hague. The Hague, Martinus Nijhoff, 1899
Raemaekers, L., *Ha! Ha! Ha! Alweer een vredesconferentie.* Amsterdam, Koster, 1907
Raffalovich, A.H., *Mémoires sur la conférence de la paix.* Paris, np, 1899
Reinsch, P.S., *Public international unions. Their word and organization.* Boston, Ginn, 1911
Renault, L., *L'oeuvre de la Haye en 1899 et en 1907.* Stockholm, P.A. Norstedt, 1908
Report of the international conference on the situation in the Near East. Held in London on 29 June 1904. London, London Office of 'Pro Armenia', 1904
Reventlow, E., *Weltfrieden oder Weltkrieg! Wohin geht Deutschlands Weg? Politisch-militärische Betrachtungen vor der Haager Friedenskonferenz.* Berlin, Karl Curtius, 1907
Les résultats de la conférence de la Haye. Conférence faite devant la Société des Amis de l'Université de Lyon 14 janvier 1900. Paris, A. Storck, 1900
Results of the Hague conference. New York, North American Review, 1899
Rich, N., M.H. Fisher, eds, *The Holstein Papers.* Volume 4, Cambridge UP, 1963
Rolin, A., *Les origins de l'Institut de Droit International 1873–1923. Souvenirs d'un témoin.* np, 1923
Roosevelt, T., *African and European addresses.* New York, G.P. Putnam, 1910
Rümelin, G., *Politics and the moral law.* New York, MacMillan, 1901
Ruxton, I.C., ed., *The diaries and letters of Sir Ernest Satow (1843–1929).* Lewiston, Edwin Mellen, 1998
Saint-Maurice, Comte de, *La deuxième conférence de la paix. Etude critique de ses travaux.* Paris, Librairie des Publications Officielles du Bulletin des Lois, 1908
Schmidt, F.A., *Von den Haager Friedensabkommen bis zum Kellog-Pakt.* np, 1931
Schücking, W., *The international union of the Hague conferences.* Oxford, Clarendon Press, 1918 [1912]
Schücking, W., *Das Werk vom Haag. Zweite Serie. Die gerichtlichen Entscheidungen.* Two volumes, Leipzig, Duncker und Humblot, 1917 [1912]
Scidmore, E.R., *As The Hague ordains. Journal of a Russian prisoner's wife in Japan.* New York, Century, 1914 [1907]
Scott, J.B., *The Declaration of London February 26, 1909.* New York, Oxford UP, 1919 [1912]

Scott, J.B., *The exhibit on friendship between nations sesqui-centennial exposition.* Philadelphia, np, 1926

Scott, J.B., *The Hague peace conferences of 1899 and 1907. A series of lectures delivered before the Johns Hopkins University in the year 1908.* Two volumes, Baltimore, Johns Hopkins Press, 1909

Scott, J.B., ed., *Instructions to the American delegates to the Hague peace conferences and their official reports.* New York, Oxford UP, 1916

Scott, J.B., ed., *Proceedings of the Hague peace conferences. Translated of the official texts. The conference of 1907.* Three volumes, New York, Oxford UP, 1920

Scott, J.B., ed., *Proceedings of the international peace conference. The Hague, May 18-July 29, 1899.* New edition. Washington D.C., Carnegie Endowment for International Peace, 1920

Scott, J.B., *Resolutions of the Institute of International Law dealing with the law of nations with an historical introduction and explanatory notes.* New York, Oxford UP, 1916

Selenka, M., *Die internationale Kundgebung der Frauen zur Friedens-Konferenz vom 15 mai 1899.* Munich, August Schripp, 1900

Sewall, M.W., *Genesis of the International Council of Women and the story of its growth 1888–1893.* np, 1914

Siebold, A. von, *Der ewige Krieg und die Friedenskonferenz.* Munich, August Schupp, 1899

Signatures, ratifications, adhesions and reservations to the conventions and declarations of the first and second Hague peace conferences. Washington D.C.: Carnegie Endowment for International Peace, 1914

Smit, C., ed., *Bescheiden betreffende de buitenlandsche politiek van Nederland 1848–1919. Derde period 1899–1919.* Several volumes. Dordrecht, Martinus Nijhoff, 1964

Spiller, G., ed., *Papers on inter-racial problems communicated to the First Universal Races Congress held at the University of London July 26–29, 1911.* London, P.S. King, 1911

Stead, F.H., *To abolish war at the third Hague conference. An appeal to the peoples.* Letchworth, Garden City Press, 1916

Stead, W.T., *La chronique de la conference de la Haye 1899. Accompagné du texte des conventions.* The Hague, J. Hoekstra, 1899

Stead, W.T., *Methods of barbarism. War is war and war is hell. The case for intervention.* London, Mowbray House, 1901

Stead, W.T., ed., *The M.P. for Russia. Reminiscences and correspondence of Madame Olga Novikoff.* Two volumes, London, Andrew Melrose, 1909

Stead, W.T., *Le parlement de l'humanité 1907. Biographies et photographies.* Amsterdam, Maas van Suchtelen, 1907

Stead, W.T., *The united states of Europe on the eve of the parliament of peace.* London, np, 1899

Stengel, K. von, *Der ewige Friede.* Paris, H. le Soudier, 1899

Stengel, K. von, *Weltstaat und Friedensproblem.* Berlin, Reichl, 1909

Story, R.D., *Arbitration or war? A view of the Transvaal question with a glance at arbitration in politics generally.* London, F. Parker, 1899

Suijling, J.P., *The Hague peace conferences of 1899 and 1907.* The Hague, Martinus Nijhoff, 1910

Suttner, B. von, *Die Haager Friedenskonferenz. Tagebuchblätter.* Dresden, E. Pierson, 1901

Suttner, B. von, *Memoirs of Bertha von Suttner. The records of eventful lives.* Two volumes, New York, Ginn, 1910

Suttner, B. von, *Zur nächsten Intergouvernementalen Konferenz im Haag*. Berlin, Wilhelm Süssenrott, 1907

Swift, L., *Expansion. Being Bart's best cartoons for 1899 taken from the* Minneapolis Journal. np, 1900

Swinburne, F.W.P., *Anglo-Saxon sea-sway and sonnets for the Hague conference*. Coggeshall, np, 1907

Takahashi, S., *International law applied to the Russo-Japanese War with the decisions of the Japanese prize courts*. London, Stevens, 1908

Teixeira Mendes, R., *La diplomatie et la régéneration sociale*. Rio de Janiero, Temple de l'Humanité, 1907

Tetterborn, A., *Das Haager Schiedsgericht*. Bonn, Carl Georgi, 1911

Tolstoy, L., *The way to peace and greetings to conscientious objectors*. Glasgow, Strickland Press, 1940 [1899]

Trueblood, B.F., *The development of the peace idea and other essays*. Boston, Plimpton Press, 1932

The Tsar's rescript. A series of papers issued and circulated by the Peace Society. London Peace Society, 1899

Turpin, E., *Requête à messieurs les presidents et membres de la conference de la paix à la Haye*. Paris, Chaix, 1899

Ullman, E. von, *Die Haager Konferenz von 1899 und die Weiterbildung der Völkerrechts*. Tübingen, J.C.B. Mohr, 1907

United States Department of State, *Papers relating to the foreign relations of the United States, with the annual message of the President transmitted to Congress*. Washington D.C., United States Government Printing Office, 1898–1915

Upward, A., *Secret history of today. Being revelations of a diplomatic spy*. New York, G.P. Putnam, 1904

Valk, J.P. de, M. van Fassen, eds, *Dagboeken en aantekeningen van Willem Hendrik de Beaufort*. Two volumes, The Hague, ING, 1993

Vargas, M., *Recuerdos intimos. Conferencia internacional de la paz en la Haya*. Bogota, El Correo Nacional, 1908

Vrede door Recht, *Le palais de la paix*. The Hague, Belinfante, 1913

De vredes-conferentie. Prentenboek voor oud en jong. Amsterdam, H. Gerlings, 1899

Het vredespaleis. Gedenkboek. The Hague, Belifante, 1913

Vries, J.H. de, *Pour la paix. Une presse mondiale*. Paris, Schleicher Frères, 1911

Waller, M.W., *Through the gates of the Netherlands*. Boston, Little Brown, 1907

War with China. London, 1841

Waszclewicz-van Schilfgaarde, B.J.M.C., *Internationale ontwapening. Een vrouwenzaak en een vrouwenbelang*. Amsterdam, W. Verslys, 1899

Wasklewicz-van Schilfgaarde, B.J.M.C., *Open brief aan Felix Ortt. Een word tot de Tolstoïanen en Christelijk-Anarchisten*. Amsterdam, W. Versluys, 1899

Weber, C., *Kriegspatronen und Dum-Dum Geschosse*. Stuttgart, J.E.G. Wegner, 1914

Wehberg, H., *Der Abkommen der Haager Friedenskonferenzen, der Londoner Seekriegskonferenz nebst Genfer Konvention*. Berlin, J. Guttentag, 1910

Wehberg, H., *Capture on land and sea*. London, S. King, 1910

Wehberg, H., *Deutschland und die Friedensbewegung*. Berlin, Deutsche Verlagsgesellschaft für Politik und Geschichte, 1924

White, A.D., *The first Hague conference. Reprinted from Dr White's autobiography*. Boston, World Peace Foundation, 1912

Whyte, F., *The life of W.T. Stead*. Two volumes, London, Jonathan Cape, 1925
Wilhelmina, *Eenzaam maar niet alleen*. np, Uitgeverij W. ten Have, 1959
Wyndham, H., *Victorian sensations*. London, Jarrolds, 1933
XYZ Suisse, *Discours nécessaires à la conférence de la Haye*. Paris, Génerale Lahure, 1906
Yarmolinsky, A., ed., *The memoirs of Count Witte*. New York, Doubleday, 1921
Zorn, P., *Die Ergebnisse der Haager Konferenzen das Kriegsverhütungsrecht*. Stuttgart, W. Kohlhammer, 1915
Zorn, P., *Die Fortschritte des Seekriegsrechtes durch die zweite Haager Friedenskonferenz*. Tübingen, J.C.B. Mohr, 1908
Zorn, P., *Weltunionen, Haager Friedenskonferenzen und Völkerbund*. Berlin, Ferd. Dümmlers, 1925

Secondary

Unpublished

Cooper, S.E., 'Women's participation in European peace movements. The struggle to prevent World War I' Unpublished paper, Berkshire Conference on the History of Women, June 1984 (National Library of Australia Microfiche)
Genin, V., 'La diplomatie belge et le droit international face à la Conférence de la Paix de la Haye en 1899. Attraits et méfiances' Unpublished paper, 'International Law and Arbitration from the Hague conferences to the League of Nations' seminar, University of Antwerp, 2 June 2015
Higgins, A.R., 'Law not war. James Brown Scott's interest in and representation of the 1899 and 1907 Hague peace conferences' Summer Scholar Research Essay, University of Auckland, 2014
Mamolea, A., 'The United States and the Hague tradition. Myth and reality' Unpublished paper, 'War, peace and international order. The legacies of the Hague conferences of 1899 and 1907' conference, University of Auckland, 19 April 2016

Online

Berger, J., 'European freemasonries, 1850–1935: networks and transnational movements' *European History Online*. www.ieg-ego.eu, December 2010 (accessed March 2016)
'Peace Palace opening 1913' youtube. https://www.youtube.com/watch?v=ULCrzpruEXQ (accessed October 2017)
Rydell, R.W., 'World's Columbian Exposition' *Encyclopedia of Chicago*. http://encyclopedia.chicagohistory.org/pages/1386.html (accessed March 2015)
'Tentoonstelling *De Vrouw 1813–1913*' in *Atria. Kennisinstituut voor Emancipatie en Vrouwengeschiedienis* 2015. https://www.atria.nl/nl/publicatie/tentoonstelling-de-vrouw-1813–1913 (accessed October 2016)
'Treaties, State Parties and Commentaries' *International Committee of the Red Cross*. https://www.icrc.org/applic/ihl/ihl.nsf/Article.xsp?action=openDocument&documentId=568842C2B90F4A29C12563CD0051547C (accessed May 2016)
Tyrrell, I., 'The Woman's Christian Temperance Union and internationalism' *Women and Social Movements, International. 1840–Present*. Electronic database, Alexandria VA, Alexander Street Press (accessed April 2016)

Books and Edited Collections

Abbenhuis, M., *Age of neutrals. Great power politics 1815–1914*. Cambridge UP, 2014

Abbenhuis, M., C.E. Barber, A.R. Higgins, eds, *War, peace and international order. The legacies of the Hague conferences of 1899 and 1907*. New York, Routledge, 2017

Acker, D., *Walther Schücking*. Münster, Aschendroffsche Verlagsbuchhandlung, 1970

Aerts, R., H. de Liagre Böhl, P. de Rooij, H. te Velde, eds, *Land van kleine gebaren. Een politieke geschiedenis van Nederland 1780–1990*. Nijmegen, SUN, 1999

Afflerbach, H., D. Stevenson, eds, *An improbable war. The outbreak of World War I and European political culture before 1914*. New York, Berghahn, 2007

Albertini, L., *The origins of the war of 1914*. Three volumes. Oxford UP, 1965

Alonso, H.H., *Peace as a woman's issue. A history of the US movement for world peace and women's rights*. Syracuse UP, 1993

Anderson, M.S., *The rise of modern diplomacy 1450–1919*. London, Longman, 1993

Andrew, C., *Théophile Delcassé and the making of the Entente Cordiale. A reappraisal of French foreign policy 1898–1905*. New York, St Martin's Press, 1968

Ballentyne, T., A. Burton, *Empires and the reach of the global 1870–1945*. Cambridge, Bellknap, 2012

Bank, J., M. van Buuren, *Dutch culture in a European perspective. Volume 3. 1900 the age of bourgeois culture*. Assen, Royal van Gorcum, 2004

Bank, J., M. Mathijsen, eds, *Plaatsen van herinnering. Nederland in de negentiende eeuw*. Amsterdam, Bert Bakker, 2006

Bartlett, C.J., *Peace, war and the European powers, 1814–1914*. New York, St Martin's Press, 1996

Belanger, C., J.G. Guiral, F. Terrou, eds, *L'histoire générale de la press française*. Three volumes, Paris, Presses Universitaires de France, 1972

Bell, D., ed., *Victorian visions of global order. Empire and international relations in nineteenth-century political thought*. Cambridge UP, 2007

Bell, D.A., *The first total war. Napoleon's Europe and the birth of warfare as we know it*. Boston, Houghton Mifflin, 2007

Ben-Canaan, D., F. Grüner, I. Prodöhl, eds, *The transcultural past of Northeast China*. Heidelberg, Springer, 2014

Bentley, J.H., R. Bridenthal, A.A. Yang, eds, *Interactions. Transregional perspectives on world history*. Honolulu, University of Hawai'i Press, 2005

Best, G., *Humanity in warfare. The modern history of the international law of armed conflict*. London, Methuen, 1983

Best, G., *War and law since 1945*. Oxford, Clarendon Press, 1994

Bickers, R., R.G. Tiedemann, eds, *The Boxers, China and the world*. Lanham, Rowman and Littlefield, 2007

Blaas, P.B.M., *Geschiedenis en nostalgie. De historiografie van een kleine natie met een groot verleden*. Hilversum, Verloren, 2000

Bond, B., *War and society in Europe 1870–1970*. Gloucestershire, Sutton, 1984 [1998]

Bourke, J., *Deep violence. Military violence, war play and the social life of weapons*. Berkeley, Counterpoint, 2015

Boyce, G., J. Curran, P. Wingate, eds, *Newspaper history from the seventeenth century to the present day*. London, Constable, 1978

Boyd, R.W., ed., *Information beyond borders. International cultural and intellectual exchange in the belle époque*. London, Taylor & Francis, 2014

Boyle, F.A., *Foundations of world order. The legalist approach to international relations (1898–1922)*. Durham, Duke UP, 1999

Brake, L., M. Demoor, *Dictionary of nineteenth-century journalism in Great Britain and Ireland*. London, Academia Press and The British Library, 2009

Brake, L., R. Luckhurst, J. Mussell, eds, *W.T. Stead. Newspaper revolutionary*. London, British Library, 2013

Brake, L., E. King, R. Luckhurst, J. Mussell, eds, *W.T. Stead. Newspaper revolutionary*. London, British Library, 2012

Bridgen, P., *The Labour Party and the politics of war and peace 1900–1924*. Woodbridge, Boydell Press, 2009

Brock, P., *Twentieth-century pacifism*. New York, Van Nostrand Reinhold, 1970

Burris, J.P., *Exhibiting religion. Colonialism and spectacle at international expositions 1851–1893*. Charlottesville, Virginia UP, 2001

Burton, A., I. Hofmeyr, eds, *Ten books that shaped the British empire. Creating an imperial commons*. Durham, Duke UP, 2014

Buttsworth, S., M. Abbenhuis, eds, *Wars, myths and fairy tales*. London, Palgrave Macmillan, 2017

Campbell Jnr, C.S., *Anglo-American understanding 1898–1903*. Baltimore, Johns Hopkins Press, 1957

Campo, J. del, *A history of the world for rebels and somnabulists*. London, Telegram, 2008

Ceadel, M., *The origins of war prevention. The British peace movement and international relations 1730–1854*. Oxford UP, 1996

Ceadel, M., *Pacifism in Britain 1914–1945. The defining of a faith*. Oxford UP, 1979

Ceadel, M., *Semi-detached idealists. The British peace movement and international relations 1854–1945*. Oxford UP, 2000

Chatfield, C., P. van den Dungen, eds, *Voices prophesying war 1763–1984*. Knoxville, University of Tennessee Press, 1988

Childs, T.W., *Italo-Turkish diplomacy and the war over Libya 1911–1912*. Leiden, Brill, 1990

Claeys, G., *Imperial sceptics. British critics of empire 1850–1920*. Cambridge UP, 2010

Clark, I., *International legitimacy and world society*. Oxford UP, 2007

Clarke, I.F., *Voices prophesying war 1763–1984*. Oxford UP, 1966

Claude Jnr, I.L., *Swords into plowshares. The problems and progress of international organization*. New York, Random House, 1956

Conrad, S., *Globalisation and the nation in imperial Germany*. Cambridge UP, 2010

Cooper, S.E., ed., *Arbitration or war? Contemporary reactions to the Hague peace conference of 1899*. New York, Garland, 1972

Cooper, S.E., ed., *Internationalism in nineteenth-century Europe. The crisis of ideas and purpose*. New York, Garland, 1976

Cooper, S.E., *Patriotic pacifism. Waging war on war in Europe 1815–1914*. New York, Oxford UP, 1991

Cooper, S.E., ed., *Peace activities in Belgium and the Netherlands*. New York, Garland, 1972

Craven, M., M. Fitzmaurice, M. Vogiatzi, eds, *Time, history and international law*. Leiden, Martinus Nijhoff, 2007

Crook, P., *Darwinism, war and history*. Cambridge UP, 1994

Cunha, P.P. da, *A diplomacia da paz. Rui Barbosa em Haia*. Rio de Janiero, Ministério da Educaçao e Cultura, 1977

Czyzewska, M., *Der Allgemeine Deutsche Sprachverein und das Fremdwort*. Dresden, Neisse, 2008

Daudet, Y., ed., *Actualité de la conference de la Haye de 1907, deuxième conférence de la paix*. The Hague, Martinus Nijhoff, 2008

Davis, C.D., *The United States and the first Hague peace conference*. Ithaca, Cornell UP, 1962

Davis, C.D., *The United States and the second Hague peace conference. American diplomacy and international organization 1899–1914*. Durham, Duke UP, 1975

Deacon, D., P. Russell, A. Woollacott, eds, *Transnational lives. Biographies of global modernity 1700-present*. New York, Palgrave, 2010

Delissen, A.J.M., G.J. Tanja, eds, *Humanitarian law of armed conflict challenges ahead. Essays in honour of Frits Kalshoven*. Dordrecht, Martinus Nijhoff, 1991

Dipper, C., A. Gestrich, L. Raphael, eds, *Krieg, Frieden und Demokratie. Festschrift für Martin Vogt zum 65 Geburtstag*. Frankfurt, Peter Lang, 2001

Drolet, J.-F., J. Dunkerley, eds, *American foreign policy. Studies in intellectual history*. Manchester UP, 2017

Dülffer, J., *Regeln gegen den Krieg. Die Haager Friedens-Konferenzen 1899 und 1907 in der internationalen Politik*. Berlin, Ulstein, 1980

Duranti, M., *The conservative human rights revolution. European identity, transnational politics, and the origins of the European Convention*. Oxford UP, 2017

Eckley, G., *Maiden tribute. A life of W.T. Stead*. Philadelphia, Xlibris, 2007

Elleman, B.E., *Modern Chinese warfare 1795–1989*. London, Routledge, 2002

Epkenhans, M., G.P. Gross, eds, *The Danish straits and German naval power 1905–1918*. Potsdam, Militärgeschichtliches Forschungsamt, 2010

Eyffinger, A., *The 1899 Hague Peace Conference. The parliament of man, the federation of the world*. The Hague, Kluwer Law International, 1999

Eyffinger, A., *The 1907 Hague Peace Conference. 'The conscience of the civilized world'*. The Hague, JudiCap, 2007

Eyffinger, A., *The Hague. International centre of justice and peace*. The Hague, Jongbloed Law, 2003

Eyffinger, A., *De hele wereld bijeen. De eerste Haagse vredesconferentie van 1899. Mesdagkwartier lezing III*. np, 1995

Eyffinger, A. *The trusteeship of an ideal. The Carnegie Foundation, vignettes of a century*. Amsterdam, Joh. Enschede, 2004

Fasseur, C., *Wilhelmina. De jonge koningin*. Amsterdam, Balans, 1998

Finch, G.A., *Adventures in internationalism. A biography of James Brown Scott*. Clark, Lawbook Exchange, 2012

Fink, C., *Defending the rights of others. The great powers, the Jews and minority rights 1878–1938*. Cambridge UP, 2006

Gellately, R., B. Kiernan, eds, *The spectre of genocide. Mass murder in historical perspective*. Cambridge UP, 2003

Geppert, D., W. Mulligan, A. Rose, eds, *The wars before the Great War. Conflict and international politics before the outbreak of the First World War*. Cambridge UP, 2015

Geyer, M.H., J. Paulmann, eds, *The mechanics of internationalism. Culture, society and politics from the 1840s to the First World War*. London, German Historical Institute, 2001

Glenny, M., *The Balkans 1804–1999. Nationalism, war and the great powers*. London, Penguin, 2000

Göhring, W., *Verdrängt und Vergessen. Friedensnobelpreisträger Alfred Hermann Fried*. Vienna, Kremayer and Scheriau, 2006

Goldstein, R.J., ed., *War for the public mind. Political censorship in nineteenth-century Europe*. Westport, Greenwood, 2000

Gong, G.W., *The standard of 'civilization' in international society*. Oxford, Clarendon Press, 1984

Grabar, V.E., *The history of international law in Russia 1647–1917. A bio-bibliographical study*. Oxford, Clarendon Press, 1990

Grant, J.A., *Rulers, guns and money. The global arms trade in the age of imperialism*. Cambridge, Harvard UP, 2007

Gray, T., *Champions of peace. The story of Alfred Nobel, the peace prize and the laureates*. Birmingham, Paddington, 1976

Grossi, V., *Le pacifism européen 1889–1914*. Brussels, Bruylant, 1994

Gubin, E., L. van Molle, eds, *Women changing the world. A history of the International Council of Women*. Brussels, Racine, 2005

Halévy, E., *The rule of democracy 1905–1914*. London, Ernest Benn, 1961

Hamann, B., *Bertha von Suttner. A life for peace*. Syracuse UP, 1996

Hamilton, K., E. Johnson, eds, *Arms and disarmament in diplomacy*. London, Vallentine Mitchell, 2008

Hampton, M., *Visions of the press in Britain 1850–1950*. Urbana, University of Illinois Press, 2004

Havighurst, A.F., *Radical journalist. H.W. Massingham (1860–1924)*. Cambridge UP, 1974

Headrick, D., *The tools of empire. Technology and European imperialism in the nineteenth century*. Oxford UP, 1981

Herman, S.R., *Eleven against war. Studies in American internationalist thought, 1898–1921*. Stanford, Hoover Institution Press, 1969

Hess, S., *The government/press connection. Press officers and their offices*. Washington D.C., Brookings Institute, 1984

Hilton, S.L., S.J.S. Ickringill, eds, *European perceptions of the Spanish-American War of 1898*. Frankfurt, Peter Lang, 1999

Hinsley, F.H., ed., *British foreign policy under Sir Edward Grey*. Cambridge UP, 1977

Hinsley, F.H., *Power and the pursuit of peace. Theory and practice in the history of relations between states*. Cambridge UP, 1963

Hofmeyr, I., *Ghandi's printing press*. Cambridge, Harvard UP, 2013

Holbraad, C., *Internationalism and nationalism in European political thought*. London, Palgrave MacMillan, 2003

Holl, K., A.C. Kjelling, eds, *The Nobel Peace Prize and the laureates. The meaning and acceptance of the Nobel Peace Prize in the prize winners' countries*. Frankfurt, Peter Lang, 1994

Hough, H.G., *First Sea Lord. An authorized biography of Admiral Lord Fisher*. London, George Allen and Unwin, 1969

Howard, M., G.G. Andreopoulos, M.R. Shulman, eds, *The laws of war. Constraints on warfare in the western world*. New Haven, Yale UP, 1994

Huffman, J.L., *Creating a public. People and press in Meiji Japan*. Honolulu, University of Hawai'i Press, 1997

Huffman, J.L., *Japan and imperialism 1853–1945*. Ann Arbor, Association for Asian Studies, 2010

Hull, I.V., *A scrap of paper. Breaking and making international law during the Great War*. Ithaca, Cornell UP, 2014

Hunt, L., *Inventing human rights. A history*. New York, W.W. Norton, 2007

Hutchinson, J.F., *Champions of charity. War and the rise of the Red Cross*. Boulder, Westview Press, 1996

Hutt, A., *Changing newspaper. Typographic trends in Britain and America 1622–1972*. London, Gordon Fraser, 1973

Iriye, A., *Cultural internationalism and world order*. Baltimore, John Hopkins Press, 1997

Ishay, M., *The history of human rights from ancient times to the globalisation era*. Berkeley, University of California Press, 2004

Jackson, P., *Beyond the balance of power. France and the politics of national security in the era of the First World War*. Cambridge UP, 2013

Johns, A., *War, journalism and the shaping of the twentieth century*. London, I.B. Tauris, 2006

Johnson, G., ed., *The Foreign Office and British diplomacy in the twentieth century*. New York, Routledge, 2005

Joll, J., *The second international 1889–1914*. Second edition. London, Routledge and Kegan Paul, 1974

Kalyva, S.N., I. Shapiro, T. Masoud, eds, *Order, conflict and violence*. Cambridge UP, 2008

Kassimeris, G., ed., *The barbarization of warfare*. New York UP, 2006

Kaul, C., ed., *Media and the British Empire*. London, Palgrave, 2006

Kemperink, M., L. Vermeer, eds, *Utopianism and the sciences 1880–1930*. Leuven, Peeters, 2010

Kennedy, P., *The parliament of man. The United Nations and the quest for world government*. London, Allen Lane, 2006

Kern, S., *The culture of time and space 1880–1918*. Cambridge, Harvard UP, 1983

Kiernan, B., *Blood and soil. A world history of genocide and extermination from Sparta to Darfur*. New Haven, Yale UP, 2007

Killy, W., ed., *Dictionary of German Biography*. Volume 9, Munich, K.G. Saur, 2005

Kingsberg, M., *Moral nation. Modern Japan and narcotics in global history*. Berkeley, University of California Press, 2014

Kirkby, D., C. Coleborne, eds, *Law, history, colonialism. The reach of empire*. Manchester UP, 2001

Kramer, A., *Dynamic of destruction. Culture and mass killing in the First World War*. Oxford UP, 2007

Krebs, P.M., *Gender, race and the writing of empire. Public discourse and the Boer War*. Cambridge UP, 1999

Krieken, P.J. van, D. McKay, eds, *The Hague. Legal capital of the world*. The Hague, T.M.C. Asser Press, 2005

Koskenniemi, M., *The gentle civilizer of nations. The rise and fall of international law 1870–1960*. Cambridge UP, 2001

Kuehl, W.F., *Seeking world order. The United States and international organization to 1920*. Nashville, Vanderbilt UP, 1969

Lachs, M., *The teacher in international law. Teaches and teaching*. Second revised edition, The Hague, Martinus Nijhoff, 1987

Laidler, C.V., *A segunda conferência sa paz de Haia 1907*. Rio de Janiero, Casa de Rui Barbosa, 2010

Laity, P., *The British peace movement 1870–1914*. Oxford, Clarendon Press, 2001

Langer, W., *The diplomacy of imperialism, 1890–1902*. New York, Knopf, 1951 [1935]

Langhorne, R., *The collapse of the concert of Europe. International politics 1890–1914*. New York, St Martin's Press, 1981

Lanza, A., *La santa sede e le conferenz della pace dell'aja del 1899 e 1907*. Rome, Lateran UP, 2002
Laqua, D., *The age of internationalism and Belgium, 1880–1930. Peace, progress and prestige*. Manchester UP, 2015
Larson, T.A., *History of Wyoming*. Second edition, University of Nebraska Press, 1990
Lemarchand, R., ed., *Forgotten genocides. Oblivion, denial and memory*. University of Pennsylvania Press, 2011
Lesaffer, R., ed., *Peace treaties and international law in European history. From the late Middle Ages to World War One*. Cambridge UP, 2004
Lettevall, R., G. Somsen, S. Widmalm, eds, *Neutrality in twentieth-century Europe. Intersections of science, culture, and politics after the First World War*. New York, Routledge, 2012
Leventhal, F.M., *The last dissenter. H.N. Brailsford and his world*. Oxford, Clarendon Press, 1985
Löhr, I., R. Wenzlhuemer, eds, *The nation state and beyond. Governing globalization processes in the nineteenth and early twentieth centuries*. Berlin, Springer, 2012
Long, D., B.C. Schmidt, eds, *Imperialism and internationalism in the discipline of international relations*. State University of New York Press, 2005
Mackay, R.F., *Fisher of Kilverstone*. Oxford, Clarendon Press, 1973
MacKenzie, J., *The partition of Africa 1880–1900*. Third edition. London, Routledge, 2005
MacMillan, M., *The war that ended peace. How Europe abandoned peace for the First World War*. London, Profile Books, 2013
Maguire, P., *Law and war. International law and American history*. Revised edition, New York, Columbia UP, 2010
Marchand, C.J., *The American peace movement and social reform 1898–1918*. Princeton UP, 1972
Martin, M., *Images at war. Illustrated periodicals and constructed nations*. Toronto, Unviersity of Toronto Press, 2006
Mazower, M., *Governing the world. The history of an idea, 1815 to the present*. London, Penguin, 2013
McCarthy, H., *Women of the world. The rise of the female diplomat*. London, Bloomsbury, 2014
McCormack, T.L., M.J. Tilbury, G.D. Triggs, eds, *A century of war and peace. Asia-Pacific perspectives of the centenary of the 1899 Hague peace conference*. Boston, Kluwer Law, 2001
McGann, T.F., *Argentina, the United States and the inter-American system 1880–1914*. Cambridge, Harvard UP, 1957
McLuhan, M., *Understanding media. The extensions of man*. London, Sphere Books, 1967
Meier, H.K., *The United States and Switzerland in the nineteenth century*. The Hague, Mouton, 1963
McGetchin, D.T., *Indology, Indomania and orientalism. Ancient India's rebirth in modern Germany*. Madison, Fairleigh Dickinson UP, 2009
Miller, B., *From liberation to conquest. The visual and popular cultures of the Spanish-American War of 1898*. Amherst, University of Massachusetts Press, 2011
Minohara, T., T. Hon, E. Dawley, eds, *The decade of the Great War. Japan and the wider world in the 1910s*. Leiden, Brill, 2014
Moses, D., D. Stone, eds, *Colonialism and genocide*. New York, Routledge, 2007
Mösslang, M., T. Riotte, eds, *The diplomats' world. A cultural history of diplomacy 1815–1914*. Oxford UP, 2008

Motte, D. de la, J.M. Przyblyski, eds, *Making the news. Modernity and the mass press in nineteenth-century France*. Amherst, University of Massachusetts Press, 1999
Muir, N., *Dimitri Stancioff. Patriot and cosmopolitan 1864–1940*. London, John Murray, 1957
Mulligan, W., *The great war for peace*. New Haven, Yale UP, 2014
Nabulsi, K., *Traditions of war. Occupation, resistance and the law*. Oxford UP, 1999
Nasaw, D., *Andrew Carnegie*. New York, Penguin Press, 2006
Neu, C., *The troubled encounter. The United States and Japan*. New York, John Wiley, 1975
Nevakivi, J., ed., *Neutrality in history. Proceedings of the conference on the history of neutrality organized in Helsinki 9–12 September 1992 under the auspices of the Commission of History of International Relations*. Helsinki, Finnish Historical Society, 1993
Newton, D.J., *British labour, European socialism, and the struggle for peace 1889–1914*. Oxford UP, 1985
Ninkovich, F., *The United States and imperialism*. Malden, Blackwell, 2001
Oberhauser, C., W. Knapp, eds, *Hinter den Kulissen. Beiträge zur historischen Mythenforschung*. Innsbruck UP, 2012
Ogle, V., *The global transformation of time 1870–1950*. Harvard UP, 2015
Pallua, U., *Eurocentrism, racism, colonialism in the Victorian and Edwardian age*. Heidelberg, Winter, 2005
Paris, M., *Warrior nation. Images of war in British popular culture*. London, Reaktion, 2002
Patterson, D.S., *Toward a warless world. The travail of the American Peace Movemement 1887–1914*. Bloomington, Indiana UP, 1976
Peet, A.J. van der, *Belangen en prestige. Nederlandse* gunboat diplomacy *omstreeks 1900*. Amsterdam, De Bataafsche Leeuw, 1999
Penson, L.M., H.W.V. Temperley, *A century of diplomatic blue books 1814–1914*. London, Routledge, 1966
Pick, D., *War machine. The rationalisation of slaughter in the modern age*. New Haven, Yale UP, 1996
Pinker, S., *The better angels of our nature. A history of violence and humanity*. London, Penguin, 2011
Pollock, J., *Kitchener. The road to Omburman and saviour of the nation*. London, Constable & Robinson, 1998
Potter, S., *News and the British world. The emergence of an imperial press system 1876–1922*. Oxford UP, 2003
Pretorius, F., ed., *Verskroeide aarde*. Capetown, Human & Rousseau, 2001
Prins, G., H. Tromp, eds, *The future of war*. The Hague, Kluwer Law, 2000
Prost, M., ed., *Mélanges offerts à Marc Orange et Alexandre Guillemoz*. Paris, Collège de France, 2010
Pustogarov, V.V., *Our Martens. F. F. Martens international lawyer and architect of peace*. The Hague, Kluwer Law International, 2000
Rayward, B., ed., *Information beyond borders. International cultural and intellectual exchange in the belle époque*. London, Taylor & Francis, 2014
Read, D., *The power of news. The history of Reuters 1849–1989*. Oxford UP, 1992
Reinink, A.W., *K.P.C. de Bazel*. Amsterdam, J.M. Meulenhoff, 1965
Ricard, S., ed., *A companion to Theodore Roosevelt*. London, Blackwell, 2011
Robbins, K., *Britain and Europe 1789–2005*. London, Hodder Arnold, 2005
Roberts, C.M., *The Washington Post. The first 100 years*. Boston, Houghton Mifflin, 1977

Robinson, W.S., *Muckraker. The scandalous life and times of W.T. Stead, Britain's first investigative journalist*. London, Biteback, 2012

Rodogno, D., *Against massacre. Humanitarian intervention in the Ottoman Empire 1815–1914*. Princeton UP, 2011

Röhl, J.C., *Kaiser Wilhelm II, 1859–1941. A concise life*. Cambridge UP, 2014

Rosenberg, E.S., ed., *A world connecting 1870–1945*. Cambridge, Harvard UP, 2012

Rosenne, S., ed., *The Hague Peace Conferences of 1899 and 1907 and international arbitration. Reports and documents*. The Hague, T.M.C. Asser Press, 2001

Rossi, C.R., *Broken chain of being. James Brown Scott and the origins of modern international law*. The Hague, Kluwer Law International, 1998

Rüger, J., *The great naval game. Britain and German in the age of empire*. Cambridge UP, 2007

Rybachenok, I.S., *Rossiia i pervaia konferentsiia mira 1899 goda v Gaage*. Moscow, Russian Academy of Sciences, 2005

Saler, M., ed., *Fin-de-siècle world*. New York, Routledge, 2014

Salerno, E., *Genocidio in Libia. Le atrocità nacoste dell'avventura colonial 1911–1933*. Milan, Sugarco Edizione, 1979

Sarkin, J., *Germany's genocide of the Herero. Kaiser Wilhelm II, his generals, his settlers, his soldiers*. Cape Town, UCT, 2011

Sarkissian, A.O., ed., *Studies in diplomatic history and historiography in honour of G.P. Gooch*. London, Longmans, 1961

Schaus, G.P., ed., *Onward to the Olympics*. Waterloo, Wilfrid Laurier UP, 2007

Schirbel, G., *Strukturen des Internationalismus. First Universal Races Congress London 1911*. Volume 1, Münster, Lit Verlag, 1991

Schircks, R., *Die Martens'sche Klause. Rezeption und Rechtsqualität*. Baden-Baden, Nomos, nd

Schlichtmann, K., *Japan in the world. Shidehara Kijūrō, pacifism, and the abolition of war*. Volume 1. Lanham, Rowman & Littlefield, 2009

Schou, A., *Histoire de l'internationalisme. III Du Congres de Vienne jusqu'à la première guerre mondiale (1914)*. Oslo, H. Aschenhoug, 1963

Schuyt, B. van der, *De 's Gravenlandseweg en zijn bewoners*. Hilversum, Verloren, 2005

Segesser, D., *Recht statt Rache oder Rache durch Recht? Die Ahndung von Kriegsverbrechen in der internationalen wissenschaftlichen Debatte 1872–1945*. Paderborn, Ferdinand Schöningh, 1998

Semmel, B., *Liberalism and naval strategy. Ideology, interest and sea power during the Pax Britannica*. Boston, Allen & Unwin, 1986

Sheehan, J., *Where have all the soldiers gone? The transformation of modern Europe*. Boston, Houghton Mifflin, 2008

Sherwood, M., *Origins of Pan-Africanism. Henry Sylvester Williams, Africa and the African diaspora*. New York, Routledge, 2011

Silva, L.A., *O discurso modernizador de Rui Barbosa (1879–1923)*. np, Universidade Federal de Juiz de Fora, 2009

Simms, B., D.J.B. Trim, eds, *Humanitarian intervention. A history*. Cambridge UP, 2011

Sluga, G., *Internationalism in the age of nationalism*. Philadelphia, University of Pennsylvania Press, 2013

Spender, J.A., *The life of the Right Hon. Sir Henry Campbell-Bannerman*. Two volumes, London, Hodder & Stoughton, nd

Spennemann, D.H.R., *The heritage of nineteenth-century Samoan newspapers. A bibliographical documentation*. Albury, Johnstone Centre, 2003

Spiers, E.M., *The Victorian soldier in Africa*. Manchester UP, 2004
Steele, D., *Lord Salisbury. A political biography*. London, University College London Press, 1999
Stolleis, M., M. Yanagihara, eds, *East Asian and European perspectives on international law*. Baden-Baden, Nomos, 2004
Tate, M., *The disarmament illusion. The movement for a limitation of armaments to 1907*. New York, MacMillan, 1942
Tilchin, W.N., C.E. Neu, eds, *Artists of power. Theodore Roosevelt, Woodrow Wilson and their enduring impact on US foreign policy*. Westport, Praeger Security International, 2006
Tompkins, E.B., *Anti-imperialism in the United States. The great debate 1890–1920*. Philadelphia, University of Pennsylvania Press, 1970
Totten, S., W.S. Parsons, eds, *Centuries of genocide. Essays and eyewitness accounts*. Fourth edition, New York, Routledge, 2013
Trentmann, F., *Free trade nation*. Oxford UP, 2008
Tuchman, B.W., *The proud tower. A portrait of the world before the war 1890–1914*. New York, Ballantine Books, 1962 [1996]
Ugbaoaja Ohaegbulam, F., *West African responses to European imperialism in the nineteenth and twentieth centuries*. Lanham, UP of America, 1984
Uhlig, R., *Die Interparlementarische Union 1899–1914*. Wiesbaden, Franz Steiner, 1988
Verwaest, R., *Van Den Haag tot Genève. België en het internationale oorlogsrecht (1874–1950)*. Brugge, Die Keure, 2011
Vick, B.E., *The Congress of Vienna. Power and politics after Napoleon*. Cambridge, Harvard UP, 2014
Villiot, P., *Le recours au siege apostolique et la première conférence international de la paix. Les enseignements des archives du Quai d'Orsay*. Paris, Collection Archétypes Contemporaines, 1999
Vries, J. de, ed., *Nederland 1913. Een reconstructive van het culturele leven*. Meulenhoff, Landshof, 1988
Wank, S., ed., *Doves and diplomats. Foreign offices and peace movements in Europe and America in the twentieth century*. Wesport, Greenwood, 1978
Ward, A.W., G.P. Gooch, *Cambridge history of British foreign policy, 1783–1919*. Volume 3, Cambridge UP, 1923
Westwood, J.N., *Russia against Japan 1904–1905. A new look at the Russo-Japanese War*. State University of New York Press, 1986
Widenor, W.C., *Henry Cabot Lodge and the search for an American foreign policy*. Berkeley, University of California Press, 1980
Wild, A., *Baron d'Estournelles de Constant (1852–1914)*. Hamburg, Europea-Kolleg, 1973
Wilkinson, G.R., *Depictions and images of war in Edwardian newspapers, 1899–1914*. Houndsmills, Palgrave MacMillan, 2003
Williams, K., *Read all about it! A history of the British newspaper*. London, Routledge, 2010
Wilson, J., *CB. A life of Sir Henry Campbell-Bannerman*. London, Constable, 1973
Wilson, K., ed., *British foreign secretaries and foreign policy. From Crimean War to First World War*. London, Croom Helm, 1987
Wilson, K., ed., *The international impact of the Boer War*. Chesham, Acumen, 2001
Winter, J., *Dreams of peace and freedom. Utopian moments in the twentieth century*. New Haven, Yale UP, 2006
Wolfke, K., *Great and small powers in international law from 1814 to 1920*. Wroclaw, np, 1961

Women in a changing world. The dynamic story of the International Council of Women since 1888. London, Routledge and Kegan Paul, 1966

Young, R.J., *Marketing Marianne. French propaganda in America 1900–1940*. New Brunswick, Rutgers UP, 2005

Zanders, J.P., ed., *Innocence slaughtered. Gas and the transformation of warfare and society*. London, Uniform Press, 2015

Zang, X., *The origins of the modern Chinese press*. London, Routledge, 2007

Journal Articles

Abrams, I., 'Bertha von Suttner (1843–1914). Biographical notes' *Peace and Change* 16, 1, 1991, 64–73

Abrams, I., 'Bertha von Suttner and the Nobel Peace Prize' *Journal of Central European Affairs* 22, 1962–63, 286–307

Abrams, I., 'The emergence of the international law societies' *Review of Politics* 19, 3, July 1957, 361–380

Accioly, H. 'O barão do Rio Branco e a 2a conferência de Haia' *Revista do Instituto Histórico e Geográfico Brasileiro* 187, 1945, 61–104

Agøy, N., 'It will serve to increase our Union difficulties. Norway, Sweden and the Hague peace conference of 1899' *Historisk tidsskirft* 79, 2000, 181–208

Aldrich, G.H., 'The laws of war on land' *American Journal of International Law* 94, 4, 2000, 42–63

Aldrich, G.H., C.M. Chinkin, 'A century of achievement and unfinished work' *American Journal of International Law* 94, 1, 2000, 90–98

Alvarez, D., 'The Holy See and the first Hague peace conference (1899)' *Archivum Historiae Pontificiae* 26, 1988, 431–438

Anderson, A.M., '"Jacky Fisher" and the 1899 Hague conference. A reassessment' *New Zealand Journal of Research on Europe* 11, 1, March 2017, 54–92

Baker, R., 'Bertha von Suttner as author. The Harriet Beecher Stowe of the peace movement' *Peace and Change* 16, 1, 1991, 74–96

Barcroft, S., 'The Hague peace conference of 1899' *Irish Studies in International Affairs* 3, 1, 1989, 55–68

Baylen, J.O., A. Conan Doyle, 'Sir Arthur Conan Doyle and W.T. Stead. The novelist and the journalist' *Albion* 2, 1, 1970, 3–16

Bederman, D.J., 'Appreciating a century of scholarship in the *American Journal of International Law*' *American Journal of International Law* 100, 2006, 20–63

Best, G., 'Peace conferences and the century of total war. The 1899 Hague Peace Conference and what came after' *International Affairs* 75, 3, 1999, 619–634

Bettez, D., 'Unfulfilled initiative. Disarmament negotiations and the Hague peace conferences of 1899 and 1907' *RUSI Journal* 133, 3, 1988, 57–62

Bradlow, E., 'Idealism and realism. Conan Doyle, imperialism and the Anglo-Boer War' *Kleio* 35, 1, 2003, 19–40

Brailey, N.J., 'Sir Ernest Satow and the 1907 Second Hague Peace Conference' *Diplomacy & Statecraft* 13, 2, June 2002, 201–228

Callahan, K., '"Performing inter-nationalism" in Stuttgart in 1907. French and German socialist nationalism and the political culture of an international socialist congress' *International Review of Social History* 45, 2000, 51–87

Caron, D.D., 'War and international adjudication. Reflections on the 1899 peace conference' *American Journal of International Law* 94, 4, 2000, 4–30

Cassese, A., 'The Martens Clause. Half a loaf or simply pie in the sky?' *European Journal of International Law* 11, 1, 2000, 187–216

Ceadel, M., 'Enforced pacific settlement or guaranteed mutual defence? British and US approaches to collective security in the eclectic covenant of the League of Nations' *International History Review* 35, 5, 2013, 993–1008

Cooper, S.E., 'The origins and development of European peace movements. From Vienna to Frankfurt' *Wiener Beitrage zur Geschichte der Neuzeit* 11, 1984, 75–95

Crespo, E., 'La segunda conferencia de paz de la Haya (1907) y la posición de España' *Revista Española de Derecho Internacional* 60, 1, 2008, 113–128

Davy, J.A., 'Pacifist thought and gender ideology in political biographies of women peace activists in Germany 1899–1970' *Journal of Women's History* 13, 3, 2001, 34–45

Dawson, G., 'Preventing "a great moral evil". Jean de Bloch's *The Future of War* as anti-revolutionary pacifism' *Journal of Contemporary History* 37, 1, 2002, 5–19

Douma, M.J., 'Ethnic identities in a transnational context. The Dutch American reaction to the Anglo-Boer War 1899–1902' *South African Historical Journal* 65, 4, 2013, 481–503

Dülffer, J., 'Die Haager Friedenskonferenzen von 1899 und 1907 im internationalen Staatensystem' *Die Friedens-Warte* 74, 1–2, 1999, 98–112

Dungen, P. van den, 'Een interessante probleem: Jean Bloch en de eerste Haagse vredesconferentie' *Transaktie* 10, 1981, 189–214

Dungen, P. van den, 'The making of peace. Jean de Bloch and the first Hague peace conference' *Occasional Paper Series of the Center for the Study of Armament and Disarmament* 12, 1983, np

Dungen, P. van den, 'Preventing catastrophe. The world's first peace museum' *Ritsumeikan Kokusai Kenkyu* 18, 3, March 2006, 449–462

Eyffinger, A., 'A highly critical moment. Role and record of the 1907 Hague Peace Conference' *Netherlands International Law Review* 54, 2007, 197–228

Filene, P., 'The world peace foundation and progressivism, 1910–1919' *New England Quarterly* 36, 4, December 1963, 478–501

Fitzmaurice, A., 'Liberalism and empire in nineteenth-century international law' *American Historical Review* 117, 1, 2012, 122–140

Ford, T.K., 'The genesis of the first Hague Peace Conference' *Political Science Quarterly* 51, 3, September 1936, 354–382

Frei, G.A., 'Great Britain, contraband and future maritime conflict' *Francia* 40, 2013, 409–418

Genell, A.G., 'The well-defended domains. Eurocentric international law and the making of the Ottoman Office of Legal Counsel' *Journal of the Ottoman and Turkish Studies Association* 3, 2, November 2016, 255–275

Griffiths, A., 'Winston Churchill, the *Morning Post* and end of the imperial romance' *Victorian Periodicals Review* 46, 2, 2013, 163–183

Gullace, N., 'Sexual violence and family honor: British propaganda and international law during the First World War' *American Historical Review* June 1997, 715–742

Hanson, I., '"God'll send the bill to you". The costs of war and the God who counts in W.T. Stead's pro-Boer peace campaign' *Journal of Victorian Culture* 20, 2, 2015, 168–185

Harris, S.M., 'The global construction of international law in the nineteenth century. The case of arbitration' *Journal of World History* 27, 2, June 2016, 303–325

Hasian Jnr, M., 'Alice Seeley Harris, the atrocity rhetoric of the Congo reform movements, and the demise of King Léopold's Congo Free State' *Atlantic Journal of Communication* 23, 2015, 178–192

Heerikhuizen, A. van, 'Een Haagsche salon met toekomstige Nobelprijswinnaars' *Working Papers in European Studies* University of Amsterdam, 2007

Heerikhuizen, A. van, 'William Thomas Stead, Den Haag en wereldvrede' *De Negentiende Eeuw* 29, 2, June 2005, 135–146

Hepp, J., 'James Brown Scott and the rise of public international law' *Journal of the Gilded Age and Progressive Era* 7, 2, April 2008, 151–179

Herren-Oesch, M., C. Knab, 'Die Zweite Haager Friedenskonferenz und die Liberalisierung des politischen Informationsmarktes' *Die Friedens-Warte* 82, 4, 2007, 51–64

Holquist, P., 'Dilemmas of an "official with progressive views". Baron Boris Nolde' *Baltic Yearbook of International Law* 7, 2007, 211–249

Hucker, D., 'British peace activism and "new" diplomacy. Revisiting the 1899 Hague Peace Conference' *Diplomacy & Statecraft* 26, 2015, 405–412

Hucker, D., 'International history and the study of public opinion. Towards methodological clarity' *International History Review* 34, 4, 2012, 775–794

Hutching, M., 'Mothers of the world. Women, peace and arbitration in early twentieth-century New Zealand' *New Zealand Journal of History* 27, 2, 1997, 173–185

Hutchinson, J.F., 'Rethinking the origins of the Red Cross' *Bulletin of the History of Medicine* 63, 4, 1989, 557–578

Ito, F., 'One hundred years of international law studies in Japan' *Japanese Annual of International Law* 19, 1969, 19–26

Jochnick, C. af, R. Normand, 'The legitimation of violence. A critical history of the laws of war' *Harvard International Law Journal* 35, 1, 1994, 49–95

Kaiser, W., 'Transnational mobilization and cultural representation. Political transfer in an age of proto-globalization, democratization and nationalism 1848–1914' *European Review of History* 12, 2, 2005, 403–424

Kalshoven, F., 'De eerste Haagse vredesconferentie van 1899' *Militair Rechtelijk Tijdschrift* 42, 8, September 1999, 257–265

Kätzel, U., 'A radical women's rights and peace activist. Margarethe Lenore Selenka, initiator of the first worldwide women's peace demonstration in 1899' *Journal of Women's History* 13, 3, Autumn 2001, 46–69

Keefer, S.A., 'Building the palace of peace. The Hague Conference of 1899 and arms control in the progressive era' *Journal of the History of International Law* 8, 2006, 1–17

Keefer, S.A., 'Explosive missals. International law, technology and security in nineteenth-century disarmament conferences' *War in History* 21, 4, 2014, 445–464

Keefer, S.A., 'An obstacle though not a barrier. The role of international law in security planning during the *Pax Britannica*' *International History Review* 35, 5, 2013, 1031–1051

Kennedy, W.M., 'The imperialism of internment: Boer prisoners of war in India and civic reconstruction in Southern Africa, 1899–1905' *Journal of Imperial and Commonwealth History* 44, 3, 2016, 423–447

Knab, C., 'Civil society diplomacy? W.T. Stead, world peace and transgressive journalism' *Comparativ* 23, 6, 2013, 22–51

Knee, S.E., 'Anglo-American understanding and the Boer War' *Australian Journal of Politics and History* 30, 2, 1984, 196–208

Kuehl, W.F., 'Concepts of internationalism in history' *Peace and Change* 11, 1, 1986, 1–10

Kussbach, E., 'Heinrich Lammasch, scholar of public international law and Austrian statesman' *Miskolc Journal of International Law* 1, 2, 2004, 63–77

Landauer, C., 'The ambivalence of power. Launching the *American Journal of International Law* in an era of empire and globalisation' *Leiden Journal of International Law* 20, 2, June 2007, 325–358

Laurence, R.R., 'Bertha von Suttner and the peace movement in Austria' *Austrian History Yearbook* 23, 1992, 181–201

Leanza, U., F. Mucci, 'La partecipazione dell'italia alla prima conferenza per la pace del'aja del 1899' *La comunità internazionale* 54, 1999, 3–12

Lee, E.Y.-J., 'Early development of modern international law in East Asia-with special reference to China, Japan and Korea' *Journal of the History of International Law* 4, 2002, 42–76

Leeuwin, E.W., 'The arts of peace. Thomas H. Mawson's gardens at the peace palace, The Hague' *Garden History Society* 28, 2, Winter 2000, 262–276

Lentföhr, C., 'Die Haager Landkriegsordnung vom 18 Oktober 1907' *Humanitaeres Völkerrecht* 2, 2, 1990, 86–90

Lesaffer, R., 'The temple of peace. The Hague peace conferences, Andrew Carnegie and the building of the Peace Palace (1898–1913)' *Preadviezen. Mededelingen van de Koninklijke Nederlandse Vereniging voor Internationaal Recht* 140, November 2013, 1–38

Mack, J., 'Nicholas II and the rescript for peace of 1898. Apostle of peace or shrewd politician?' *Russian History* 31, 1–2, 2004, 83–103

Mamadouh, V., A. Meijer, J.D. Sidway, H. van der Wusten, 'Toward an urban geography of diplomacy. Lessons from The Hague' *Professional Geographer*. 2015, doi: 10.1080/00330124.2014.987184

Mangoldt, H. von, 'Verrechtlichung? Vom Haager System zum Völkerbund' *Die Friedens-Warte* 69, 1–2, 1993, 7–38

Meron, T., 'The Martens Clause, principles of humanity, and dictates of public conscience' *American Journal of International Law* 94, 1, January 2000, 78–89

Morrill, D.L., 'Nicholas II and the call for the first Hague conference' *Journal of Modern History* 46, 2, June 1974, 296–313

Murase, S., 'The most-favored nation treatment in Japan's treaty practice during the period 1854–1905' *American Journal of International Law* 70, 2, April 1976, 273–297

Murase, S., '1907nen hāgu heiwakaigi saihō: kankoku kōtei no shōsetsu' *Gaiko Forum* 6, 227, 2007, 56–63

Murase, S., 'The presence of Asia at the Hague peace conference of 1907' *Colloquium. Topicality of the Hague peace conference of 1907*. The Hague, MArtinus Nijhoff, 2007, 85–101

Osterhammel, J., 'Europe, the "West" and the civilizing mission' *German Historical Institute London. The 2005 annual lecture*. London, German Historical Institute London, 2005, 5–44

Porsch, D., 'Die *Friedens-Warte* zwischen Friedensbewegung und Wissenschaft' *Die Friedens-Warte* 74, 1–2, 1999, 39–78

Praet, C. van, C. Verbruggen, '"Soldiers for a joint cause". A relational perspective on local and international educational leagues in the 1860s' *Low Countries Historical Review* 130, 1, 2015, 4–24

Readman, P., 'The Conservative Party, patriotism and British politics. The case of the general election of 1900' *Journal of British Studies* 40, 1, 2001, 107–145

Rindfleisch, A., 'Das Seekriegsrecht und die "Zivilisierung der Menscheit". Debatten zur zweiten Haager Friedenskonferenz und ihre Folgen' *Die Friedens-Warte* 82, 2007, 83–95

Rodogno, D., 'European legal doctrines on intervention and the status of the Ottoman Empire within the "family of nations" throughout the nineteenth century' *Journal of the History of International Law* 18, 2016, 5–41

Rupp, L.J., 'Constructing internationalism. The case of transnational women's organizations, 1888–1945' *American Historical Review* 99, 4, December 1994, 1571–1600

Sarkin, J., 'The historical origins, convergence and interrelationship of international human rights law, international humanitarian law, international criminal law and public international law and their application since the nineteenth century' *Human Rights and International Legal Discourse* 125, 2007, 125–172

Schlichtmann, K., 'Japan, Germany and the idea of the Hague peace conferences' *Journal of Peace Research* 40, 4, 2003, 377–394

Schultz, M., '"A harmony of frenzy". Maori in Manhattan, 1909–10' *Theatre Studies* 67, 3, October 2015, 445–464

Schulz, M., 'Vom Direktorialsystem zum Multilateralismus? Die Haager Friedenskonferenz von 1907 in der Entwicklung des internationalen Staatensystems bis zum Ersten Weltkrieg' *Die Friedens-Warte* 82, 4, 2007, 31–50

Segesser, D.M., 'Die Haager Landkriegsordnung in der internationalen wissenschaftlichen Debatte über Kriegsverbrechen im Ersten und Zweiten Weltkrieg' *Die Friedens-Warte* 82, 4, 2007, 65–82

Segesser, D.M., '"Unlawful warfare is uncivilised". The international debate on the punishment of war crimes, 1872–1918' *European Review of History* 14, 2, 2007, 215–234

Sluga, G., 'Turning international: foundations of modern international thought and new paradigms for intellectual history' *History of European Ideas* 2014, 1–14

Spiers, E.M., 'The use of the dum dum bullet in colonial warfare' *Journal of Commonwealth and Imperial History* 4, 1, 1975, 1–14

Vagts, D., 'Hague conventions and arms control' *American Journal of International Law* 94, 4, 2000, 31–41

Veeser, C., 'A forgotten instrument of global capitalism?' *International History Review* 35, 5, 2013, 1136–1155

Theses

Barber, C., 'The evolution of global politics and the pacific settlement of international disputes 1794–1907' PhD thesis, University of Auckland, 2017

Fitzsimons, T., 'Wellington's newspaper space, 1896–1912' BA(Hons) dissertation, Victoria University of Wellington, 2012

Graham, M.J.A., 'Defence debates in the *Royal United Services Institute Journal*. Readying the British military for war in the hope of preserving peace, 1898–1914' MA thesis, University of Auckland, 2015

Halcrow, J., 'Drugs, empire and international law. British debates over the First Opium War, 1839–1842' MA thesis, University of Auckland, 2017

Higgins, A.R., 'Petitioning for peace. The British public movement in support of the proposed first Hague peace conference, 1898–1899' MA thesis, University of Auckland, 2016

Hutching, M., '"Turn back this tide of barbarism": New Zealand women who were opposed to war, 1896–1919' MA thesis, University of Auckland, 1990

Junk, A., *Die Mächte auf der ersten Haager Friedenskonferenz (1899). Inaugural-Dissertation zur Erlangung der Doktorwürde der Philosophischen Fakultät der Universität Frankfurt a. M.* Borna-Leipzig, Universitätsverlag Robert Noske, 1928

Keefer, S.A., 'Great Britain and naval arms control. International law and security 1898–1914' PhD, London School of Economics and Political Science, 2011

Moon, M. 'The origins of the first "International Parliament". Perceptions of the first Hague peace conference and concepts of universality 1898–1899' BA(Hons) dissertation, University of Auckland, 2012

Munro, T., 'The Hague's war, 1914–1929' PhD thesis, University of Auckland, forthcoming, 2018

Ward, M., 'Popular perceptions of the second Hague peace conference, 1907, in the American and British press' BA(Hons) dissertation, University of Auckland 2014

Index

Aberdeen Free Press 138
Aberdeen, Lady Ishbel 55, 64, 137, 138
abolitionism of slavery 16, 92, 143
Abyssinia (Ethiopia) 60
Academy of International Law (The Hague) 183
Adam, Paul 91–2
Adler, Arthur 166
Admiralty (Britain) 57, 84, 100
Advocate of Peace 34, 38, 121
aerial warfare 26, 84, 139, 155, 165, 180
Afghanistan 56
Africa 5, 10, 11, 12, 16, 17, 31, 98, 102, 103, 107, 157
African Standard 111
Africans *see* Africa
Ahmed, Rafiuddin 23
Alaska 56
Alexander I, Tsar 32, 33
Alexander II, Tsar 32, 43
Algeciras crisis (1906) 141, 146, 155
Algemeen Dagblad 106
Algemeen Handelsblad 93, 146
Algeria 23, 25–6
Alianza Intelectual (Madrid) 156
Alsace-Lorraine 23, 24, 26, 56, 157
Amaral, Crispin do 110
American (New York) 151
American Association for International Conciliation 140
American Humane Society 156
American International Law Association 135
American Journal of International Law 123
American Monthly Review of Reviews 40, 61, 116, 131
American Peace Society 15, 30, 38, 64
American Social Science Association 30
American Universal Peace Union 64
American Women's Council 53
Amsterdam 79, 81, 156, 159, 176
Amsterdammer, De 47, 54, 148, 149, 150
anarchism 17, 22, 23, 56, 58, 64, 92, 156
Anderson, Alan 82
Anglo-Boer War, second (1899–1902) *see* Boer War
Anglo-Saxon Review 91
Anti-Imperial League (American) 18
Anti-Revolutionary Party (Netherlands) 81
Appleton, Lewis 33
Apponyi, Count Albert 52, 94, 95, 124, 129, 132, 139
Arabs 111–12
arbitration 2, 47, 87, 98, 102, 103, 114, 120, 130, 181 *see also* Permanent Court of Arbitration
  and activism 8, 15, 16, 18, 28, 38–9, 48–53, 54, 87, 116, 121–2, 125–6, 130, 136–9, 155–6, 178
  and governments 14, 18, 39–40, 61, 63, 64, 87, 89–90, 115, 118, 132, 148, 152, 167, 181
  and The Hague 3, 20, 22, 32, 33, 38, 39, 44, 48, 52, 55–6, 61, 63, 72, 73, 74, 76–7, 82, 83, 87–90, 91, 92, 93–4, 95, 114–17, 102, 121, 124, 126, 132, 133, 137, 153–4, 156, 158, 159, 160, 161, 164, 167, 169, 178, 180, 181
  treaties 14, 87, 104, 114, 133, 137, 160, 180
Arbitrator 29, 166
architecture 171–2, 174, 175
Ardagh, Major John 61, 84, 85, 90, 108, 109, 110, 111, 133
Argentina 31, 137, 138, 160, 162, 174
Armenia 70, 81–2, 101, 119
armies, size of 26, 29, 30, 31, 56–7
armistice 86
arms limitation 1, 20, 21–2, 24, 25, 26, 27, 28, 29, 30, 31, 32, 33, 40, 48, 52, 55, 56–7, 64, 73, 114, 126, 137, 140, 169, 183

at The Hague (1899) 74, 77, 82–5, 87, 90, 91, 94, 121, 139
at The Hague (1907) 149, 151–3, 159, 162–3, 165
at The Hague (1915) 180
arms race 32, 114, 120, 147, 148, 149, 150, 151, 152, 162 *see also* arms limitation
Arnaud, Émile 76
Asahi 116
Asia 5, 10, 11, 12, 22, 24, 25, 27, 30–1, 32, 115, 140, 147
Asser, T.M.C. 52, 58, 82, 131, 142, 159, 160, 179, 180
Associated Press 12
Association des journalists-amis de la paix (Association of Journalist Friends of Peace) 124
Atlanta Constitution 131, 132
Auckland Star 25, 148, 149
Australasia 5, 12, 46
Australasian (Melbourne) 23, 24–5, 67–8, 69, 70, 140
Australia 13, 23, 25, 53, 114, 138, 140, 146, 156, 174
Austria-Hungary 26, 27, 29, 32, 36, 49, 52, 53, 58, 62, 64, 68, 75, 91, 94, 95, 106, 113, 121, 123, 124, 131, 137, 139, 146, 152, 156, 167, 180

Bain, Wilhelmine Sheriff 138
Balfour, Sir Arthur 103
Balkan Wars (1912–1913) 113, 176, 178
Balkans 157, 166
balloons as weapons 26, 84, 139, 155, 165
Bangor City 110
Bar, Carl Ludwig von 98, 100–1
Barbosa, Rui 160
Barclay, Thomas 133, 135
Barthold, Richard 174
Basili, Count Alexander de 33, 63, 131
Basili, Nicolas de 33
Bavaria 59
Bazel, A.K.P.C. de 174
Beales, A.C.F. 33
Beaufort, Willem Hendrik de 46, 60, 64, 79, 94, 156, 160, 180
Bebel, August 119
Beer Portugael, General de 83
Beernaert, Auguste 52, 63, 74, 82, 83–4, 86, 142, 161
Beldiman, Alexander 77, 82
Belgium 15, 27, 39, 48, 52, 58, 63, 64, 74, 76, 101, 102, 114, 119, 133, 160, 174, 175, 181, 182
Belgrade 180
Bengal 111, 145
Benoit, Raoul 26
Berlage, Hendrik Petrus 171, 175
Berlin 49, 52, 61, 87, 113, 133, 138, 178
Berlin Post 89
Berlin, Congress of (1884–1885) 15, 33
Berlin, Treaty of (1878) 6
Berlin, University of 154
Berliner Börsenzeitung 146
Berliner Tageblatt 26, 92, 138, 146, 166
Berne 15, 58, 175
Bieberstein, Baron Marschal von 160, 163
Bihourd, Georges 62
Bildt, Baron Carl Nils Daniel 76, 83–4, 90
Bille, E. 84
Binnenhof 69, 159
Bismarck, Otto von 6, 33
Bjørnson, Bjørnstjerne 38, 53
Blackwood's Edinburgh Magazine 91
Bliss, Edwin Munsell 40
Bloch, Ivan 17, 31, 32, 33, 55, 64, 65, 78, 81, 133, 134
blockade 116, 161, 162, 163, 164, 180
Boardman, Dana 64
Boer War (1899–1902) 60, 95, 97–106, 107, 108, 109, 110, 111, 112, 115, 120, 123, 124, 132, 225 n.99
Bolivia 60
bombardment 85, 90, 112, 139, 150, 155, 161, 162, 164, 180, 181, 182
Bond, Brian 38
Booth, General William 29
Borel, Colonel 162
Bosch, A. ten 173, 175
Bosnia-Herzegovina 56, 146, 167
Bosphorus 56
Bourgeois, Léon 48, 62, 69, 74, 76, 82, 84, 91, 92, 94, 123–4, 129, 131, 132, 160
Bourke, Joanna 99, 108, 112
Boxer Rebellion (1899–1900) 100, 101, 106–8, 115, 119, 120, 123, 132

Braakensiek, Johan 37, 54, 104, 150, 159, 173
Brailey, Nigel 8
Brailsford, H.N. 13, 119, 183
Brazil 31, 160, 174
Breukelman, J.B. 48
Bridgman, Raymond L. 166
Britain 7, 11, 14, 16, 18, 25, 26, 27, 28, 30, 33, 34, 39, 40, 44, 46, 49, 50, 51, 57, 59, 60, 61, 65, 76, 84–5, 87, 91, 93, 94, 97–106, 107, 108–13, 114, 115, 116–17, 118, 120, 133, 141, 145, 148, 151–3, 154, 156, 161, 162–3, 164, 167–8, 174, 176, 180, 181
British Foreign Arbitration Association 33
Bruges 160
Brugman, Hajo 180
Brussels 12, 58, 136, 175
Brussels Conventions (1874) 20, 22, 40, 55, 82, 85, 90, 95
Bryan, William Jennings 180
Bryce, James 145, 154
Budapest Journalist Society 124
Budapest Tagblatt 95
Buddha 128
Bulgaria 33, 52, 59, 60–1, 63, 68, 79, 90
bullets 84, 110 *see also* dum-dum bullets
Bülow, Count von 88
Bustamente y Sirven, Antonio S. de 160
Butler, Nicholas Murray 130

Calcutta 23, 84
Campbell-Bannerman, Sir Henry 102, 152, 153
Canada 107, 133
Canevaro, Felice Napoleone 59
cannon 26, 37, 56, 84, 148, 149
Caricature, La 109, 110
Carnegie Endowment for International Peace 18, 135
Carnegie Stichting (Carnegie Foundation) 171, 172, 173, 175
Carnegie, Andrew 18, 125, 130, 155, 166, 170, 171, 172, 175, 178
Casablanca 145, 146
Cassini, Count 49
Catherine the Great, Tsarina 32
Catholicism 27, 58, 59, 60, 116 *see also* Vatican
Catholic World 59
Ceadel, Martin 15, 38, 126
censorship 13, 14, 32, 109, 110, 180
Channing, William Elery 33
charity *see* war charities, philanthropy
chemical warfare *see* gas
Chicago Daily Tribune 29–30, 80, 106, 123, 132, 138, 142
Chickering, Roger 126
Chile 162
China 11, 16, 18, 22, 56, 62, 106–8, 115, 135, 137, 140, 141, 147
Choate, Joseph 142–3, 148
Chun, Yi 157
Church Times 93
Churchill, Winston 104
civil rights 17, 157
civilians in wartime 86, 98, 103, 105, 107, 112, 181
civilization 3, 10, 11, 15, 16, 18–20, 25, 26, 41, 48, 51, 67, 73, 80, 84, 87, 91, 93, 97–101, 103–14, 118–20, 121, 123, 124, 127, 132, 142, 151, 154, 163, 176, 179, 181, 182
Clark, I. 8
Clarke, I.F. 38
Claude, Inis Jnr 8
Cobden Club 46
Colenbrander, H.T. 180
collective security 126, 153, 154, 183
Cologne Gazette 77, 92, 155
Columbia 160
Columbia University 61, 130
Columbian Exposition (1893) 14, 16
commission of enquiry 88, 113, 117, 153, 160 *see also* arbitration
Committee of Boer Independence 102
Conan Doyle, Sir Arthur 29, 105–6
concert of Europe 9, 33, 58, 147, 167, 181 *see also* diplomacy
Concordia 78
conflict resolution 2, 5, 9, 52, 73, 87, 97, 121, 123, 134 *see also* arbitration, good offices, mediation
Confucius 128
Congo 15, 60, 101, 119, 145
Congregational Union of New Zealand 46
Conrad, Joseph 32
conscription 20, 26, 120

conservatism 9, 23, 27, 28, 29, 40, 95, 167–8
contraband 117, 133, 161, 164
Cooper, Sandi 126
Cooperative Societies (Britain) 52
Copenhagen 53, 58
Cordonnier, Louis Marie 171–2, 175
Correo Español, El (Mexico) 31
Courrier de la Conférence de la Paix (Hague) 155
Courrier de Tlemcen (Algeria) 23
Crimean War 16
Crozier, Captain William R. 61, 85
Cuba 16, 160, 167
Current Literature 51, 155
Cyprus 103
Czegka, Bertha 152

Dagblad van Zeeland en 's Gravenhage 82
Daily Express 106, 115, 124
Daily Mail 103, 109–11, 125
Daily Mirror 120
Daily News 27, 59
Daily Telegraph 107
Damaraland Treaty (1885) 118
Danger, Henry 128
Darby, William Evans 49, 64, 74, 97, 98
Davis, Calvin DeArmond 8
defensive warfare 13, 97, 101, 102
del Campo, Jesus 1–2
Delcassé, Théophile 44, 55–6
Delft 80 *see also* 4 July 1899
Deming, W.C. 125
democracy 17, 22, 136
Den Haag *see* Hague, The
Denmark 48, 53, 58, 84, 114, 138, 174
Descamps, Baron Eduoard 15, 52, 63, 76, 82, 131, 133
Desjardin, Arthur 40, 92, 111
Diligentia 78
Dillon, E.J. 107
Dillon, John 102
diplomacy 56, 82, 103, 142, 157, 158
  cultural 78–81, 115, 159–60, 172, 174, 178
  democratization of 7, 58, 60, 64, 122, 125, 147, 165–7, 183
  great power 6–7, 15, 19, 40, 45, 58, 59, 95, 102, 106–7, 141, 147, 160, 165, 167, 181
  gunboat 162
  multilateral 169
  public diplomacy 3, 6–7, 18, 22–3, 25, 44–6, 51, 55–7, 59, 63–4, 73–7, 79–84, 89–90, 94–5, 100, 106–7, 112, 114, 115, 118, 127, 131, 135, 146, 151, 153–4, 158, 180, 181, 184, 193 n.106
  secret diplomacy 74–6, 147, 158, 165, 183
disarmament *see* arms limitation
Disraeli, Benjamin 6
Doggerbank incident (1904) 116–17, 132, 150–1
Dominions (British) 167
Drago doctrine 162, 164
Drago, Louis María 159, 160, 162
Dreyfus Affair 1, 19, 101, 120
Ducommun, Élie 49, 124
Dum-Dum arsenal 84
dum-dum bullets 33, 84–5, 90, 91, 103, 108–14, 117, 118, 162
Dunant, Henri 38
Dupuis, Charles 111
Dutch East Indies 13, 61, 103, 106, 108, 112, 113, 119
Dutch Peace Society 59
dynamite 17, 26, 141

Echo de Paris 26, 47
Eckstein, Anna 178
economic warfare *see* maritime warfare
Economist 93
Edinburgh Review 93, 115, 165
Edward VII, King 22, 120
Egypt 17, 57
'18 May' movement 53–4, 136, 137, 138–9, 142, 182
Eijkman, P.H. 174–5
Eijs, J.C.N. van 75
Emma, Queen 59, 178
English Church (The Hague) 78
Entente Cordiale
  Anglo-French (1904) 114, 115, 130
  Anglo-Russian (1907) 7, 160
Erasmus 128
Esperanto 16, 174
Estournelles de Constant, Baron d' 52, 62, 82, 94, 116, 120, 130–1, 132, 133, 135, 142, 171, 173

Europe 5, 8, 11, 14, 15, 16, 17, 18, 19, 20, 24, 25, 26, 27, 29, 30, 31, 34, 35, 38, 39, 44, 45, 48, 50, 53, 54, 55, 56, 60, 64, 65, 68, 83, 97, 98, 99, 102, 103, 107, 108, 109, 110, 112, 114, 115, 121, 125, 126, 129, 130, 132, 135, 140, 141, 167, 176, 178
Evening News (Britain) 125
Evening Post (Wellington) 46
Evening Star 46
exploding bullets *see* dum-dum bullets
Eyffinger, Arthur 8, 171

Fabianism 17
Familieblad 48
family of nations 16, 46, 99
Ferdinand of Bulgaria, Prince 68
Finland 36, 37, 81, 97, 101
Finlay, Sir Robert 116
Fiore, Pasquale 40
First Nations (of America) 99
First World War 6, 8, 13, 99, 168, 169
  origins 8, 19, 146–7, 170, 180–1
  and The Hague 100, 113, 114, 133, 135, 170, 178, 181–4
Fisher, Admiral Jacky 61, 68, 79, 82
flags of truce 86, 103
Fonbelle, Georges 23
Fondation International 157, 174, 175
foodstuffs 117, 167, 168
Foster, John W. 135, 148
4 July 1899 celebration (Delft) 79–81, 172
franc-tireurs 103, 105
France 14, 19, 22, 23, 24, 25, 26–7, 34, 36, 40, 44, 48, 49, 52, 55–6, 62, 69, 84, 91, 94, 102, 106, 109, 110, 114, 115, 117, 120, 130–1, 141, 145, 147, 156, 162, 174, 176, 181
France-Britain Expo (1908) 115
Franco-Prussian War (1870–1871) 23, 86
Franz Josef, Emperor 62
freedom of the seas *see* open seas
Freemasonry 139
French revolution (1789) *see* revolution
Fried, Alfred H. 27–8, 64, 92, 121, 122, 123, 134–5, 142, 179
Friedens-Warte, Die 121, 138
Friend of India & Statesman (Calcutta) 23, 24, 32, 72, 91
Friends, Society of 28, 64
Fry, Sir Edward 160, 162

Gall, A. 65
gas 84, 85, 90, 114, 182
Gaulois, Le 103
Gazette Algerienne (Bône) 23
Geneva 58, 175, 184
Geneva Conventions
  (1864) 16, 20, 22, 38, 39, 82
  (1906) 153, 161, 163
  and The Hague 55, 63, 73, 82, 85–6, 90, 161, 163
Genin, Vincent 39
genocide 118–19
Georgia 81
Georgia, University of 131
German South-West Africa 118–19, 195 n.29
German Women's Association 53
Germany 6, 14, 23, 25, 26, 27, 28, 32, 34, 44, 48, 49, 52, 53, 59, 60, 61, 62, 63, 64, 83–4, 87–90, 90–1, 92–3, 94–5, 98, 99, 102, 106, 107, 109, 113, 116, 117, 118–19, 121, 123, 126, 130, 131, 132, 133, 135, 138, 141, 145, 146, 148, 151–3, 158, 161, 162, 174, 180, 181, 182, 195 n.28, 195 n.29
Gesellschaft für Reform und Kodification des Völkerrechts (Association for Reform and Codification of International Law) 48
Gilinsky, General 83
Gironde, La 102
Glasgow 106
global governance 6, 14–15, 18, 82, 96, 122, 126, 133, 140, 147, 148, 153, 161, 166, 167, 169, 174, 175, 183–4
globalization 5–6, 10–15, 18–19, 142, 145, 154, 167
Gobat, Albert 52
good offices 22, 55, 73, 87, 88, 98
Goschen, G.J. 57
Graphic (Britain) 176
Grazer Tageblatt 91
Great Exhibition (1851) 14
Grey, Sir Edward 116, 153
Grieg, Edvard 53
Grotius, Hugo 80, 172 *see also* 4 July 1899 (Delft)

guerrilla warfare 98, 103
Guiyesse, Charles 36
Gündell, General Erich von 158

Haarlem 78
Hague (Peace) Conferences 3, 169, 174, 184 *see also* Hague, The
  First (1899) 2, 4, 22, 38, 53, 57–65, 67–95, 97, 99, 108, 109, 115, 120, 132, 137, 142 *see also* rescript
  historiography of 3, 5, 7–8, 27, 28, 32, 33, 38, 50, 52, 63, 72, 126, 140, 147, 165, 179
  institutionalization of 136, 151, 165, 167, 169, 170, 175, 183–4
  Second (1907) 60, 95–6, 118, 126–7, 128, 129, 133, 135, 141, 136, 140, 142, 145–68, 171, 172, 174
  Third (1915) 136, 165, 167, 168, 169, 178, 180, 183
Hague, The ('s Gravenhage) *see also* Hague (Peace) Conference, international law internationalism
  and academics 134–5, 165, 166–7
  city 4–5, 22, 57, 58–9, 64, 65, 68, 69, 72, 78, 79, 136, 139, 140, 156, 157, 159, 166, 169, 170–5, 176, 178, 184
  Conventions (1899) 73, 84, 85, 86–7, 90, 101, 109, 114, 118, 132, 135, 136, 137, 154
  Conventions (1907) 114, 135, 148, 161, 164–5
  delegate activism for 94–5, 129–133
  delegations at 61–4, 82, 90, 128, 131, 142, 148, 149, 153, 155–6, 157, 159–64, 180
  idea of 2–6, 9–10, 73–4, 77, 80–1, 86–7, 95, 96, 97–120, 122–42, 147–67, 169–80, 183–4
  institutions 2, 122, 168, 169, 171, 174, 178, 183
  municipal council 72, 78, 169
  and newspapers 4–5, 45, 50, 70–4, 75–7, 79, 80, 81–2, 89–90, 91–4, 97–120, 121–34, 140–1, 145–67, 171–4, 176, 178–9, 184
  public support for/against 1–3, 6, 7, 32, 38, 44–56, 60, 72–4, 78, 90–4, 97, 101, 111, 121–9, 140–1, 147–67, 178, 180, 181–4 *see also* internationalism
  ratification of 85, 95, 97, 118, 131, 164, 167–8, 215 n.28
  and small states 64, 136, 147, 154, 157, 160, 167
  and state violence 3, 9, 98–114, 118–20, 126, 170
  and war 1–2, 3, 9, 13, 20, 25, 26, 28, 31–2, 34, 39, 40, 45, 48, 52, 53, 55, 56, 57, 63, 67, 69, 71, 72, 73, 74, 75, 78, 81–7, 90–3, 95, 97–114, 116–20, 140, 155, 158, 169, 170, 178, 180–4
Hahn, Albert 113, 126, 127, 179
Haiti 174
Hale, Edward Everett 23, 49, 132
Hamburg 139
Hamburger Nachrichten 171
Hamilton, Keith 63
Hanotaux, G. 181
Hart, Sir Robert 107
Havas 12
Hawai'i 146
Hawera & Normanby Star 141
Hawke's Bay Herald 39, 141–2
Hay-Pauncefote Treaty (1897) 61
Hay, John 45, 49
Hayashi, Baron Tadasu 62
Herald of Peace 29, 50, 78, 140
Herero 118–19
Herman, Sondra 8
Herren-Oesch, Madeleine 6
Hershey, Amos 117–18
Herzl, Theodor 64, 81
Hessaptchieff, Major Christo 63
Hevinson, Henry 165
Higgins, Annalise 51
Hill, David Jayne 49, 63, 80, 123
history 21, 22, 30, 64, 69, 138, 139, 142, 148
  diplomatic 2, 6, 73, 117
  global 2, 5, 18–19, 36, 61, 145, 154
  legal 8
  public opinion 3–4
HMS Dreadnought 145, 151, 153
Hobhouse, L.T. 182
Hobson, J.A. 5–6
Hoffmann, Admiral 167
Hofstad, De 69

Holguin, Jorge 160
Holland, T.E. 12–13, 135
Holls, Captain Frederick W. 61, 87, 94, 131–2, 171
Holstein, Friedrich von 89
Hoo-Wei-Teh 62
Horrix, Paul 174–5
Hotel des Îndes 92
Howoth, Sir Henry 29
Hucker, Daniel 8
Hugo, Victor 21
Huis ten Bosch 22, 68, 69, 76, 77, 92, 115, 159
Huizinga, Johan 180
Hull, Isabel 86, 99, 119
human rights 6, 16, 92, 108, 130, 138 *see also* civil rights
humanitarianism 1, 8, 16, 22, 24, 26, 30, 32, 45, 82, 84, 85, 86, 92, 96, 108–9, 122, 127, 163 *see also* internationalism
Humanité Nouvelle 52
Hungary *see* Austria-Hungary
Hunt, Lynn 6
Hunter, Robert 29

Illustrated London News 126, 128, 129, 155
immigration 145, 146
imperial policing 84, 110, 118 *see also* state violence
imperial warfare 84, 109, 145, 147, 157 *see also* state violence
imperialism 11, 15, 18, 97, 99, 118, 147, 157
  critique of 16, 40, 92, 107–8, 111–13
indemnities 107
Indépendance Belge 27, 76
India 18, 23, 24, 54, 91, 108, 110, 111, 137, 157
Indonesia *see* Dutch East Indies
Institut de droit international (Institute of International Law) 4, 16, 20, 52, 80, 133, 140, 180
Institut International de la Bibliographie (International Bibliographic Institute) 12
Inter-Parliamentary Union (IPU) 4, 15, 17, 32, 50, 52, 64, 78, 120, 121–2, 123, 130, 136–7, 140, 150, 156, 178
Interessante Blatt (Vienna) 137
International Academy for Hygiene 174
International Arbitration and Peace Association 28
International Association of Academies 17
International Bureau of American Republics 18
International Committee of the Red Cross (ICRC) 16, 156
International Congress of Historical Studies (1913) 154
International Congress of Master Cotton Spinners (The Hague, 1913) 178
International Congress of Public School Teachers 139
International Council of Women (ICW) 4, 16, 38, 50, 52–5, 120, 136, 137–40, 156, 178
International Court of Justice (ICJ) 169, 180, 183
international courts 122, 140, 154, 169
International Criminal Court 183
International Crusade of Peace *see* International Peace Crusade 50
International Eastern Question Association 119
international institutions or unions 11–12, 14, 122, 169 *see also* Non-Government Organisation
international law 96, 148 *see also* arbitration, Hague Conventions; internationalism; arms limitation; mediation
  codification of 11, 15, 16, 82, 100, 132, 153, 161, 166
  and diplomacy 13, 73, 82, 100, 134, 146, 161, 166, 169, 181
  international impact of 8, 11, 74, 98–9, 100, 116–18, 123, 134, 169, 180–4
  and lawyers 8, 9, 11, 12, 15, 16, 28, 39, 48, 49, 52, 55, 85, 98, 132, 135, 154, 182
  library 171
  as norm 8, 9, 15, 17, 41, 49, 98–120, 146, 161, 169, 181, 182
  private 180
  and silences 87, 99–100, 108, 112, 119
  and state violence 98, 99–120
  treaty law 11, 20, 82, 99, 169, 181
  violation of 103, 105, 109, 116, 118, 136, 181–2

of war 2, 8, 9, 20, 22, 32–3, 38–9, 40, 55, 73, 74, 85–7, 90, 92, 111, 112, 114, 117–18, 122, 134, 136, 153, 161, 162–5, 181
International Literature and Art Association 178
International Lodging Congress (The Hague, 1913) 178
International Opium Commission and Congress 157, 178
International Peace and Arbitration Association (London) 156
International Peace Bureau (IPB) 15, 50
International Peace Congress 15
International Peace Crusade 29, 50
International Pharmaceutical Congress (The Hague, 1913) 178
international police force 179, 180
International Postal Union 11
International Prize Court (IPC) 161, 164, 168
International Students' Congress (The Hague, 1913) 178
International Telegraph Union 11
International Tourism Congress (The Hague, 1913) 178
International Tuberculosis Congress 174
International Women's Congress (1915) 178, 183
International, the 17
Internationale Vereeniging Vrede-Tentoonstelling (International Association for a Peace Exhibition) *see* Plan 1913
internationalism *see also* Hague
  activism 4, 6, 10, 14, 15, 17–18, 21, 24, 25, 28, 34, 38, 49–52, 60, 64, 92–3, 121–40, 155–8, 166, 169, 170, 175, 179, 182–4 *see also* petitions, public meetings
  anti-war 98–106, 107, 126, 148
  and art 65, 70, 71, 78, 93–4, 115, 141, 176, 178
  and Britain 27, 28–9, 133, 139, 156, 178
  and China 18, 137, 140
  conferences 14, 15, 178, 183
  and education 18, 49, 121, 137, 139, 156, 175, 176, 178, 183
  and Europe 102
  and France 133, 139, 148, 156
  and Germany 27, 28, 53, 133, 138, 153, 156
  government response to 19, 158, 165, 183–4
  at the Hague 76–8, 81, 82, 174–5
  and Japan 18, 53, 54, 137, 139, 156
  liberal 4, 7, 15, 41, 52, 67, 74, 101, 114, 122–40, 142, 166, 169, 182
  and Netherlands 47–8, 102, 139, 156, 173, 174–5, 179–80
  and newspapers 76–7, 121, 124–5, 134–7, 139, 140–2, 155–68, 179
  nineteenth-century 9–10, 15–19
  organisations 15–19, 135–40, 170, 178, 183 *see also* Non-Government Organisation
  peace through law 16, 48, 52, 78, 92, 101, 114–15, 122–40, 142, 147, 154, 165, 166, 168, 169, 174, 179, 182, 183, 184 *see also* international law, pacifism
  and race 17, 81, 98, 107, 119, 140, 157
  radical 17, 64, 119
  and religion 15, 17, 18, 29, 46, 48, 51, 52, 58–60, 78, 98, 107, 132, 139, 156, 159, 201
  and Russia 53
  and United States 27, 52, 53, 99, 102, 126, 130, 131, 132, 135, 137, 139, 148, 155, 170, 178
  and women 16, 46, 49, 52–4, 137–40, 176, 178, 183, 203 n.89 *see also* International Council of Women, Women's Christian Temperance Union
  working-class 17, 27, 46
internment 20, 86, 98, 105
Ireland 114, 157
Ireland, Archbishop 64
Ishay, M. 112
Islam 61
Italo-Ottoman War (1911) 111, 119–20
Italy 14, 16, 25, 27, 34, 37, 40, 49, 53, 56, 59, 62, 87, 102, 106, 111–12, 116, 119–20, 137, 160, 162, 174

Japan 11, 12, 18–19, 22, 45–6, 53, 54, 62, 70, 91, 92, 106, 107, 112, 115, 116–18,

119, 137, 139, 140, 141, 145, 146, 147, 148, 149, 150, 155, 156, 157, 174
Japan House Tax 116
Japan Times 51, 70, 92, 115, 119, 140, 146, 155, 157
Jaurès, Jean 130
Jenkins, Howard M. 64
Jiji 116
Jochnik, C. af 99, 108–9
Jordan, David Starr 17
Journal de l'Haye 82
Journal de St.-Petersbourg 14, 43, 78, 165
Journal des Débats Politiques et Littéraires (Paris) 27, 80, 108–9
Journal des Économistes 40
Journal Gaulois 26
journalism 13, 68, 75–6, 77, 79, 124, 125, 160, 173
  and language 81–2, 179
  special correspondents 13, 24, 30, 31, 32, 74, 80, 103, 104, 106, 107, 134, 138, 157
Journalistenkring (Council of Journalists, Netherlands) 77
Joyce, James 34
Jugend 56

Karnebeek, Baron A.P.C. van 76, 80, 83, 85, 131, 171
Kay-Shuttlesworth, Sir U. 51
Keefer, Andrew Scott 108
Kellogg, Vernon 17
Kern, Stephen 8
Kerr, H.S. 13
Khartoum 26
Khuepach zu Reid, Lieutenant-Colonel Victor 62
Kikeriki (Vienna) 75
Kipling, Rudyard 32, 34
Kirchoff, Arthur 49
Kitchener, Lord 24, 106
Knab, Cornelia 6
Knobel, F.M. 182
Kobe 139
Kohler, Josef 178, 182
Kojong, Emperor 157
Kokumin 91
Kölnische Zeitung 26
Koo, Johannes de 47
Korea 11, 37, 157
Krebs, Paula 14
Kristiana *see* Oslo
Kruger, Paul 100, 102, 103, 110
Kuehl, Warren 6, 8, 155
Kuijper, Abraham 81
Kuropatkin, Count Alexei N. 32, 45, 55
Kyoto 139

Labouchere, Henry 57
Lagos Weekly Record 119
Lammasch, Heinrich 52, 62, 90, 131, 158, 183
Landsdowne, Lord 109
Langhorne, Richard 8
Lapradelle, Gerard de Geouffre 67, 74, 101, 123, 135
Latin America 18, 31, 147, 157, 160, 162
law of war *see* international law
Lawrence, T.J. 121, 123, 135, 168
Le Figaro (Paris) 12, 26
League of Nations 183, 184
Leeuwarder Courant 93
Leo XIII, Pope 59 *see also* Vatican
Leopold II, King 119
Les annals de la jeunesse laïque 34
Lesaffer, Randall 165
Levysohn, Arthur 92
liberalism 9, 15 *see also* internationalism
Liberia 60
Liberty Review (Britain) 32
Libre Parole 27
Liebknecht, Karl 27, 156
Liège 175
Ligue des femmes pour le désarmement (Women's League for Disarmament) 47, 53
Linten, C. te 180
Linzer Montagpost 23
Lokal Anzeiger (Berlin) 132
London 14, 24, 29, 30, 52, 54–5, 63, 106, 115, 137, 139, 140, 156, 178
London Peace Society 15, 28, 50, 78, 140
London, Declaration of (1909) 164, 167–8, 180
Los Angeles Times 70, 72, 75, 80, 89, 91
Low, Seth 61, 94, 95
Low, Sidney 29
Loyalist League of Victoria 114

Luegger, Karl 137
Luiscius, J.M. van Stipriaan 48
Lustige Blätter, Der 93, 149, 178
Luxembourg 39
Lyon, University of 135

Macedonia 22, 56, 81, 90
MacMillan, Margaret 8
Mafeking Mail 118
Magna Carta 148
Mahan, Captain Alfred Thayer 61
Mahdi of Sudan 101
mail 11, 24, 81, 117, 156, 159, 164, 176
Malloch, G.R. 119
Manchester Guardian 80, 132, 133, 137, 140, 167
Manchuria 113
Marchand, C.J. 126
maritime warfare 55, 90, 117, 133, 139, 153, 160–1, 163–5, 168 *see also* naval warfare
Martens Clause (1899) 86–7, 90
Martens, Fyodor 52, 55–6, 58, 63, 74, 82, 85, 86, 90, 94, 107, 131, 132, 133, 153, 160, 161, 171
Martinus Nijhoff 78
Marxism 17
Massingham, H.W. 119
Mataura Ensign 56
Matin, Le (Paris) 70, 72, 142, 145–6, 147–8
Mawson, Thomas 174
Maxse, Leopold 40
Mazower, Mark 8, 170
Mazzini, Guiseppe 14
McKinley, President William 22, 48, 106–7
Mead, Edwin 6, 33, 119, 133, 225 n.99
Mead, Lucia Ames 6, 133, 139, 225 n.99
media *see also* newspapers, public opinion
  communications revolution 10–11, 13, 18
  global 5, 10, 13, 82, 118, 160
mediation 22, 73, 77, 87, 88, 115, 120, 122, 147, 155, 160, 169, 181
Mediterranean 157
Melbourne 24
Mérey von Kapos-Mére, Kajetan 62
Méringhac, A. 123–4, 132, 135
Meurer, Christian 135
Mexico 31, 116
might makes right 10, 28, 61, 82
militarism 3, 6, 8, 9, 18–19, 27, 61, 83, 92, 93, 101, 118, 120, 125–6, 141, 146
  critique of 20, 83, 101, 112, 120, 149, 156, 159
military budget 26, 56–7, 83
military deterrence 28, 39, 83
military necessity 28, 86, 87, 99, 105, 106, 108, 109, 111 *see also* might makes right
Mill, John Stuart 16
Milwaukee Sentinel 30
Minneapolis *Journal* 62
Moch, Gaston 49
moderation *see* restraint
Molinari, G. de 135
Moloch, B. 70
Monsell, B.E. 168
Montbard, George 69, 71
Moore, John Bassett 117
Morning Post (Britain) 27, 104
Morocco 141, 145
Moscheles, Felix 32, 48, 64, 76
Moscheles, Greta 64, 76
Motono, Ichiro 62
Mounier, General 62
Mouravieff, Count Mikhail 21, 22, 32, 36, 44, 55–6, 58, 115
Mügge, Maximilian 183
Mulligan, William 13, 102
Munro, Thomas 181
Münster, Count Herbert von 44, 55, 61–2, 63, 64, 68, 88–90
murder 58, 113, 119, 145, 155

Naber, Johanna 180
Nagao, Ariga 62, 112
Nama 119
Nanchang Riots (1906) 115
Napoleon III 14, 33
Napoleonic War 9, 15
Natal Witness 165
Nation (London) 152
National Arbitration and Peace Congress (New York, 1907) 155
National Council of Women (New Zealand) 46 *see also* International Council of Women

national honour 87, 158, 161, 179 *see also* sovereignty, vital interests
National Liberal Federation (Britain) 46
nationalism 6, 8, 9, 18, 19, 23, 49, 114, 125, 126, 141, 145, 165, 179, 180
naval warfare 63, 84–5, 86, 116–18, 150, 151, 164, 182
Nederlands Anti-Oorlog Raad (Netherlands Anti-War Council, NAOR) 182, 183
Nederlandsche Dagblad 21
Nelidov, Count Aleksandr 156, 157–8, 162, 163, 167
Netherlands, the 13, 22, 47, 52, 58, 59–61, 74, 77, 78–9, 80, 81–2, 83, 93, 95, 97, 102, 103, 104, 107–8, 114, 123, 139, 146, 150, 151, 156, 158–9, 160, 170, 171, 172, 173, 175–80
Neue Freie Presse 27, 106, 146
Neue Hamburger Zeitung 97, 106, 107, 139
Neue Wiener Tageblatt 27, 146
Neumann, Amelia 137
neutrality 3, 12, 48, 58, 85, 86, 103, 114, 117, 122, 123, 133, 134, 148, 150, 151, 168, 179, 181, 182, 183
  and The Hague 58, 86, 88, 100, 103, 113, 118, 133, 136, 151, 153, 156, 161, 162, 163–5, 169, 179, 180, 181
  permanent 48, 56, 63, 64
New South Wales 156
New York 49, 101, 138, 155
New York Bar Association 49
New York Times 30, 80–1, 123, 130, 131–2, 133, 140, 141
New York Tribune 61
New Zealand 7, 11, 13, 25, 39, 46, 53, 56, 119, 134, 138, 141–2, 146, 181
New Zealand Herald 46
Newel, Stanford 61
newspapers 4, 12–14, 23–7, 29–31, 125, 145–6, 176, 195 n.29
Nicholas II, Tsar 1, 21, 22, 24, 27, 32, 34–5, 36, 43–4, 47, 55, 58, 68, 101, 106–7, 122, 145, 151, 152, 162
Nieuwe Kerk (Delft) 80
Nieuwe Rotterdamsche Courant 106
Nieuwenhuis, Domela 64, 78, 92, 156
Nigra, Count Constantino 62, 68, 76, 79, 81, 82, 88, 94, 131
Nippold, Otfried 135
Nobel Peace Prize 17, 131, 135, 141–2
Nobel, Alfred 17, 128, 141
Non-Government Organisation (NGO) 7 *see also* internationalism
Norddeutsche Algemeine Zeitung 93
Norddeutscher Lloyd 160
Norman, Louis E. van 116
Normand, R. 99, 108–9
North American Shipping Company 160
North China Herald 12, 30–1
Norway 38, 48, 53, 114, 116, 141, 160, 174
Notovich, Nikolai 34
Novicow, Jacques 17, 64
Novosti 30
Nuovo Antologia 40

occupation (military) 20, 86, 157, 180
Odier, Edouard 88, 131
Ohinemuri Gazette 134
Ohio 156
Okolicsány, Alexander von 62, 76
Okuma, Shigenobu 22
Olympic Games 14, 136
open seas 10, 12, 117, 161, 163, 164, 183
opening of hostilities 161, 162, 164, 180
Opium War, First (1839–41) 16
Oppenheim, Lassa 8, 178
Orange Free State 60, 97
Organisation centrale pour une paix durable (Central Organization for Durable Peace, CODP) 183
Osaka 139
Oscar II, King 56, 160
Oslo 122, 139
Ottoman Empire 11, 16, 22, 60, 70, 81, 101, 103, 111–12, 119–20, 157
Oxford Manual 20
Oxford University 132

Pacific 12, 25, 140, 147, 181
pacifism 15, 38, 40, 52, 86, 101, 126, 133, 134–5, 153, 179 *see also* internationalism
Palestine 137
Pall Mall Gazette 50
pamphlets 1, 2, 3, 18, 23, 29, 34, 45, 49, 61, 100, 103, 104–5, 122, 136, 138, 140, 156, 160, 175, 179, 182

Pan-African Association 17
Pan-American Union 14, 33, 147
Pan-Slavism 17
Panama Canal 115
Papeete 181
Paris 12, 14, 44, 55, 61, 63, 65, 69, 70, 102, 115, 124, 145, 175
Paris Exposition (1900) 70, 136
Paris peace negotiations (1919) 65, 167
Paris, Declaration of (1856) 20
Passy, Frédéric 49, 92, 125, 135
patriotism *see* nationalism
Patterson, D.S. 126
Pauncefote, Sir Julian 61, 63, 76, 79, 82, 87, 131
peace activism *see* internationalism, pacifism, petitions
Peace Museum (Lucerne) 65, 134
Peace Palace (The Hague) 4, 18, 130, 136, 141, 155, 166, 170–4, 175, 176, 177, 178, 179, 180, 182
peace symbol 36, 80, 141, 169, 170, 171, 173, 174, 176, 178, 184, 205 n.161
Peirce, Herbert H.D. 45
Peking 107, 145
Pêle-Mêle (France) 117, 182
Péphau, Rear Admiral 62
Permanent Court of Arbitral Justice (PCAJ) 161, 165
Permanent Court of Arbitration (PCA) 4, 18, 47, 48, 73, 76, 87, 88–9, 90, 91, 93, 95, 102, 103, 107, 114–17, 118, 119, 122–3, 130, 131, 134, 136, 137, 142, 151, 153, 155, 158, 161, 162, 169, 174 *see also* arbitration
Permanent Court of International Justice (PCIJ) 183
Persia 56, 137
Pester Lloyd 124
Petersburgskija Vledomosti 94
Petite République 26
petitions 2, 3, 13, 25, 29, 30, 34, 38, 45, 46–7, 48–54, 70, 81, 102, 137, 139, 155–7, 178
Philadelphia Press 30
philanthropy 17, 25, 26, 123, 170, 171
Philippines 16, 99
Pichon, Stéphen 147
Pick Me Up 37
pilgrimage 47, 50, 155, 169, 170, 178
Pious Funds of the Californias 116, 130
Pirquet, Baron 64
'Plan 1913' 175–9, 180
pogrom 37
Poland 17, 81, 146
police 68, 81, 110, 112, 138, 156 *see also* imperial policing, international police force
Pollock, Sir Frederick 29
Port Arthur 12, 117, 150
Portsmouth, Treaty of (1905) 115–16, 132
Portugal 64, 85, 114
post *see* mail
Poverty Bay Herald 59
Pratt, Hodgson 52
press office 14, 76, 157
prisoners of war (POWs) 20, 86, 98, 103, 105, 117
private property 105, 107, 112, 139, 150, 153, 161, 164
privateering 92, 164
prize, law of 161, 164
progressivism 16, 17, 27, 74, 111, 115, 126, 129, 135, 148, 154, 166, 182 *see also* internationalism, liberalism
public meetings 2, 13, 17, 29, 38, 45, 48–9, 50, 53–5, 64, 102, 122, 136, 137–8, 140, 155–6, 176
public opinion 3–7, 12, 13–14, 18, 23, 44–61, 74, 120, 124–5, 166, 180
Puck 170
Pulchri 65, 78
Punch (Melbourne) 148

Quakers *see* Friends, Society of
Quidde, Ludwig 101

Raemaekers, Louis 159, 178
Raffalovich, Arthur 84, 94
Rahusen, Eduard 52
rape 107, 105
Reay, Lord Donald Mackay 133, 160
Red Cross 86, 104 *see also* International Committee of the Red Cross (ICRC)
Reed, Thomas B. 64
refugees 103, 157
Reich, Emil 29
Reid, Whitelaw 68, 90

Reinsch, Paul S. 10, 16, 166
Renault, Louis 52, 62, 90, 142, 147, 161, 179
rescript
first (1898) 1–2, 13, 21–2, 23–32, 32–8, 43–56, 73, 91, 101, 107, 137, 142, 170, 185 n.3
second circular (1899) 22, 32, 38, 39–41, 52, 55–6, 83, 85
resolutions *see* petitions
restraint 1, 100, 181
Reuters 12
Review of Reviews 50
Revista Moderna (Brazil) 31
revolution 9, 36, 56, 152 *see also* communications revolution, media
1848 16
French (1789) 23, 36, 130
Russian (1905) 36, 120, 151
Revue des Deux Mondes 40, 92
Rhodes, James Ford 64
Rhodesia Herald 119
Richet, Charles 64
Richmond River Express & Casino Kyogle Advertiser 156
Rodin, Auguste 115
Roëll, J.A. 180
Rogier, Count de Grelle 63
Rome 56
Roosevelt, President Theodore 12, 115, 116, 118, 130, 135, 136, 142, 150–1, 153, 154, 155
Root, Elihu 142, 148, 179, 182
Rotterdam 65, 160, 176
Royal Academy of Academic Research 174
Royal Navy (Britain) 27, 57, 61, 84, 151
Russell, Lord 29
Russell, Rolo 29
Russia 7, 12, 14, 17, 18, 21, 22, 24, 25, 30–3, 34, 36, 37–8, 43, 44, 45, 49, 52, 53, 54, 55–6, 57, 58, 59, 60, 63, 68, 74, 77, 83, 84, 87, 89, 91, 94, 97, 98, 100, 101, 102, 106, 107, 112, 113, 115, 116–18, 120, 130, 132, 133, 141, 145, 149, 150, 151, 153, 155, 157, 160, 162, 164, 174, 180
Russian High Seas Fleet 116
Russian revolution (1905) *see* revolution
Russo-Japanese War (1904–1905) 12, 13, 36, 100, 112, 115, 116–18, 123, 130, 133, 142, 147, 150, 152, 155, 164

Sakamoto, Toshiatsu 62
Salisbury, Marquis of 28, 29, 46
Salvation Army 29
Samoa 23, 25, 56, 195 n.28
Samoan Weekly Herald (Apia) 23, 25
Satow, Ernest 8, 160, 163
Scandinavia 48, 53, 56, 64
Scheveningen 77, 79, 80, 170, 171, 174, 176
Schilfgaarde, Johanna Waszklewicz van 47–8, 54, 55, 64, 133, 225 n.99
Schücking, Walther 135, 166
Schwarzhoff, Colonel Gross von 83–4
Scotland 116
Scott, James Brown 9, 16, 135
sea mines 12, 117, 161, 163, 164, 180
Second World War 183
Segesser, Daniel 102
Selenka, Margaretha Lenore 53–4, 138
self-determination 17, 81, 156, 167
Serbia 22, 53, 64, 180
Sewall, May Wright 53, 55, 138
's Gravenhage *see* Hague, The
Shaw, George Bernard 29, 32
Siberia 37
Sinn Fein 114
Sino-Japanese War (1894) 86
slavery *see* abolitionism
Sluga, Glenda 8, 126
Snijders, General W.F.G. 112
social Darwinism 19
socialism 17, 27, 52, 60
Soerabaijasch Handelsblad 106
Sol de Domingo, El (Argentina) 31
Somalia 111, 112
Sophia 52
South Africa 59, 60–1, 81, 92, 136 *see also* Boer War, Orange Free State, Transvaal
South African Women and Children's Distress Fund (Britain) 103
South America *see* Latin America
South China Morning Post 159
sovereignty 3, 11, 61, 62, 64, 82, 86, 88, 95, 99, 107, 108, 116, 122, 148, 153, 158, 163, 166, 178, 181

Spain 1, 16, 22, 25, 34, 53, 54, 85, 86, 102, 147, 162, 174
Spanish-American War (1898) 16, 22, 34, 85, 86, 147
Speaker (Britain) 31
Spectator 51, 91
Spokane Spokesman Review 148, 149
sport 79, 176, 178 *see also* Olympic games
St Louis 61, 136, 137, 150
St Petersburg 1, 21, 22, 39, 44, 45, 57, 58, 59, 60, 62, 63, 146
St Petersburg Declaration (1868) 20, 33, 40, 82, 85, 108
Staal, Baron George de 53, 63, 68, 74, 77–8, 83, 89, 122, 129, 131
Stancioff, Dimitri 33, 63, 68, 79, 90
Standard 27
Star (Christchurch, New Zealand) 106
state violence 97, 99 *see also* genocide, imperial warfare, imperial policing
Stead, W.T. 28–9, 32, 33, 47, 49, 50–2, 55, 64, 72, 78, 92, 104–5, 106, 119, 133, 153, 155, 171, 175, 225 n.99
Stengel, Karl von 28, 40, 49, 61, 205 n.161
Steyn, Martinus Theunis 102–3
Stockholm 53, 100
Stop the War Committee (Britain) 103
Strachan, Douglas 174
Subject Races Committee 17, 156
Sudan 24, 26, 57, 101
Sumatra Post 97, 107–8, 112, 134, 140, 141
Sunday Sun (Sydney) 119
Sunday Times (Britain) 33
Surinam 24, 26–7, 47
Surinamer (Paramaribo) 24, 26–7
Suttner, Baroness Bertha von 17, 32, 33, 38, 54, 55, 64, 74, 76, 79, 81, 90, 92, 93, 128, 133–4, 138, 141, 142, 151, 169, 170, 225 n.99
Sviet 30
Sweden 56, 76, 83–4, 100, 114, 138, 156, 160, 176
Swedish Peace Party 32
Swinderen, Renée de Marees van 178
Switzerland 85, 88, 114, 123, 134, 156
Sydney 25, 119

Tadasu, Hayashi 45
Taft, President William Howard 135
Tages-Post (Linzer) 146
Tahiti 181
Taku 107
Tasmania 138
Tate, Merze 7, 126
Tcheraz, Minas 81–2
Telegraaf 70, 72, 81, 82, 97, 140
Telegraph (Brisbane) 146
telegraph communication 1, 10, 11, 12, 25, 79, 117, 154, 160
Temps, Le (Paris) 23
Ten Kate, Jan 65, 78, 176
territorial waters 116, 180
Thames Advertiser (New Zealand) 46
Thames Star (New Zealand) 7
Thomson, Major 111
Tijd De 48, 79
Times, The (London) 27, 57, 125, 132, 134, 146, 165
Toché, M.M. 115
Tokyo 54, 139
Tolstoy, Leo 17, 32, 55
Tornielli, Count 161
Toronto 137
tourism 134, 159, 160, 175–9
trade unions 27, 29, 38, 45
Trades Union Congress, Bristol (1898) 24, 25, 45
Transvaal 56, 61–2, 82, 97, 102, 215 n.28
Tripoli 56, 111–12, 120
Trotha, Ludwig von 119
Trueblood, Reverend Benjamin T. 30, 64
Tryon, James L. 126
Tseng-Tsiang, Lou 62
Tübingen, University of 84–5, 133
Tuchman, Barbara 7, 21 n.21
Tung-chow 107
Twain, Mark 23, 32
Twee Steden hotel 160

U-boat 182
Uehara, Yusaka 62
Uilenspiegel 37
Ullmann, E. von 154
Union for the Protection of Industrial Property 11
United Kingdom *see* Britain
United States 10, 14, 15, 16, 17, 18, 19, 23, 25, 27, 29–30, 33, 34, 39, 49, 52, 53,

61–2, 63, 68, 72, 76, 77, 79–81, 85, 87, 94, 95, 99, 102, 106, 111, 113, 116, 117, 119, 130, 131, 132, 135, 139, 141, 145, 147, 148, 150–1, 153, 154, 155, 156, 162, 172, 174, 176, 180, 181
Univers 27
Universal Peace Congress (UPC) 106
Universal Races Congress (1907) 17, 130, 140
universities 11, 12, 17, 49, 61, 84, 90, 130, 131, 132, 133, 135, 154, 156, 179
Upward, Allan 33
Utah 49

Vaderlander (Netherlands) 21
Vagt, Detlev 114
Valvérane, Louis Denis 182
Vargas, Marceliano 160
Varick, A. van Dhaene van 78
Vaterland (Austria) 27
Vatican, the 27, 58–60, 140
Vejstnik Jewrozy 120
Venezuela 60, 116, 132, 162
Venloosche Bode 60
Verbande der Presse im Dienste des Friedens (Peace Press Association) 124
Vereshchagin, Vasily 32
Versailles, Treaty of (1919) *see* Paris peace negotiations (1919)
Vickery, James Harris 94
Victoria, Queen 109, 110
Vie Illustrée, La 68–70, 71
Vienna 23, 55, 62, 131, 136–7, 146
Vienna, Congress of (1814–1815) 6, 33
Vita Internazionale, La 34
vital interests 40, 85, 87, 95, 168 *see also* military necessity, national honour, sovereignty
Vledomosti 30
Vogue 101, 139
Volk, Het 106, 113
Volksbond 59
Vollenhoven, Cornelis van 179–80
Vossische Zeitung 119, 140, 167
Vrede door Recht (Peace through Law) 47, 179
Vries, Johan de 125

Wahre Jacob, Der 75, 91
Wairarapa Daily Times 123
Wank, Solomon 102
War Against War 50
war charities 28, 85, 103
war limitation 2, 20, 57, 73, 86–7, 90, 164 *see also* arms limitation, Martens Clause (1899), restraint
War of Italian Unification, Second (1859) 16
War Office (Britain) 57, 84, 85, 105, 108, 109, 111
Washington D.C. 18, 150, 174, 175
Washington Post 76, 132, 133, 138, 140, 145–6, 158
weaponry 10, 26, 36, 83, 84, 109, 111, 114, 134, 150
Webster, Andrew 114
Wehberg, Hans 39, 135, 178
Welserheimb, Count Rudolph von 62, 68
Wesleyan Conference, Melbourne (1899) 46
White House 145
White, Andrew D. 52, 61, 68, 76, 78, 79, 80–1, 82, 94, 171
Wiener Zeitung 70, 72, 137, 146
Wiesbaden 89
Wilhelm II, Kaiser 22, 28, 44, 61–2, 63–4, 87–8, 94
Wilhelmina, Queen 22, 58, 59, 79, 95, 159, 172, 178
Wilson, President Woodrow 65, 183
Witte, Count Sergei 32, 55
Wolff 12
women *see* International Council of Women, internationalism, Women's Christian Temperance Union
Women's Christian Temperance Union (WCTU) 16, 25, 38, 46, 50, 52–3
Women's Suffrage Pilgrimage (London) 178
Women's Tribune 49
Woolsey, Theodore S. 12, 155
Workmen's Peace Association *see* International Arbitration and Peace Association 28
world city 169, 174–5, 178
World Fair (St Louis, 1904) 136
World Fair, Paris (1889) 14, 15, 16, 17
World Peace Congress (The Hague, 1913) 178

Würzburg, University of 135
Wylie, Neville 86
Wyndham, George 109
Wyoming State Tribune 125

Yale University 132, 155
Yihequan 106
Yorodzu 141
Young Turks 81
Yü, Yang 62

Zillesen, H. 78
Zionism 64, 81, 140, 156
Zola, Emile 19
Zorn, Phillip 52, 61, 87, 94, 131, 133, 135